DC 148 .L4131 v.2
Lefebvre, Georges, 1874-1959

The French Revolution.

12/7/18

THE FRENCH REVOLUTION

Volume II

From 1793 to 1799

GEORGES LEFEBVRE

THE FRENCH REVOLUTION

(In two volumes)

I. From its Origins to 1793

II. From 1793 to 1799

THE
French Revolution

Volume II

FROM 1793 TO 1799

BY

Georges Lefebvre

TRANSLATED FROM THE FRENCH
BY JOHN HALL STEWART
AND JAMES FRIGUGLIETTI

NEW YORK: Columbia University Press

Published 1964

This is a translation of the last three parts and the Conclusion of *La Révolution française* (deuxième édition, revue et augmentée, de la nouvelle rédaction, 1957) , by Georges Lefebvre, Volume XIII of the series 'Peuples et Civilisations', published by Presses Universitaires de France.

ISBN *0-231-02519-X Clothbound*
ISBN 0*-231-08599-0 Paperback*

Library of Congress Catalog Card Number: 64-11939
Printed in the United States of America

Thirteenth cloth and fifth paperback printing.

Clothbound editions of Columbia University Press books are Smyth-sewn and printed on permanent and durable acid-free paper.

Contents

II. THE VICTORIOUS OFFENSIVE OF THE REVOLUTION

Preface

AS INDICATED on the copyright page, this book is a translation of the last three parts and the Conclusion of the 1957 edition of Georges Lefebvre's *La Révolution française*. It completes the work begun by Elizabeth Moss Evanson in her translation of the Introduction and the first three parts, *The French Revolution from Its Origins to 1793*, produced by the same publishers in 1962. My collaborator and I have endeavoured to follow the general pattern established by Mrs. Evanson, but instead of continuing the numbering of the 'Books' to conform to the French version (IV, V, VI), we have identified them as I, II, and III; and we have renumbered the chapters in regular sequence from one through seventeen. An attempt has been made to correct factual errors, but no references to such alterations are included. As in the Evanson volume, the bibliographical references, amplified by the 'Additions' given in the 1957 edition, are placed at the back of the book; and a few untranslated words are explained in the list on p. xiii.

Georges Lefebvre is seldom a subject of real controversy among historians. As a person he was charming, considerate, generous—a man of integrity. As a scholar he was the leader of his generation in his field of study—erudite, industrious, perceptive, and original. Moreover, whatever his mild bias, he was doubtless as objective as any Frenchman can ever be when dealing with one of the most significant epochs of the history of his native land, the Great French Revolution.[1] Yet anyone who has read much of his writing, and certainly those few of us who have endeavoured to translate portions of it, must admit, however reluctantly, that he was no stylist. Perhaps he was so busy that he was content simply to commit the results of his vast and valuable researches to paper and get on with the next job. Whatever the reason, the fact remains that in general he did not

[1] See Paul Beik's Foreword to Mrs. Evanson's translation.

write well—at least in *La Révolution française*. Carl Becker is alleged to have said that if the writer doesn't sweat the reader will. In the present instance the translators did the real sweating.

Perhaps we have taken too many liberties with words; and there is no denying that we have done violence to the sentence and paragraph structure of the original. At all times, however, we have endeavoured to seek the answers to three basic questions: What does the text say? How may the same statement be made in clear, modern, idiomatic English? Have we succeeded in making such a statement without losing the sense of the original? We hope that our shortcomings will be offset by the fact that at long last this essential work is available in English.

JOHN HALL STEWART

Western Reserve University
Cleveland, Ohio

Acknowledgments

ALTHOUGH James Friguglietti and I were seeking appointment as translators of this book long before we were assigned the task, in the last analysis we owe the achievement of our goal largely to Shepard B. Clough of Columbia University, Elizabeth Moss Evanson, whose translation of the first part of the work appeared in 1962, and Henry H. Wiggins of the Columbia University Press.

Appreciation is due the officers of Western Reserve University, who made it possible for me to obtain a leave of absence for the spring session of 1962–63 so that I could accept a visiting professorship at the University of Texas, where most of my share of the work was done.

In a sense, however, my prime acknowledgment is to the Department of History at the University of Texas—John Rath, Joe Frantz, Archie Lewis, and the rest—for providing me with an opportunity to effect comfortably, for the first time in more than thirty years, a satisfactory balance between teaching and writing, without (at least to my knowledge) serious damage to either. I am also grateful to the departmental secretary, Colleen Kain, for her excellent work in typing the manuscript (after office hours), and to Theodore Andersson, Chairman of the Department of Romance Languages, for his most generous assistance in helping me over many of the treacherous hurdles in translation. May all these Texans live long and thrive mightily.

I thank my collaborator (one of my former prize students) for doing the difficult work of preliminary translation, for correcting errors in the original text, and for enduring the tribulations to which I have too often subjected him. And both of us are grateful for suggestions made by Marc Bouloiseau of the Institut d'Histoire de la Révolution Française at the University of Paris, and Louise Lindemann of the Columbia University Press.

Finally, as usual, I can never quite express my great indebtedness to my wife, Helen Doolittle Stewart. Since the publishers have assumed the responsibility for making the index, she is spared that task in the present instance; but proofreading is still in the offing, and I hereby thank her in advance for helping with that particular drudgery.

J. H. S.

Definition of French Terms Used in Text

aides	taxes, chiefly on beverages
assignats	originally, bonds issued by the Constituent Assembly; later a forced paper currency
avocat	a type of lawyer
avoué	a type of lawyer
banalité	obligation requiring peasants to use manorial services such as grist mills
biens nationaux	'national property'; property confiscated by the state from the clergy, the nobles, and others during the Revolution
cahiers	statements of grievances presented by the deputies to the Estates General in 1789
Carmagnole	a name applied in the plural to groups of revolutionaries; also a revolutionary song and dance
cens	a manorial tax, usually paid annually and in money; a kind of quitrent
champart	a manorial tax, consisting of a portion of the produce of the land; a field rent
chouannerie	risings of peasants in the Vendée and elsewhere; see *chouans*
chouans	a name for rebellious peasants in the Vendée and elsewhere; derived from one of the peasant leaders, Jean Cottereau, known as Chouan
ci-devants	literally 'the former ones'; a term applied to the former aristocrats of France
collège	a type of secondary school
compagnonnages	brotherhoods of workmen
congéable	a legal term meaning 'held under tenancy at will'
corvée	manorial obligation on the part of the peasants to do certain types of labour, mainly for the seigneur
décade	the ten-day week under the revolutionary calendar
droits casuels	contingent, or occasional, dues or fees

emigrés	opponents of the Revolution who left France
Enragés	literally 'madmen'; a small, noisy group of radicals in the National Convention
franc-fief	literally 'freehold' or 'free fief'; actually, a fee paid by a non-noble on acquiring property
gabelle	a tax on salt
ideologues	literally 'ideologists'; a term applied to a group of thinkers during the Directory
jeunesse dorée	literally gilded youth; the name applied to groups of young aristocrats who went about assaulting Jacobins; in a sense, reactionary vigilantes
lettre de cachet	'sealed letter'; a form of warrant for arbitrary arrest and imprisonment prior to the Revolution
livre	basic unit of French money before the Revolution
lycée	a type of secondary school
Merveilleuses	term applied to extravagantly dressed women of the period of the Thermidorian reaction; feminine counterpart of *Muscadins*
métayer	sharecropper
Muscadins	fops or dandies; male counterpart of *Merveilleuses*
'notables'	persons of note; those who had played a prominent part in the earlier days of the Revolution; sometimes a term of contempt
octroi	a municipal tax assessed for the privilege of bringing commodities into a town for commercial purposes
patente	a tax, mainly in the form of a licence for engaging in commerce or industry
Patrie	homeland, motherland; not usually translated
philosophes	general term applied to the leading French thinkers of the prerevolutionary period
procureur-général-syndic	a subordinate royal officer at the law courts
rentier	one who enjoys an income from a *rente*; a bondholder or pensioner
sans-culottes	persons who did not wear the *culottes*, or knee-breeches, of the pre-revolutionary aristocrats; a name applied to radical republicans
vingtième	a tax, nominally of one twentieth, usually on revenues from land during the Old Regime

I

THE COALITION AND THE REVOLUTION TO THE TREATIES OF 1795

CHAPTER ONE

The European Coalition (1793–1795)

EVEN THOUGH MOST of the European states were now at war with France, they had not yet joined forces. It was England that formed the Coalition; but partly because of her own errors she did not succeed in making it effective. The Allies never reached an agreement concerning their war aims, and they failed to concentrate their troops. Poland and the maritime and colonial war engrossed them as much as, or more than, the Continental assault against France. The result was that after a few successes their armies either halted or retreated. Then, in 1794, they gave way before the revolutionary offensive, and like the Austro-Prussian alliance after Valmy and Jemappes, the European Coalition began to disintegrate.

Yet disputes among the Allies do not in themselves suffice to explain their failure. There were deeper causes which, by comparison, pointed up the singular nature of the Revolution. The members of the Coalition never fully exploited their resources. They did not perceive the novelty of the war, and they waged it according to custom, without modifying their political procedures or their military tactics. Nor did their ineffectiveness stem solely from old habits. They hesitated to ask too much from their subjects because they feared that concessions would be demanded in return for sacrifices; and they had no intention of having victory thus turned against them.

THE EUROPEAN COALITION (1793–1795)

FORMATION OF THE COALITION

When England entered the war against France, tradition ordained that she would support the latter's enemies on the Continent, with money if necessary. Holland was already her ally, and since November, Grenville had been making overtures to Austria. After the declaration of war (February 1, 1793) she gradually united with all the belligerents: with Russia on March 25; with Sardinia on April 25; with Spain on May 25; with the Bourbons of Naples on July 12; with Prussia on July 14; with Austria on August 30; and with Portugal on September 26. In March, 1793 (after the Holy Roman Empire had decided to declare war on France), Baden and the two Hesses also reached an understanding with England. As for Hanover, it belonged to George III. Thus step by step, the so-called First Coalition took form. It existed only because of England. If the struggle against a common enemy created a certain solidarity among the powers, it was never manifested in a general pact; and the idea of a unified command or a pooling of resources was never even contemplated.

An obvious inequality prevailed among England's allies. Sardinia, Naples, Portugal, Hanover, Baden, and the Hesses furnished contingents in return for subsidies; and Pitt regarded them as his mercenaries. Holland helped finance the war, but could not defend herself without aid. Prussia and Austria, on the contrary, even while hoping to obtain financial aid sooner or later, did not intend to take orders. The treaties with Spain and Russia merely anticipated the organization of a blockade. Had the unity of Germany and Italy already been achieved, those two nations, turning all their power against France, might, indeed, have assumed direction of the Continental war, and the Revolution probably would have succumbed. Under existing circumstances, however, the Coalition could prove effective only if England and the states outside her hegemony were in agreement concerning objectives. But this was not the case.

WAR AIMS OF THE ALLIES

Two war aims might have produced Allied unanimity. The first, long extolled by Burke and the émigrés, consisted of saving

European civilization (that is, the domination of the aristocracy) by destroying the work of the Revolution in France. This was a would-be idealistic crusade and, in reality, a class war. The other, which Pitt and Grenville preferred, was limited to restoring the law of nations—France would have to respect treaties and renounce propaganda—and to re-establishing the European balance of power—she would have to return her conquests. This was a political war.

Lest we be misled, it should be pointed out that neither of these objectives had been repudiated by the Allies. Pitt refused to publish the manifesto proposed by Burke, for the English aristocracy was neither inclined towards idealism nor concerned with avenging the French nobility. Moreover, any attempt to re-establish the Old Regime in France would make victory more difficult. The Continental Powers were nonetheless agreed upon effecting counter-revolution, and at conferences at Antwerp in April, 1793, the English did not oppose their plan. It was carried out particularly in the department of Nord, where a council of Austrian functionaries—the 'junta' of Valenciennes—governed a portion of the region for a year. It re-established the tithe and manorial rights, recalled the non-juring clergy and the religious orders, restored the available national property to them and announced that more would be recovered. These actions suggest what might have happened had France been conquered.

Pitt was determined, at least in his own mind, to restore the monarchy and the constitutional predominance of the nobility and the upper bourgeoisie after the pattern of Great Britain. As for the political war, he felt that the Continental Powers were certainly far less interested than he. Not all of them felt wronged by the French conquests, which the growing states of Russia, Prussia, and Sardinia would have tolerated had they received as much themselves. They all knew why England clung to the balance of power: it assured her the rule of the seas. Nevertheless Pitt's principles seemed so reasonable that nobody ever questioned them.

This did not prevent each of the Allies from hoping to obtain a territorial indemnity. Burke predicted that such aims would produce dissension among them and arouse the national spirit of France. Yet Pitt could not preach disinterestedness, for he had to have allies, and the question of indemnities, incidental at the outset, had become so much the chief preoccupation of the Continental Powers that they had decided upon them even before England entered the war. Moreover, it was soon apparent that Pitt adhered to the principle, for he counted upon aggrandizing the British Empire by seizing Corsica and the French colonies. Despite his protests to the contrary, he was suspected of wishing to annex Dunkirk and Toulon as well.

In any case, at the Antwerp conferences the English, like the others, protested against the prince of Coburg's manifesto, which, in order to favour Dumouriez's undertaking against the Convention, guaranteed the territorial integrity of France. Consequently, in the department of the Nord the Austrians refused to proclaim Louis XVII, or even to permit the return of émigrés who had not been resident there. At Toulon, Howe had recognized Louis XVII and had raised the white flag, but Pitt refused to sanction his actions and denied the count of Provence access to the city. With conquest exposed as the chief aim of the Allies, events took a more unfortunate turn than even Burke had foreseen.

Obviously the Revolution could be crushed only on the Continent; but eager to occupy the colonies of France, to destroy her navy, and to conquer her markets, Pitt disregarded the fact. By so doing he irritated Spain, which was concerned with a war of principles, and gave her cause for alarm regarding her own maritime and colonial interests. So much was this the case that the naval war, lacking sincere Spanish cooperation, produced no decisive results, and Charles IV finally abandoned the Coalition. England's example encouraged her allies to look first to their own interests. Geographically, however, they could not, or would not, all help themselves in France, and Spielmann's plan[1] acknowledged the fact. When, therefore, efforts should have been made to unite against their common enemy, Russia and Prussia, if not Austria as well, were more interested in attacking Poland. Spielmann's plan at least imposed on the first two the moral obligation to interest themselves in the war in the west. Before the Netherlands could be exchanged they would have to be retaken from the French;

[1] See Evanson's translation, pp. 250–51 [trans.].

and, by the treaty of January 23, 1793, Catherine in effect obliged the king of Prussia to be an accessory.

Unhappily for Pitt, from the moment he admitted the principle of indemnities, he could not entirely dissociate himself from their methods. He held Poland to be of little account. At the end of 1792, and again on January 12, 1793, Grenville protested against the partition; but in July, at the moment of reaching an agreement with Prussia, he had to grant his approval. Pitt, on the contrary, was intractable when it came to the exchange of the Netherlands. To encourage Austria to retain them, he suggested that they be extended as far as the Somme. But this new plan did not appeal to Prussia. She used it as a pretext for avoiding her obligations; and Austria, humiliated, was goaded into moving part of her forces back to the east.

Thus the great Continental Powers divided their troops between Poland and France. England devoted herself principally to maritime and colonial war, without being able to deal a decisive blow to the Revolution. The other allies, aware that the 'Big Four' scarcely thought of letting them play a part, limited their contribution to the bare minimum. This was one of the basic reasons for the triumph of the Revolution.

THE COALITION AND POLAND (APRIL, 1793–OCTOBER, 1794)

The second partition of Poland was not completed until September, 1793. On April 4 the Prussian occupation was terminated by the capitulation of Danzig. Three days later, annexation manifestoes were issued, but they still required ratification by the Diet. Sievers, charged by Catherine with this task, succeeded only with difficulty. Despite his refined cunning and bribery, twenty-five Patriots were elected, and once the Diet met, Stanislas and the confederates, ashamed of their role, secretly engaged in obstructionist tactics. To put an end to these activities Sievers sequestered the king's revenues, arrested several deputies, and threatened opponents with seizure of their property. On July 22 the agreement with Russia was ratified. So far as Prussia was concerned, resistance continued, especially since Sievers now became conciliatory,

Finally, on September 2, on Catherine's orders, troops surrounded the Diet, and it yielded upon condition of commercial concessions, which Prussia rejected. On the 23rd violence recurred. The silence of the unfortunate Poles, faint from exhaustion, was taken as consent, and on September 25 the treaty was signed. Already, however, on the 22nd, the exasperated Frederick William had set out for Poland, forsaking the war against France and virtually abandoning the Coalition.

Indeed, hostility between Prussia and Austria had increased during the interval. After the partition had been proclaimed at Vienna in February, 1793, announcement of the terms was delayed; the campaign in the Netherlands having begun, Austria might be unable to march into Poland. When finally, on March 23, the content of the treaty was divulged, it unleashed a storm, for the acquisitions of the two accomplices exceeded all expectations. Cobenzl and Spielmann were dismissed on the 27th, and were succeeded by Thugut, who was named director of foreign affairs. Thugut was a parvenu, devoted solely to his own fortune. He believed his success would be assured if he satisfied the territorial appetite of the Habsburgs by acquiring territory forcibly or through dubious transactions. He proved superior to his predecessors; yet in substituting his greedy and ferocious egotism for the inefficient laxity of Cobenzl and Spielmann, he weakened the bonds of the Coalition.

To begin with, he engaged in a violent controversy with Haugwitz, who was accused of duplicity. But the Prussians had the last word—they would wait for their ally to return to her senses. Catherine indicated that Austria, by being obstinate, had reason to fear abandonment by Frederick William. Thugut was fully aware of this, and he had no intention of refusing his approval of the treaty of January 23. He only postponed it, hoping that he would be formally guaranteed some compensation. Prussia's obligations were limited to the campaign in progress, and he foresaw a third one. Having secretly renounced the exchange of the Netherlands under pressure from Pitt, he had to obtain the lines of the Somme and the Moselle in France.

Frederick William's ministers, invoking the situation in Poland, urged their master not to strengthen the emperor. They were delighted to learn from the English that Austria had renounced the exchange. When negotiations opened in August, Lucchesini declared that Prussia, on the contrary, would adhere to it; and now that Belgium was reconquered, she considered that her duty as an ally had been loyally fulfilled. Then, because the situation was becoming more serious in Warsaw, the king finally was persuaded to inform Austria that he was no longer bound by the treaty of January 23; accordingly she might take what she wished from France. A final qualm prompted him to admit that he would agree to a third campaign if the wherewithal were provided for him. Thereupon he left the Rhine. Behind him Brunswick left Wurmser to carry on the fighting, and soon yielded the command to Möllendorf, one of the most resolute advocates of peace with France.

Although abandoned, Thugut did not lose hope of a conquest in France (thanks to the support of England); but he began to seek an easier prey, and turned his eyes towards Venice, as Joseph II had done before him. He was aware that Catherine's attitude towards Prussia was now very cool. Having helped enlarge Prussia, the tsarina thought it opportune to contain it by bringing Russia closer to Austria. Thugut favoured this development by recognizing the treaty of January 23 insofar as it affected Russia. On February 27, 1794, plans were made for a new Austro-Russian alliance which would deliver Venice to Francis II in lieu of conquests in France. Moreover, Thugut certainly had one reservation in mind—a Poland still remained. The war in the west obviously interested him less and less; and that very day he rejected the demand for subsidies presented by Frederick William and recommended by England, and declared himself satisfied with the 20,000 men due him from Prussia according to the treaty of February 7, 1792. The king parried by ordering Möllendorf to withdraw into Westphalia. If his troops took part in the campaign of 1794, it was because Pitt undertook to maintain them—a sacrifice that was pure waste, because the Polish crisis reopened.

The Patriots had not resigned themselves to allowing their country to be dismembered without putting up a fight. Kosciusko, a refugee in Saxony, prepared an insurrection, and when the disbanding of Polish regiments precipitated it in March, 1794, he hastened to Cracow. On April 4 the Russians were beaten at Raclawice; Warsaw rose, and they evacuated it on the 19th. Almost immediately troops infiltrated Prussian Poland. But Kosciusko judged his defeat certain if he did not secure the neutrality of the two German powers. He offered to negotiate, leaving them the provinces they had acquired in the two partitions. Frederick William refused to parley, however, and Thugut made a dilatory reply. Indeed, it was obvious that those who crushed the national movement would confiscate what remained of Poland. This time, however, Catherine was at a disadvantage. She had only a few troops there, and it would take time to bring Suvorov's army from the Ukraine. The advantage lay with the Austro-Prussians. Thugut rushed precipitately from the Netherlands, and the emperor was not long in following him. All available forces, between 15,000 and 20,000 men, were turned towards Galicia.

The Austro-Russian agreement was specific: Austria would occupy the southern palatinates, particularly Cracow; but the Prussians moved first. News of the insurrection brought a meeting of the minds between the ministry and the army. The king himself set out with 50,000 men. By June 3, 1794, he was at Wola, and on the 15th his troops entered Cracow. In July, 25,000 Prussians and 13,000 Russians encircled Kosciusko, who was entrenched in Warsaw. Unhappily, the Poles were divided among themselves. A democratic constitution on the French model was being prepared and there was talk of emancipating the peasants; but the aristocracy would not agree to this. Bloody clashes occurred between the 'friends of liberty' and the 'royalists'. Nevertheless the besieged put up a stout defence, and, as in 1792, the slowness of transport and the indecision of the king prevented the Prussians from winning. Entrenchment was not begun until July 26; it progressed slowly, and a rising in Posen threatened communications. On September 6, Frederick William raised the siege. Immediately Dombrowski seized Bromberg, and the Prussians began to wonder if they could hold the Vistula and protect the Oder.

Finally the Russians arrived. In October, 1794, Suvorov defeated the Poles at Maciejowice and captured Kosciusko. On November 4 he took Praga and slaughtered its inhabitants; and Warsaw, in a state of tumult, capitulated on the 6th. Thugut, having lost the Netherlands, had notified the English in August that he would leave the reconquest to them. The

Prussians still occupied Cracow, and he had not a moment to lose. Thenceforth he gave his full attention to outwitting Catherine and preparing for the third partition. If Frederick William found himself excluded from it, Austria would have had her revenge.

This was fully understood in Berlin. The only way to parry the blow was to negotiate with France, so that all the Prussian troops might be moved to the east. If they were there in force, Austria, exposed to the thrusts of the revolutionaries, would not dare come to blows. Foreseeing this, on July 31, Möllendorf had made overtures to Barthélemy, who represented France at Basel. The king hesitated a long time, but the retreat from Warsaw and the maladroitness of Pitt, who just at this moment cut off Prussian supplies, completed the work of Valmy. On October 25, 1794, Frederick William ordered negotiations with the regicides.

Thus the Polish crisis kept not only Russia, but part of the Prussian and Austrian armies as well, away from France. It eventually broke up the Coalition on the Continent. At the price of her independence Poland contributed to the salvation of the Revolution.

THE WAR AGAINST FRANCE: VICTORIES AND DEFEATS OF THE ALLIED ARMIES (1793–1794)

Nevertheless the assault against France in 1793 seemed formidable. Coburg entered the campaign with 5,500 Austrians and 11,000 Prussians. Gradually he was reinforced, first with English and Dutch, then with Hanoverians and Hessians, and by August he had 110,000 soldiers between the North Sea and the Meuse. The king of Prussia marched on Mainz with 42,000 men and left 33,000 in Westphalia, while Wurmser supported him with 24,000 Austrians, who were to be joined by 14,000 Germans. England subsidized 20,000 Sardinians and 6,000 Neapolitans. Spain armed some 50,000 men, and Portugal sent a division. If the danger to the Revolution did not abate until autumn, however, it was as much because of attacks from the rear by its internal enemies, who lent a helping hand to the Allies. In March the Vendée appealed to the English, and after June 2 the entire south of France was in arms, to the advantage of the Sardinians and the Spanish.

Yet the campaign ended in victory for the Carmagnoles. Contemporaries laid a share of the blame on Prussia and Austria. The Prussians in Westphalia had left for Poland, while those in the Netherlands went to join the Army of the Rhine, which nonetheless remained inactive. Consequently, in order to reinforce Wurmser, Thugut brought back from Italy the troops which were supposed to embark for Toulon to support the Sardinians. These latter, uneasy, did not fully commit themselves, and no more than 1,600 appeared at Toulon. The blame also fell upon Pitt, and not without reason. As a diplomat he had already seen his star wane in 1791; and as a war leader he showed only one of the qualities that had distinguished his father—tenacious perseverance. If his will was not broken by events, his spirit remained incapable of dominating them.

Pitt did not perceive the novelty of the war, that it was no longer a matter of wresting peace from a weary king. The Jacobins rejected all compromises, and would choose only between victory and death. Accordingly no negotiations could be entered upon until their government was overthrown—and that necessitated taking Paris. Burke saw this clearly. 'It will be a long war and a dangerous war,' he said. Pitt and Grenville, on the other hand, underestimated the power of their adversary; in their opinion one or two campaigns would suffice. They failed to see the weaknesses of the Coalition. As in a dream, Pitt computed the promised forces on paper. He counted on 34,200 men at Toulon by the end of October; only 17,000 appeared, and of those but 12,000 were of any value.

Sure of an easy and immediate victory, Pitt was thus preoccupied above all with assuring England's share of the spoils, and consequently, with relying upon tradition to determine his country's role in the conduct of the war. To the Allies and mercenaries belonged the war on the Continent; to England, the seas and the colonies. British troops might undoubtedly participate in European operations, but only to serve English interests directly or to seize pawns—and never at more than token strength. Nothing is more instructive than Pitt's attitude in the campaign in Belgium, the very country from which he was still so intent upon driving the French. The duke of York set out only on February 20, 1793, and he took a mere four battalions, with orders not to cross the Dutch frontier. After

Neerwinden he was finally authorized to march on Antwerp and Ghent, but by the end of April he still had only 6,500 English. True, Pitt had very few troops available; but at least he should have avoided dispersing them.

Pitt's policy produced two fatal consequences. First, he missed one of the best opportunities offered the Coalition—to respond to the appeal from the Vendée. England alone could help that region. Burke and Windham pointed out that even if the enterprise did not go off smoothly, because the British fleet lacked control of the sea, the risk would be worth running nonetheless. Their efforts were in vain. A popular uprising brought only derision from the military, and the ruling classes never viewed it with approval. A new prospect was presented when Admiral Hood, on his own initiative, responded to an appeal from the royalists of Provence and occupied Toulon. This time Pitt was roused to action, because this port constituted a pawn and yielded half the French fleet. The measures he applied, however, were inadequate—he sought troops and vessels at Turin, at Milan, and at Naples, and finally, in December, he drew reinforcements from Ireland. But it was too late. On November 26, 1793, 7,000 men had embarked for Haiti.

Elsewhere the affliction that paralyses coalitions—the great difficulty they experience in co-ordinating the movement of their armies—ran its course unchecked. At a time when communications were so slow that it took at least eleven days to transmit an order from London to Toulon, perfect synchronization of operations on all fronts was unattainable. Nevertheless on the north-eastern front, the decisive area of operations, the leaders were able to plan a simultaneous advance. Some possibly insurmountable obstacles undoubtedly stood in the way: the antagonism between Prussia and Austria; the incapacity of the leaders, who were obsessed with the idea of taking fortresses instead of seeking out and destroying the enemy; and the concern for seizing pawns, which encouraged generals in their outmoded strategy. It was no less true, however, that with England the heart of the Coalition, Pitt, who spoke in her name, alone was capable of trying to accelerate and co-ordinate the general offensive; but he did not even think of it. In any case, it would have required England to send a strong army to the Netherlands, and not to set an example of suspending a war of movement in order to seize Dunkirk.

In reality, if the Coalition triumphed for several months, it was only because the French forces were divided and poorly led. Between the armies of Custine and Dumouriez, Brunswick and Coburg occupied a central position suitable for an offensive. Custine was overextended at Mainz, and Dumouriez's army was scattered behind a weak cover guarding the Roer. As a crowning misfortune, on February 16, 1793, just as Coburg was about to get under way, Dumouriez invaded Holland. The genius of Mack, Coburg's chief of staff who directed the campaign, was pompously extolled; he had only to press forward. On March 1 the Allies routed the enemy on the Roer and drove upon Liége. Dumouriez finally resigned himself to withdrawing from Holland, and gave battle before he had concentrated his troops. Beaten at Neerwinden on March 18, then at Louvain, he was able to defend the line of the Scheldt; but having just broken with the Convention, he wished to march on Paris. He concluded an armistice with Mack and evacuated Belgium; and in keeping with the agreement, Coburg halted at the frontier.

Assembled an Antwerp, the diplomats of the Coalition protested, on April 8, against this attitude which obstructed conquest, and Thugut, after ratifying the armistice on the 9th, renounced it the next day. When Dumouriez's defeat invalidated it, Coburg had already crossed the frontier. Still, reinforcements were slow in arriving. Dampierre resisted Coburg for several weeks in the forest along the Scarpe, and the camp of Famars held out until May 23. Then the French withdrew to Caesar's Camp between the Scheldt and the Sensée, and Coburg was left free to besiege Condé and Valenciennes undisturbed. He spent two months there, for his depots and munitions were not at hand. He forced the surrender of Condé on July 10, and that of Valenciennes on the 28th. At last in August he planned a great manoeuvre to outflank Cambrésis; but instead of taking Cambrai or crossing the Scheldt to the north, he took the city from the south, and without using his cavalry. The French army, still 40,000 strong, was able to retreat behind the Scarpe. Nevertheless the road to Paris was clear, and Coburg now had 100,000 men in open country.

During this time the Prussians, having crossed the Rhine north of Bingen, were encircling Mainz. Wurmser also crossed the river, south of Mannheim. Custine, taken from behind, retreated hastily to Landau. The siege of Mainz began, and lasted as long as those of the northern forts, ending only on July 23, 1793. In August, Landau was blockaded, and Wurmser penetrated the Bienwald between the Queich and the Lauter. On other fronts the Allies were equally successful. The Sardinians were advancing in the Tarentaise, Maurienne, and Faucigny; but the siege of Lyons had scarcely begun. On August 29 the royalists handed Toulon over to the English, but failed to do likewise with Marseilles. To the west of the Pyrenees, Caro had reached the Nivelle. Ricardos had captured the forts which protected Roussillon, and in September he invested Perpignan. Finally the Vendée beat off all assaults. True, the revolutionary government was being formed, but Coburg still had time to act.

At this very moment, however, his army broke up. The English had agreed reluctantly to postpone the siege of Dunkirk. They had become impatient, and the duke of York received orders to take the town. The Dutch followed him, and the Prussians went to reinforce Brunswick. Coburg, weakened, contented himself with the capitulation of Le Quesnoy, on September 12, after which he attacked Maubeuge. Likewise, since Brunswick remained on the defensive in the Palatinate, Wurmser dared not cross the Rhine south of the Lauter. First he had to make a frontal attack on the lines of Wissembourg. He decided upon it only on October 13, and then he could advance only as far as the Zorn; but he was too late. The French had profited from his inaction to group their forces in the north, and to defeat the disorganized corps of York and Coburg at Hondschoote, on September 6 and 8, and at Wattignies, near Maubeuge, on October 16. Then Wurmser was attacked and driven back upon the lines of Wissembourg, from which he was finally dislodged, and he was forced to raise the siege of Landau at the end of December.

Events followed the same pattern in the south of France. The Sardinians, lacking Austrian support, halted, and after Lyons fell on October 9, they were driven from Savoy. On the Pyrenees front, Caro retreated as far as Bidassoa, and Ricardos to the camp of Boulou. The French were now able to press the siege of Toulon, the fall of which, on December 19, 1793, marked the end of the campaign. The Allies had reconquered Belgium and the left bank of the Rhine, and they held three fortresses in the north of France. But the revolutionary armies, taking the offensive again, had shown themselves to be far more formidable than heretofore.

Pitt, it must be admitted, finally endeavoured to improve the methods of the Coalition. He roundly criticized Coburg's incapacity, and unable to secure his replacement, had him attached to Mack, who, wounded, had returned to Austria in May of 1793. It was agreed that Francis II would go in person to the Netherlands to ensure a unified command. Conferences were held, first in Brussels and then in London, to prepare the impending campaign between the Rhine and the sea. Mack insisted that all available forces be concentrated in the Netherlands—at least 200,000 men—to march on Paris. Because the Prussians threatened to withdraw, the prospects did not seem bright. Pitt temporarily reunited the Allies by sending Lord Malmesbury to the Prussians. Thugut having refused his quota of 22 million thaler demanded by Frederick William for the maintenance of 100,000 men, Möllendorf at first received orders to cross the Rhine again. Malmesbury intervened, however, and conducting Haugwitz to the Hague, induced him to sign a treaty on April 19, 1794. England undertook to subsidize 62,400 Prussians, at a cost of £50,000 a month, plus £300,000 to be paid at once.

Still the situation remained virtually unchanged. England had only some 12,000 men in the Netherlands, and her authority there was very weak. The advisers of Francis II discredited Mack. When the Polish crisis brought the emperor back to Vienna towards the end of March, Mack left the fray, and the command returned to its previous status. Pitt could not offset the consequences of events in Poland, but by his clumsiness he contributed mightily to Prussia's defection. He ratified the treaty concluded by Malmesbury only on May 22, and then claimed the right to use the troops in his pay as he saw fit. Finally he decided to bring them from the Palatinate into the Netherlands, an obviously wise move; but the king of Prussia was offended because his soldiers were shifted without his being consulted, and Möllendorf had a good excuse for refusing to undertake this flanking march in the presence of the French.

Since Thugut sent no reinforcements, Coburg could range only 185,000 men from the North Sea to Luxembourg. The French opposed him with almost as many. Coburg attacked their centre, but did not concentrate his forces sufficiently. He first took the offensive on the Sambre and seized Landrecies. Then he pushed a spearhead against Lille and was beaten at Tourcoing on May 13, 1794. Möllendorf's inaction, similar to Brunswick's in 1793, determined the outcome. The French brought down the Sambre a part of the Army of the Moselle, which, united with that of the Ardennes, attacked Coburg from the rear. The battle of Fleurus, on June 26, reopened Belgium to the republicans.

Pitt had abandoned none of his illusions. He calculated that the Austrians would move 100,000 men into the Netherlands at the end of the year. When, however, he saw them in retreat towards the Rhine, while the duke of York, withdrawing from his sector, re-entered Holland, he lost his composure. Throwing responsibility for the disaster on the Prussians, on October 17 he withdrew all subsidies. This was the deciding factor which prompted Frederick William to negotiate with the French. Undoubtedly some may think that Pitt could not have saved the Coalition. Nevertheless he did so little to assure its victory, and so manifestly contributed to its ruin, that he cannot be said to have acted as a great statesman.

MARITIME AND COLONIAL WARFARE

The essential task that Pitt had reserved for himself seemed less arduous. In order to re-establish the balance of power during the American War of Independence, France had needed the aid of Spain and Holland. By turning against her they made her defeat certain. Nevertheless, during the first years of this war England did not enjoy absolute control of the seas, and she experienced several setbacks.

Her allies gave her little assistance. Holland possessed 49 mediocre vessels, which were used for convoys and blockading. Naples had only 4 to offer, and Portugal 6, which were staffed with British officers. Spain alone could have been very helpful with her 76 ships of the line, 56 of which were in commission in 1793. Her alliance opened the Mediterranean to the English, and by supporting them resolutely there, Spain would have permitted them to use the major part of their own forces in the Channel and on the Atlantic. But she distrusted them, and did not attempt to help them take Corsica. At Toulon, Langara quarrelled with Hood, who wanted to bring out the French squadron, and ultimately Hotham received no aid from Spain. The Spanish were even more disturbed by the English annexation of the French Antilles, and above all, of Haiti; and Valdes, minister of the navy, was frankly anti-English.

True, the English fleet possessed an obvious numerical superiority over the French: at the beginning of the war, 115 available ships of the line as against 76. Although its ordnance was proportionately less powerful, it did enjoy several technical advantages—lighter masts, better rigging, flexible ramrods which were valuable in the event of boarding. It fired to sink rather than to dismast. But it was not adequate for all purposes—fighting, maintaining a blockade, and protecting commerce against privateers. In any case, it was not entirely ready. Great difficulties were experienced and years were required to bring it to the point of readiness.

Shipbuilding procedures had altered but little. The ship of the line remained unchanged—200 feet in length and 50 feet at mid-beam, with 2 fighting decks, 74 guns, and a crew of 600. Lord Spencer, successor to Chatham as first lord of the admiralty from 1794 to 1801, was able to solve construction problems easily. To English oak and fir, or the Norway pine of Scotland, which was not yet scarce, were added Baltic woods (which the French could no longer buy) as well as American white pine. But England's arsenals were mediocre, and of 24 ships of the line built from 1793 to 1801, only 2 left the state dockyards. She also had difficulty in recruiting sailors. In 1792, naval personnel comprised 16,000 men, and 9,000 more were added in December. Yet in 1790 the squadrons mobilized against Spain had carried 40,000, and in 1799 there were more than 120,000. If the English took the upper hand at once, it was because the French fleet was disorganized as a result of emigration, treason, and lack of discipline. Nevertheless at the outset they had to limit themselves to keeping watch on the enemy, so that most of their ships could be used for patrol and escort duty. Only gradually did they assume the offensive, and in 1795 they had not yet cleared the sea of republican squadrons.

Until that date, it is true, Chatham and Richmond, the administrative chiefs of the navy, appeared as unconcerned as they were incompetent, and the command made poor use of its forces. Yet it was superior to the army. Since many officers were needed, birth was not scrutinized too closely, and some were even drawn from the merchant marine. Men of great valour who were to revolutionize tactics were already in the lower ranks—Collingwood, Cornwallis, Troubridge; and Nelson, destined to become the most famous, was then a captain of thirty-four. Among the admirals trained in the American War of Independence were such able leaders as Duncan and Jervis. But Howe and Hotham, especially the latter, were not equal to their tasks. The Admiralty ordered that the enemy should be sought out and destroyed, but Howe thought only of sparing his ships. He obstinately refused to blockade the French in their ports because such activity was too hard on his vessels; and he continued the same old tactics of line combat, ship against ship. Hood, although more skilful, achieved no great success.

The new feature of the war during these first years was the importance of Mediterranean operations, which the English were able to undertake, thanks to the alliance with Spain. Hood did not succeed in bottling up Trogoff in Toulon until July; but when treason delivered the French squadron, he had four vessels brought out, and at the time of the evacuation, he burned nine others. Now he was at leisure to conquer Corsica, where Paoli was directing a separatist movement and had offered the crown to George III. Since, however, he lacked landing troops, three fortresses held out for a long time. Calvi fell into Nelson's hands only in August, 1794. The English leaders acted no more in unison than they had at Toulon, and Pitt sent them hardly any reinforcements. Meanwhile the French were at work, and in June, 1794, they put out to sea again. Hood drove them back into Juan Gulf without being able to attack them, and when, at the beginning of 1795, six vessels arrived from Brest, his situation became critical. He complained and was recalled. His successor, Hotham, although reinforced, found himself challenged by Admiral Martin in Corsican waters in May and July, but he did not risk a decisive battle. The blockade of Toulon was re-established by Jervis only in November.

Nor did the English win any decisive advantages on the Atlantic. In July, 1793, Howe declined to engage Morard de Galles in the waters off Belle-Isle. Afterwards he refused to do blockade patrol before Brest. Roundly criticized, he set sail in May, 1794, to intercept the large convoy that France was expecting from America, and encountered Villaret-Joyeuse, who had gone to protect it. The two squadrons clashed on May 26 and 29 and June 1. Although Howe captured six ships and still had fifteen serviceable vessels against Villaret's nine, the latter was able to re-enter Brest, and the convoy arrived safely. In December, Villaret set out again, but a storm, not the enemy, drove him back into port. In the summer of 1795, Bridport and Cornwallis forced him to take refuge in Lorient during the disembarkation at Quiberon. Nevertheless, in January, 1796, Hoche's expedition succeeded in reaching Ireland.

Under these circumstances, France carried on the colonial war longer than might have been expected. Since the British were particularly covetous of the sugar islands, the French concentrated on the Antilles. Ever since the slave insurrection in Santo Domingo, the planters had been calling for help from the outside world. The Spanish aided the insurgents solely out of hatred for the Revolution. Pitt held back until the war, and then dealt with the colonists in order to promote what he hoped would be a permanent conquest; and he used troops which could have been of great assistance at Toulon and in the Vendée. Beginning in September, 1793, they gradually occupied various ports in Santo Domingo, and in June, 1794, Port-au-Prince. In May, however, Toussaint L'Ouverture had broken with Spain and had come to the aid of General Lavaux; and the abolition of slavery by the Convention brought the Negroes to the side of the French. Furthermore, illness decimated the English, and by the end of 1795, confined to the coastal towns, they looked forward to leaving Haiti.

They were more successful in the Windward Islands. In April, 1793, they occupied Tobago without firing a shot. At

Martinique there were setbacks at first, but in March, 1794, Jervis arrived to take it. Then St. Lucia and Guadeloupe suffered the same fate. Victor Hugues reversed the situation somewhat by reconquering Guadeloupe, knew how to keep it, and from this base greatly harrassed the enemy. Once Holland had been taken over by the republicans, the Dutch colonies offered new opportunities; and the English occupied the Cape of Good Hope on September 16, 1795, and Dutch Guiana as well. The scales were tipping more and more in their favour. Still, the last word had not been said, for after the fall of Holland, Spain abandoned the Coalition.

ECONOMIC WARFARE

For a long time Pitt and Grenville used French distress to justify their own optimism: famine and the collapse of the assignats would bring France to her knees; and the time was not far distant. In 1792 the émigrés had asked the king of Prussia to counterfeit assignats, but he had refused. Pitt did not have the same scruples, and he had vast quantities printed for distribution in France. Meanwhile, in August, 1793, he was accused in the Convention of opening credits to bankers so that they might sell London stocks in Paris and thus depress French exchange by encouraging an export of capital. The accusation was probably well founded; certainly Pitt kept in touch with Parisian financiers, such as the Englishman Boyd and the Swiss Perregaux. But experience presented him with a still more effective means of weakening France—the blockade, the principles of which had been developed during the Seven Years' and the American Revolutionary wars.

On June 8, 1793, Pitt, assuming that the French government had now acquired all the resources of the country through requisitioning, and that imports could thereby be turned to the profit of the army, added grain to the list of war contraband. In fact, this measure (which he renewed on April 25, 1795) for the first time treated the civilian population of an entire country like that of a besieged town. Moreover, the blockade was made more stringent than before. In earlier wars the land frontiers of France had largely remained open, many Continental states had remained neutral or had joined her, and the

Mediterranean had not come under British control. Now the Allies strove to close their ports to the French, to confiscate their goods, to forbid the profitable shipment of merchandise covered by the blockade, and to prohibit all loans and payments. Armies sealed off French frontiers, except on the Swiss border, and the English patrolled the Mediterranean. France was almost completely isolated, and banking relations, which were to continue during the subsequent Napoleonic era, were interrupted, at least in principle.

Still, the blockade was far from being airtight. The Allies did not apply the necessary measures with equal zeal. The emperor, for example, waited until March 17, 1794, to forbid payments to the French in the Netherlands. In vain the Diet admonished the Senate of Hamburg, which permitted merchants and bankers to deal with the Republic. It took an ultimatum and extended cruises to close Leghorn. Even in Holland the blockade was evaded. In the days of sailing ships, moreover, there were many ways of eluding it, and coasting trade, especially with Genoa, was not greatly disturbed. There was no international organization of commercial espionage—to say nothing of means of communication—to keep the blockaders informed. Finally, there were the neutrals. Some—Swedes, Danes, and Americans—observed the blockade only when they were forced to do so. Others—the Genoese and the Swiss—escaped it because of their geographical location. Through Switzerland, France was able to buy in Germany, Austria, and Italy.

It must be observed, moreover, that in the hands of the English the blockade was not aimed solely, or even primarily, at the enemy's military resistance. Added to the mercantile system, it freed the English from French competition and permitted them to confiscate French markets. Through the draconic regulation applied to merchant vessels, it tended to eliminate the neutrals and even the Allies, to the profit of the British. The Order in Council on colonial trade, November 6, 1793 (renewing that of 1756), brought out this aspect of the blockade. It forbade neutrals to trade with French colonies which were closed to them before the war but which the Convention had opened to them. England thus arrogated to herself a monopoly over colonial goods.

From the mercantilist point of view an airtight blockade would have been absurd; if profit were to be gained by preventing the enemy from selling, there was also some to be made by shipping English merchandise to it. This would permit the extraction of specie or the securing of needed products from France. Consequently the government distributed licences for enemy ports as circumstances warranted. In truth, the Convention had proscribed trade with Great Britain, but merchandise was easily 'neutralized'. This operation was practised on a large scale at Emden, for example, and it cost only a commission of 1 or 2 per cent. As for transport, the English in turn resorted to neutral vessels. In fact, exports to France and the Netherlands (15 per cent of the total English exports in 1792) had fallen only three points by 1800. It even seems that, to take care of mercantile interests, the authorities looked indulgently upon war contraband. Since the neutrals performed services, notably in evading privateers, it was necessary to make concessions to them. Even the ban on grain imports into France was repealed in August, 1794. Thus the English would willingly have eased the blockade in order to continue exporting, but the will of the French and, above all, their controlled economy, prevented them from so doing.

As it was, the blockade created problems for the Allies. First, it embroiled them with the neutrals. The Danish minister, Bernstorff, and the Swedish regent energetically maintained their rights. Finally, on March 27, 1794, they concluded an agreement which provided for the arming of sixteen vessels for the protection of their commerce, and even for closing the Baltic to belligerents. Grenville was not greatly alarmed, because he knew that Bernstorff did not wish a break, and in any case no action could be taken until the following spring. At the moment the United States appeared to be a greater threat.

After 300 of their ships trading with the French Antilles had been captured, the Americans had placed an embargo on British vessels. When, on April 29, 1794, the Scandinavians informed the Americans of their agreement, rumours began to circulate that the latter would subscribe to it. But the attitude of the French representative antagonized Washington, and Hamilton, secretary of the Treasury, wished to avoid a conflict with England at all costs. In June, 1794, Jay arrived in London, and on November 19 he concluded the treaty that bears his name. The United States agreed to admit no more French privateers into her ports, and to keep the ports open to British vessels and prizes. The agreement made no mention of the blockade, but it was tacitly admitted. Jay had even consented to reduce American trade with the Antilles to almost nothing, and to renounce the shipment of colonial produce to Europe. The Senate refused to accept these latter capitulations, but it ratified the remainder of the pact, partly in the interests of peace, partly because England promised to evacuate the posts which she still occupied in the north of the United States.

On the other hand, the measures adopted by France, combined with the activity of her privateers, caused serious damage to Allied commerce. Despite sailing in escorted convoys, the English lost more than 600 ships a year in 1794 and 1795. Insurance rates rose greatly, and neutral trade with British ports increased in tonnage from 10 per cent in 1792 to 25 per cent in 1793. Nevertheless England's great difficulties were experienced only during the first year. The declaration of war, by tightening credit, brought about numerous bankruptcies and the collapse of a hundred banks. The reserves of the Bank of England were reduced to £4 million in February, 1793. In the course of the year the aggregate tonnage of the ports declined by 17 per cent, and exports fell from £24 million to £19 million in 1792. The price of colonial goods slumped, and Hamburg was glutted with them.

But the Bank held firm, discounted commercial paper freely, and issued five-pound notes to mitigate the hoarding of specie. Gold was leaving France, and almost £4 million was bought by the Bank, so that the reserves rose again. Its advances permitted Pitt to devote £5 million to aiding business leaders. Once the crisis had passed, imports and exports no longer lagged. The latter rose to £25 million in 1794 and 1795, and to £28 million in 1796. The slave trade, which had made a prodigious advance in 1792, following the troubles that paralysed the French Antilles, continued to flourish. Twenty-seven thousand slaves were imported in 1792, as contrasted with 11,000 in 1789; and 14,000 more were brought in in 1794.

True, some industries were jeopardized—the silk and brocade

weavers at Spitalfields, for example, were thrown out of work. But the Continentals suffered far more. Some, such as the Italians and the Spanish, who were customers of France, experienced privations. Others, such as the Germans, who furnished France with precious metals and chemical products, found themselves deprived of this market. The Polish crisis, coinciding with the blockade, made matters worse. The textile industry in Germany, especially in Silesia, was reduced to nothing. In certain areas provisioning became difficult. Little grain was available from Prussia and Poland, while Holland and the Austrian Netherlands, obliged to feed armies, no longer had any to sell. At Barcelona, 'hungerbread' of mixed grain (*pain d'amalgame*) was being used as early as the spring of 1793. The situation became worse when, in 1794 and 1795, harvests were not good throughout western Europe. England in particular felt the effects. The price of wheat rose constantly until it reached 6 guineas per quarter in 1796, or 28 livres per French quintal, twice the maximum of the Year II. In 1795 prices exceeded those of 1790 by 26 per cent, and they continued to rise. Evil years were beginning for Britain.

Unemployment and high prices produced the same effects everywhere. As in France, the masses were roused. This was what the Old Regime governments most dreaded, and their fears affected the conduct of the war by preventing the Coalition from 'popularizing' it, from making it a national war after the pattern of the French revolutionaries.

THE WAR GOVERNMENTS OF THE ALLIES

The immediate causes of the failures of the Coalition were its lack of unity and the mediocrity of its diplomats, who were incapable of changing their habits, but the real cause lay in the Old Regime. For a long time this war, conducted by the French along such new lines, brought no change in the Allies' methods of government.

Monarchs and aristocrats, ossified by inheritance, privilege, and prejudice, could neither invent nor utilize new methods. To be sure, it is not astonishing that the Continental governments were not reformed. Apart from Catherine, whose counter-revolutionary passion remained platonic, their princes were, for the most part, undistinguished. The two most powerful were the emperor and the king of Prussia. The former, Francis II, allowed himself to be led by the empress, daughter of Ferdinand of Naples, and by a Lorrainer, General Rollin, his aide-de-camp, who, in league with Thugut, made the military decisions and was responsible for Mack's dismissal. The king of Prussia, Frederick William II, was the only Prussian who wished to continue the war against France after the battle of Valmy. His ministers, supported by Prince Henry, constantly criticized him. As for the army, it was a state within a state, to such an extent that Möllendorf, its chief, finally negotiated with the French on his own authority.

It is more astonishing that the government of England, which did not suffer from the same anarchy, was not more speedily impelled by the demands of war to make necessary reforms. Pitt had, indeed, modified his ministry; but he did so by parliamentary tactics. The war eventually consummated the Whig split. Although Fox, Sheridan, and Lansdowne periodically presented motions in favour of peace, Windham would have agreed to participate in the government. Pitt was willing to include him, but Dundas, who was head of the Home Office, minister of war, secretary for Ireland, and treasurer of the navy, obstinately refused to reduce his extravagant pluralism. Dundas, however, merely held the *title* of minister of war. Knowing nothing about the army, he turned it over to Yonge, first secretary of the War Office, who was not a member of the cabinet. Actually Pitt and Grenville directed operations, but they were not always in agreement, even on diplomacy, and nothing had prepared them for the prosecution of a war. George III took advantage of the situation to have things done as he wished. He forced the siege of Dunkirk, thought he could bring Möllendorf into the Netherlands in 1794, and for more than a year prevented the recall of the duke of York, even though the latter was the laughingstock of the army.

The navy fared little better. Of its two masters, Lord Chatham, Pitt's brother, was known to be a sad nonentity, and the duke of Richmond was notoriously lazy and incompetent. The fleet took no part in the siege of Dunkirk, and at the very time that Toulon clamoured for reinforcements, Lord Moira was left immobilized at Portsmouth, and four regiments were inactive in the Channel Islands. When the troops from Ireland were ready, there were no ships to transport them. It required the defeat at Fleurus and the loss of Belgium to make Pitt realize that change was necessary. Dundas finally gave up the administration of the war, and a secretaryship for the purpose was established for Windham. The duke of York was soon recalled. Spencer replaced Chatham, and Cornwallis succeeded Richmond. These last choices were good ones, but Windham proved to be a mediocre minister. He hastened to organize the expedition to the Vendée which he had long advocated and which ended in disaster at Quiberon.

The Allies changed nothing in their manner of recruiting. In 1794 there was much talk in Germany of a general arming of the people; but it was only talk. With volunteers becoming increasingly scarce, levies by lot became frequent everywhere. The difficulties which accompanied them explain in part the shortage of effective manpower and the slowness with which reinforcements were supplied. Until 1794 England was content to depend upon volunteers. The aristocracy furnished the officers, who purchased their commissions. Thirty-four new regiments were established, and Protestant Ireland proved her loyalty by sending 25,000 men. The militia, increased to 30,000, was to provide territorial defence under the supervision of the gentry, and volunteer companies were formed to maintain order or to co-operate with the militia. To the volunteers, accepted without regard to national origins, the navy added all men, sailors or not, who were picked up by the press gangs, and despite the law and in the face of American protests, foreigners as well. It also embarked convicts, and after the suspension of habeas corpus, it included political suspects as well.

Finally it was necessary to resort to the drawing of lots: first, in 1794, for the militia—and this in itself was sufficient to increase disturbances; then, in 1795, for 30,000 sailors; and eventually, in 1796, for the army of the line. Of course the procedure contained the same abuses that were found on the Continent, and the burden fell upon the poor. Since the new conscripts were virtually without training, they were sent to the colonies to replace professional soldiers, and there they were decimated by the climate. The untrained sailors suffered even more evils—wretched food, curtailed by peculation; no medical service; no shore leaves. No wonder that mutiny was commonplace in the British navy.

Although the effectives mustered by each power were not comparable to those of the French, all the Allies experienced much difficulty in arming, equipping, and even in feeding them in the customary manner. Nowhere, however, was civilian mobilization attempted, and everywhere the population, indifferent to the war, met requisitions with inertia. In the Netherlands the Austrians had no success. Insufficient finances were almost always at the root of these troubles. Prussia, a poor state, hard hit by the closing of the Polish market, experienced a considerable decline in revenue. Since she exported from 18 million to 20 million thaler annually for the needs of the army, she soon found herself in the grip of a monetary crisis. Moreover, Struensee, minister of finance, encountered great administrative obstacles. Frederick II, by reserving to himself the administration of the 'Privy Purse' (*Dispositionskasse*), in which were placed funds not specifically allocated, and by turning into it the revenues from Silesia (the only province that was really productive), had weakened the centralization so painfully achieved by his father, the 'sergeant king'.

Actually Struensee controlled only the coffers of the army and the crown lands, the resources of which, earmarked in advance and never adequate, should have been augmented by outlays from the 'Privy Purse', which Frederick William II handed over to Wöllner. Only with great difficulty did Struensee succeed in having expenses for luxuries reduced. Moreover, it was necessary to use up the 19 million thaler still held by the war fund at the end of 1792, and also to borrow in Holland and Frankfort—5 million gulden in 1793 and 8 million in 1794, not counting short-term advances. In 1795 an internal loan failed woefully. English money alone enabled Prussia to hold out. When she was deprived of that resource, Struensee, in October, 1794, saw no remedy other than to suppress privileges. The war was leading to revolutionary expedients, and there was no choice but to conclude peace.

The distress of the emperor, who was obliged to conciliate Belgium and Hungary, was no less great. The deficit, which was chronic, reached 30 million gulden in 1793 and 66 million in

1795. Beginning in 1793, loans were floated at home and abroad. From 362 million gulden in 1789, the debt rose to 477 million in 1796. Austria was able to survive only by issuing paper money, of which 23 million gulden were circulating in 1789 and 35 million in 1796. She could not have continued the war if, after the treaties of Basel, Thugut had not obtained subsidies from England.

As for Spain, she dispensed the government bonds (*vales reales*) of the Bank of St. Charles (Banco de San Carlos) lavishly. In 1794 part of the church silver was seized, and in 1795, with the permission of the pope, the king took over the revenues of vacant benefices and decided to fill none of them for a year. This was a step in the direction of selling clerical property. Having denounced the expedients of the French, the Spanish now likewise yielded to necessity and ended by imitating them.

It might have been supposed that well-to-do Englishmen, who approved the war and profited from it, would be willing to pay for it. But Pitt spared them this obligation as long as he could, by making good the growing deficit through loans. Receipts were far from increasing—£14,284,000 in 1792 and £13,557,000 in 1795; while naval expenditures rose from £1,985,000 to £6,315,000, and those of the army from £1,819,000 to £11,610,000. Borrowing furnished £4·5 million in 1793, almost £13 million in 1794, and £19·5 million in 1795. Pitt maintained the Sinking Fund, however, and nourished it with loan funds at ever-increasing rates of interest. Available capital was exhausted. Similarly, the Bank of England consented to advances, and accepted Exchequer bills to a total of £18 million in 1793. England, too, was headed towards a monetary crisis, in which Pitt's reputation as a financier would be put to the test.

THE EUROPEAN REACTION

Not daring to imitate the methods of the Jacobins, the aristocracy thought it best to evince indignation and to make a scapegoat of them. Throughout Europe novelists, writers, orators, and preachers denounced the 'cannibals' who, by threats of the guillotine, forced their compatriots into military service, ruined them through paper money, starved them through requisitions, and in short, reduced them to barbarism.

The émigrés contributed to this propaganda. At Verona, d'Antraigues fabricated incriminating documents, which were translated and distributed widely. The Abbé Barruel prepared to assemble the charges that Hoffmann had directed against the Freemasons and the *Illuminati*, and to these he now added the Protestants. Soon Joseph de Maistre, who was then directing Piedmontese espionage from Lausanne, was to make a synthesis of all this work and project the shadow of Satan behind the Revolution. The Genevans, d'Ivernois and Mallet du Pan, and constitutionalists such as Mounier, indoctrinated the liberal bourgeoisie. This propaganda had a profound effect. It alarmed self-interest even more perhaps than it did conscience. No matter how much one was a friend of liberty and equal rights, he would have to agree completely that the French were paying dearly for them. To all who were contemplating the inferno from afar the Terror also seemed indefensible. The boldest attempted only to explain it, while at the same time condemning it.

Fear or pity increased the recantations, but everywhere liberals and democrats survived, and the war, owing to its unforeseen consequences, was soon to provide them with new opportunities. Everything the French were blamed for—conscription, requisitions, paper money, unemployment, high prices, poverty—gradually appeared here and there throughout Europe. The rich or well-to-do saw an abyss between France and the Allies, because the Old Regime, in contrast with the Terror, spared them as much as possible. But the common people, who suffered, also made comparisons; moreover, their suffering was enough to spur them to revolt. As the war lengthened the reaction thus became worse, and occasionally it was accompanied by bloodshed. On the Continent this was quite in keeping with the prevailing despotism. In England, the suspension of constitutional liberties showed that, as in France, these liberties were only relative. To protect themselves the British aristocracy instituted their own dictatorship through terror, and tried to reduce popular anger through a kind of minimum wage—at the same time stigmatizing the French demagogues who had established a maximum for commodities.

In the north and east of Europe opponents disappeared early. Catherine closed Masonic lodges, imprisoned Novikov, and sent Radishchev to Siberia for having considered the abolition of serfdom. At Stockholm, in January, 1793, the lawyer Thorild was arrested; at Copenhagen, Baggesen now wrote odes against the Terror, and Malte-Brun fled to France; and in Norway the trial of Lofthus, leader of the peasant movement, was proceeding.

In Spain the war brought no changes. Those who had not succumbed to the Inquisition had fled to France—the Convention had given asylum to Olavide. At the beginning of hostilities Godoy succeeded, thanks to the clergy, in making the war popular; but when the sans-culottes failed to appear, the people soon relapsed into apathy, and discontent gradually spread among them. The dominant classes and the army also became provoked, chiefly because of the distrust inspired by the English. Godoy's enemies sought to make use of this to overthrow him. In 1795 he claimed to have discovered a plot to secure a meeting of the Cortes. It is probable that if he had not concluded peace he would have been unable to continue in office; but it does not appear that the opposition could have assumed a revolutionary character.

The symptoms became more threatening in Italy If the liberals had not disappeared, at least they were reduced to silence or had abjured. The two Pindemontes (Giovanni and Ippolito) changed sides. Alfieri, having complained of the revolutionaries in April, 1793, during his stay in Paris, broke with the French, 'born for servitude', although his *Misogallo* was not published until later. After the murder of Bassville, Monti flattered the reaction in his *Bassvilliana*, which was the principal literary event of the day. The centre of counter-revolutionary propaganda remained in Rome where the Frenchmen Bernis and Hesmivy d'Auribeau were active; but everywhere academies and newspapers worked along the same lines.

Still the unrest persisted. Tuscany long remained open to the French, and the smuggling of books and gazettes continued at Genoa, one of the principal trade centres of the Committee of Public Safety. Through Genoa, Piedmont became infected, and Turin, Saluzzo, Asti, and Vercelli served as the chief points of dissemination. Discontent increased in the army, and the prying activity of the secret police exasperated everyone, as in the rest of Italy. The court itself would have signed a peace treaty out of hatred for Austria if it had not been afraid of her. In the Romagna and in Venice feelings were rising likewise. At Bologna two young men raised the Italian tricolor in November, 1794, and called the people to insurrection.

The Neapolitan government also was disturbed. It seems that a plot was discovered at Palermo in 1795, and the peasants rose in Basilicata, shouting, 'We want to do what the French have done.' But the Terror had been rampant in that kingdom since 1793. A special junta instituted 813 trials and ordered 51 executions. In 1794 the king of Sardinia resorted to the same tactics, and an 'extraordinary' court returned fourteen death sentences in July. The two Bolognese were hanged; but others took their place. It was no longer simply a matter of overthrowing tyrants and putting an end to privilege. As would soon be apparent, Italian national unity was being fused with the revolutionary ideal.

Switzerland also was stirring. At the end of 1791 repression began in Vaud and Valais, where five death sentences were passed. Agrarian movements were taking form in the domains of the abbot of St. Gall at the end of 1793. In 1794 the people of Grisons rose. At Geneva an insurrection succeeded on July 19, 1794, and a revolutionary tribunal sentenced eleven persons to death. Perhaps encouraged by this example, the inhabitants of Stäfa, in the canton of Zurich, presented their grievances to the patriciate in 1795, and it responded with mass arrests. Lavater's intervention prevented executions, but 260 condemnations were pronounced.

In Germany the attitude of the Rhenish Club accentuated and justified the reaction. Since October, 1792, the emperor had proscribed French newspapers within his domains. In February, 1793, he proposed that the Diet forbid propaganda in all forms, with special reference to the clubs. A proclamation of April 30 denounced 'the dangerous principles of the Revolution, advocated and disseminated by ignorant philosophers'. On June 14 the Diet suppressed student associations. Spying and informing spread everywhere. The police opened letters and increased their searching of homes. Many municipalities forbade 'any untimely discussions at inns and in the streets'. Bookshops were closely watched, and at Vienna the archbishop assumed direction of censorship. Here and there Masonic lodges came under fire, and the one in Karlsruhe was closed.

In 1794 the terror became worse in Bavaria, where a great treason trial was organized, and especially in Vienna and Budapest, where blood was shed. A propaganda committee had undertaken to distribute copies of a republican catechism drafted by Martinovics. He was prosecuted for conspiracy, and in November, 1794, a large number of suspects was arrested. Seven liberals, including Martinovics and Laczkovics, went to their deaths in May, 1795, and many others remained in prison. The teaching staff at Buda was purged, and the works of Kant were banned and burned. Thugut reduced Alxinger and Sonnenfels, friends of Joseph II, to silence, while Hoffmann, now supported by Gentz, continued his campaign.

The terror thinned the ranks of the liberals. Ewald had to leave Detmold, and Posselt abandoned his chair at Karlsruhe. Fichte, called to the University of Jena in 1794, soon found himself the target of attacks. Rebmann fled to Altona, whence he reached Paris, and Cramer, Reichardt, and Baron von der Trenck followed him there. Elsewhere events in France discouraged the friends of the Revolution. Klopstock and Herder denounced the Terrorists, and Goethe and Schiller became openly hostile to these 'executioner's assistants'. Yet the liberal movement did not disappear entirely. Anonymous pamphlets continued to circulate. Kant persisted in his fidelity to the principles of 1789, and Richter still extolled the Girondins. Wieland at least remained opposed to armed intervention, while Dalberg and Mounier took up the defence of Freemasonry and the Enlightenment. At Brunswick, Benjamin Constant, now a court chamberlain, clung to sympathy for the republicans out of disgust with the obscurantists.

Finally, as elsewhere, the war eventually stirred up public disturbances. In the spring of 1793 the weavers of Silesia joined in violent reprisals against the businessmen who, deprived of export trade, had reduced them to beggarly wages. In 1794 the workers of Breslau rose in rebellion, the province was occupied by troops, and the outbreak was drowned in blood. No one in Germany undertook to exploit these conditions to the advantage of the Old Regime. In 1793 the towns of Saxony and the bourgeois and peasants of Hanover confined themselves to calling for fiscal equality, but without success. In 1794, in the provincial Diet (*Landtag*) of Bavaria, the nobles presented a list of grievances, and the Diet of Württemberg continued to quarrel with the duke; but the privileged classes (*Stände*) thought only of themselves.

Circumstances were different in England. Hence the history of that country assumes a special interest. The Whig schism showed that the war had accentuated counter-revolutionary feeling among the ruling classes. On the other hand, Fox, his friends, and Wilberforce, who censured the war, were visibly embarrassed by the annexations of the Convention, by the death of the king, and by the excesses of the Terrorists. At first the poets held fast. Wordsworth approved the execution of Louis XVI and pronounced himself in favour of the Republic. This state of mind was manifested in *The Borderers*, as well as in Southey's *Wat Tyler*. Nevertheless, when blacklisted by 'society', they gradually became discouraged. In 1794 Coleridge and Southey wept over their broken dreams, and the former celebrated the fall of Robespierre. The democratic leaders, on the contrary, were not affected. Clubs continued to multiply. Hardy and his lieutenant, the tailor Place, sold 200,000 copies of Paine's *Rights of Man* in 1794. Thirty popular societies existed at Norwich, and those of the Sheffield district enrolled 5,000 members.

Tory opinion promptly demanded prosecution. At first Pitt refrained from extraordinary measures and contented himself with allowing Dundas and Chancellor Loughborough to collaborate with voluntary associations in organizing repression. These groups organized themselves in watch committees and resorted to civic denunciation, spying in public places, and searching for subversive pamphlets and placards. The judges eagerly welcomed their information and freely dispensed sentences of fines, the pillory, and prison. In Scotland, Braxfield and Dundas, the nephew of the minister, became notorious for their partiality and skill in packing juries. 'God help the people who have such judges!' cried Fox. They gladly used *agents provocateurs*, but a simple offence against public opinion was usually sufficient. All propaganda on behalf of reform was seditious.

The Scots were bolder than the English, and they were the first to be struck. The lawyer Muir, arraigned on January 2, 1793, when he was about to leave for France, was sentenced on his return to fourteen years' transportation to Australia, despite an eloquent defence. The pastor Palmer of Dundee suffered the same fate simply for having written a placard. The excitement grew. In October a new Scottish Convention brought together thirty-five societies, in which York, London, and Ireland were represented. At the same time an assembly met in London to demand universal suffrage and annual Parliaments. At the end of November *agents provocateurs* persuaded the Scottish Convention to vote for the organization of a general convention of the United Kingdom. Dundas and Braxfield dispersed it by force and took advantage of the situation to obtain three more condemnations.

The English clubs held protest meetings, and on March 27, 1794, they decided to convoke a new Convention. After the Whigs had refused to defend the wishes of the democrats in Parliament, it was claimed that the democrats would resort to violence, and that they were secretly making weapons; but proof was never furnished. Watt, executed for having plotted an uprising at Edinburgh, was an informer who seems to have allowed himself to become enmeshed in his own provocative intrigues. This time, however, Pitt intervened in person. It was just at this moment that the coalition of Tories and Old Whigs was officially formed, an act that illustrates the underlying solidarity between the two political parties that constituted Parliament.

On May 12, 1794, Hardy, Tooke, Thewall, and several others were arrested, and the papers of the clubs were seized. These papers were examined by a Parliamentary committee, and in accord with it, Pitt had the Habeas Corpus Act suspended on May 16. Still he dared not set up a special jurisdiction, and no attempt was made to pack the juries in London, or, if one were made, it was not successful. Erskine conducted the defence magnificently, and in October the trial resulted in acquittal. Only one of Hardy's companions was punished, later, with two years in prison. The government withdrew its prosecutions, but henceforth it was able to arrest and detain suspects arbitrarily or to ship them off as sailors on warships.

Nevertheless the democrats were not entirely reduced to impotence. This was because economic unrest affected the people. There was unemployment, and the cost of living was increasing. From 1793 speculation by grain merchants had been violently denounced, as in France, and Pitt secured the right to pre-empt cargoes of grain destined by neutrals for France. The poor harvests of 1794 and 1795, and the difficulty of importing grain, aggravated the situation. In 1795 it became disturbing. Revolts increased, particularly in London, Birmingham, and Dundee. In the rural areas justices of the peace were threatened. Enclosures provoked disorders, and agrarian crimes occurred. The drawing of lots for the militia produced uprisings, and at Liverpool the use of the press gang had to be discontinued. With the army becoming increasingly susceptible to propaganda, executions for insubordination were initiated. Furthermore, the failures of the Coalition exerted a depressing influence.

The crisis reached its peak in October, 1795, when Parliament was opening. Following a great meeting held on the 27th, the king and Pitt were insulted by rioters on the 29th. Then the reaction increased. On November 4 a proclamation prescribed that seditious assemblies and publications should be prosecuted. On December 14 a bill subjected assemblies of more than fifty persons to a declaration and the presence of a magistrate. Huge meetings protested in vain, but to the very end, and much to the regret of Malmesbury, the democrats abstained from insurrection.

Henceforth their influence began to decline, less as a result of repression than of the relative improvement in living conditions. For one thing, the harvest of 1796 was satisfactory; for another, the expedient of aiding English workers against the high cost of living was adopted. On May 6, 1795, the justices of the peace in Berkshire established a cost-of-living index of articles essential to a worker, based upon the price of bread and taking into account the size of his family; and to assure their supply, they eventually decided to supplement wages at the expense of the taxpayers. In December, Whitbread advised the establishment of a minimum wage at the employer's expense.

The House of Commons rejected the measure, but Pitt gave his approval to the system adopted in Berkshire, and in November, 1796, he proposed to make it law. He even added an authorization for parishes to provide their indigents with cows, and to found industrial schools. Parliament thought this overly generous.

All the counties at least imitated the example of Berkshire. It may be that religious feeling commended it as a paternalism reconcilable with the interests of the ruling classes; but the result was no less obvious. The democrats were thus disarmed, and the aristocratic regime was consolidated for a long time. Simultaneously, manufacturers were assured of cheap manpower at the expense of the middle class, which in large part paid the costs of the 'relief'. The landed proprietors sold their wheat dearly. Purveyors to the army and navy, and manufacturers rid of French competition, realized respectable profits; and thanks to the high-interest loans to which they themselves subscribed, both escaped the costs of the war. True, the Coalition was beaten, but the aristocracy and the upper middle class did not suffer in their businesses.

Events took a different turn in Ireland. In January, 1793, Pitt yielded to reform agitation and granted the franchise to Catholics. This concession appeared sufficient to restore calm. The Catholic Committee dissolved, and Grattan was able to assure England of Irish loyalty in the conflict with France. When, however, the Whigs entered the ministry, they stipulated the nomination of Fitzwilliam as viceroy of Ireland; and he announced his intention of giving power to Grattan and of emancipating the Catholics. The Irish lords protested loudly, and the king imposed his veto.

As usual, Pitt yielded, and Fitzwilliam, who arrived in Dublin on January 4, 1795, was recalled on February 19. Already the Catholics were aroused, and they presented their demands. When the new viceroy, Camden, disembarked, disturbances broke out in Dublin. The Ulster Orangemen responded by attacking the Catholics. In 1796 famine plunged Ireland into anarchy. In 1795 the Committee of Public Safety had dispatched a former pastor, Jackson, to Ireland, and when arrested he took poison. Wolfe Tone collected funds in the United States, and Fitzwilliam negotiated with the French at Hamburg. The storm rumbled in Ireland at a time when it had subsided in Great Britain. If, after 1794, England had had its Vendée, the aristocracy would have run a great risk, and the terror might perhaps have become bloody instead of remaining 'dry'.

The Allies, comparing themselves to France, prided themselves on their benignity, and indeed it may be argued that through their precautionary measures, they were spared greater rigours. Moderate as they may have been, however, they nonetheless tended to repress the democratic spirit. Consequently, they refrained from appealing to national sentiment and 'popularizing' the war. This gave them another pretext for shutting themselves up within their traditional prejudices and routine mediocrity, at the very moment when the Revolution was giving free rein to individual talents and mobilizing all the energies of the French nation. As Mallet du Pan wrote, 'They feared their subjects almost as much as they feared the enemy.' This was the basic cause of their defeat.

CHAPTER TWO

The Revolutionary Government (1793–1794)

SCARCELY HAD THE REVOLUTION declared war upon Europe than it found itself in mortal danger: the foreign menace, civil war, and economic crises all pushed it towards the abyss. It had dreamed of freeing the world. Now it saw itself driven from Belgium and the Rhineland, on the point of being attacked in France itself, and (as Michelet said) stabbed in the back by the Vendée. It replied by organizing the revolutionary government.

Legally this was intended as a temporary regime that would disappear once a new constitution was adopted; in this sense it dated from August 10, 1792. But it was also a war regime, destined to defend the Revolution against its enemies, at home and abroad, by special measures which limited or suspended the rights of man and citizen. So its severity increased or decreased with the danger. After Valmy and Jemappes the Girondins had disavowed the expedients adopted in August and September, while in 1793 the Mountain revived and developed them. Finally, although a constitution had been voted, the regime acquired a certain degree of permanence, and it was agreed that it should last until the peace. Created gradually under the pressure of circumstances, it passed through a long and confused period of development. This we shall examine first. Then we shall consider the nature and accomplishments of the system.

FALL OF THE GIRONDINS: THE REVOLUTION OF MAY 31 AND JUNE 2, 1793

It was only on January 25, 1793, that a report by Dubois-Crancé revealed the necessity of raising 300,000 men to make the army 500,000 strong, and of unifying the military organization by amalgamating the volunteers and the infantry of the line; the cavalry and artillery would continue to be recruited through voluntary enlistments. The Convention adopted the 'amalgam' in principle. It had been prepared, on December 21, 1792, by the standardization of pay, followed by that of uniforms—the blue of the National Guard—and promotions, as well as of new names for regiments and ranks; but with the campaign opening, the formation of new 'demibrigades' was postponed. Only on February 24, 1793, was the levy of the 300,000 men decided upon, for bachelors and widowers between the ages of twenty and forty. No one seems to have anticipated that although military service was unpopular, it would provoke violent resistance.

There could be no illusions about the outlook for the naval war, or consequently, about the fate of the colonies. Corsica itself was lost to the Republic. The Constituent Assembly had permitted Paoli (erstwhile leader of resistance against the Genoese and French) to return home. Regarding the island as his fief, he decided, in league with the *procureur-général-syndic*, Pozzo di Borgo, to secede, and appealed to the English. At least the privateers could be counted upon, but even though they inflicted damage upon the enemy, the merchant marine of France suffered greatly. Neutral vessels became the essential intermediaries in her foreign trade.

In previous wars the king had posed as defender of the 'freedom of the seas'. He had maintained, along with the neutrals, that 'flag covers cargo', thereby assuring himself of their help in evading the British blockade. The Convention adopted the opposite policy. Not content with repudiating commercial treaties with its adversaries—principally that of 1786—and with excluding many English commodities, on May 9, 1793, it decreed that if neutrals submitted to the orders of Great Britain, enemy property aboard their ships would henceforth be lawful prize. The protectionist manufacturers, especially those dealing in cotton, rejoiced; their spokesman, in the *Moniteur* and as Barère's advocate, was the former consul, Ducher. The upper bourgeoisie in the ports, on the other hand, lamented, but in vain. In this respect, too, the intransigence of the Convention attests the weakening of the Gironde.

Thus reinforced, the blockade could only aggravate the economic situation. Already life was becoming increasingly difficult, because the death of the king and the general war had provoked a decline of the assignats. At the beginning of January they still retained from 60 to 65 per cent of their nominal value; in February they fell to 50 per cent, and the decline continued until October. The revolutionaries blamed the foreign bankers (Baring of London, Hope of Amsterdam, and Parish of Hamburg), who speculated by mutual agreement—and, also, it was said, on behalf of Pitt—with the complicity of Parisian financiers, most of whom likewise were foreigners.

It was obvious, however, that quite a few Frenchmen had similar schemes, and that many others, chary of paper money, bought at any price. Prices continued to rise so rapidly that wages were unable to keep pace. In January the workers of Lyons demanded fixed prices. The distracted populace completely halted the movement of grain. The government did what it could to remedy the situation with the aid of grain purchased abroad, but the supply was limited. In Paris the Commune continued to maintain bread at three sous a pound by extorting funds from the Convention; but from February 25 to 27, grocers' shops and barges carrying soap were pillaged.

Meanwhile the government was weakening. The Girondins lost Roland, who resigned on January 22, 1793; but, in February, they succeeded in driving Pache from the war ministry. Beurnonville, who replaced him, having played a deceptive game with both parties, expelled the sans-culottes from the bureaux and gave the contractors a free hand. Garat, who took the post of minister of the interior, sympathized with the Right, but he had no intention of compromising himself; and Gohier, now minister of justice, and Monge both posed as

Jacobins. Lebrun and Clavière found themselves increasingly attacked, and Lamarche, director of assignats, was impeached.

On January 1, 1793, the Convention had, indeed, created a Committee of General Defence, in which the Girondins were dominant. Out of consideration for the separation of powers, however, it was accorded merely the right of surveillance over the ministers, who responded only with a greater tendency towards inertia. In February, Condorcet presented his report on a proposed constitution. It was little appreciated, and the Montagnards felt that circumstances were not propitious. Debate began only in April, when the Girondins conceived the idea of hastening promulgation of the constitution. They believed that the elections would eliminate the Montagnards. In reality neither side was interested in creating a strong government in which its adversary could become entrenched. The struggle between them continued inexpiably and without results. The decision was to come from outside.

Ever since the king's trial the sans-culottes had been constantly assailing the 'appealers' (*appelants*), and quickly came to desire their expulsion from the Convention. If this were achieved, the government could recover the energy to enable it to deal with the aristocratic plot by arresting suspects and establishing a revolutionary tribunal. In direct contact with the lower classes, the popular leaders realized that the masses were interested chiefly in survival. Therefore they demanded price controls over commodities, the requisitioning of grain, assistance to the poor and to families of soldiers, and the formation of a revolutionary army, which would have the double advantage of assuring their authority and of providing work for the unemployed. The wherewithal would be secured by taxing the rich.

Such measures were advocated particularly by those who were called the *Enragés* (madmen)—the priest Jacques Roux, Varlet, a well-to-do postal worker, and their provincial counterparts, Chalier and Leclerc at Lyons, and the lawyer Taboureau at Orléans. They did not demand the 'agrarian law'; in any case, a decree of March 18 punished such proposals with death. In their eyes, however, social questions overshadowed political problems. The people were now sovereign. But what good was this if they died of hunger? The members of the clubs already in office, or noted journalists such as Hébert and Marat, were jealous, but eventually imitated them. Most sans-culottes turned towards the Montagnards and the Jacobins, awaiting their cue. Yet there was no lack of impatient men, notably Varlet, who thought them overly cautious and too moderate and deemed it necessary to take the initiative. Such men would not hesitate to disperse the Convention and seize power. Some, who perhaps had taken part in the September massacres, even wanted to profit from the crisis to bring the Girondins and suspects before a revolutionary tribunal or provisional popular courts.

Until the last moment Danton hoped to re-establish republican unity. Robespierre and the Montagnards, whom the Jacobins and the Commune followed, believed such a union impossible. Like the sans-culottes, they thought that the Girondins had to be dealt with, and that public safety required a dictatorial government. Since they were threatened with expulsion and arraignment by their adversaries, their personal security impelled them to the same goal. Agreement upon a social programme was more difficult, because it involved price regulation; as bourgeois committed to economic freedom, the Montagnards did not believe in the virtues of controls. In their opinion politics outweighed other matters. At the time of the February riots Robespierre grew indignant that 'paltry merchandise' was diverting attention from counter-revolutionary intrigues; and in the Commune, Chaumette merely proposed the prosecution of hoarders and the creation of large-scale public works to give employment to the jobless. In April they yielded, but their reluctance persisted, as was seen in the course of the following months; and the understanding was never complete.

It remained to be seen whether the Plain would bring itself to eliminate the Girondins. Robespierre seems to have cherished this hope for a long time. His motives were doubtless doctrinaire—to force the Convention was not in keeping with the representative system, and the consequences of an insurrection were uncertain. As before August 10, he continued to maintain that the responsibility of the people was not less than that of its representatives, and that through legal displays of its will, it had the power to make them comply therewith. This was a great illusion. The Jacobins applauded, but the sans-culottes in the galleries treated him like an *endormeur* (someone who sought to lull them to sleep). In fact, he had to consent to a threatening demonstration that would compel the Assembly to yield.

What if it stood firm? The Montagnards did not want to disperse it; and they desired, even less, a repetition of the scenes of September, which would cause them to lose power to the Commune and the sans-culotte agitators. This the provinces would not tolerate; so, to rally them, the Convention would have to be maintained for the dictatorship of the Montagnards. These divergent tendencies are of far-reaching significance. They explain why the fall of the Gironde came only after four months. Since they continued, the stability of the revolutionary government was never assured, and they contributed to its fall.

After the relative calm that followed the death of the king, the crisis was renewed when danger appeared simultaneously on the frontiers and in the interior. On March 1, 1793, when Dumouriez had just entered Holland, his cover on the Roer was destroyed by Coburg, who soon occupied Liége and crossed the Meuse. For several days Beurnonville and the Girondins issued reassuring statements, but on the 8th, Danton, who had hastened back from Belgium, spread the alarm. During the ensuing days he reiterated the language of 1792: 'I know only the enemy; let us beat the enemy.' With time pressing, he demanded a new effort from the patriots of Paris to save Belgium. When they replied, as they had in September, that they would not leave the city exposed to the plots of traitors, Danton proposed the creation of a revolutionary tribunal to forestall new massacres, and on the 9th, Pache, in the name of the sections, supported him.

At the same time an insurrectionary movement was developing outside the Assembly. On the evening of the 9th the offices of several Girondin newspapers were attacked, and delegates from the sections assembled at the Bishop's Palace (Évêché). On the 10th, Varlet induced the Cordeliers to take the initiative for a 'day'. It failed, because neither the Commune nor the Jacobins associated themselves with it. On the basis of a report by Lindet the Convention established a special tribunal from which there would be no appeal or review. It reserved to itself the choice of judges and jurors, and particularly the issuing of indictments. Danton also asked it to create a committee invested with executive power, and this was approved by both Robespierre and Cambacérès. The Girondins cried 'dictatorship', and on the 11th, La Revellière-Lépeaux had the motion rejected. In essence the crisis came to naught.

In Belgium during this time the commissioners whom the deputies on mission had sent to the provinces were busily confiscating public funds and church treasures. The populace protested or resisted, and anarchy became widespread. Dumouriez, having returned from Holland, hastened to Brussels, took the clergy under his protection, and treated members of the clubs severely. Then, on March 12, 1793, he sent the Convention a threatening letter in which he recapitulated his complaints and placed particular blame on the decree of December 15. The Committee of General Defence deliberated the matter on the 15th. Intervening, Danton undertook to make the general realize his mistakes. He returned disappointed, but kept silent.

Beaten at Neerwinden on the 18th, and at Louvain on the 21st, Dumouriez concluded an armistice with the Austrians so that he could march on Paris and restore Louis XVII and the Constitution of 1791. The Committee had decided to summon him to appear before the bar, and on the 30th, the Convention sent Beurnonville and four of its members to inform him of its decree. On April 1, Dumouriez handed them over to the enemy. Seeing nothing to bar his way to Paris, he wished to imitate Lafayette's attempted *coup*; but his army refused to follow him, and on April 5 he crossed the frontier. At the same time Custine, vanquished on the Nahe on March 27 and 28, abandoned the left bank of the Rhine and withdrew to Landau, leaving the Prussians to besiege Mainz.

Within France itself the levy of 300,000 men caused trouble. The decree had provided that potential conscripts might determine the personnel of the required contingent. Some resorted to elections, which produced absurd results. In most cases they sought paid volunteers. Elsewhere there were fruitless disputes, and in more than one instance they agreed to deride the authorities whom the Convention had exempted, and even to revolt. On March 9, 1793, a general mission of eighty-two representatives was established to apply the law, and a decree of the 19th pronounced the death penalty for instigators of rebellion.

In general the situation was rapidly dealt with, even in Brittany; but from March 10 to 15 the Vendée rose *en masse*. The peasants there were neither royalists nor partisans of the Old Regime; but the religious schism and the severity of the administrative bodies and of the Jacobins in the towns towards the refractory clergy incensed them. The Reformation had gained a large following in Poitou, and since the end of the seventeenth century the missionaries of the Company of Mary (the *Mulotins*), founded by Grignion, and the Daughters of Wisdom had been ardently catechizing the population. In August, 1791, the peasants had not supported the revolt of the nobles; nor had they risen in 1792 to protect the 'good' priests from deportation. Recruiting, however, provoked an initial popular uprising among them in August, and it was foreseen that they would not consent to fight for the Republic. All the troops, however, had gone to the frontiers.

Breaking out simultaneously, the uprisings would seem to have been co-ordinated; but they appear to have surprised the nobles, who, contemplating an insurrection of their own, deemed them premature. Several chief towns of districts were overrun (notably Cholet, on March 14), their administrations dispersed, and the bourgeois who composed them manhandled or (as at Machecoul) tortured and put to death. Nobles soon assumed the leadership, without completely eliminating commoners, such as Stofflet and Cathelineau. Former officers, they easily took control and divided up the sectors. Charette was master of the Marais, while Royrand and the Sapinauds held the Bocage. The Mauges remained the domain of the 'royal Catholic' army, commanded by Bonchamps, d'Elbée, Stofflet, Lescure, and La Rochejaquelein. In collaboration with Abbé Bernier, they organized a government, and they were even joined by a self-styled bishop, Guillot de Folleville. An appeal was immediately made to the English. Some wanted to march on Paris, others to enter Brittany. But they did not succeed in forming a permanent army: the peasants hastened forth when the 'Blues' were reported, but after a victory they returned to their homes. It was this fact that saved the Republic.

Nevertheless the insurrection won striking successes; the

woods (*bocages*), with their sunken roads and their isolated farms (surrounded by trees which obstructed vision), lent themselves admirably to defence and surprise attacks, the more so since there were few roads. Like the volunteers, the Vendéans spontaneously practised tactics suitable for such improvised troops: sharpshooting or ambush, then a mass attack upon a disorganized enemy. For weeks the Convention sent only National Guards or recruits against them. Except for Noirmoutier, the coast was held or reconquered. During the summer the 'Blues' won three victories before Luçon. The offensive against the Layon in April was essential, but it failed. The Vendéans occupied Bressuire and Parthenay, and on May 5, 1793, they seized Thouars. Routed before Fontenay, they took revenge by pillaging the town. On June 9 they won Saumur, then entered Angers, but finally, on June 29, they failed before Nantes.

In May the government had become resigned to effecting troop withdrawals from the frontiers, but the numerous representatives installed at Saumur and Tours neither succeeded in agreeing nor in working in harmony with the other base established at Niort, where Biron resided. Westermann took Châtillon on July 3, but was routed there on the 5th; on the 18th the same fate overtook Santerre at Vihiers. Rossignol then took the command, seconded by Ronsin, but these sans-culotte generals were no luckier, and the Vendéans remained unvanquished in their home territory until October.

Domouriez's treason and the civil war roused the republicans. It was like a new 'fear', and once more suspects were arrested. The two events exasperated them even more than the invasion and caused them to take special measures. These latter met less and less resistance in the Convention itself. On March 18, 1793, the death penalty on mere verification of identity was decreed for émigrés and priests subject to deportation who were arrested on the territory of the Republic; and on the following day, for rebels caught bearing arms. On the 21st the watch committees appeared. They were elected and were charged only with supervising passports, strangers, and foreigners; but they came to be called 'revolutionary', and if there were numerous sans-culottes on them, they soon dominated the political police. On the 28th a law defined emigration, inflicted civil death on émigrés and reserved to the Republic for fifty years any share they might have in the estates of their relatives. Those who returned to France would be punished with death. Finally, on April 5, the Convention renounced the right to refer cases to the Revolutionary Tribunal (except where ministers and generals were involved), and turned this duty over to the public prosecutor, Fouquier-Tinville.

In the provinces, on the other hand, the administrative bodies, under pressure from the Jacobins, spontaneously created committees of public safety (under various names) for the organization of the levy and security measures. On April 19, 1793, the department of Hérault adopted a decree which became famous: it empowered such a committee to choose 5,000 men to form a regiment that would be at its disposal, and to assess a forced loan of 5 million livres. The deputies dispatched on March 9, and those who succeeded them with the armies on April 30, aided in the initiation of revolutionary measures and, to a certain point, in their co-ordination. Because the Girondins had judged it shrewd to select these deputies from among the Montagnards, in order to weaken opposition in the Convention, the device was turned against them.

The instructions of May 6 authorized the deputies on mission to name delegates and to surround themselves with a council, which they naturally chose from among the Jacobins of the clubs. They purged the administrations, arrested suspects, levied taxes, and prescribed requisitions. More than once their activities encountered the violent anger of local authorities who had remained Girondins or who styled themselves as such. A conservative bourgeois such as Carnot recognized the necessity of the struggle until death. 'No genuine peace can be expected from our enemies,' he wrote on March 18, 'even less from those within than from those outside. . . . We must crush them or be crushed by them.'

Yet what good were these efforts if the government remained powerless? Dumouriez's treason had accentuated the animosities of the extremist parties, and the Girondins were compromised by their close connection with him. Nor can it be doubted that those who exploited his name would have applauded the success of his *coup d'état*. To parry the attack they took the offensive. In the entourage of Dumouriez there were friends and relatives of Philippe Égalité, whose own son, the duke of Chartres, was numbered among the lieutenants of the traitor, whom he followed in his flight. This provided an excellent pretext for reviving the charges of Orléanism against the Montagnards. Danton himself gave cause for the suspicion by reason of his missions to Belgium and the silence he had maintained since his last return. On April 1, 1793, Lasource denounced the plot and drew a crushing reply from Danton, who, instead of defending himself, served notice (to the wild applause of the Montagnards) of his break with those who had wished to save the tyrant. In vain did Robespierre propose the next day that charges be brought against them.

The Plain had no intention of following Robespierre, but circumstances drew it to Danton. On April 6 it finally created the Committee of Public Safety, which he had demanded, and to fill it, elected him, along with men—notably Barère and Cambon—who had more or less rallied to the Mountain but were still regarded as independents. This first Committee of Public Safety seemed to be a second Danton ministry, so obvious was his dominant position in it. Despite his outburst of April 1, he pursued his policy of conciliation and evasion. This suited the Plain, which, in instituting the Committee, forbade it to order arrests, and reduced it to the surveillance of ministers whose authority was needlessly diminished. This was not the solution that the Mountain had desired; and the Gironde likewise repudiated it. The struggle continued.

On April 1, 1793, Birotteau had obtained the enactment of a decree stating that immunity did not cover any deputy who was suspected of high treason. This opened the way for the proscriptions which would decimate the Convention. Birotteau's friends intended to turn it against the Montagnards, and the occasion was not long in coming. On April 5, in a circular signed by Marat as president, the Jacobins urged the patriots in the provinces to come to the aid of a Paris menaced by Dumouriez, and denounced the 'appealers'—those members of the Convention who during the king's trial had called for the appeal to the people—as the traitor's accomplices. The Girondins replied, on April 13, by having the Convention arraign Marat before the Revolutionary Tribunal.

Meanwhile, on April 10, 1793, the Halle au Blé section had taken the initiative in a petition aimed at bringing the 'appealers' before their electors, so that their mandates might be withdrawn. The Plain would surely not agree to this; besides, the Girondins continued to demand similar measures against the Montagnards. Robespierre protested against this imbroglio, but the section commissioners adopted the text, which originated with friends of Danton. Philippeaux, another of his supporters, proposed that the Convention reject it, and on April 20 that body declared it calumnious to the 'appealers'. It seemed evident that Danton was sowing discord, still hoping to win over the Gironde. As for Marat, he was acquitted on the 24th.

One important fact, however, had recently altered the situation: the Montagnards had openly joined with the sans-culottes of the sections and the Cordeliers in supporting the controlled economy. Robespierre would justify this implicitly by proposing, on the 24th, to incorporate into the Declaration of the Rights of Man four articles that defined property as 'the portion of goods . . . guaranteed by law', and limited its extent, stipulating that it could not prejudice 'the security, the liberty, the existence, or the property of our fellow men'. On April 11 the Convention banned double prices and trade in specie, and punished refusals to accept assignats. On the 18th the representatives of the various authorities of the department of Paris issued a petition in favour of fixing prices. The members of the Convention discussed it in committee until the 25th, and then on the floor. On April 30 a deputation from the Faubourg St.-Antoine appeared at the bar, and the women from Versailles next came to their aid. On May 4 a law instituted a 'maximum' on grain and fodder in the departments, and directed that they be inventoried and requisitioned by the districts in order to supply the markets, to which their trade was henceforth limited.

At this moment, however, the sans-culottes were faced with unrest, which had originated in the disasters in the Vendée. On April 25, 1793, the Bon Conseil section demanded the dispatch of a Parisian contingent against the 'brigands'; and at the beginning of May the Commune voted a levy of 12,000 men and a forced loan, entrusting them to the revolutionary committees in the same manner as the decree of the department of Hérault, which the Convention had just approved. Violent disturbances spread throughout Paris. The sans-culottes wanted to enroll the law clerks and 'shop hands' first. These young men strenuously resisted, and from the 4th to the 6th of May they held meetings at the Luxembourg gardens and the Champs Élysées.

Nor were the members of the National Guard themselves willing to go. Taking advantage, as usual, of direct democracy, they claimed the right to choose the method, and the Convention eventually approved their stand. As was customary, 'heroes at 500 livres' were raised, and to hasten the procedure, demands were made that funds be advanced. This the Assembly did with no hope of being repaid. Beginning with these days, section meetings were frequently stormy, since the opponents of the sans-culottes decided to appear at them; the two parties each lent support to their adherents in one neighbourhood after another, and they did not hesitate to come to blows. On May 8, Robespierre pointed out the danger and demanded the formation of a revolutionary army, at the expense of the 'golden knee-breeches' (*culottes dorées*).

These events showed that the masses were unenthusiastic about fighting for the Republic. The government would have to compel them to do so, even while it depended upon them. This contradiction boded no good. For the moment, however, the attention of the Montagnards and the sans-culottes centred upon the impending 'rising of the sections' in Paris, examples for which had already been set in many towns. It dated from the first Terror and was rekindled by the death of the king. The Girondins had encouraged it by their appeals for help; the Montagnard representatives had done likewise by angering the 'notables'. Recruiting (and in the ports, the blockade, which was causing unemployment) gained supporters for it.

Some departments sought to form battalions to go to Paris, and Finistère sent one. From March 16, 1793, onward, at Orléans, deputies on mission were insulted, and one of them, Léonard Bourdon, was assaulted and injured. Slowly the watchwords became 'aid to the section assemblies' (which had hitherto been disdained) and 'permanent sessions'. These permanent sessions had existed in Paris since July, 1792—why not in the provinces? Action was taken without waiting for the consent of the Convention.

At Bordeaux the sections contented themselves with a threatening address on May 9. At Marseilles, where the Jacobins had broken with Barbaroux, they lost control of the city, and on April 29 the deputies escaped. The sections formed a general committee, and directed against the sans-culottes the popular tribunal which had been created without legal authorization in September, 1792. It was worse at Lyons. On May 29 an insurrection attacked the Jacobin commune, and after street fighting the deputies suspended it and Chalier was imprisoned. On May 24 the department of Jura had proposed that the alternate deputies meet at Bourges. Ain agreed, and Côte-d'Or suggested that an army be sent to protect them. At Caen, on May 30, the dispatch of a battalion to Paris was discussed.

Sincere republicans, hostile (like the Plain) to extreme democrats, played a part, albeit as a minority, in the section movement. The strength of the latter came from the bourgeoisie who had remained monarchist, from supporters of the refractory clergy, and from partisans of the Old Regime. All called themselves Girondins, but this was only camouflage. 'The two main factions tearing us apart are abominable,' wrote Griolet, *procureur-général-syndic* of Gard; 'Brissot, Pétion, and Guadet are as much to be feared as Marat, Danton, or Robespierre.' If the Girondins had triumphed, thanks to such allies, the reaction would have overtaken them rapidly. As Michelet said, 'They no longer possessed the genius of the Revolution.'

The sans-culottes could not ignore the fact that the majority of the nation, attached to the work of the Constituent Assembly but impatient to resume its easy, peaceful life, would have accepted a compromise peace. If the section movement grew at Paris while it spread in the provinces, the Girondins would, one day or another, dictate their will to the Convention in its name. Thus the revolution of June 2, 1793, was a new defensive and punitive response to the 'fear' which was awakening what the Montagnards and sans-culottes regarded as a manifestation of the aristocratic plot.

With their habitual flightiness, the Girondins hastened the final crisis before they had secured the means of assuring their success. When the Commune decided to form a revolutionary army and to arrest suspects, as Robespierre had recommended, representatives from the watch committees met, and the proposals miscarried. Two police officials even proposed, on May 19, to kidnap the leading Girondins, put them to death secretly, and claim that they had been émigrés. Protests were raised, and Pache tabled the motion. But Guadet, aware of the secret meeting, again denounced the popular conspiracy on the 18th, and Barère, entering the fray, had a commission of twelve members named to investigate.

Composed of Girondins, there could be no doubt as to the findings of the commission. On the 24th it had four sans-culottes arrested. These included Varlet and Hébert, a deputy public prosecutor of the Commune, whose newspaper, *Le Père Duchesne*, was enjoying a wide vogue. The Commune protested the next day, and Isnard, now president of the Convention, burst into threats against Paris in a 'new Brunswick manifesto'. On the 27th a mob slowly formed around the Tuileries, where the Convention had been sitting since May 10, and that evening it invaded the hall. At midnight, when Danton intervened, a decree suppressed the 'twelve'. The following day the Girondins obtained their restoration. In truth, the Convention soon afterwards disavowed them by releasing the prisoners, but the deed was done. That same evening, at the Bishop's Palace, a group of sans-culottes formed an insurrectionary committee, the mainspring of which was probably Varlet.

During the night of May 30–31, 1793, the section commissioners quashed the Commune, then reinstated and joined it. Hanriot took command of the National Guard. Orders were given to arrest or disarm all suspects. The Montagnards, in agreement over the elimination of the Girondins, were nonetheless disturbed. The proposals put forth on May 19 at the meeting of the revolutionary committees called attention to what might happen if the Convention resisted. Its dissolution had to be avoided, and above all, the September massacres must not be repeated. The department therefore summoned the authorities and made sure that a commission was designated which would join that of the insurgents. Pache and Chaumette acted as moderators. The sections were very slow in getting under way. May 31 fell on a Friday, so the workers were at their jobs. The demonstration took shape only in the afternoon and scarcely intimidated the Assembly. Again the 'twelve' were suppressed, and the petition demanding the arrest of the Girondins was referred to the Committee of Public Safety for examination and report within three days. This was a defeat.

Next day, after a new address that had no greater effect, the insurrectionary committee decided to invest the Convention on Sunday, June 2, and to exact an immediate solution. This was the best-organized 'day' of the Revolution. Danton let events take their course this time, and the Committee of Public Safety, divided, offered no resistance to the National Guards, who surrounded the Tuileries. A critical moment came, however, when the Convention was persuaded to leave, in regular procession, in hopes of carrying the day. The smallest incident would have destroyed it, but to Varlet's great regret, Hanriot was satisfied with blocking its path. It returned inside and resigned itself to ordering the arrest of twenty-nine deputies, as well as Clavière and Lebrun. The revolutionary army was also created in principle. No action was taken on the social programme of the *Enragés*.

The Montagnards had been victorious. They rid themselves of the insurrectionary committee, replacing it, on June 8, with a committee of public safety for the department of Paris. Varlet and his friends were excluded from it. With the Convention still in existence, the Montagnards governed in its name. In reality it never forgave them. Moreover, although it placed the Girondins under house arrest, it did not arraign them. This was the sole method of expulsion compatible with the representative system. The sans-culottes, on the contrary, were left empty-handed. The Montagnards were in danger of coming between two fires, and for them the 'revolution of May 31' was but one step on the path to power.

REVOLUTIONARY CRISIS DURING THE SUMMER OF 1793

Montagnard success soon seemed to be brought into question. Seventy-five deputies signed a protest; others left Paris or deserted the Assembly; and the opposition of the National Guard to the levies for the Vendée and the revolutionary army revived. The news from the Vendée soon gave cause for alarm. As early as June 6, Barère and Danton (that is, the Committee of Public Safety) proposed that the watch committees be suppressed and that hostages be sent to departments from which the deputies had been arrested. Robespierre had such measures rejected, but the Montagnards, although disturbed, continued to temporize. The number of the Girondins arrested grew slowly, but their fate was left in doubt. Even on July 8, Saint-Just advised that only those who were fomenting civil war be punished. The revolutionary army was not organized, and the deliberations over the forced loan came to naught. Above all, there was hasty discussion of the Constitution of 1793, which was concluded on June 24.

Prefaced by a new Declaration of Rights, which amplified that of 1789 with provisions for religious liberty and economic freedom, the Constitution instituted political democracy: a legislative body, elected by direct, universal suffrage, with single-member districts; and an executive council, chosen by the legislative body from among candidates designated by its own electors. As Condorcet had proposed, following the example of certain American states, the exercise of popular sovereignty was enlarged by the introduction of the referendum—the Constitution would be ratified by the people. But such consent was not required for urgent decrees, and where laws were concerned, it was subordinated to extremely narrow limits. Social democracy was not insisted upon; the Declaration simply proclaimed that the aim of society was 'the general welfare', and poor relief 'a sacred obligation', a right of the poor.

Since its meeting the Convention had, moreover, constantly affirmed the principle of national solidarity, promising pensions to disabled veterans, granting benefits to the next of kin of the 'defenders of the *Patrie*', and having the state assume the expense of damages caused by the war and collective disasters. Robespierre breathed not a word of the famous articles of his previous proposition which might alarm the bourgeoisie, and on June 27, Barère inveighed against the partisans of the 'agrarian law', whom a decree of March 18 had already made liable to capital punishment. The Montagnards hoped that the Constitution would dispel fears of a dictatorship by the Paris sans-culottes. Yet they did not overlook the peasants. It was to these latter that the revolution of May 31 (like those of July 14 and August 10) brought a substantial and permanent profit.

On June 3 the sale of the property of émigrés, in small parcels and payable in ten years, was decreed; on the 10th, the optional division of common lands by head; and on July 17, the abolition, without compensation, of all that remained of manorial rights.

Despite everything, a new civil war could not be avoided. In May, as has been seen, the section movement had already taken the initiative. By being the first to act in Paris, the Montagnards necessarily kindled the spirit of rebellion. Provincial jealousy of the capital, and the survivals of particularism, undoubtedly aided it. Moreover, the local authorities, having broken with the Convention, set themselves up as sovereign. This action made it possible to accuse them of federalism, since they opposed the unity and indivisibility of the Republic.

It cannot be denied that the federalist idea did seduce certain revolutionaries—Billaud-Varenne himself in 1791—and particularly Girondins such as La Revellière-Lépeaux; but the federalists simply wanted to seize power. Under the pressure of circumstances they pushed to the extreme the decentralization which had prevailed since 1789, and manifested the independent initiative which the revolutionaries had always displayed and to which the Jacobins, for their part, continued to resort. Like the section movement, which their revolt was prolonging, they gathered together the bourgeoisie worried about property, the Feuillants hostile to universal suffrage, the Catholics attached to the refractory clergy, and the partisans of the Old Regime. To these they added the democrats, who were indignant at the outrage perpetrated against the national representation, and whose adherence singularly strengthened their ranks.

The complexity of such a group undermined its cohesion. Attachment to the Revolution of 1789 and a concern for national independence were incompatible with civil war, and the Girondins refused to ally themselves with the Vendéans or to seek help abroad. So the *fait accompli* was accepted without much difficulty by some thirty departments around Paris and in the Loire valley (alarmed by its proximity to the Vendée) and along the frontiers, while the insurrection persisted in the south-east, where the counter-revolutionaries, alien to these scruples, assumed its leadership.

The fact remained, however, that in Brittany, Normandy, Franche-Comté, and the south, the departmental administrative bodies had seceded. Each of them joined with the authorities of the chief town, appealed to other districts, and even convoked primary assemblies and called their delegates together. Having become federalists, the fomenters of the section movement continued to imitate the Jacobins. They formed committees of public safety or watch committees, arrested suspects, closed the clubs, and decided upon levies of troops. At Lyons, Marseilles, and Toulon 'popular' tribunals ordered patriots guillotined or hanged. The results were piteous. The struggle between Girondins and Montagnards was of no concern to the masses.

Like the Convention, the leaders of secession encountered the resentment aroused by military service and the discontent created by scarcity. Besides, success would have required that a new central government be organized by convening at Bourges the convention of alternates which had been contemplated. But the loyalist departments lay between the north-west and the south, the Vendée between Brittany and Aquitaine. Lyons was separated from Côte-d'Or by Saône-et-Loire, which supported Allier, and from Provence by Drôme, which rallied Isère to its side. Even regional co-operation was not achieved. Toulouse eventually rebuffed the entreaties of Bordeaux, thus breaking the link between Aquitaine and lower Languedoc. Finally, everywhere there were districts and municipalities that refused their allegiance, and patriotic functionaries, like Descombels at Toulouse, who thwarted rebellion, or like Joseph Payan at Valence, who rallied the sans-culottes. Prompted by impotence and the voting of the Constitution, which gave them hope that the forthcoming election of the legislative body would rid them of the Convention, many federalists took advantage of the period of grace that the Montagnards had prudently granted and made amends.

For the Convention the immediate danger lay in Normandy. No troops covered Paris, and shipments of food to the capital ceased. Meeting at Caen, Buzot, Pétion, and Barbaroux urged the departments to act. But Seine-Inférieure failed them and permitted grain to pass. The capture of Saumur on June 9, 1793, secured Orne and Maine; only Finistère showed any enthusiasm. Before the Bretons could join them, the Normans set out. On July 13, near Pacy-sur-Eure, as they rested without posting guards, several thousand men, painfully gathered by the Committee of Public Safety, appeared. The Normans fled without a fight. The whole north-east submitted, and the Girondins left Caen, and then Brittany, for Bordeaux. Nor was there further need for waging war in the east against Côte-d'Or, Doubs, Haute-Saône, Jura, and Ain, or in the south against Toulouse and lower Languedoc. Isolated, Bordeaux permitted the deputies to enter on August 19, and then drove them out. The Jacobins did not regain the advantage until October, when the city was occupied on the 16th. At least it had not resisted by force of arms.

It was the south-east which really endangered the patriots' cause. The Army of the Alps and that of Italy were cut off from behind. Précy, whom the Lyonese had placed in command, appealed to the Sardinians; Marseilles and Toulon to the English, as Paoli had done in Corsica. When Carteaux, supported by the clubs of Drôme, had repulsed the army from Marseilles and retaken Avignon on July 27, the Lyonese rebels were surrounded, except in the west, where they occupied the department of Loire until September. At the end of August, Carteaux resumed the offensive, and on the 25th he seized Marseilles just in time to forestall the English. Such was not the case at Toulon, which welcomed the enemy and handed over the Mediterranean squadron on August 29. The deputies re-entered Lyons only on October 9, and Toulon held out until December 19. In this region the civil war took on the same ferocity as in the Vendée, and led to the same bloody reprisals. From August on, the peril was at least localized; but in July it had seemed that France was disintegrating.

The danger appeared no less on the frontiers. Since his return to power Danton had been negotiating. On April 13, 1793, at his demand, the Convention implicitly repudiated the decree of November 19, 1792: the Republic would not interfere in the internal affairs of other peoples. If Danton was attempting to win over Sweden, Turkey, Piedmont, and even Kosciusko, or to cajole the courts of Naples and Florence, it was by fair means; but the small powers did not willingly lend an ear to the vanquished. He was also seeking peace with England,

Prussia, and Austria. Grenville contemptuously referred him to the general staffs, and Forster, charged with reaching them, was unsuccessful.

What could Danton offer? The abandonment by the Republic of its conquests? The Coalition had already retaken these, expected to dismember France, and mocked the ridiculous proposals of a regicide at bay. This diplomacy, often praised by posterity, presupposed victory or capitulation disguised as compromise. The Montagnards also suspected Danton of considering the surrender of the queen and her children—even the restoration of the monarchy. On April 13 he stipulated that the sovereignty of the people should be recognized; it was not incompatible with royalty. Nevertheless Robespierre prevailed upon the Convention to prohibit, under penalty of death, all negotiations which might jeopardize the republican regime, and to confirm the annexations. On the 10th he had already demanded that Marie Antoinette be brought before the Revolutionary Tribunal.

In June, 1793, an article of the Constitution declared that the French people would not make peace with an enemy that occupied its territory. Danton still persisted, however, and in the meantime war production was not progressing, and attacks against the contractors increased. In July, following a report by Dornier, the arrest of d'Espagnac was ordered. One reverse followed another. Since Dumouriez's failure Coburg had been besieging Condé and Valenciennes. Dampierre's attacks in the Raisme and Vicoigne forests miscarried, and he was killed. On May 23 his successor had to evacuate the camp at Famars and withdraw to Caesar's Camp, between the Scheldt and the Sensée, thereby leaving Cambrai unprotected and the route to Paris open.

Although Custine had vainly attempted to resume the offensive to aid Mainz, the Committee of Public Safety nonetheless charged him with returning to the command of the Army of the North. He applied himself to it, and not without success; but this great lord treated the government airily. He heaped scorn upon the minister of war, Bouchotte, a mere lieutenant-colonel; upon his secretary, the Hébertist Vincent; upon his commissioners with the armies; and upon the Jacobin officers who, at Lille, had upheld the commanding officer,

Favart, against General La Marlière. He soon became suspect, despite the support of the deputies on mission, and was recalled to Paris on July 12 without having accomplished anything. The Sardinians threatened Savoy and Nice; and the Spaniards, forcing the Pyrenees, advanced towards Perpignan and Bayonne. In the west, Westermann, initially victorious at Châtillon-sur-Sèvre, was routed there in July. Then it was Santerre's turn at Vihiers.

The economic crisis increased daily. The law of May 4, 1793, was not applied properly. The authorities, often moderates, delivered requisitions simply as a matter of routine, so that the Maximum succeeded only in emptying the markets. Since price regulation was a departmental matter, and the costs of transportation were not taken into account, regions poorly supplied no longer received anything. In this universal anarchy the local administrations banned the exit of grain. Far from enforcing the law, the Convention abandoned it. On July 1 it permitted the authorities to purchase outside the markets, and the armies supplied themselves in the same way. The deputies on mission and the departments were allowed to suspend the Maximum. In Paris and the larger towns there were queues outside the bakers' shops, and disorders occurred Still, the assignats fell to less than 30 per cent of their face value in July. Capital fled abroad, and there was frenzied speculation on the stock exchange. Commodities were hoarded, and prices rose constantly. From June 25 to 28 the increase in soap prices provoked new outbreaks in Paris.

The more impotent the Convention proved, the more numerous and insistent the petitions became. A new effort was necessary to make the government equal to the situation. No peace was possible, for the Coalition wanted to restore the Old Regime, and in the department of the Nord the Austrians already were striving to do so. Forced to choose between victory and subjection, the sans-culottes demanded a war to the bitter end—'liberty or death'. In this supreme peril, why delay in bringing the full power of the country into play? The idea of a levy *en masse* was gaining ground, and was favoured, moreover, by the egalitarian instinct and the memory of Jemappes. The 'selfish rich' became suspect, and the death penalty against hoarders, the closing of the stock exchange, and the suppression of joint-stock companies were now being demanded. The movement gained in strength, because it seemed easy to curb speculation through restraint.

A national reaction was taking shape as well: the revolutionaries were coming to scorn and hate the 'slaves' who blindly followed their tyrants, the foreigners who carried off goods for export. It seemed quite simple for France to forbid them to do this and to keep their produce. The *Enragés*, reinforced by Leclerc d'Oze from Lyons, and supported by the Society of Revolutionary Women, led by the actress Claire Lacombe, aroused popular anger. On June 25, Jacques Roux, speaking at the bar of the Convention in the name of the Cordeliers, reproached it with pathetic violence for its inertia. 'Deputies of the Mountain, do not end your careers ignominiously!' He was treated as a counter-revolutionary. Robespierre denounced him at the Jacobin Club, while Marat, Hébert, and Chaumette joined the chorus, delighted that they could strike at their enemies. Soap riots occurred opportunely, and Jacques Roux was blamed for them. The Commune and the Cordeliers abandoned him.

Yet if all those who were later called Hébertists—although Hébert was never the leader of a party—were preaching a war to the death and the extermination of the aristocrats, they soon adopted the social programme of the *Enragés*, because the sans-culottes approved it. If they preferred agreement with the Montagnards, so long as they could hope to control the Convention through them, they had by no means yet disavowed a new 'day' that, perhaps, would bring them to power. They dominated the Cordeliers, filled Bouchotte's bureaux, and could carry the Commune with them. The Convention would be at their mercy.

This situation presented grave dangers. The Republic owed its salvation to the ardour of the sans-culottes, whose succinct ideas, bluntness, and needs pushed them into the foreground. 'Dare!' Saint-Just was to cry some time later; but in July, 1793, the Convention sulked and the Montagnards debated. Popular enthusiasm could accomplish nothing without a government that would discipline it, without the co-operation of the middle class (upper or lower) that provided its plan. The salvation of the Revolution, the work of the Third Estate, depended upon the unity of the latter. The Convention was its symbol, for it represented the only authority recognized by all patriots. The Constitution, voted by it and ratified by 1,800,000 votes, reunited the republicans. To dissolve or to impair the Assembly once again would be to risk renewed civil war and to allow the revolutionary effort to exhaust itself in anarchy.

Pitt perceived this. The banker Perreguax distributed money on his behalf to those who undertook to 'fan the flames'. At the end of July the portfolio of an English spy, whose mission was to foment disorder, was found at Lille. An audacious adventurer, the self-styled Baron de Batz, who, after having attempted to save the king was planning the queen's escape, also thought that the Revolution could be dealt with only by provoking the republicans to destroy one another. As eager to speculate as to conspire, he succeeded in gaining the confidence of numerous individuals corrupted by dissipation or gambling, too often inclined to fish in troubled waters—deputies, club orators, foreign refugees—who were not always the last to advocate extreme measures. At the same time they played a bear market in stocks of companies which Delaunay, in July, and Fabre d'Églantine, in August, attacked from the speaker's rostrum. From the very outset Robespierre suspected that there were counter-revolutionary agents among the extremists.

At last France saw a government take shape. At the beginning of July, 1793, the continued aggravation of the situation intensified criticism; moreover, General Dillon was accused of planning a rising on behalf of the queen and her son. This was, perhaps, the final stroke. On July 10 the Convention renewed the Committee of Public Safety and eliminated Danton. Yet two months were required for the great Committee of the Year II to take form. Loyal to Custine, Gasparin withdrew quickly; Danton's friend Thuriot followed in September; and Hérault de Séchelles, lover of Madame de Bellegarde (whose husband was serving in the Sardinian army), promptly became suspect.

Couthon, Saint-Just, Jeanbon Saint-André, and Prieur of Marne formed a nucleus of resolute Montagnards who rallied Barère and Lindet, then successively added Robespierre on July 27, Carnot and Prieur of Côte-d'Or on August 14, and Billaud-Varenne and Collot d'Herbois on September 6.

Agreement among them was lacking on more than one point. Lindet disliked terrorism; Billaud-Varenne and Collot d'Herbois inclined towards the sans-culottes. Although they all belonged to the bourgeoisie, it was primarily social leanings that separated Robespierre or Saint-Just, who were partisans of a social democracy, from Carnot or Lindet, who were distinctly conservative.

Temperaments also differed, and personal affronts eventually turned into hatreds. Still, for months the peril to the Revolution delayed the split that would destroy them. These men were honest, hard-working, and authoritarian. They had a few clear ideas to which they clung: to command, to fight, and to conquer. Their work in common, the danger, the taste of and pride in power created a solidarity that made the Committee an autonomous organism. They reacted against the forces within the Convention and the Third Estate which tended to sow dissension among them in order to cause their downfall. Most of them devoted themselves primarily to administrative work which became a heavy burden. There have been those who pretended to praise them in order to draw a contrast with the others—as if they could have remained indifferent to the stability upon which their success depended.

It was Robespierre above all who, aided by Barère, Saint-Just, and Billaud-Varenne, assured them of some degree of permanence by defining and defending their policy in the Convention and at the Jacobin Club. Born in Arras, where, after brilliant studies as a scholarship holder at the Collège Louis-le-Grand, he had enjoyed an honourable reputation at the bar, Maximilien Robespierre had been elected to the Estates General in 1789. Since that time, by his unflagging defence of democratic principles before the Constituent Assembly, at the Jacobin Club, and in the press, he had won the esteem of the revolutionaries. He was unable, however, to prevent them from yielding to a passion for propaganda and war, which the eloquence of the Girondins had inspired. Now that all his fears had been justified, by a tragic reversal he, more than any other person, assumed the terrible responsibility for saving the Republic at the height of the storm which he had vainly sought to avert.

The patriots' confidence was well placed. As much from

personal dignity as from conviction, Robespierre courageously attested his respect for the principles he professed, but he was by no means the abstract theoretician he has been made out to be. On the contrary, in the long crisis which followed he appeared singularly attentive to circumstances, and he was able to meet them with the dexterity of a statesman. He had long maintained that to remain stable, revolutionary authority should be exercised in the name of the Convention, but to remain strong, it must do this in close communion with the sans-culottes. The Committee must set itself above both, and must choose those popular demands which were most suitable for achieving the Assembly's aims: to crush the enemies of the Republic and dash the last hopes of the aristocracy. To govern in the name of the Convention, at the same time controlling it, and to restrain the people without quenching their enthusiasm —this was a gamble.

As experienced politicians, Robespierre and his colleagues also knew how to arrange a 'day'. They succeeded in lasting for a year amidst the frightful torment. Yet we must not be misled. If, in July, 1793, the Robespierrists were moved by certain guiding principles, the application of these principles needed to be specified. The essential part of their method was still lacking. It was imposed upon them, in large part, during the summer by popular passions provoked by political, military, and economic crises.

ORGANIZATION OF THE MONTAGNARD DICTATORSHIP (JULY–DECEMBER, 1793)

With the new Committee barely installed, disasters increased, and it narrowly avoided being overthrown by the Convention. On July 13, 1793, Marat was assassinated by Charlotte Corday, a young royalist from Normandy, and on the 16th the rebels at Lyons beheaded Chalier. A furious outcry demanded reprisals and the Girondins were the first to suffer. Federalism was about to collapse in the north-west, but on July 18 the Vendéans routed Santerre's army at Vihiers. The deputies on mission on the Loire were not in agreement with Biron, commander at Niort, and their disputes over the sans-culotte leaders, Ronsin and Rossignol, reflected those of the Convention. Philippeaux denounced them and Choudieu supported them. Soon Ronsin was sent back to Paris and Rossignol was arrested. It was worse on the frontiers: Condé capitulated on the 10th, Mainz on the 23rd, and Valenciennes on the 28th.

The Committee recalled Biron, and on July 22 it arrested Custine. At once the friends of these generals, and those deputies who supported them, protested violently, and Gasparin abandoned his colleagues. At the same time abuse was heaped upon Bouchotte, his bureaux, and the sans-culotte officers. It was even decided to replace the minister. Robespierre's intervention saved the day, and it was at this point that he entered the Committee. On July 25, Rossignol replaced Biron; on the 28th, Custine and the Girondins were indicted and the fugitive deputies outlawed.

Terrorist measures were decidedly taking precedence on August 1. The Convention sent Marie Antoinette to the Revolutionary Tribunal and ordered the destruction of the royal tombs at St.-Denis. It prescribed that the Vendée be devastated after the evacuation of patriots, and sent to that region the Mainz garrison, which had been liberated by the Prussians. After Barère denounced English espionage, it was decided, on August 3, to arrest all British subjects; and on the 7th, Pitt was declared the 'enemy of the human race'. Heretofore the people of Lyons had been treated leniently, and by the end of July they appeared willing to accept reconciliation in exchange for an amnesty. But on July 12 the Convention had refused to pardon the ringleaders, and on August 4 the Committee of Public Safety ordered Kellermann to undertake the siege of the town.

Despite these severities, disturbances still continued. Counter-revolutionary resistance in the sections persisted. Rumour spread once more that a St. Bartholomew's massacre of patriots was being prepared and that only a new slaughter of suspects could prevent it. A great festival, prepared by David, was to celebrate the anniversary of August 10 and the promulgation of the Constitution; and the commissioners of the primary assemblies were arriving to report the results of the plebiscite. This might be the occasion for a 'day', and the food shortage might contribute to its success. The Committee was able to maintain order, however, and the ceremony took place without incident.

Now that the commissioners had solemnly committed the 'ark' containing the Constitution to the care of the Convention, would the elections be prepared? Danton's friend Delacroix demanded them; the *Enragés*, Hébert, and numerous popular leaders were of the same opinion, and henceforth continually criticized their postponement. Did any of these imagine that the vote would favour them? This was pure nonsense, unless all those who disapproved of the revolution of May 31 were barred from voting. The desire to oust the members of the Committee of Public Safety blinded them. It took only one speech by Robespierre at the Jacobin Club to bring about the implicit postponement of the Constitution until peace had been made.

The commissioners and the sans-culottes of the sections were not satisfied; they heatedly demanded the arrest of suspects, the levy *en masse*, and a general maximum on commodities of prime necessity. Here and there in the provinces these measures were adopted spontaneously. On August 4, 1793, the deputies on mission resorted to the first two in the north, and unleashed the Terror; the same thing happened in Alsace on the 18th. There was no difficulty where suspects were concerned: on Danton's recommendation the Convention ordered their internment on August 12. As for the levy *en masse*, the Committee hesitated, and the Convention equivocated: What would be done with such a mob? Still, it was necessary to give way, and Carnot, summoned for the purpose, drafted the decree of August 23. The call was limited to unmarried men between the ages of eighteen and twenty-five; all other citizens were subject only to eventual employment in war industries and service behind the lines. Thus the role of the Committee began to be defined. Popular impetus had placed the entire power of the nation at its disposal, but from the summary idea of the levy *en masse* the Committee drew an organized mobilization.

What about the Maximum? At the moment it seemed to be a matter of course, for the levy *en masse*—requisitioning of persons—inevitably led to requisitioning of things. Spending promised to be enormous, and only price controls could restrain inflation. Thus the interest of the state coincided with the popular will. Yet the Committee and the Convention, desperately clinging to the principle of a free economy, yielded only gradually. On July 26 a decree ordered death for 'hoarders', that is, those merchants who, as holders of commodities and merchandise of prime necessity, failed to declare them and to post lists on their doors. Each municipality had to name commissioners specially charged with seeking them out. Would this police inquisition not in itself be enough to curb prices?

On August 1, 1793, the export of capital was forbidden, and on the 15th the exportation of many products was suspended. This resulted in an embargo which interrupted the maritime traffic hitherto maintained by the neutrals. On the 9th a new decree ordered the creation of public granaries for the harvest. In the last two weeks of the month the institution of a maximum on fuel, salt, and tobacco was finally adopted with reluctance. Contractors and financiers were hard hit. The stock exchange had been closed since June 27; at the end of July the postal service and military transport were brought under state supervision; and a decree of August 24 suppressed the Bank of Discount (Caisse d'Escompte), the East India Company, and all stock companies.

Cambon used the time thus won to reduce both the excessive amount of paper money and expenditures. On July 31 he demonetized all assignats bearing the royal portrait; these now served only as payment for taxes and national property. On August 24 he undertook a large transaction that was both political and financial: all state debts were 'republicanized' by registration in the Great Book of the Public Debt, in the name of each bearer, for the total of the annuity (not the capital), without distinction as to origin. Life annuities were excepted, but later, on 23 Floréal, Year II (May 12, 1794), they met the same fate.

Because of these circumstances numerous securities could not be presented, and, moreover, dividend coupons were subject to the same tax through deductions as landed property. Undying hatred became attached to the name of Cambon, the 'executioner of bondholders'. In addition, the forced loan of one billion finally went into effect on September 3, 1793. To it was added an unlimited voluntary loan through registration in the Great Book, good for the purchase of national property and exemption from the forced loan. But the deficit remained no less appalling; there was no avoiding the fact that until peace was made the Republic was condemned to inflation. How could requisitioning and price controls be avoided thereafter? This question could be answered only by another crisis.

Although crops were good, disturbances jeopardized the harvest. Then, at the end of August, drought and calm stopped the mills. The *Enragés* once more raised their voices, and Hébert added his fulminations. As usual, while poverty was rousing the mob, its leaders were thinking primarily of politics. Custine mounted the scaffold on August 28, but demands for the trial of the queen and the Girondins came to naught; and the *endormeurs*, including Danton and Robespierre, were denounced. On top of this came the news of unprecedented treason: Toulon and its squadron had been handed over to the enemy. In this crisis Billaud-Varenne and Collot d'Herbois, the Commune and the Jacobins determined to act. On September 4, at the Hôtel de Ville, invaded by the sans-culottes, they chose the following day for their rising.

On September 5, 1793, the Convention, surrounded by demonstrators, made terror the 'order of the day'. It adopted a programme to which the Committee finally agreed and which was put into effect during the ensuing days. From the 6th to the 8th enemy nationals were arrested and their property was confiscated, and seals were placed on the houses of bankers and stockbrokers. On the 9th the revolutionary army was organized under the command of Ronsin. On the 17th the Law of Suspects was passed. It defined suspected persons so generally that the revolutionary committees were all-powerful. And four days later, wearing of the tricolor cockade was made obligatory. The controlled economy progressed rapidly. On September 11 the regulation of grain and fodder was reorganized, and price controls on them were made uniform throughout the Republic. On the 21st a navigation act, after the English pattern, barred neutral ships and made importation by sea virtually impossible. And on the following day debate began on the general maximum on commodities of prime necessity and wages.

Nor was this all. Nothing had yet been said about the great trials, and the *Enragés* recriminated more than ever, because, on September 5, Danton had had the permanence of section assemblies suppressed and their meetings reduced to two per week. On the other hand, a premium of forty sous was to be distributed henceforth to the sans-culottes who attended such meetings. So the Committee, having skilfully gained the support of Billaud-Varenne and Collot d'Herbois, deemed that the moment had come to dispose of the *Enragés*, and Roux and Varlet were arrested. Leclerc disappeared, and in October the society of Clair Lacombe was suppressed.

Far more dangerous appeared the Montagnard opposition which was taking shape in the Convention. Chabot, Julien, and other 'rotters' (*pourris*) had had decrees and orders against foreigners and financiers annulled or curtailed. On September 14 they were ousted from the Committee of General Security, where they had entrenched themselves. But the Committee of Public Safety had alienated many other representatives by recalling them and placing them under suspicion: Reubell and Merlin of Thionville, just back from Mainz; Briez, returned from Valenciennes; Duhem, a supporter of Custine; and Bourdon of Oise, who had arrested Rossignol. Since the victory at Hondschoote the campaign had taken a turn for the worse. Houchard allowed the English to escape, and was beaten at Menin; Le Quesnoy capitulated; and while attempting to relieve Avesne-le-Sec, the garrison of Cambrai was annihilated. Its general was dismissed and arrested.

At this news a great assault on the Committee began. Thuriot resigned and, on September 25, 1793, broadening the debate, he attacked the extension of the controlled economy and the growing influence of the sans-culottes at the expense of the 'notables'. The Convention applauded and added Briez to the Committee. Then Robespierre arose. If such were to be the case, let the Convention renew the Committee. It was one of his finest speeches. 'I promised you the whole truth, and I shall give it. The Convention has not shown all the vigour it should have. . . . I tell you this: He who was at Valenciennes when the enemy entered is not fit to be a member of the Committee of Public Safety. . . . That may seem harsh, but what is even worse for a patriot is that in two years 100,000 men have been butchered because of treason and weakness. It is weakness for traitors that is destroying us.' The Convention, stupefied, declared that the Committee retained its full confidence; but some politicians never pardon those who, with such vigour and vividness, compel them to assume their responsibilities. It was what they called the 'tyranny of public opinion'.

Nevertheless this time the die was cast. On the 29th the general maximum was decreed. On October 9, English merchandise was prohibited, Britishers interned, and their property confiscated; and a week later, the arrest of all enemy subjects was ordered again. The great trials began. On October 10, on the basis of a report by Saint-Just, the Convention finally proclaimed officially that the 'government of France is revolutionary until the peace'.

Henceforth the terrorists ruled in Paris with the approval of the Committee. Until September, 1793, the Revolutionary Tribunal had proceeded somewhat slowly, and its president, Montané, had compromised himself by tempering its severity. Out of 260 persons, 66 (26 per cent) had been condemned to death. During the 'day' of September 5 it was decided to increase the personnel and to divide the court into four sections. Herman became its president and Fouquier-Tinville remained as public prosecutor. From October to December executions were accelerated. The queen was guillotined on October 16. A special decree stifled the defence of the 21 Girondins, including Vergniaud and Brissot, and they perished on the 31st. The extermination of the party continued during the ensuing months, in Paris and in the provinces. Prominent among those beheaded were Madame Roland, Rabaut, and Lebrun. Others—Roland, Clavière, Pétion, Buzot—committed suicide. Several Feuillants, Bailly and Barnave for example, as well as Philippe Égalité and Biron, also went to the scaffold.

During the three months, of 395 accused, 177 (45 per cent) were sentenced to death. The increase is explained by the proscription of the party leaders. Arrests continued: from 1,417 on August 1, the number of prisoners grew to 4,525 on 1 Nivôse, Year II (December 21, 1793). The section committees, popular societies, and administrative bodies did their best to purge themselves, and although the Convention refused to deprive aristocrats of their civil rights *en masse*, they were maintained in their posts only during good behaviour.

Paris became calmer, because the sans-culottes were gradually finding ways to subsist; the levy *en masse* and the formation of the revolutionary army were thinning their ranks; many were now working in arms and equipment shops, or in the bureaux of the committees and ministries, which had expanded enormously; the sections were supporting others from revolutionary wages as permanent National Guards, commissioners, and guards over property under seal; and their benevolent committees distributed relief. Attempts were also made to induce respect for the Maximum through careful police surveillance, and the Commune instituted the rationing of bread and sugar by means of food cards. Once emptied, however, the shops were not replenished. Chaumette threatened merchants and manufacturers with nationalization of their establishments. After the drive against the 'selfish rich' came that against merchants, even against sans-culottes. This was indeed what the Committee had feared.

The authority of the Committee remained precarious. In fact, the sans-culotte leaders, coming into the inheritance of the *Enragés*, re-established permanent section meetings by creating neighbourhood popular societies. In the Paris region the revolutionary army was developing, and its leader, Ronsin, at the head of his Carmagnoles, was believed capable of imitating Cromwell. It was becoming obvious that the Committee, having adopted the controlled economy, intended to reserve principal benefits therefrom for the army and public services, and that it was not preoccupied with popular consumption except to insure bread, the essential food.

Technical difficulties partly explain this policy, but there was also the desire to conciliate the peasants and the lower middle class of artisans and shopkeepers, as well as the well-to-do buyers. Thus, on 2 Brumaire, Year II (October 23, 1793), the Convention decided that the sale of livestock would remain free, and the Commission on Provisions (*subsistances*) never secured the repeal of this concession, which made a mockery of price controls on meat. For its part, the Committee of Public Safety forbade house-to-house searches for provisions in Paris, took no precautions against illicit trade, and gave no support to the commissioners who were trying to check the hoarding of food. With provisioning remaining insufficient and irregular, the exasperation of the sans-culottes kept the government in constant danger of a crisis.

Other difficulties existed in the provinces. There no sans-culottes contested or threatened the authority of the Convention and the Committee, but decisions were often made without consulting them. A large mission of deputies directed the levy *en masse*. Invested with discretionary power, they acted 'revolutionarily', that is, rapidly and through exceptional measures, on their own responsibility, to compel all citizens to work for the common safety. The very extent of their powers, the slowness of communications, and urgency enabled them to act independently, and the Committee was unable to control their activity. It must be granted that they were more or less motivated by the spirit of the Mountain, and to some extent they resembled the intendants of Richelieu and Colbert as instruments of centralization under extraordinary circumstances. They reached an agreement with the popular societies concerning the purging of the authorities. They had suspects arrested, and raised recruits, equipped and armed them as best they could by requisitioning, and fed the population in the same way.

But circumstances varied from one region to another. They also presented a wide variety in inclinations and temperaments, and even in morals. Many limited themselves to measures indispensable to security and national defence; others energetically applied the social policy that prevailed at Paris. Fouché in Nièvre, Baudot and Taillefer in the southwest, and Isoré and Chasles in the north organized the unemployed into revolutionary armies, taxed the rich, established workshops, workrooms, and almshouses, and saw that the Maximum was respected. They were not the only ones—far from it.

The most noticeable differences were apparent in the application of the Terror, which became really sanguinary only in exceptional cases. Most of the deputies were satisfied with arrests, while others (such as Dumont in Oise) caused more fear than harm. Or again, like Lebon on his first mission, they punished severely only insurgents or traitors. The federalists in particular were treated in different ways. Some were guillotined, while a reconciliation was effected with others. In Normandy, Lindet and Frémanger took no action against them, but some deputies established revolutionary tribunals on their own initiative. In the civil war regions a few, such as Collot d'Herbois, Fouché, Barras, and Fréron at Toulon, conducted mass executions. At Nantes, Carrier ordered prisoners to be put to death without even a summary trial. And there was good reason for questioning the integrity of Barras and Fréron in Provence, of Rovère in Vaucluse, and of Tallien at Bordeaux.

If the system thus varied in place and time with its representatives, there was scarcely any less diversity within the jurisdiction of each. Being unable to do or to see everything, they relied upon local Jacobins and the commissioners of August 10, who had been sent back to their homes by the Convention with the mission of co-operating in the levy *en masse*. The deputies approved their efforts, or assumed their responsibilities (like Carrier, for example), so far as the noyades were concerned. They filled the administrative bodies with them, delegated their powers to some of them, and formed committees of public safety—Couthon at Ambert—and departmental or district revolutionary committees not provided by law.

Left to themselves, the sans-culottes applied the revolutionary measures energetically, but by doing as they pleased, and frequently by anticipating or exceeding the decrees. Like the deputies, they differed from one another, and, established in the cities, they could supervise only from a distance the small towns and villages, where they had few reliable and capable men. Here the Jacobin impetus was followed submissively but unenthusiastically. Only a few suspects were discovered; elsewhere they were imprisoned on the slightest pretext. Even in the cities the two tendencies were frequently encountered. The most violent were not always the democrats of yesterday, but rather new sans-culottes who wanted to live down their Feuillantism, evade revolutionary taxes, or enjoy power. The moderates and the extremists, the *citras* and the *ultras*, shared the different administrative bodies. Watch committees, municipalities, and districts came into conflict. They quarrelled over the popular societies, and the deputies on mission were circumvented to effect a purge and to have opponents arrested. Even the most patriotic did not feel safe.

Often, too, there were conflicts between the deputies and the dominant parties: Saint-Just and Lebas proscribed Euloge Schneider and the Alsatian extremists; Hentz and Guiot, those in the Nord. Opposite inclinations were not always the only question at issue. When Barras and Fréron pronounced the dissolution of the Convention of the Popular Societies of the South, and when Tallien and Fouché fell out with the local terrorists, it appears that rivalry over authority and personal jealousy played a large part. The provincial Jacobins, especially at Lyons, wanted to remain masters of their own houses, and they disliked Parisian intrusion. Nor must it be forgotten that in certain regions different missions had to collaborate, and more than once they quarrelled: Lebas and Saint-Just with Baudot and Lacoste; Hentz and Guiot with Chasles and Isoré in the Nord. Finally, deputies succeeding each other in the same area showed different leanings, each more or less modifying the work of his predecessor, dismissing or punishing some, releasing or favouring others.

When the government failed to act, it was the impetus of the Jacobins and deputies on mission that saved the Republic in the summer of 1793. They re-established national unity, recruited and supplied the armies, and fed the population. Nevertheless there had been a surfeit of authorities and a lack of co-ordination and discipline. Arrests and taxes were causing anger, the revolutionary armies might be turned against the Convention, and local conflicts threatened to disorganize administration, or at least to reduce the effectiveness of the revolutionary war effort. The spontaneous popular action had been salutary, but (as Levasseur noted) 'anarchy' could not continue. The Committee deemed it necessary to organize the regime and to reinforce centralization. The question was whether in so doing it would break revolutionary ardour, restrict the spirit of initiative, and weaken the repression. Yet, while admitting that politics might cause it to hesitate, the economic situation left it no choice.

The decree of September 29, 1793, provided that district administrations should regulate the prices of commodities at one-third higher than the rates of 1790. It also charged the municipalities with fixing wages at not more than 50 per cent higher than those of the same year. The most shocking inequities in the rates were immediately apparent: it seems that the districts generally assessed the articles produced in the country at the highest possible price, and vice versa. Moreover, the decree said nothing about costs of transport or the rate of business profits; nor was it clear concerning the application of price controls to producers, wholesalers, or retailers. Distribution and production slowed or stopped entirely. On the other hand, the decree of September 11 established a national maximum on grain and fodder, and included transport costs. But the harvest, which had been good, was partially destroyed by war or absorbed by the army, and the departure of recruits delayed the threshing. Accordingly the districts were careful to claim only what was absolutely essential for the markets, and even this was obtained with great effort. Naturally it was only with difficulty that they authorized purchases which benefited their neighbours.

Certain regions, the south in particular, seemed condemned to famine, inasmuch as all importing from abroad appeared to be virtually impossible. Still, life had to go on, and foreign commerce revived spontaneously. At Bordeaux, in October, and Marseilles, in December, the deputies on mission, in collaboration with the merchants, created committees charged with purchasing grain abroad through the medium of neutrals. Since the latter refused to accept assignats, the committees permitted the exportation of certain merchandise, requisitioned foreign bills of exchange, struck money from precious metals taken from the churches, or even prescribed the compulsory exchange of specie for paper money, in the hope that the value of the latter might rise.

It was impossible to renounce regulation, for this would have meant breaking with the sans-culottes and playing into the hands of the extremists. Having undertaken vast war manufactures, and being obliged to feed its armies, the Committee could not get along without requisitioning. Without price controls the assignats would have collapsed, while the Maximum, on the contrary, brought them up to 50 per cent of par in December. The economic government remained to be organized by standardizing the Maximum on commodities and by distributing resources equitably throughout all regions of the Republic through requisitions determined by the central government. Foreign commerce also had to be nationalized. From the very outset the Committee had decided to import raw materials and provisions from all sources. Consequently it repressed local initiative that threatened to exhaust foreign exchange for the special benefit of certain departments. Even more than political needs, economic necessity forced the Committee to assume absolute and unprecedented authority over the entire life of the nation.

From October to December, 1793, the Committee gradually developed a doctrine, a plan of action, and the agencies for its execution. In his report of 28 Brumaire, Year II (November 18, 1793), Billaud-Varennes, following Saint-Just, defined the principles and aim of the revolutionary government. Its chief features were set out in the great decree of 14 Frimaire, Year II (December 4, 1793). All initiative, foreign or contrary to the law, was condemned; all collaboration between local administrations or popular societies was forbidden; every delegation of power, even to the deputies on mission, was banned. The revolutionary armies of the provinces were to be dismissed, and revolutionary taxes abolished.

On October 22, 1793, the Commission on Provisions had been created to take charge of the economic government; on November 18 it was given the monopoly on imports, and on December 10, the task of authorizing exports. Beginning with 24 Pluviôse, Year II (February 12, 1794), it alone would retain the right of requisitioning, except in the provisioning of local markets. A decree of 10 Brumaire, Year II (October 31, 1793), had charged it with establishing a national price schedule for merchandise at the place of production, and for this purpose it began a comprehensive inquiry. The Convention refused to withdraw specie from circulation, but on 5 Nivôse, Year II (December 25, 1793), Cambon requisitioned the foreign exchange of bankers. By year's end the revolutionary government was taking form. Still, the existence of the Committee of Public Safety, its keystone, could be sustained only at the price of constant vigilance. The disintegration of the Montagnard party, apparent in September, grew more serious daily, and each of the two factions claimed to be subordinating itself to the Committee, while waiting to take its place.

DECHRISTIANIZATION

In November violent dechristianization provoked an unexpected disturbance and inaugurated the final crisis. During the course of this crisis, which lasted all winter, the attitude of the Committee changed several times.

The causes of the movement were deep-seated. Except for a certain number of 'red curés', the constitutional priests had been alarmed by the religious consequences of August 10. Approving neither the death of the king nor the fall of the Girondins, they became suspect; and on October 25, 1793, the Convention, in codifying the penalties against refractory clergy, also ordered the deportation of constitutional clergy who were denounced by six citizens. On the other hand, a growing number of republicans deemed it useless to pursue the experiment attempted by the Constituent Assembly. As early as November, 1792, Cambon vainly proposed that payment of the clergy cease. Since there were doubts that the state could dispense with the church, and since the majority of sans-culottes themselves might be lacking in respect for religious ceremonies, this revolutionary cult, which had evolved since 1789 and heretofore had been associated with that year, was gradually set up in opposition to the traditional form of worship.

For the first time the festival of August 10, 1793, was purely secular. The new religion endowed itself with symbols and a form of liturgy, honoured the 'holy Mountain', and venerated its martyrs, Lepeletier, Marat, and Chalier. On 3 Brumaire, Year II (October 24, 1793), on recommendations by Romme and Fabre d'Églantine, the Convention adopted the revolutionary calendar. It attempted to dechristianize daily life by substituting the date of September 22, 1792, the first day of the Republic, for the Christian era; by replacing references to religious ceremonies and the saints with names borrowed from tools and products familiar to the French; and above all, by eliminating Sunday in favour of the Tenth Day (*décadi*). On 15 Brumaire, Year II (November 5, 1793) a report by Marie-Joseph Chénier on civic festivals constituted the prelude to the official organization of the national religion.

As yet the Catholic faith had not suffered any legal restrictions. Nevertheless some Montagnards tolerated it only with impatience. At Nevers on September 22, 1793, in collaboration with Chaumette, who had come to breathe the 'air of his birthplace', Fouché celebrated a festival in honour of Brutus in the cathedral itself. On October 10 he forbade all religious ceremonies outside churches, and secularized funeral processions and cemeteries. Upon his return to Paris, Chaumette recommended identical measures to the Commune. Other deputies adopted similar arrangements, as did the revolutionary armies. A few priests resigned their posts. The district of Corbeil declared that the majority of persons under its jurisdiction no longer desired the Catholic form of worship, and on 16 Brumaire, Year II (November 6, 1793) the Convention accorded the communes the right to renounce it.

Then some extremists precipitated events. On the night of 16–17 Brumaire, Year II (November 6–7, 1793) they compelled Gobel, the bishop of Paris, to resign, and on the 17th he came with his vicars to the Convention to confirm his action officially. A Festival of Liberty was planned for 20 Brumaire, Year II (November 10, 1793). To celebrate the victory of philosophy over fanaticism, the Commune seized Notre Dame, a mountain was built in the choir, and an actress impersonated Liberty. Informed of this, the Convention proceeded to the cathedral—now called the Temple of Reason—and attended a second celebration of the civic festival. Some sections followed this example. On the 30th (November 20) the citizens of the Unity section (the former Four Nations), adorned with priestly symbols, paraded before the Convention, singing and dancing. Then, on 3 Frimaire, Year II (November 23, 1793), the Commune closed the churches.

In adopting the republican calendar the majority of the Convention had shown its hostility to Christianity, but these masquerades offended it. The abolition of Catholic worship seemed to it a political mistake—the Republic faced enough enemies without throwing all devout Catholics into the opposition. The Assembly refused to discontinue the salaries of priests, and the Committee of Public Safety supported its decision. Moreover, it is probable that conservatives like Carnot believed, as Voltaire had and as Bonaparte would later, that religion was necessary to prevent social upheaval. In Robespierre's eyes the question was more significant. Behind dechristianization he suspected atheism—a doctrine of the rich and alien to the people—which did not differentiate between public and private immorality. He had had the bust of Helvétius banned from the Jacobin Club.

A more pressing anxiety, however, intervened for the Committee of Public Safety: Did dechristianization conceal some political manoeuvre? There was no doubt that it responded to the feelings of the sans-culottes who had taken part in the 'days'. This is proved by the fact that henceforth hostility towards the clergy persisted among the common people, among whom the Voltairianism of the upper social classes had hitherto found few adherents. Thus the crisis aggravated the agitation in the sections and the clubs and threatened the Committee. Even worse, about October 12, 1793, Fabre d'Églantine, having fallen out with the extremists, denounced them as accomplices in a 'foreign plot' for the benefit of Pitt and Baron de Batz. The Committee was closely watching the refugees, notably Proli, a rich Belgian, who was believed to be a natural son of Kaunitz. Guzman had already been imprisoned. Among those who had recently provoked Gobel's abdication were the German baron Cloots and the Portuguese Pereira. Furthermore, among the deputies who favoured the dechristianizers, some, such as Chabot, were suspected of stock speculation, while others, such as Danton's friend Thuriot (who, at the moment, was leading the attack against the Committee in the Convention), were distrusted as moderates.

The execution of the Girondins had caused a vague uneasiness among the deputies. In future, would they allow the Committee to arrest one of their members, and then order the Assembly to indict him without a hearing or a study of the evidence? Might it not be able to escape their control through the Terror that decimated the Convention? On 19 Brumaire, Year II (November 9, 1793) Osselin had to be surrendered for having protected an aristocrat who had become his mistress. The next day, withdrawing its approval, the Convention decided that henceforth it would hear accused deputies, and only with difficulty did Barère succeed in getting this decree revoked on 22 Brumaire. Thereupon, Chabot, violently criticized since his recent marriage to the sister of the Freys, Austrian Jews who were very suspect, wished to protect himself. On the 24th (November 14) he made revelations to the committees, which Basire confirmed and which justified Fabre d'Églantine's accusations. He explained that Delaunay and Julien of Toulouse, in collaboration with Batz, had offered him a bribe to persuade

Fabre d'Églantine himself to sign the falsified draft of the decree ordering the liquidation of the East India Company. The committees of Public Safety and of General Security decided to arrest both accuser and accused.

Danton, who had remarried during the preceding summer and had been staying at Arcis since October, at once returned hurriedly on 30 Brumaire, Year II (November 20, 1793), apparently to come to the aid of Basire and Fabre d'Églantine, his close friends. The Committee began to suspect that the 'foreign plot' was a link between the two factions—on one hand, the Hébertists (with whom Chabot had become associated), and on the other, the peculators (whose accomplice the same Chabot had been) who, as associates of Baron de Batz and friends of Danton, secured the aid of the members of the Convention who were hostile to the 'men of blood'.

The combination must have appeared formidable, for Robespierre veered to the right in order to fight dechristianization in collaboration with Danton. Fabre d'Églantine explained that he had signed the false decree prepared by Delaunay without reading it, and far from being affected, he was made a party to the investigation. The embezzlers were not brought to trial. Robespierre led the Jacobins against the dechristianizers, and Danton entreated the Convention to 'put up the barrier'. On 16 Frimaire, Year II (December 6, 1793), a decree affirmed the existence of freedom of worship, and on the 29th a law declared education also free and did not exclude priests. A memorandum of the Committee, 4 Nivôse (December 24), pointed out the dangers of violence.

Actually the Committee's success was entirely relative. On 18 Frimaire, Year II (December 8, 1793), the Convention stipulated that the decrees of deputies on mission who had closed the churches would remain in effect. The Commune allowed the constitutional clergy to practise their worship in private, but the churches of Paris remained closed. Some deputies on mission conformed to the Committee's intentions, but most of them felt that security measures should not be confused with violence. Since they considered the influence of the constitutional priests detrimental, they bullied or imprisoned those who refused to resign. On 6 Germinal, Year II (March 26, 1794), the Convention itself suspended the payment of ecclesiastical pensions, and more than one district stopped paying clerical salaries.

Nevertheless dechristianization followed the uneven course already noted, for it depended greatly upon the local authorities. Some churches were closed hastily, but this did not prevent the arrest of those who had not previously attended masses celebrated by constitutional priests. Elsewhere worship was suspended only tardily and with regret. In several regions the resulting unrest gave reason for prudence. In Thermidor some churches still remained open, but these became increasingly rare. In the last analysis the Hébertist spirit triumphed. The Montagnard dictatorship gained nothing from this obstinacy, for dechristianization could only sow dissension among the lower classes.

The Committee's victory was primarily political. It had smashed the intrigue that it suspected was destined to drive it to extremes and thus overthrow it. This was a Pyrrhic victory, for the moderates who were helping Robespierre fight the sans-culottes hoped to win him over to their view in order to upset the Committee. The military situation provided them with an argument. The need to conquer justified the revolutionary government; but with one victory following another, had it not lost its reason for existence? For the Committee this was a new danger.

FIRST VICTORIES OF THE REVOLUTIONARY GOVERNMENT (SEPTEMBER–DECEMBER, 1793)

During the summer the requisition of the levy of 300,000 men was finally completed, and by July the total strength of the army reached 650,000. It was with these troops that the Committee of Public Safety completed the campaign of 1793, although the men of the levy *en masse* who could not be armed were left in their garrisons. Yet the difficulties were tremendous. War production, begun in September, produced no important results until the end of the year. The army command was in the midst of a purge. A new generation, sprung from the diverse elements of the Third Estate, as well as from the poor nobility, was moving to the top ranks. Peerless leaders came to the fore, but many incompetent ones were beaten. Even as it was preparing for future victories, the Committee still had to improvise some immediate ones to halt the invasion and end the civil war. Whatever its power, it needed both time and luck. These were provided by the Polish insurrection, the divisions among the Allied Powers, and the mediocrity of the Coalition generals.

In August, 1793, the Allied army fell apart, and sieges immobilized it. The duke of York particularly wished to take Dunkirk, which British shipowners had detested, because of its privateering, since the time of Louis XIV. Coburg laid siege to the small fortress of Le Quesnoy. Carnot, a military engineer, also ascribed vital importance to fortresses. If he was able to take advantage of the masses which the Republic had mobilized, by concentrating them, he did not dream of giving Coburg a decisive battle that would open Belgium. He reinforced Houchard's army and sent it to the aid of Dunkirk, where the situation seemed alarming. Houchard repulsed Freytag, who was covering the siege, and beat him at Hondschoote on September 8; but instead of cutting off the retreat of the Anglo-Hanoverians, he allowed them to escape. Shortly afterwards he was beaten at Menin, and was guillotined.

With Le Quesnoy taken, Coburg attacked Maubeuge, and established himself south of the Sambre to halt any reinforcements. Since Brunswick did not prove very enterprising, Carnot drew part of the Army of the Moselle to the north. A tactical formation was assembled near Guise under Jourdan's command, and Carnot himself joined it on October 8. On the 15th the Carmagnoles made a frontal assault upon Coburg's troops, which repelled them; but the next day they turned their left wing at Wattignies. Maubeuge was relieved; its garrison had done nothing, and its commander, General Chancel, was guillotined. Meanwhile the Austrians, who had been battling the Army of the Rhine north of the Lauter since July, took the offensive. On October 13, Wurmser stormed the entrenchments known as the Wissembourg lines, and after investing Landau, invaded Alsace. The French were thrown back in the Vosges and beneath the guns of Strasbourg.

Happily for them, the less aggressive Brunswick did not yet seek to take the Saar line from the Army of the Moselle. Saint-Just and Lebas hastened to Strasbourg, while Baudot and Lacoste in Lorraine had time to prepare a counterblow. With the campaign ended in the north, Carnot redeployed his forces to the east. Pichegru now received the command of the Army of the Rhine, and took the offensive on November 18, but without great success. Hoche, who had distinguished himself at Dunkirk, was sent to the Army of the Moselle. He attacked Brunswick at Kaiserlauten between the 28th and the 30th. The Prussians repulsed him, but failed to follow up their victory. Hoche then crossed the Vosges, and debouched through Froeschwiller and Wörth behind Wurmser, who beat a retreat. Rejoined by Pichegru, and appointed general-in-chief by Baudot and Lacoste, Hoche recaptured the Wissembourg lines, relieved Landau on December 28, and occupied Spire. Everywhere the invasion had been driven back or halted. The Spanish retreated south of Bayonne, and in the eastern Pyrenees they retired behind the Tech. Kellermann had liberated Savoy in October.

At this same time the royalist insurrections were reduced, but it required almost as much effort as did the frontiers. In August, Dubois-Crancé had forecast the prompt capitulation of Lyons. Actually, even bombardment did not end the resistance. Moreover, the investment of the town was not completed on the western side until September 17, after the arrival of the army raised in Auvergne by Couthon. The decisive attack of the 29th yielded the heights of Fourvière to the republicans, who entered Lyons on October 9. The Committee grew violently angry at this long delay, which was jeopardizing the Army of the Alps and had prevented Carteaux from saving Toulon.

The last straw was the escape of Précy. True, his troops had been cut to ribbons, but it was feared that he might reach Provence. Hence the Committee recalled Dubois-Crancé. The Convention declared that Lyons would be called 'Freed City' ('*Ville Affranchie*'), and the houses of the rich would be demolished. Robespierre organized the repression, and Couthon carried it out with moderation; but in November, Collot d'Herbois and Fouché replaced him, and thenceforth executions increased. By March, 1,667 death sentences had been pronounced by the revolutionary committees. After the fall of Lyons it was possible to press the siege of Toulon. Prepared by Dugommier, assisted by the artillery captain Bonaparte, the final attack began on December 15. On the 19th the town fell to the republicans, and Barras and Fréron had several hundred rebels shot.

At the same time, after many vicissitudes, the first war in the Vendée ended. The arrival of the garrison from Mainz facilitated the striking of a fatal blow against the royal Catholic army. Even so, two attempts were necessary, because the deputies on mission and the generals directing the encircling attacks were at odds. Ronsin and Santerre were beaten at Coron, and Kléber at Torfou (September 18 and 19). At last, on October 17, the blue armies met at Cholet, and crushed the 'Whites', who lost most of their leaders. But La Rochejaquelein and Stofflet crossed the Loire with some 20,000 to 30,000 men, who were joined in Maine by the bands of Jean Chouan. They were met at Entrammes (south of Laval), on October 27, by the republicans, whom they defeated decisively. The 'Whites' were then able, without interference, to reach Granville (November 13 and 14), which was defended by the deputy Le Carpentier. Repulsed, they returned southward and ambushed the scattered columns that attempted to halt them. They finally reached Angers, where they failed once more (December 3 and 4).

Marceau now commanded in place of the sans-culotte generals, and he hastened the reformed army into action. The Vendéans took the road to Le Mans, where terrible street fighting finished them. The remnants dragged themselves as far as Savenay, and there they were annihilated on the 23rd. Again La Rochejaquelein and Stofflet recrossed the Loire, and Charette had not left the Marais. He even surprised Noirmoutier, which Haxo recaptured on January 3, 1794. Thus the guerrilla war was prolonged, and Turreau, who took command, threw the 'infernal columns' across the Vendée in order to effectuate the plan of devastation decreed on August 1.

The military commissions condemned a large number of 'brigands'; and at Angers a 'commission of review' ('*commission de recensement*') put more than 2,000 others to death without a trial. The deputy on mission, Francastel (less well known than Carrier), proved equally implacable. The most notorious summary executions had begun at Nantes before the final rout. The military commissions were unequal to the task, so the prisoners had been herded there; and the courts at Nantes were similarly overwhelmed. Since the prisons became centres of infection and the prisoners could not be fed, they were disposed of, without formalities, by being drowned in the Loire. The first noyade may have been the work of local terrorists, but Carrier let them continue. The number of mass drownings and that of the dead—refractory clergy, suspects, 'brigands', and common-law prisoners—remains debatable, and legend has even increased the horror of this nocturnal slaughter; but during December and January at least 2,000 to 3,000 persons perished.

The Vendée was not completely vanquished, and there could be no doubt that the Coalition would make a new effort in the spring; but the immediate peril had been dissipated. Was it necessary, therefore, to strain the energies of the government still further? The Committee replied that it was, that the decisive victory would be dearly won, and that events would prove it was right. Could the repression at least not be moderated? Many members of the Convention thought so, and some Montagnards were willing to agree, whereupon the sans-culottes cried treason. Once again the Committee found itself caught between two fires.

TRIUMPH OF THE COMMITTEE OF PUBLIC SAFETY (DECEMBER, 1793–MAY, 1794)

The disavowal of dechristianization caused confusion among the extremists. Accusing Chaumette of defection, the Cordeliers Club excluded him. Danton's friends, with the tacit approval of Robespierre, pressed the attack against them. Camille Desmoulins issued a new newspaper, *Le vieux Cordelier*, the first numbers of which enjoyed an astonishing success. Fabre d'Églantine, Bourdon, and Philippeaux violently attacked Ronsin and Vincent, and on 27 Frimaire, Year II (December 17, 1793) had their arrest ordered.

At the same time the moderates were plotting. The third number of *Le vieux Cordelier* attacked the Law of Suspects on 25 Frimaire (December 15); five days later a crowd of women implored the Convention to release prisoners who were unjustly accused, and Robespierre himself had a committee named to review the arrests. On 2 Nivôse (December 22) a businessman condemned for food speculation was freed by the Convention, and shortly thereafter, the decree of July 26, 1793, was suspended.

The secret implications of this offensive were revealed by attacks against Bouchotte, minister of war, and Héron, a government agent. As early as 22 Frimaire, Year II (December 12, 1793), Bourdon even proposed that the Committee of Public Safety be purged, and Merlin of Thionville suggested that it be renewed by one-third every month. Robespierre seemed to have compromised himself with the Indulgents, and to have abandoned his role of arbitration and domination, which assured the unity of the Committee. Likewise on 22 Frimaire he had Cloots expelled from the Jacobin Club. Certainly Billaud-Varenne and Collot d'Herbois did not go along with him. Once the Committee was divided, it might be renewed, and everyone believed that Danton would once more become its head.

Danton undoubtedly assumed that, as after Valmy, with the *Patrie* no longer in danger, severity might be reduced. 'I ask that the blood of men be spared!' he cried on November 22. To end the revolutionary government was to suggest that peace was imminent, and the rumour spread that negotiations were being conducted. At Copenhagen the minister Bernstorff let it be understood that he was willing to act as an intermediary. Danton was no more the leader of a party than was Hébert, but the tactics and aspirations of the Indulgents were in harmony with his previous policy and with the conciliatory opportunism which characterized it. Unhappily, among the partisans of 'clemency' there were the 'rotters' who 'wished to tear down the scaffolds because they were afraid of having to mount them'. Since Danton was considered to be venal, it was a simple matter to transform the Indulgents into a branch of the 'foreign plot', seeking the same end as the extremists and for the same purpose, but in different ways.

The tide turned abruptly after Collot d'Herbois, who had hastened from Lyons, boldly defended the terrorists at the Jacobin Club on 1 Nivôse, Year II (December 21, 1793). Robespierre, obviously recovering his poise, once more denounced the double peril from right and left. On 6 Nivôse, Billaud-Varenne, probably with the approval of the Committee of General Security, had the 'committee of justice', or 'of clemency', suppressed. Soon *Le vieux Cordelier* was assailed at the Jacobin Club. Robespierre first pretended to treat Desmoulins as an *enfant terrible*; but the latter, hearing him advise the burning of copies of his newspaper, replied, 'Burning is not answering.' The following day, 19 Nivôse, Year II (January 8, 1794), Robespierre, returning to the theme of the two factions, served notice of the rupture—though this did not keep him from preventing Desmoulins' expulsion from the club.

But the government had a more effective means of dealing with the Indulgents. It kept as hostages the imprisoned peculators, among whom it knew they had friends. Inaction gave way to prosecution. It was decided that Fabre d'Églantine's excuse—his claim that he had signed the false decree without reading it—was not good enough, and he was arrested on the night of 23–24 Nivôse, Year II (January 12–13, 1794). With Danton protesting, as he had in November, that accused deputies should be heard, Billaud-Varenne made open threats against him. In Pluviôse, on the contrary, Mazuel, Ronsin, and Vincent emerged from prison.

Since the Committee had regained its balance, the two factions vainly fought each other for two months. Desmoulins and Philippeaux continued their campaign. The Hébertists responded by denouncing food speculators, by demanding the proscription of the 75 objectors to June 2 (whom Robespierre had spared from the Revolutionary Tribunal), the signers of the petitions of 1792 (the '8,000' and the '20,000'), and even Louis XVII. In the Committee, on the other hand, Lindet demanded that trial of the federalists be postponed until his report was presented, but it never came. The 132 men of Nantes, who were sent to Paris at the height of winter, were never tried.

In the provinces the rupture between the government and the Hébertists cast discredit on the sans-culottes. Fouché, sensing the way the wind was blowing, broke with those of Lyons, and Gouly with those at Bourg. All things considered, the Indulgents did not lose hope, for if the Committee did not yield to them at least it had repressed popular action. Jacques Roux killed himself in prison. Moreover, the deputies on mission who were known terrorists—Carrier, Tallien, Javogues, Barras,

Fréron—were recalled, and in Franche-Comté, Augustin Robespierre made Bernard of Saintes beat a retreat.

Finally uncertainty disappeared, for at winter's end the economic situation worsened and precipitated a crisis. Bread became scarce and inedible, meat was in short supply, and the peasants, frightened by the section commissioners who seized their products in order to distribute them, brought in less and less. The Hébertists incited the sans-culottes to demand stringent measures, and strikes broke out in the arms factories. Robespierre was ill, but Billaud-Varenne, Collot d'Herbois, and Saint-Just were undoubtedly counted upon. In fact, the Committee did prove conciliatory. On 13 Pluviôse, Year II (February 1, 1794), the Convention voted 10 millions for relief; on 3 Ventôse (February 21) Barère presented the new general Maximum; on the 8th, Saint-Just obtained a decree confiscating the property of suspects and distributing it among the needy; and on the 9th the plan for a new law on monopoly was read. The Cordeliers Club felt that if it increased the pressure, it would triumph once and for all. On 12 Ventôse, Year II (March 2, 1794), Ronsin talked of insurrection, and on the 14th, Hébert attacked Robespierre by name. On the 17th, Collot d'Herbois went to the Cordeliers Club, on behalf of the Jacobins, to effect a reconciliation; but the menacing proposals continued.

All that was involved was probably a new demonstration like the one in September. As always in such cases, however, the police maintained that some were arming and that a conspiracy was being planned in the prisons. It is understandable that the Committee was uneasy; but would a few arrests not be enough to reassure it? Still, it lost patience, and on 22 Ventôse, Year II (March 12, 1794), with Robespierre once more present, it decided to have done with the Hébertists. To Hébert, Ronsin, Vincent, and Momoro it added the refugees Proli, Cloots, and Pereira, so as to present them as parties to the 'foreign plot'. All were executed on 4 Germinal (March 24). The decrees of the Convention, the charges of dishonesty levelled against Hébert, the distribution of provisions, and the dispersal of the revolutionary army struck home—the sans-culottes remained passive.

Five days previously, the 'corrupt ones'—Fabre d'Églantine,

Chabot, Basire, Delaunay—had been arraigned. On the night of 9–10 Germinal, Year II (March 29–30, 1794) the Committee decided to include Danton, Delacroix, Philippeaux, and Camille Desmoulins as well. In all likelihood Collot d'Herbois and Billaud-Varenne, supported by the Committee of General Security, maintained that having struck the Left, it was necessary to intimidate the Indulgents as well. It seems that Billaud-Varenne, on returning from his mission to St.-Malo, was dumfounded at the fall of the Hébertists, and later reproached Robespierre for his resistance to the new proscription. Although Robespierre might have yielded, he nonetheless accepted the responsibility, aided Saint-Just in drawing up his report, and took it upon himself to quash the protests in the dismayed and trembling Convention on behalf of a 'long-decayed idol'.

With the Indulgents were grouped Abbé d'Espagnac, a notorious speculator; Westermann, whose past, it was said, was by no means spotless; Hérault de Séchelles, a member of the Committee who had been excluded by his colleagues on the charge of revealing their deliberations; and Guzman and the Frey brothers, in order to tie the accused to the 'foreign plot'. A planned conspiracy to snatch the accused from their prison was alleged so as to throttle Danton's defence, just as that of the Girondins had been stifled. He was guillotined with the others on 16 Germinal, Year II (April 5, 1794). As an epilogue to the alleged conspiracy came a new mixed 'batch', among whom Chaumette, Hébert's widow, and Lucille Desmoulins perished on 24 Germinal (April 13).

This crisis was decisive. In the history of the revolutionary movement the fall of the Hébertists marked the beginning of the ebb-tide. For the first time since 1789 the government had forestalled popular action by doing away with its leaders. It boldly completed its victory. The revolutionary army was disbanded on 7 Germinal, Year II (March 27, 1794); the 'provisional executive council' (that is, the ministers) was suppressed on 12 Germinal (April 1); and the Ministry of War, already deprived of Vincent, was lost to Bouchotte, who was eventually imprisoned on 3 Thermidor (July 21). The department, the municipality, the general council of the Commune, and the police administration were purged, and filled with reliable men; and the mayor, Pache, was arrested on 21 Floréal (May 10). As early as 8 Germinal, Year II (March 28, 1794) the Commission on Provisions assumed control of provisioning Paris with bread and meat. The Cordeliers Club was reduced to insignificance, and under government pressure, the section clubs, one after another, pronounced their own dissolution at the end of Floréal and in Prairial.

Henceforth the popular leaders accused of Hébertism felt suspect. In Paris, several of them were incarcerated, and some were guillotined. In Bourg, they were arrested after the departure of the representative Albitte, who was sent to Savoy. In Lyons, Fouché purged the popular society and the town government. In the Orléans region, Demaillot, an agent of the Committee, sent the terrorists to Paris under heavy guard. Thus disorganized, the sans-culottes thereafter appeared incapable of intimidating the Committee. Government authority had been re-established.

True, Robespierre and his colleagues expected to remain in harmony with the people; but they had not gauged the influence of the Ventôse tragedy on morale. Next to the *Enragés*, 'Père Duchesne' and the Cordeliers had been the real leaders of the sans-culottes. The survivors blamed the Committee for the death of their friends. Hostile to the revolutionary dictatorship from the moment that they themselves lost control of it, they fought it mercilessly and ceaselessly. Who in the crowd would not have been discouraged and disillusioned to see these patriots struck down as traitors? The economic policy of the Committee was now exposed, and, completely oriented towards the war, it was incapable of satisfying the people. Would its social policy be enough to attach the latter to the Montagnards?

The Committee, it is true, found itself at the mercy of the Convention. Having compelled the Convention to deliver the Girondins and Danton, it believed it had a safe majority. It was wrong. The Convention never forgave it these sacrifices. So many empty seats spread a secret terror, which might easily turn into rebellion. It was as mediator between the Assembly and the sans-culottes that the Committee had acquired its strength. By breaking with the sans-culottes it freed the Assembly, and to complete its destruction, it had only to split internally.

CHARACTER AND ORGANIZATION OF THE REVOLUTIONARY GOVERNMENT

From 16 Germinal to 9 Thermidor, Year II (April 5–July 27, 1794), the revolutionary government continued to develop further under the pressure of events. Nevertheless, having attained the undisputed dictatorship of the Committee of Public Safety, it henceforth presented a certain degree of stability. It was a war government; such was the fundamental idea of the Committee. The Revolution was defending itself on the frontiers and at home. 'Are our enemies at home not the allies of our enemies abroad?' cried Robespierre. It was struggling for its existence, and this necessity legitimized exceptional measures. When the victorious Republic made peace, the constitutional system would reassert its dominion.

The voting of sweeping measures is not enough for the waging of war; a government must see that they are executed, and that all efforts are co-ordinated. Even Bonaparte, on 1 Thermidor, Year II (July 19, 1794), pointed out to Augustin Robespierre 'the absolute necessity, in an immense struggle like ours, of a revolutionary government and a central, stable authority'. Time was pressing, and it was important to move 'like lightning', with the speed and urgent might of a thunderbolt. All administrative bodies would be subordinated to the government through centralization; all resistance would be broken by its 'coercive power', that is, through the Terror; and anyone disobeying its law would be an 'enemy of the people' and deserving of death.

In essence the revolutionary government was a restoration of authority. But its agents might not use it except for the salvation of the nation; their 'virtue' was the safeguard of patriots. Next to treason, falsehood was the worst of crimes. 'The soul of the Republic,' Robespierre wrote as early as 1792, 'is the love of the *Patrie*, the generous devotion which submerges all private interests in the general interest.' How could these sentiments be reconciled with private immorality? Thus the latter was suspect. The 'enemies of the Republic are the dastardly egotists, the ambitious, and the corrupt'. Montesquieu and Rousseau had already said this.

Although provisional and compelled to adapt itself readily

to circumstances, the revolutionary government needed an organic framework. Its charter was the law of 14 Frimaire, Year II (December 4, 1793), which was often commented upon: by Billaud-Varenne, on November 18 and again on 1 Floréal (April 20, 1794); by Robespierre, on 5 Nivôse (December 25, 1793) and on 17 Pluviôse (February 5, 1794); by Saint-Just, Barère, Carnot, and Couthon; in the Committee's circulars; and by the proclamations of the deputies on mission. In principle it remained democratic, for the Convention held supreme authority, and the committees governed under its control. Similarly, patriots could speak in the popular societies, and their newspapers were not subject to censorship. But the executive power was the essential organ of the regime, and nothing might contravene its actions or impair its prestige. So, after Germinal the sessions of the Convention became dreary, the committees worked in silence, and the clubs disappeared, except for the Jacobins, where most of the regulars were functionaries of the Terror. In the provinces, the revolutionary committees and popular societies aided and counselled the authorities, but criticism became suspect. The independent press disappeared.

The committees of the Convention were numerous—twenty-one in the Year II—but the committees of Public Safety and General Security were dominant. The first, reduced to eleven members with the death of Hérault de Séchelles, was re-elected from month to month without modification. It was 'at the centre of operations', ordering arrests, directing diplomacy, managing the war through its Topographic Bureau, armaments through its Commission for Arms and Powder, and economic life through its Commission on Provisions, which was replaced on 1 Floréal (April 20) by that for Commerce and Provisioning. It controlled the twelve executive commissions which had replaced the ministers after 12 Germinal. Its secretariat was gradually subdivided into a world of bureaux and agencies. Invested with regulatory power, it issued decrees for the execution of the laws, and for this reason it did not hesitate to violate them or to make them itself. The Committee of General Security applied the Law of Suspects and directed the police and revolutionary justice. In principle it was the ministry of the Terror. For a long time less stable than the Committee of Public Safety, it was now equally constant.

Organization in the provinces was simplified. Departmental administration, suspected of federalism and reduced to its directory, lost most of its powers. The principal agencies were the district and the municipality, which corresponded directly with the central government. The revolutionary committees remained, but the majority of villages possessed none. With each administrative body sat a national agent (replacing the prosecutor), elected by it but responsible for the execution of decisions by the government, to which the national agent in the district sent a report every ten days. Moreover, the role of elections was purely theoretical; as a matter of fact, purges left the choice of all functionaries to the central government and the deputies on mission. Saint-Just dreamed of a single magistrate in each district, who would govern in the name of the state.

The deputies on mission were interposed between the local administrations and the committees. A last large mission took place at the end of December, 1793, to apply the law of 14 Frimaire; but this law implicitly limited the initiative of the deputies (no more delegation of powers, or armies, or revolutionary taxes), and on 19 Floréal, Year II (May 8, 1794) their revolutionary tribunals were suppressed. By this time most of them had returned to the Convention. Fouché was recalled as early as 7 Germinal (March 27), and twenty-one others on the 30th (April 19). As Billaud-Varenne said, on November 18, 1793, increasing their numbers weakened their authority, and it became more difficult to select the right men. As a matter of fact, the independence of their colleagues and the diversity in their policies displeased the members of the Committee, because they thwarted centralization. The Committee preferred its own agents, like Jullien of Paris (the son of a deputy from Drôme), who instigated the recall of Carrier and Tallien, or having one of its own members visit the provinces or the armies when it was necessary to 'wind up the machine'.

Actually the Committee of Public Safety did not have time to push centralization to its logical conclusion. Both before and after Germinal it had to conciliate the Convention and the other committees. Cambon ruled over the Committee on Finance, and the independent Treasury was considered—not unjustifiably—a den of counter-revolutionaries. The Committee of General Security resisted the encroachments of the Committee of Public Safety, and their conflict was to lead to the fall of the regime. In the provinces, the deputies on mission pursued their personal policies, and local quarrels continued. Napoleonic order was still far distant. Nevertheless the decentralization of the Constituent Assembly was only a memory. The sans-culottes had demanded a dictatorship. Now they had one, but it was run by committees and bureaucrats. Like everyone else, they could only obey in silence.

It is true that the committees spared nothing to secure their regular support. But the theory of revolutionary government, coherent as it may have been, did not encompass all the facts; and its leaders were unable to agree fully concerning its application. The majority of the Committee of Public Safety thought solely of the war; for that reason it naturally accepted the services of all those, even aristocrats, whose allegiance was unquestionable. Let the civil rights of the rich, the businessmen, and the financiers be restored, provided they were submissive and faithful. Let regulation be limited to the strictest necessities and restrained from becoming an instrument of social reform, so as to avoid bringing the different elements of the Third Estate into conflict. 'He who is not against us is with us,' it was willing to say. This tendency is so obvious that there is some temptation to regard the revolutionary government as simply a government of national defence. It was certainly that, but not that alone, for this theory would imply a cessation of dechristianization and a moderation of the Terror after Germinal. Yet such was not the case.

The reason is to be found in the war. It was more than a *national* war—it was a *class* war as well. The Third Estate was defending the soil of the *Patrie*, while at the same time it was pursuing the struggle, begun in 1789, against the aristocracy. It had seen some of its members, rich and poor, go over to the enemy. The sans-culottes were only the more eager to complete the extermination of the enemy class and all turncoats. The 'great fear' of the 'aristocratic plot' was perpetuated, as were the defensive reaction it aroused and the punitive reaction which gave birth to the Terror. So the Hébertist spirit survived. All the sans-culottes were steeped in it, and it persisted in the Convention and the committees, where it produced division. Economically and socially the martial spirit inspired only in part the movement that created the dictatorship. If all the sans-culottes demanded regulation, it was to their advantage (even if the bourgeoisie had to suffer) far more than it was in the interests of national and revolutionary defence. By utilizing it chiefly for the benefit of the state, the Montagnard leaders eventually disillusioned them. Now, socially as well as politically, they were suspended in the void.

THE ARMY OF THE YEAR II

Yet the will to conquer was universal. Without exception the Montagnards sacrificed everything to the army. And whoever was attached to the Revolution, in whatever degree, was compelled to admit that they were right. The army of the Year II was the symbol of revolutionary unity.

Within the Committee of Public Safety two military engineers, Carnot and Prieur of Côte-d'Or, supported (until Germinal) by Bouchotte, the minister of war, undertook to organize and lead this army. Prieur occupied himself primarily with armaments, Lindet with supplies and transport. Carnot, as supreme commander, directed operations. Since the levy *en masse*, more than a million men were available, but they were of diverse backgrounds—regulars on the one hand, and volunteers and conscripts on the other, the 'white bottoms' and the 'blue crockery'.

In February, 1793, unification of forces (*l'amalgame*) had been decreed in principle, after the volunteers, though more ardent than the regulars, proved less reliable and much less disciplined. It was a difficult operation, because of the prejudices of the men and the large number of officers. The volunteers, who had enlisted temporarily to repel invaders, did not regard themselves as soldiers. The regulars viewed them with disapproval, and until the purge, their patriotism was cause for concern. Meanwhile no more new battalions were formed, and the levy of 300,000 men and the levy *en masse* were incorporated into existing formations. In the spring of 1794 the amalgamation, which required much time, was undertaken. Two battalions of volunteers joined one battalion of regulars to constitute a demibrigade, or regiment. Then the companies were regrouped to strengthen the union, and sometimes they were re-formed. At last the army was rebuilt. Only 'Blues' were left, although, because of shortages, the old uniforms were to endure for some time.

At the same time the command was reconstituted. The purge ended with most (but not all) of the nobles excluded. The decree of 27 Germinal, Year II (April 16, 1794), authorized the Committee of Public Safety to retain those whom it deemed useful. The new generation now reached the highest ranks, and the War College (*École de Mars*) received six young men from each district to improve the staff. The regular officers were of great assistance in training in 1793. Gradually they gave way to the new ones, who were drawn chiefly from the volunteers. These were younger, often more cultivated, and the war provided them with an opportunity.

By standardizing promotions for both regulars and volunteers, the decree of February 21, 1793, had recognized seniority, dear to the upper ranks, and considerably reduced that of election, which had been used for the others. The soldiers no longer elected anyone but corporals. One-third of the upper ranks were to be based on seniority, while the soldiers designated only three candidates for the remaining two-thirds. Moreover, they had to take these from among non-commissioned officers of ranks lower than the post to be filled, with incumbents of equal rank making the choice. Colonels achieved their rank through seniority. A third of the generals were named on the same basis, and the rest were elected. Would the armies on active duty pay attention to these complicated arrangements? It was doubtful; and it is probable that election prevailed as authority grew stronger. Army commanders were to be appointed by the Convention.

Similarly, an attempt was made to re-establish discipline. It was necessary to begin with the high command, which the Committee distrusted. It feared treason and military dictatorship. How could it forget Lafayette and Dumouriez? The execution of Custine, suspected of following their example, imposed upon the commanders a passive submission to the civil power. In the fearful summer of 1793 others suffered the same penalty, because incompetence and negligence implied disloyalty. The deputies on mission embodied republican authority, just as the intendants with the armies had once done for that of the king. In 1793 the commissioners of the ministry and, in the Vendée, even those of the Commune, meddled in the supervision of the high command. At the same time they distributed sans-culotte newspapers and harangued the soldiers in the clubs; but by the spring of 1794 they had disappeared.

Inspection by the deputies on mission was frequently inconvenient, inasmuch as some of them occasionally interfered in the conduct of operations. The Republic could not restore the authority of its commanders, however, without assuring itself of their fidelity. In addition, if the intervention of numerous and divided deputies in campaign plans in the Vendée left vexatious memories, such was not the case everywhere. More than one, notably Saint-Just, were the architects of victory. As for the troops, on December 21, 1793, they were forbidden to issue collective petitions. 'The armed forces do not deliberate,' said Carnot, 'they obey the laws and execute them.' The clubs ceased to intervene in the administration of the army. Juries were maintained in military tribunals, but occasionally, when circumstances seemed pressing, the deputies on mission established courts-martial, as in the Army of the Moselle on 18 Floréal, Year II (May 7, 1794).

Still, it was not the guillotine, as the reactionaries of Europe claimed, on which the Committee relied to stimulate the zeal of generals and to make discipline respected. It counted above all on their confidence in and love for the *Patrie* and the Revolution. In the Year II it became sufficiently sure of its generals that it no longer blamed their failures on treason. Once again Carnot spoke with a sublime simplicity. 'A defeat is not a crime when everything has been done to merit a victory. We do not judge men by events but by their efforts and their courage. We care only that they do not lose hope for the salvation of the *Patrie*.'

As for the military tribunals, if they were pitiless towards rebels, émigrés, and deserters caught bearing arms, as the law commanded them to be, they were, nonetheless, lenient with soldiers, and (particularly worthy of note) absentees (*insoumis*) as well. From 7 Brumaire, Year II (October 28, 1793) to 16 Ventôse (March 6, 1794), the tribunal of the Army of the Rhine judged 660 accused persons, acquitted 282, forced 188 to enlist, and pronounced 190 convictions, only 62 of which were capital. The army preserved its democratic character. The soldiers of the Year II continued to frequent the clubs, and the government kept them informed about the political situation by sending them patriotic newspapers. The Convention promised to reserve a billion in émigré property for them, and it had pensions granted to the disabled and allowances to relatives of the 'defenders of the *Patrie*'. 'You must not expect victory from the numbers and discipline of soldiers alone,' Saint-Just said. 'You will secure it only through the spread of the republican spirit within the army.'

The army of the Year II was not limited to ardent republicans; it contained many who were in complete harmony with those on the home front. It is unfair to contrast, as has often been done, the soldiers of the Year II, who were exclusively preoccupied with the salvation of the *Patrie*, with the sans-culottes, who were absorbed in hunting down aristocrats at home. The revolutionaries turned soldier did not forget their hatreds. The republicans behind the lines were not lacking in self-sacrifice and daring. Hoche had been a Maratist, Kléber and Marceau praised the activity of Carrier, and Bonaparte attached himself to the Robespierre brothers. The truth is that in the army, duty is simpler and concord easier. So, many years later, even men like Marmont and Soult were moved with emotion by the memory of the shining hours they had known in the service of the 'Indivisible Republic'.

For the first time since antiquity a truly national army marched to war, and for the first time, too, a nation succeeded in arming and feeding great numbers of soldiers—these are the novel characteristics of the army of the Year II. The technical innovations resulted chiefly from its very mass; many did not last, or they appeared only slowly and uncertainly. The armament remained that of the royal troops: the rifle of 1777, with a fire accurate at more than 100 metres, and Gribeauval's artillery, principally a cannon that shot a four-pound ball between 400 and 500 metres. In practice, tactics depended upon the training of the troops. Generally the soldiers of the Year II fought as skirmishers, utilizing the terrain; then at the favourable moment they charged with bayonets in a more or less confused mass. But the regulation of 1791 remained law for the officers. Whenever they could, particularly in decisive actions, they arrayed their men in a long, thin line. They did not deem them sufficiently trained to manoeuvre in attack columns or to form squares against cavalry. These formations reappeared in 1795, and thus, as it was formed, the Army of the Republic returned to the tactics of the Old Regime.

The chief innovation—systematic use of brigades and divisions—developed out of a superiority in numbers. As a tactical unit, the division in 1793 remained of uncertain composition; its concept became more clearly defined in 1794. From it Jourdan created a veritable army corps of two infantry brigades, two cavalry regiments, and a horse-drawn battery, not counting the guns attached to each battalion—8,000–9,000 men in all. Strategy was transformed in principle by the necessity for exploiting large numbers of men. So the old system of cordons and sieges lost its prestige. Moving between the armies of the Coalition, the French could manoeuvre, to a certain degree, along interior lines, deploy part of their troops along the frontiers, and take advantage of the inaction of any one of their enemies to beat the others. Acting in masses, and overwhelming the foe by sheer numbers—such were Carnot's principles. They were still untried, and not until Bonaparte appeared did they enjoy any great success.

Carnot and his aides (d'Arçon, for example) were engineers, who set great store by fortresses. In 1793 the 'iron frontier' remained their base of operations. Conducting the campaign as under the Old Regime, they thought first of relieving a besieged stronghold by manoeuvre, while attempting a diversion. Then, when its fall appeared imminent, they brought up a relief army, with only a portion of the available forces—40,000 men at Hondschoote and 50,000 out of some 200,000 at Wattignies—the remainder forming a cordon or garrisoning the fortresses. This plan succeeded in making the enemy retreat but not in destroying it. In 1794, fascinated by the stronghold of Ypres and the conquest of Flanders, they manoeuvred with the left wing while the right alone, debouching through Charleroi, would be able to cut Coburg's communications and annihilate him. Eventually, though cautiously, they threatened him with such a fate, but it was too late. Though beaten, Coburg evacuated Belgium, and his army survived.

Technical skill obviously played a lesser role than speed and power. These were precisely the essential attributes of the revolutionary government. Carnot, rallying the army to attack on the second day at Wattignies, and Saint-Just, indefatigably pressing the Army of the Sambre and Meuse to the assault at Charleroi 'like a pack of hounds', were the true masters of victory. On the battlefield they were moved by that same fierce stubbornness which (as will be seen) mobilized all the nation's resources to provide the army with the wherewithal for war.

The efforts of the Committee on behalf of the navy were slower and less fortunate. Lack of discipline had disorganized the dockyards, and it prevailed aboard ship, even in the face of the enemy. Few officers remained. The decree of April, 1791, admitted officers from the merchant marine to the rank of ensign after a year of service, and to that of captain after two more years. In 1793 they might hope to command a squadron. Many, such as Surcouf, preferred to become privateers. It was a former captain of the merchant marine turned pastor, Jeanbon Saint-André, who directed the naval war, first at Brest and then at Toulon. He re-established discipline, set the dockyards to work again, and sent out squadrons. Yet a fleet was not improvised as easily as an army. He was unable to recover the time lost, or repair the damage caused by the treason of Toulon.

ECONOMIC GOVERNMENT

In accepting the levy *en masse* the Committee of Public Safety realized that it would encounter extraordinary difficulties in feeding and especially in clothing, equipping, and arming such a vast multitude. Most arms factories—Maubeuge, Charleville, Douai, Klingenthal—were within reach of the enemy, and St.-Étienne was in rebel hands. State-operated gunpowder and saltpetre plants could not meet the demands, and the blockade deprived France of German steel, Indian saltpetre, Baltic potash, Spanish soda, and Italian sulphur. It was necessary to develop war production, revive foreign trade, and find new resources in France itself; and time was short.

Individual initiative would never have succeeded in overcoming so many difficulties or in restoring co-ordination among industries. Contractors would have demanded excessively high prices, and inflation would have reduced the value of the assignats to nothing by the end of 1793. Moreover, with France taking on the appearance of a besieged fortress, civilians would have fought over supplies if the Committee had not intervened to set aside the army's share, regulate the distribution of the remainder, and maintain order. Circumstances gradually compelled it to assume the economic government of the country. Along with the organization of the army (which, from one point of view, was inseparable from it anyway), this was the most original feature of its work.

Only unmarried men between the ages of eighteen and twenty-five were enrolled. Deferments and exemptions were granted to many who seemed to be needed on the home front, and this led to fraudulent practices. Numerous individuals had made themselves immune by enrolling in the transport system; and public functionaries remained at their posts. For all others the levy *en masse* was only civil mobilization. It was aimed at everyone, but to become effective it required formal requisitioning. Although improvisation developed in proportion to need, an effort was made to consider qualifications, frequently with no regard to politics. The Committee made use of Périer and Chaptal as great industrialists, and Perregaux as a banker, even though Chaptal was known to be compromised by federalism, and Perregaux was a foreigner in touch with Pitt.

A special appeal was made to scientists, many of whom had declared themselves in favour of the Revolution. Hassenfratz was one of the principal organizers of the arms industry at Paris. Monge, Vandermonde, Berthollet, Darcet, and Fourcroy perfected metallurgy and the manufacture of arms. Vauquelin, along with Chaptal and Descroizilles, directed the search for saltpetre, and new methods were devised by Carny to refine saltpetre and to manufacture gunpowder. At Meudon the Committee established a laboratory where Berthollet, Conté, and Guyton de Morveau engaged in research and where experiments were carried out with explosives for shells and with the captive balloon used at Fleurus by the first company of balloonists. Chappe resumed his experiments with the semaphore telegraph and installed the first line from Paris to the northern frontier.

All material resources were naturally subjected to requisitioning. Farmers surrendered their grain, fodder, wool, flax, hemp, and occasionally cattle. Artisans and merchants gave up their manufactured products. Private citizens were asked for their arms, National Guard uniforms, and sometimes even their tablecloths and linens. At Strasbourg, Saint-Just exacted 20,000 pairs of shoes from them. Raw materials were carefully sought out—metal of all kinds, church bells (as well as their ropes), old paper, rags and parchments, saltpetred walls, grasses, brushwood, and even household ashes for the manufacture of potassium salts, and chestnuts for distilling. All businesses were placed at the disposal of the nation—forests, mines, quarries, furnaces, forges, tanneries, paper mills, large cloth factories, and shoemakers' workshops. This did not prevent the state from establishing new factories, which were absolutely necessary for armament and munitions making. But it did compel existing enterprises to extend their production to the limit, and even to increase it by applying processes recommended by the scientists. The regime of the Year II was favourable to the development of industrial techniques.

The labour of men and the value of things were subject to price controls. The Maximum contributed its share to business profits, and left production with a bonus. Contrary to current assertions, not all enterprises operated at a loss in the Year II; but they did not realize as large a profit as they might have at national expense. No one had a right to speculate at the cost of the *Patrie* while it was in danger. Above all, clothing and equipment were assured by local authorities, who created women's workshops and set harness makers to work. The central government intervened in the matter of footwear: butchers turned over skins of slaughtered animals; tanners received tanbark from forests exploited by the nation and were required to keep their bark pits full. On the island at Billancourt that still bears his name, Seguin established a rapid tanning process which he invented. Shoemakers were obliged to produce two pairs of shoes per journeyman every ten days.

Armament caused far more concern. As early as September, 1793, efforts were made to create a large factory in Paris for rifles and sidearms. While private workshops were being used, workers were installed in the gardens of the Tuileries and the Luxembourg, on the former Place Royale, and the esplanade of the Invalides. Next, provincial factories were revived, and deputies on mission were authorized to create others. This was done, for example, by Noël Pointe in Moulins, and Lakanal in Bergerac. Périer's large factory in Chaillot began to produce bronze cannons conjointly with that of Romilly near Rouen. Ferry, Pointe, and Romme provided a sharp stimulus for the forging of cast-iron naval cannon in central and south-eastern France, at Vierzon, Le Creusot, Ruelle, and Abzac.

It was in the munitions industry, however, that the Committee undoubtedly encountered the greatest obstacles and secured the most astonishing results. Saltpetre was lacking, and it had to be found in France itself. When abundant quantities were reported in Touraine, Vauquelin was sent there on a mission. Following his instructions, Prieur of Côte-d'Or decreed the creation of a national organization, which eventually took over the administration of the commodity. In every commune the local authorities chose saltpetre workers to conduct the search for and the removal of saltpetred earth and walls, and to organize an evaporation plant. In Ventôse some of these workers were brought to Paris to receive practical instruction. Twenty-eight refineries were established, the chief one at the abbey of St.-Germain-des-Prés. Powder factories developed likewise, the largest at Grenelle and the Ripault plant near Tours.

Although the results left Europe stupefied, they still fell far short of expectations. The Paris factory, which was supposed to produce 1,000 new rifles a day, turned out no more than 600–700, including repaired guns. During the spring campaign great difficulty was occasionally experienced in supplying the army with vital munitions. Problems of many kinds did indeed arise. Lacking the statistics without which a controlled economy cannot function, the Committee had to make approximations, with the aid of hasty inquiries and much red tape. France was primarily agricultural, and since capitalist concentration was only rudimentary, industry was widely scattered. Workers had to be trained, adapted to manufacturing or to new processes, moved about, and brought together. At the same time synchronized production had to be assured.

Finally, and most important, came the problem of transport, in a country almost entirely barren of canals, where roads could not be maintained. Horses and conveyances were already supposed to be set aside for the needs of the army (in lieu of military equipment) and the provisioning of the civilian population, without, however, interfering with farming. Boatmen and carters had to be requisitioned, a national transport agency created and a beginning made in supplying it with necessities. Without the Terror, which compelled even the most indifferent to expend *some* effort, the Committee would never have been able to restrain the spirit of speculation or to overcome passive resistance.

The economy of the country was nationalized to a considerable extent, either directly by the creation of state industries or indirectly through supplying raw materials and manpower, controlling production, requisitioning supplies, and price controls. Some have claimed that the Committee socialized it deliberately in order to lead France cunningly towards communism, considered to be the consummation of democracy. In the eyes of the sans-culottes the controlled economy incontestably had some social value, but communism was not involved. It did generalize regulation, however, and on this count it constituted what today is called 'structural reform'. This is why the Commission on Provisions (until Ventôse) and certain deputies on mission could look upon statism with complacency. The Committee of Public Safety, on the contrary, saw it merely as a temporary expedient, necessitated by the requirements of revolutionary defence, and resorted to it with regret. In addition to its attachment to economic freedom (so dear to the bourgeoisie), which for months deterred the Committee from the Maximum, circumstances limited the extension of state control.

Like the local administrations, the members of the Committee (which was a political authority) assumed their economic functions only out of concern for the public safety. Intellectually these functions were foreign to them, and they entailed a crushing burden of work and responsibility, which the members wished to be rid of as soon as the crisis subsided. Practically, the state of production and transport kept them from trying to satisfy all consumer needs. After the fall of the

Hébertists their views manifested themselves unequivocally. Obviously the dispersal of industry required recourse to many small employers; and this was done in Ponthieu, Morez, and Thiers, for example, and even in Paris. At least it was up to the Committee alone to nationalize mines and multiply state factories; but it did nothing of the kind. On the contrary, Carnot opposed direct exploitation of the plants which the deputies on mission had created, because he deemed it onerous and feared the growth of an incompetent bureaucracy. There were two areas where the Committee's tendencies were clearly apparent: in foreign trade it asked nothing more than to return control to the merchants; and in civilian provisioning it showed an undeniable unwillingness to extend the powers and responsibilities of economic government.

Since November, 1793, foreign trade had been concentrated in the hands of the Commission on Provisions, which strove to revive it. It sent agents abroad to carry out its orders, requisitioned merchant ships, and opened national warehouses in the ports. Neutrals once more found themselves welcomed, for the Navigation Act had been suspended. They were accorded markets by agreement, with payment in specie or merchandise. Special committees were formed to negotiate with them at Bordeaux and Bourg Libre (St. Louis, in Alsace). In Genoa, Switzerland, Hamburg, Copenhagen, and the United States, France succeeded in making large purchases. With importation thus re-established, the Commission, to assure payment, requisitioned the wine, brandy, silks, and cloth demanded by neutrals. It used prize ships and confiscated English merchandise. It began a search for exportable jewels, furniture, and art objects in the property of condemned persons and émigrés, as well as in royal property that had passed into the national domain. Finally, on 6 Nivôse, Year II (December 26, 1793), Cambon had foreign bills requisitioned, and redeemed at par in assignats.

On 8 Ventôse, Year II (February 26, 1794), in order to obtain capital that had left France, Parisian bankers were compelled to subscribe 50 million in notes on foreign exchanges. Many French and foreign merchants were already employed, despite the hostility of the sans-culottes; but the Committee showed its hand, especially after the fall of the Hébertists. It was harmful to the Republic, and counter-revolutionary, Barère and Robespierre henceforth explained, to make war on commerce; on the contrary, it was good policy to appeal to the wisdom and zeal of the merchants. These latter were permitted, on 21 and 23 Ventôse (March 11 and 13, 1794)—the arrest of the Hébertists had been decided upon on the evening of the 22nd (March 12)—to export products which the Commission had not declared to be of prime necessity. In return they must reimport the equivalent in merchandise subject to the Maximum, with the Republic having a right of pre-emption; or they must remit to the Treasury the specie and bills of exchange drawn abroad.

The merchants of the principal commercial towns, especially the ports, were associated in commercial agencies. They were required to advance a specified sum in commercial paper, the payment for which they were supposed to assure by their exports. The Commission's commercial agents returned to France, and purchases from neutrals were entrusted to private commissioners. Nine Thermidor occurred before these measures could produce important results. The same developments took place in industry. They were further pointed up by the suppression of the Commission on Provisions, which was replaced by a Commission on Commerce and Provisioning, with a different personnel. Undoubtedly appeals to private citizens could scarcely be successful so long as the Maximum remained. The Committee at least made it more flexible by increasing numerous charges for the benefit of contractors (in disregard of the law), and it limited the application of the system, as far as possible, to the needs of the state itself. This is what its policy of provisioning indicates.

When a district seemed to possess enough grain the Commission on Provisions demanded requisitions for the army and for deficient districts. Yet its agents were but slightly concerned with the latter. Their main interest was military requisitioning. Granted that transport was difficult, yet no thought was given to distributing resources on a strictly equal basis. The Commission drew upon the areas nearest the army or the districts to be supplied, at the risk of starving the producing regions, with a promise that these latter would be helped in due time.

It showed no concern for consumers. On 25 Brumaire, Year II (November 15, 1793) the Convention regulated milling and prescribed the mixture of different kinds of grain for baking the 'bread of equality'. But the Commission did not bother to enforce this decree itself or to regulate its observation. All the more reason that it should refrain from putting the population on rationing. Its motives are readily discernible. How could it proceed to a general amalgam when statistics, means of transport, and trained personnel were lacking? How could it supervise milling, when most villages had their own mills? How could it regulate food consumption through rationing cards, if, for the same reasons, it was not possible to effect the regular distribution of the promised quota in all places? What capitalist concentration permits a firm-minded government to do now, was then technically impossible!

All these matters, then, were left to the district directories and the municipalities: the former to initiate the requisitioning for provisioning markets; the communes to put the 'amalgam' of grain for bread into practice, to watch the millers, to regulate bakeries and pastry shops, and if need be, to institute rationing. Consequently centralization remained very superficial. If the crisis had similar effects everywhere, they appeared at different times and with varying degrees of seriousness. In fertile regions markets occasionally persisted until summer, with the well-to-do continuing to bake at home, and bakers retaining a certain degree of liberty. In the large towns and throughout the south, markets disappeared early. When the peasants arrived their grain was stored, mixed, and ground under supervision of the municipality, and the flour was allotted to the bakers, who distributed the bread upon presentation of ration cards. Hence each baker became a municipal employee. Sometimes the commune itself baked the bread in the ovens of almshouses or military bake wagons. Thus in Troyes municipalization was complete.

In rural areas the exasperated farmers did their best to avoid complying, and it was necessary to resort to house-to-house searches, military occupation, the old expedient of quartering soldiers in homes, and arrests. Many villages knew the Terror in this guise. The producer, at least, succeeded in setting aside something for his own consumption. The least fortunate of all Frenchmen were the poor husbandmen, or agricultural workers. The towns closed their doors to them, and there was nothing left for them but to beg some grain from the grower, because nobody undertook to see that the Maximum was respected.

In the matter of other commodities and merchandise, the Commission on Provisions contented itself with issuing, in Ventôse, the enormous schedule of the national Maximum, in lieu of production. Each district was then supposed to add the cost of transport, the profits of the wholesaler (5 per cent) and that of the retailer (10 per cent), and have the thick catalogue printed. Work on it continued until the end of summer, and it never served any real purpose, at least for most articles. Thanks to requisitioning, the state adhered to the Maximum for those relatively few items in which it was interested. Still, the Committee of Public Safety made numerous exceptions.

As for the consumer, it was left to him to see that the schedule was observed. At first the Commission on Provisions undertook to come to his aid. At Orléans it seized sugar from the refiners, and at Marseilles it manufactured soap. Both were distributed throughout France. Soon, however, the policy of the Committee of Public Safety rejected measures of this kind and forbade local authorities to do any requisitioning. The only recourse open to the sans-culottes was to intimidate merchants through police surveillance and the threat of terror—the effect of which remained almost nil. When they did not cheat in quality and weight, the merchants managed to make secret sales. This was the peasants' favourite method, and the clandestine trade in farm products grew by leaps and bounds. Some municipalities supplied the merchants and rationed the consumers. In the spring, meat cards, similar to those used for bread, were instituted in Paris, and in Clermont-Ferrand efforts were made to municipalize the butchers' shops. Because of the lack of an overall plan, no satisfactory results were obtained.

Thus the economic government was turned essentially to the advantage of the army. It seems that it was fed, after a fashion, throughout the winter. Nevertheless the Armies of the Rhine and the Moselle helped themselves to, and thoroughly exploited, the resources of the part of the Palatinate that they occupied from January on. It appears certain that clothing, footwear, and equipment remained insufficient, and yet in all respects the soldiers suffered less in the Year II than in the Year III. The Committee, on the other hand, refrained from complete nationalization of civilian provisioning. Certainly, as has been said, the difficulties seemed insurmountable; still, the protests of the provincial authorities deserved consideration. Why, in the department of Nord, did the Committee refuse to requisition lamp oil, which was the object of frenzied speculation? For what reason did it generally insist upon purchasing livestock by private contract instead of setting a price for it, as in the case of meat? It was because it wanted to conciliate artisans and farmers. And indeed it had to, for the sansculottes were recruited chiefly from among them and not from among the workers.

In imposing the Maximum on the peasant and the businessman, the shopkeepers and artisans had not foreseen the consequences, and they grew angry when it was applied to themselves. The shoemakers and bakers were indignant at finding themselves reduced to the status of wage earners. To the peasants, in the grip of still more demands, traffic in livestock and farm produce offered some compensation. Strictly applied, the Maximum would have exasperated all these groups; and, as it was, the bourgeoisie endured the controlled economy only with impatience. This is why the Committee, concerned above all with maintaining the unity of the revolutionary Third Estate against the aristocracy, after long avoiding the Maximum, reserved its benefits to the state as much as possible.

Only to the wage earners did the Maximum seem thoroughly advantageous. It increased wages by one-half in relation to 1790, and commodities by only one-third. But since the Committee did not ensure that it was respected (except for bread), they would have been duped had they not been benefiting from the favourable conditions that a great war always offers the labour force. The Maximum on wages, established in each commune, displayed unbelievable disparities from one place to another; and since there was a fight for workers they had the upper hand. At least in enterprises subject to state control, it was impossible to give in to them without bringing the whole structure crashing down, and the assignat with it.

So agitation continued to increase. The Committee suspected (not without reason) that its opponents were seeking to take advantage of this, particularly in Paris. It met the situation by condemning strikes (just as the Old Regime and the Constituent Assembly had done), under the pretext that the workers had been requisitioned; and it threatened recalcitrants with the Revolutionary Tribunal. On the eve of the harvest it also desired to control the agricultural day labourers. It requisitioned them, and contrary to law, permitted each district to regulate their wages throughout its entire jurisdiction. In point of fact, it was not successful in fully restraining worker agitation, and employers usually resigned themselves to the inevitable. Indisputably, the revolutionary government saved the working class from extreme misery by supplying it with work and bread. It was the group that suffered most from the return to economic freedom. It could not fail to balk, however, when required to observe the Maximum, which merchants violated with impunity.

SOCIAL POLICY

Socially the Maximum had been the great hope of the sansculottes, a juridical form of the right to live. It derived from their past, and the controlled economy (the example of which the Committee of Public Safety bequeathed to future generations as the indispensable support for a national war) seemed to them the triumph of the traditional regulation, which they contrasted with the encroaching progress of capitalism. Once the failure of the Maximum became certain, it was necessary to rally them to another programme oriented to the future in order to save them from discouragement.

Sprung from the bourgeoisie, the Montagnards repudiated communism. They conceived of it only as a moralizing utopia, or equated it with the 'agrarian law', which their classical education reminded them existed in the last days of the Roman Republic and which they associated with a general division of property. They objected that it would institute but an ephemeral equality. The decree of March 18, 1793, pronounced the death penalty against partisans of the agrarian law, and Robespierre always disapproved of them. He regarded individual and hereditary property as an evil, but declared it incurable. The difficulties created by the controlled economy would have sufficed to show that communism presupposed a concentration of production that capitalism and mechanized technique had not yet provided. For the same reason the proletariat had not yet become sufficiently concentrated or coherent to constitute a class party. Sans-culottes and Jacobins formed what today would be called a 'popular front', wherein merchants, artisans, men of law, and functionaries (usually well-to-do and often rich) exercised an uncontested predominance. Besides, the landless peasants aspired only to become landowners, and the wage earners in more than one trade deemed the suppression of guilds democratic because it dazzled them with the prospect of having their own businesses.

All of them, however, including the Montagnards, were hostile to 'opulence' and the 'rich', that is, to wealth that was believed to be excessive and conducive to idleness. Robespierre, like Saint-Just, whose *Republican Institutions* were particularly explicit, followed Rousseau in considering that liberty and equality (both civil and political) disappeared for most citizens as social inequality increased. Thus the Republic owed it to itself, on the one hand, to limit fortunes and to increase the number of small landowners; and on the other, to provide everyone with the means of rising in society through education, and the underprivileged with some security through suitable national relief. The ideal remained a social democracy of small independent producers, peasants, and artisans. There was no awareness that, in contradiction to freedom of competition within the economy which made the future safe for capitalist concentration, this ideal could not be realized.

Nevertheless the Convention did pass some significant laws. Those of 5 Brumaire, Year II (October 26, 1793), and 17 Nivôse (January 6, 1794), assured the division of estates. This they achieved by instituting absolute equality among heirs (including natural children), placing no time limit on the contesting of wills, and authorizing wills which provided only for outsiders. Moreover, division into small shares (which had been prescribed for émigré property on June 3, 1793) was extended, on 2 Frimaire, Year II (November 22, 1793), to all national property. The amount of this had been increased by the nationalization of the property of charitable and educational institutions, as well as by the confiscation of property of condemned persons and deported priests, who were classed with the émigrés.

The distribution of land enabled a certain number of peasants to become landowners, or more frequently, to round out their holdings. Since, however, sale by auction continued, the great majority received no benefits. Such was not the case in the division of common lands into individual shares (authorized on June 10, 1793); each person received his share. But common lands did not exist everywhere. In some places they were deemed unsuitable for farming, and in other regions division was rejected as detrimental to stock raising. True, the law of June 3 granted the poor an *arpent* (about one-and-one-half acres) on payment of an annual rent. On September 13, however, with financial concerns taking precedence, this concession was replaced by the remittance of a note for 500 livres, which was received in payment for national property and was repayable in twenty years without interest. The chances of profiting from this arrangement were so slight that nobody took advantage of it. Some clear-sighted administrators reported the disillusionment that this illusory generosity caused in the rural areas, but to no avail.

It is doubtful that most members of the Convention were distressed by the situation. They had not forgotten that the large farmers, as well as manufacturers, were looking for a labour supply. They felt that in an individualistic society, in which both population and capitalism were growing, it was chimerical to desire the transformation of all proletarians into independent producers. Some asserted, besides, that large concerns alone sold enough grain to feed the towns. Of course the bourgeoisie coveted these lands; and more than one district, through connivance or negligence, continued to sell them without dividing them, although the Committee had taken them to task for this during the summer.

The poor, nevertheless, continued to demand that part of the national property be made available to them at a reasonable price, or in rent, or even free. In this connection, however, those who had been able to purchase some land, and, naturally, the well-to-do cultivators who held the day labourers in dependence, had no interest in encouraging them. The peasant solidarity that had compelled the Convention to decree the outright abolition of manorial rights vanished. Moreover, the Montagnards, to whom the defence of the assignats appeared of prime necessity, were able to turn a deaf ear.

The Robespierrists alone seemed to perceive that it was indispensable to give some satisfaction to the poor sans-culottes. In Ventôse, Saint-Just had it decreed that 'indigents' would be 'indemnified' through the distribution of property confiscated from suspects. There may have been 300,000 of these 'enemies of the Revolution'. Did the Convention look with favour upon this vast expropriation? Hardly—for with this promise it simply hoped to counteract Hébertist propaganda. In his speech Saint-Just announced free grants of land, but the decree made no mention of this; and on 22 Floréal, Year II (May 11, 1794), Barère's report on national beneficence indicated rather that these, too, would be subject to the difficulties of auctions. In any case, the methods of its execution were never specified, and had this been done, they would not have satisfied as many peasants as might have been thought.

Many suspects possessed no landed property, and consequently in many villages the decree would remain meaningless. Moreover, would sharecroppers and peasants who already owned a bit of land be included among the 'indigent'? They continued to demand the division of large farms into small holdings, and the reform of sharecropping. The former gave rise to the same objections as the fragmentation of national property. The latter was urgent, because the Convention, like the Constituent and Legislative assemblies, reserved to landowners the profits from the disestablishment of tithes and manorial rights collected prior to the division of the harvest. The sharecropper, on the contrary, henceforth claimed his portion from the entire crop. In Gers, disturbances resulted. These were put down, and the bourgeoisie retained all the advantages from the freeing of the soil in its possession.

Since the Robespierrists thought the peasants poor, it was all the more characteristic that they did not take their petitions into consideration. Their education, which bound them to economic freedom, was partly responsible for this; they probably disliked agrarian regulation as much as the Maximum.

But they did not even try to repeal the decree of April 24, 1793, which condemned the collective purchase of national property by rural communities, although nothing prevented association and collusion among private individuals. They did not have a deep knowledge of the realities of rural life. No one mentioned the possibility of expropriating large estates, with compensation, on grounds of public utility, so as to divide them. The confiscation of private property by the Revolution had no motive other than punishment for treason or rebellion. In short, the Robespierrists, like the *Enragés* and the Hébertists, lacked an agrarian policy capable of appealing to the peasant masses.

As for the urban proletariat, once the Maximum was permitted to weaken, there was nothing to offer them, not even the power to form unions and the right to strike. True, requisitioning did not permit the use of strikes; but if the Montagnards had been interested in the working-class movement, they would have abrogated the Le Chapelier Law. They did at least try to hold to the promises of the Constituent Assembly. The law of 22 Floréal, Year II (May 11, 1794), nationalized relief and opened the 'book of national beneficence' ('*livre de bienfaisance nationale*'). Establishing the principle of 'social security', it instituted free medical assistance in the home, pensions to the aged, and aid for mothers of large families.

The law of 29 Frimaire, Year II (December 19, 1793), ordered the establishment of compulsory, free, and secular primary schools. The creation of institutions for scientific research and higher education continued; but the Montagnards postponed the reorganization of secondary education until later. They yielded to the necessity of educating the people, in order to develop a public spirit, to strengthen national unity. The decree of 8 Pluviôse (January 27, 1794), prescribed the teaching of French in those regions where it was still not spoken. Unhappily, there was a shortage of teachers and equipment. Much time and money were required to organize relief and public education.

The Montagnards were not relying entirely upon the schools. The Tenth Day worship and patriotic festivals were supposed to augment them. As the foundation of the republican doctrine that would be propagated in them, Robespierre intended to establish the existence of the Supreme Being, and for their support, the rewards of the afterlife presumed by the immortality of the soul. The decree of 18 Floréal, Year II (May 7, 1794), which instituted the festivals, recognized, in the name of the French people, these metaphysical propositions, which Robespierre bluntly contrasted with the materialism of some Encyclopedists and the positive philosophy. They expressed his personal convictions, but he also justified them on pragmatic grounds, and injected into them a pessimistic concern for the fate of the disinherited, who must not be deprived of their expectations of another world. No one ventured to contradict him, but many members of the Convention, although they did not believe a word of all this, also suspected him of thus making overtures to the Catholics.

The Festival of the Supreme Being (arranged by David) in which Robespierre (now president of the Convention) appeared as a kind of pontiff of the new religion (stemming directly from Rousseau), was celebrated on 20 Prairial, Year II (June 8, 1794). It corresponded to the Corpus Christi procession, and in more than one place the conclusion was drawn that dechristianization was coming to an end. Associating the new cult and Catholicism constituted a chimerical undertaking. Spiritualistic propaganda was insufficient to win over the rural proletariat, whom, in the last analysis, the revolutionary government had not succeeded in satisfying, and still less the sans-culottes of the towns, who had created it, and whom it had deceived and then subjugated.

During the summer the economic situation worsened. There was scarcity even in fertile regions like Beauce, Limagne, and coastal Flanders. The harvest period, always long in this era because of the use of flails in threshing, threatened to be prolonged, since workers were scarce. Then prospects darkened, for the crop was poor. The Committee had made great efforts to assure that land would be cultivated, charging the municipalities with providing requisitioning if necessary. The Convention prescribed the draining of marshes and the planting of 'pleasure gardens'; and an active propaganda, for which the *Feuille du cultivateur* was used, sought to improve agricultural methods and to develop cultivation of potatoes. Occasionally there was intervention to prevent the peasants from abandoning cereal grains for crops that were not subject to price controls, or for stock raising.

In this respect, fear of famine was the useful tool of the government. Still, it could not labour under any illusions. A considerable part of the soil remained uncultivated or poorly tilled for want of ploughs, implements, or manpower, and also because of the ravages of war. Finally, bad weather took its toll. It might have been foreseen that the Year III would be a time of famine. Furthermore, although inflation had been reduced, it continued, and again the assignats were depreciating. By Thermidor they had fallen to 34 per cent of their face value in the department of Seine.

The revolutionary government had gained a year—time in which to succeed. It was now threatened with being brought down by an economic crisis, just as the Old Regime and the Girondins had been. Since peace was still far off, it deemed it necessary to maintain the system. This is why it kept terror as the order of the day.

THE TERROR

In the revolutionary mentality, as has been noted, the punitive will was associated from the beginning with the defensive reaction against the 'aristocratic plot'. They were inseparable elements, although one might predominate and the behaviour that resulted might differ greatly as the result of circumstances and individual temperaments. Repressive action arose as early as July, 1789. The permanent committees confined themselves to surveillance and to investigations made on suspicion, but in a few cases summary executions by the aroused mob occurred. The deployment of the police force was not always enough to prevent these, and it was necessary to check the agitation through the all-out pursuit of conspirators and by prompt and severe penalties. The assemblies instituted committees of investigation or of general security, and referred crimes against the nation (*lèse-nation*) to a special jurisdiction, first Le Châtelet, then the High Court, and finally the tribunal of August 17, 1792.

During this first period, however, repression was not made uniform. In times of calm, with the danger fading and the bourgeoisie disliking hasty procedures that threatened individual security, the penalties seemed absurd; but a local incident was enough to cause renewed popular executions. With the war and invasion these multiplied, and in Paris they culminated in the September Massacres. The response of the Girondins, far from bringing about the reinforcement of governmental action, was to suppress it. The High Court disappeared, then the tribunal of August 17, so that political trials returned to the jurisdiction of ordinary courts.

The crisis of 1793 posed the problem once again, for the punitive will was joined with the defensive reaction to give birth to the revolutionary government. It aroused its leaders as much as its partisans. The September Massacres had nearly destroyed them, however, and resolving not to tolerate a repetition they undertook to organize the Terror. By so doing they opened a second period. At the lowest level, the watch committees, created on March 21, 1793, assumed the power to arrest suspected persons; and after the law of September 17 they were left full discretion, under the control of the Committee of General Security. If there were grounds for indictment, the Revolutionary Tribunal (instituted on March 10, reorganized on September 5, and appointed by the Convention) intervened. For some crimes the criminal court of each department, sitting 'revolutionarily', followed the same methods. Finally, in the areas of civil war, military commissions became active. Procedure was simplified in all cases. The grand jury was replaced by judges, and recourse to appeals disappeared. Moreover, the Convention reduced trials to a simple verification of identity and pronouncement of the death penalty for individuals who had been outlawed, rebels, émigrés, and deported priests who returned to the territory of the Republic.

In reality the government lost some control over the repression. Like administration, it was decentralized by the emergency. Nothing could serve better than local committees, because of the information which their members had long since acquired. The centrifugal tendency was curbed in principle by the deputies on mission. For months concentration of powers was displayed chiefly at this regional level, but in many communes the revolutionary committees were established solely for appearances, or never existed. Having difficulty in recruiting competent and reliable administrations in the villages, the deputies often preferred to leave political policing either to the committee of the chief town of the district or canton, or to the committees of public safety created spontaneously by the revolutionaries of the locality. By virtue of their full powers, however, the deputies on mission claimed to direct the Terror as they pleased. At times they collaborated with the local terrorists; at times they opposed them. The result of this inconsistency was that the scope of repression was expanded, but its severity varied greatly.

Suspicion was directed not only towards probable authors of acts already committed, on grounds of definite circumstances susceptible of discussion and of proof, but also towards the possible perpetrators of eventual crimes, who were believed capable of them because of their opinions or even their real or simulated indifference. The margin for uncertainty and the risk of arbitrary action, which normal judicial procedure reduced only slightly (because of its attention to detail and its slowness), increased enormously. The dangers were multiplied in a singularly perilous fashion when it came to arraignment. In investigating the past of persons concerned, acts or declarations that were irreproachable in their time (such as the petitions of the '8,000' and the '20,000'), or that were justified according to law (notably the protests against August 10, 1792, or June 2, 1793), were introduced. Although no subsequent opposition could be charged to these Feuillants or federalists, many of them were imprisoned and even guillotined.

Yet the 'aristocratic plot' was not the sole factor involved. The economic situation and its social consequences now revealed other 'enemies of the people'—the rich who hid their money or sent it abroad, the producers who evaded the Maximum, and those who refused assignats. The Terror thus became the prop of the controlled economy on which the sansculottes depended for their own existence. Undoubtedly crimes of an economic nature did not all fall within the special jurisdiction. Still, they exposed their authors to detention as suspects; and if their opinions and circumstances tended to impute counter-revolutionary intentions to them, their lives were at stake.

Nevertheless nothing contributed as much to spreading the Terror as dechristianization. Former clergy, constitutional priests, and practising faithful were treated as dangerous or culpable. Thus conceived, the terrorist repression was unquestionably effective, because it intimidated, reduced to impotence, or suppressed many enemies. Yet it was no less responsible for injuring, or far more frequently, for disturbing and vexing a host of people who, although hostile to the revolutionary government for various reasons, were resigned to obeying it, and who, in any case, dreamed neither of conspiracy nor of revolt.

Even making great allowances for the opinions of those who applied the Terror, its harshness depended upon their character and upon circumstances. Personal hatreds, the desire for vengeance that had permeated the punitive will from the outset, and particularly the impulsive authoritarianism of certain individuals occasionally aggravated its severity or rekindled it after a period of calm. Conversely, forbearance, friendships, and political spirit often tempered it, and numerous deputies on mission confined themselves to setting a few examples or making a few imprisonments. Likewise, the commissioners of the committees varied in their behaviour: in the district of St.-Pol one arrested 141 persons in the canton of Frévent, while his colleagues elsewhere apprehended only one or two.

Yet circumstances exerted a more considerable influence. An estimate of the relative danger, and not temperament alone, prompted some deputies to assume responsibility for establishing revolutionary tribunals or popular commissions. These, ignoring the Paris tribunal, precipitated executions. In the matter of suspects, mass arrests coincided with specific events: those of August, 1793, period of the greatest peril and the levy *en masse*; those of the autumn, when terror had just been made the 'order of the day'; and those of Ventôse, at the opening of the campaign. The role of circumstances is more clearly evident from the statistical analysis of death sentences made by Donald Greer. Seventy-one per cent occurred in the two areas of civil war—19 per cent in the south-east and 52 per cent in the west—as against only 15 per cent in Paris. Moreover, this agrees with an examination of the motives for these condemnations:

in more than 72 per cent of the cases they were due to rebellion. Six departments, on the other hand, had no executions, thirty-one had fewer than ten, and fourteen fewer than twenty-five.

Of course it is not percentages but the figures themselves that account for the impression made on public opinion. Greer's statistics are limited to death sentences, which he estimates at almost 17,000; but the number of deaths was far higher. Apart from rebels who fell in combat, it is necessary to add the executions without trial, whether by order, as at Nantes and Toulon, or by refusal to grant quarter on the battlefield, in pursuit, or in police roundups. Besides, conditions in the prisons caused a high mortality. Since an exact computation is impossible, Greer suggests an estimate of 35,000–40,000 dead. It is well to recall that the property of condemned persons, of émigrés, and of deported priests was confiscated, and that of relatives of émigrés was sequestered until the inheritance belonging to the fugitives was deducted. Finally, suspects should not be forgotten. The district of St.-Pol confined 1,460 of them, and the total number of 300,000, although hypothetical, is not improbable. The fright and rancour of contemporaries, and the indelible memory which they handed down to posterity, are quite understandable.

Greer's findings are important particularly because they confirm the nature of the Terror. It was in the two areas where counter-revolutionaries took up arms and committed open treason that it raged with the greatest fury. Despite the elements that spread it thoughtlessly or abused it, it remained until the triumph of the Revolution just what it had been at the outset—a punitive reaction indissolubly linked to the defensive spirit against the 'aristocratic plot'. Some will object that 85 per cent of the known dead—bourgeois, artisans, peasants—belonged to the Third Estate, while the clergy accounted for only 6·5 per cent, and the nobility 8·5 per cent; but in such a struggle, turncoats were treated more harshly than original enemies.

Yet to a large extent this is merely the outward aspect of the Terror. Another may be revealed within if it is observed that, associated with the revolutionary government, it conferred upon the latter the 'coercive power' that restored the authority of the state and allowed it to impose upon the nation the sacrifices indispensable to public safety. If the majority of Frenchmen clung to the Revolution and detested foreign intervention, their civic education was not enough to repress selfishness and make them all submit to discipline. The Terror forced it upon them and contributed greatly to developing the habit and feeling of national solidarity. The Montagnards undoubtedly shared the punitive will of the sans-culottes, but the fact remains that from this point of view the Terror became an instrument of government that regimented the nation, without making even occasional exception for the sans-culottes themselves. This was, so to speak, its internal aspect.

Henceforth, as the dictatorship of the Committee asserted itself, a third aspect was revealed. Some Montagnards condemned the harshness of the system, and some sans-culottes reproached it for not doing enough for them. This time the Terror was turned against those who had created it. The drama of Ventôse and Germinal thus marked a new stage in its history. It appeared destined to maintain in power the small group of men who, entrenched in the committees, embodied the revolutionary dictatorship.

Still, its earlier characteristics persisted during this third period. Centralization had progressed slowly. The Committee of General Security required justificatory reports on imprisonments, the Committee of Public Safety sent agents here and there to investigate (Jullien of Paris to Nantes and Bordeaux, and Demaillot to Orléans), and the most notable terrorists (Carrier, Barras, Fréron, Fouché, and Tallien) returned one after another. Now the decree of 27 Germinal, Year II (April 16, 1794), ordered the suppression of revolutionary tribunals in the provinces, and most of them were terminated on 19 Floréal (May 8).

Once more, circumstances produced exceptions. In the north the campaign took a turn for the worse: Landrecies surrendered on 11 Floréal, Year II (April 30, 1794), and Cambrai was threatened. Dispatched to the army, Saint-Just and Lebas appealed to Lebon, who established a branch of his Arras tribunal, which was then allowed to remain until 22 Messidor (July 10). In Provence, when Maignet declared it impossible to transfer thousands of prisoners to Paris, the Committee, on

21 Floréal (May 10), created the popular commission of Orange, which was still functioning on 9 Thermidor. On the other hand, with the Committee of Public Safety and that of General Security both directing the repression, centralization drove the former to dispossess the latter; and at the end of Floréal it established a Bureau of General Police. Its rival did not give way, and as will be seen, this rift within the revolutionary government hastened its downfall.

As an instrument of government, the terrorist methods might have given the victorious committees cause for reflection. All authoritarian regimes, and others, too, resort to them in time of war or insurrection. But it is a rule among politicians to confine themselves to setting a few examples that assure the submission of the multitude without reducing it to desperation. There were signs that some members of the Committee perceived the danger. Robespierre had opposed the trial of the deputies arrested following their protest against the 'day' of June 2; and thanks to Lindet, a general proscription of federalists was avoided. The vain efforts against dechristianization, and the recall of the worst terrorists, were steps in the same direction.

On 5 Nivôse, Year II (December 25, 1793), it was agreed to 'perfect' the Revolutionary Tribunal. Did this mean that the crimes to be repressed would be precisely defined, that guarantees for the defendant would be increased, and that arrests would be reviewed? Such was not the case. Once more, circumstances were decisive. Until the end of June, victory remained doubtful and required an all-out effort. The moment did not seem ripe for any slackening of energy. On the contrary, the decree of 27 Germinal, Year II (April 16, 1794), expelled nobles and foreigners from Paris and the fortified towns. In proscribing Indulgents and extremists, however, the committees had no intention of sparing the counter-revolutionaries. They shared the sans-culottes' urge to punish, and had no desire to risk being accused of treason.

In Paris, in Floréal, notable trials—those of the deputies compromised by their attitude in 1789, of the farmers-general (who included Lavoisier), and of Madame Elisabeth—proved that the Terror, faithful to its origin, had not become simply an instrument of government. The widespread belief in the 'aristocratic plot', extended to all those accused of hostility towards the regime, explains the increasing practice of the 'amalgam'. This, by denying all truly judicial procedure, threw together under the same sentence accused persons who did not know each other, and whose deeds or words had nothing in common other than their supposed solidarity in the 'conspiracy against the French people'. Finally, with this state of mind exaggerated because of attacks threatening the personal safety of revolutionary leaders, terrorist procedure was altered, but only to be even more greatly simplified.

Late on 3 Prairial, Year II (May 22, 1794), a certain Admirat fired his pistol at Collot d'Herbois, but missed his target. On the evening of the 4th, Cécile Renault, who insisted upon seeing Robespierre, was arrested. She refused to reveal her intentions, but voiced her hopes of victory for the Coalition. Earlier that day Barère had denounced Admirat as the agent of the plot, financed by Pitt, against the Republic. On the 7th (May 26), the Convention forbade the granting of quarter henceforth to British and Hanoverian soldiers. This was an unprecedented step, and the army could scarcely apply it; but it attested the emotion aroused by the memories of the assassination of Lepeletier and Marat. This feeling was again expressed in the appeal from the Committee of Public Safety to Saint-Just, on the 6th, in the midst of the campaign: 'Liberty is exposed to new dangers. . . . The Committee needs to unite the knowledge and energy of all its members.'

Obviously, in the eyes of the revolutionaries these assassination attempts, which they linked (without any convincing proof) to the intrigues of the elusive Baron de Batz, foreshadowed some attempt to disorganize the national defence on the eve of decisive battles. Saint-Just arrived on the 10th, but discussions (of which we know nothing) and preparations for the Festival of the Supreme Being (set for the 20th) delayed the result. This took shape on 22 Prairial (June 10), when Couthon presented the famous law, the draft of which is in his handwriting. Robespierre, who was presiding, stepped down to the tribune to secure the approval of the Convention. Later, when threatened by the reactionaries, the members of the Committee of Public Safety ascribed the initiative for the law to their vanished colleagues, and declared that they themselves had not been consulted. But the Thermidorians did not believe them. It is at least certain that the Committee of General Security was not called upon to give its opinion, and that it did not forgive this oversight.

Suppressing all preliminary questioning, leaving the summoning of witnesses to the discretion of the court, and refusing the accused the aid of counsel, the law succeeded in destroying the judicial guarantees for the defence. Furthermore, the court was left with no choice but acquittal or death. Considered as an instrument of government in the service of revolutionary defence, the Terror did not require such reinforcement. Besides, Couthon had said, 'It is not a matter of setting a few examples, but of exterminating the implacable henchmen of tyranny.' This was scorning the point of view of a statesman, a yielding completely to the passion for repression, which the threat of assassination tinged with personal animosity.

In the Convention, on the other hand, the law brought a long-felt uneasiness to its height. The opponents of the Committee claimed, on the 23rd, that the law implicitly authorized it to arraign deputies without referring the matter to the Assembly. On the next day, not without difficulty, Robespierre secured the repudiation of such a charge; but doubts persisted. For this reason the conviction spread that the Committees were accelerating the Terror in order to maintain themselves in power. So the new trend, which had been foreseen on the day following the deaths of Hébert and Danton, now prevailed.

The Law of 22 Prairial, Year II (June 10, 1794), gave birth to the 'Great Terror'. As early as the 29th it was applied to a 'batch' of 54 persons who had been implicated in the assassination attempts and the Batz conspiracy. Yet it was the anxious attention paid to the prisons which extended its scope. This was nothing new: it had been admitted in July, 1789, and September, 1792, that a prisoners' revolt was part of the 'aristocratic plot'. The great number of imprisoned suspects—now more than 8,000 in Paris—could only increase this fear. The prison system justified it. A report in Prairial acknowledged, in short, that the prisoners were virtually free to revolt. Such a plan had been charged to the Hébertists, and later to Dillon and Lucille Desmoulins. In June, after a planned escape was denounced at the Bicêtre prison, three 'batches' were brought before the Revolutionary Tribunal on these grounds.

Since the attacks of Prairial were linked to the counter-revolutionary conspiracy, it is not astonishing that the prisons were again made the order of the day. But the intention to 'exterminate', expressed by Couthon, also explains why denunciations by informers were welcomed complacently. With the approval of the Committee of Public Safety, and under the direction of Herman, the head of the Commission on Civil and Judicial Affairs, seven 'batches' were taken from the Luxembourg, Carmes, and St.-Lazare prisons between 19 Messidor, Year II (July 7, 1794), and 8 Thermidor (July 26). (André Chénier was included in one of them.) In all, the 'Great Terror' cost the lives of 1,376 persons, while only 1,251 had been executed in Paris from March, 1793, to 22 Prairial.

Public opinion was shaken, and the practices of the repression abetted the fear. The tumbrils slowly transported the condemned across the Faubourg St.-Antoine as far as the Trône-Renversé gate, the new emplacement for the scaffold. The executions were public, and the guillotine, cutting off heads and spattering blood, struck the imagination. But precisely because the victory of the Revolution no longer appeared in doubt, fear of the 'aristocratic plot' faded, the punitive will was dulled, and the popular fever subsided.

REVOLUTIONARY VICTORY (MAY–JULY, 1794)

The Committee of Public Safety has been reproached for abandoning Danton's policies and for not seeking to temper the cost of victory through diplomacy. It would have had to exploit the divisions among the Allies, support the Poles, and press the Scandinavians into action—all at the same time. Grouvelle was supplying it with information from Copenhagen, Barthélemy and Bacher from Switzerland. In their opinion Prussia and Austria were inclined to negotiate, and Bernstorff, the Danish minister, was offering his good offices. The Committee turned a deaf ear. At home negotiations would have encouraged the Indulgents and slackened the national war effort.

By the end of 1793 rumours of peace negotiations were spreading, and there was talk of 'clemency'. Abroad it would have secured nothing. Only after the victory of the regicides did the king of Prussia resign himself to negotiating with them. As for the Poles, the Committee allowed Parandier to send them Kosciusko, but refused all subsidies. It sketched a plan for a league of neutrals, and contributed, through Grouvelle, to the union of Denmark and Sweden. There was even talk of financing Swedish armament, but where would the money come from? It was known, moreover, that like the Americans, the Scandinavians thought solely of trading in peace. By yielding at the first sign of danger, the English would have made French sacrifices meaningless. The Poles might prove more useful, but how could they be helped? Their aristocratic and royal 'republic', furthermore, did not attract the sympathy of the revolutionaries. The Committee probably had some reservations, for if negotiations with Prussia were to occur Poland would have to be sacrificed; and it was thus more honest to promise her nothing.

If it did not attach great importance to diplomatic manoeuvres, nevertheless the Committee did conceive a foreign policy. This consisted of conciliating the neutrals and of avoiding everything that might increase the number of its enemies. Renewing tradition, Robespierre, on 27 Brumaire, Year II (November 17, 1793), reminded the small states that their independence would not survive the fall of France. He bitterly reproached the dechristianizers for alienating international opinion. Trade relations were resumed with the neutrals, whose vessels were respected.

Above all, propaganda was renounced. Switzerland chiefly had been alarmed, so Robespierre cut short the schemes of Hérault de Séchelles, who, within a stone's throw of Basel, was seeking to annex Mulhouse. The principality of Montbéliard opted for annexation, which did, in fact, take place; but the Convention did not ratify it. At Geneva, where Soulavie represented France, the democrats actually overthrew the patriciate, but the Committee refrained from occupying the town. Barthélemy was able to allay the mistrust of the cantons, and a crowd of agents placed orders with them. The Swiss, moreover, were supplied with the salt and products they needed. The counter-revolutionary schemes of Steiger, leader of the Bernese aristocracy, encountered the resistance of the cantons of Zurich and Basel, which continued to trade freely with France. In the United States, Genêt, the Girondin envoy, allied himself with the republicans against Washington, in order to drag their country into war; and he had armed privateers in American ports. A rupture was imminent, all the more regrettable because the United States' debt constituted the only credit that France had available abroad. Genêt was replaced, and did not return home.

The Committee was not merely being prudent when it renounced propaganda. The apathy of the 'slave' peoples and the 'foreign plot' revived the national egoism and discredited the cosmopolitan universalism that had marked the beginnings of the Revolution. The mercantile interests congratulated themselves that the treaty of 1786 had been broken and the country closed to British commerce. The Committee hastened to exploit this sudden change of mind. It 'nationalized' or 'popularized' the war. In his 'carmagnoles', Barère continued to ridicule the enemy and flatter national pride. 'I, for one, do not like the English!' Robespierre cried to the Jacobin Club.

Since the peoples did not disavow their governments, henceforth they would be treated accordingly. As early as September, 1793, the Committee prescribed that the armies take over all the resources of occupied countries and send back to France whatever they did not consume. During the winter the Palatinate was thoroughly exploited. When the offensive was imminent the Committee established an 'evacuation agency' for each army (24 Floréal, Year II—May 13, 1794), and the operation was organized definitively on 30 Messidor (July 18). The conquered countries were systematically despoiled, and in the Spanish Pyrenees, foundries that could not be utilized were destroyed. The government thus opened the way to the annexationist policy of the Thermidorians, which perpetuated the conflict; but its own plan was far different. It saw quite clearly that the country was becoming exhausted ('The people grow weary' when the struggle is prolonged, Robespierre had predicted to the Girondins) and fearing a military dictatorship the Committee had no intention of making the war permanent. We must finish it this year, wrote Carnot; otherwise 'we shall perish of hunger and exhaustion'.

Pichegru, commander of the Army of the North, had been

given some 150,000 men, with orders to attack in Flanders, so as to take Ypres and reach Nieuport. On the extreme right, the Army of the Ardennes, which numbered 25,000 men, was to threaten Charleroi, and that of the Moselle, with 40,000 men, was to advance towards Liége. It was the strategy of the Old Regime. The army strung itself out parallel with the enemy and aimed at fortresses. It manoeuvred Coburg into a position of retreat by threatening the ends of his lines, instead of making a mass attack on Charleroi to cut off his retreat and annihilate him. Pichegru proved inferior to his reputation, however, and procrastinated for a month. Leaving the initiative to the enemy, the republicans, with two-thirds of their troops massed on their left, risked being smashed in the centre and exposing the road to Paris. This was what Mack had advised. The Austrians took Landrecies, and beat the French near Le Cateau. Coburg carried the offensive to Lille, but his troops were repulsed at Tourcoing by Pichegru's lieutenants on 29 Floréal, Year II (May 18, 1794). During this time Saint-Just turned the diversion to the right into a genuine assault. The Army of the Ardennes gradually increased to 50,000 men, and four times he led it unsuccessfully against Charleroi.

As in 1793, the immobility of the Prussians decided the campaign. Jourdan, with a part of the Army of the Moselle, was able to advance across the Ardennes, and pursuing Beaulieu, he veered towards Dinant. The Committee then decided to unite his army with that of the Ardennes. This group of 90,000 men was soon to become famous under the name of 'Sambre and Meuse'. After another defeat, Jourdan finally forced the surrender of Charleroi. At this moment Pichegru was taking Ypres. The classic manoeuvre of turning the flank thus succeeded through trial and error. Coburg withdrew, but it was too late to bar his path by debouching from Charleroi. Realizing the danger, he attacked Jourdan at the gates of the town, in the plain of Fleurus, on 8 Messidor, Year II (June 26, 1794). Although repulsed, he still remained free to evacuate Belgium undisturbed. Pichegru and Jourdan joined forces at Brussels. Still, Robespierre and Saint-Just had to reject Carnot's absurd plan to remove a strong contingent from Jourdan's army for a coastal attack against Zealand.

The Allies had separated, with the Austrians withdrawing to

Aix-la-Chapelle, the Anglo-Hanoverians and the Dutch to the lower Rhine. The French followed suit. Jourdan pursued the former, and Pichegru the latter. They entered Liége and Antwerp simultaneously on 9 Thermidor, Year II (July 27, 1794). Then they halted to organize their bases in Belgium, while behind them the strong points in the north were retaken. In September, Jourdan resumed his march, beat Beaulieu on the Ourthe and the Roer, and reached the Rhine. At this moment the Prussians returned to Westphalia, and the Armies of the Rhine and the Moselle advanced and besieged Mainz. Pichegru waited until the rivers were frozen before invading Holland, and in December and January he occupied it without a struggle. The English had withdrawn into Hanover.

In the eastern Pyrenees, Dugommier had captured the Boulou camp on 12 Floréal, Year II (May 1, 1794), retaken the fortresses, and invaded Catalonia. In the west, Moncey, having turned and dispersed the enemy, occupied Fuenterrabia and San Sebastian (14–17 Thermidor—August 1–4). At one point the invasion of Italy appeared imminent. Now general of a brigade, Bonaparte imposed his plan upon Carnot through the two Robespierres; but after 9 Thermidor, Carnot returned to his own scheme of reinforcing Dugommier. In November, at the battle of Black Mountain, the Spanish were routed. Figueras capitulated, and Pérignon, replacing Dugommier, who had been killed, was able to besiege and take Rosas.

Things did not go so well at sea. Thanks to the aid of Spain and Naples, the English dominated the Mediterranean, imposed their will upon Tuscany and Genoa, and with Paoli's connivance, achieved the conquest of Corsica. In the Atlantic, however, republican squadrons still managed to put to sea. When, at the beginning of Prairial, a great convoy of grain arrived from the United States, Howe attempted to capture it, and Villaret-Joyeuse hastened from Brest to give battle on the 9, 10, and 13 Prairial, Year II (May 28 and 29, and June 1, 1794). French losses were the heavier, and it was here that the *Vengeur* sank; but Howe abandoned the fray, and the convoy escaped.

In the colonies the English occupied the trading factories of India, and St. Pierre and Miquelon; but they disregarded Senegal, and did not touch the Mascarene Islands. The struggle was concentrated in the West Indies. On September 24, 1791, the Constituent Assembly had once more left to the colonial assemblies the problem of regulating the status of Negroes. As yet there was no question of abolishing slavery, but its commissioners succeeded neither in re-establishing order nor in subduing the rebellious Negroes. The Girondins accorded all Negroes full citizenship on March 28, 1792, and dispatched new commissioners, the most notable of whom was Sonthonax. When they reached Haiti, the news of August 10 drove the whites to counter-revolution. The representatives of the Legislative Assembly supported the mulattoes, while certain generals —d'Esparbès and then Galbaud—leaned in the opposite direction. The civil war caused the destruction of Port-au-Prince and Cap Français (now Cap Haïtien). With the connivance of the colonists, the English, who were negotiating at London with their emissaries (Malouet or Dubuc from Martinique), undertook to occupy the port towns, and Sonthonax resigned himself to promising freedom to those Negroes who would help drive out the enemy.

Then, on 16 Pluviôse, Year II (February 4, 1794), the Convention abolished slavery outright. The law was never applied either in the Windward Islands (except for Guadeloupe) or in the Mascarene Islands, where the planters held it to be null and void. In Santo Domingo, however, it produced the effect the republicans expected. Already Toussaint L'Ouverture, the most remarkable of the Negro leaders, had broken with the Spanish, and rallied to General Lavaux. All the others followed his example, and by the end of 1795 the reconquest was completed. Of the Windward Islands the French retained only Guadeloupe, which had been retaken by Victor Hugues. Goyrand added St. Lucia, which he lost again in 1796 after a long resistance. Hugues gave the English no rest. Without succeeding in retaking Martinique, he inflicted severe losses upon their commerce.

Although Great Britain rallied, France did not consider herself out of the fight. To overcome the mistress of the seas, she would have to re-establish peace on the Continent. This was not impossible, for Prussia and Spain were disposed to negotiate, the Austrian Netherlands possessed great resources, and through them trade with Hamburg and the Baltic was resuming. The

Republic could delay financial and economic disaster, and through a supreme effort, crown its triumph by compelling Austria to come to peace. But this would require the continuation of the revolutionary machinery.

9 THERMIDOR (JULY 27, 1794)

The greatest part of the nation opposed such a policy. This was to be expected of those who had resisted the Third Estate in 1789, or who, because of injury to interests or self-esteem, attachment to royalty, fidelity to the refractory clergy and religious feeling, or fear of the 'agrarian law' had progressively turned against the Revolution. Such was the case for many others as well—those who, while remaining faithful to the Revolution in principle, wished to recover freedom of enterprise and profits, or more often still, were weary and wanted peace. The Jacobins of the clubs, whose numbers have been estimated at one million, were in disagreement. Artisans and shopkeepers evaded the Maximum when they could, while sans-culottes, disappointed and reproaching the committees for the proscription of their leaders, began to rouse in their shops, and showed their disaffection in various ways.

Sprung from the bourgeoisie, the Convention, for its part, desired to be done with the controlled economy and to re-establish the political and social authority of its class. It did not forgive the Montagnards, either for having imposed themselves by popular force or for having decimated the Assembly. Ever since the Law of 22 Prairial, Year II (June 10, 1794) the rumour of a new purge had alarmed it. Since the Montagnards had broken with the sans-culottes, the Convention felt that it could now recover itself. As long as the Revolution was in danger, it had hesitated to compromise the national defence, and the terrible difficulty of the task had tempered ambitions. Henceforth victory overrode its scruples and unleashed cupidity. Who did not deem himself worthy of sitting on the Committee of Public Safety, to garner the rewards proudly after having modestly avoided risks for so long?

All who detested the revolutionary government held Robespierre particularly accountable. Nothing was more natural. It was he who had defended the policies of the committees, with as much clear-sightedness as courage, in the Convention and at the Jacobin Club. The cult of the Supreme Being and the Law of 22 Prairial had made him conspicuous. Since the latter appeared to be a means of maintaining the present leaders in power, the charge was directed specifically against him, and he was suspected of preparing a personal dictatorship. In truth, he exercised no power of his own in the Committee of Public Safety. He was one of the last to enter it, he did not choose its members, and he did not even preside. He acted only with the approval of his colleagues. Nevertheless, his undeniable ascendancy, his imperious eloquence, his inflexible refusal to compromise (which won him praise as 'incorruptible'), his pitiless severity towards traitors, and his tendency to suspect all opponents of being connected with them earned him, even at the Jacobin Club, the accusation of exercising a 'tyranny of public opinion'.

Because neither an independent press nor elections any longer existed, the outcome depended upon the Convention, which each month prolonged the powers of the committees. But in an assembly where, in the absence of organized parties, each man felt isolated and feared for himself, who would dare to charge these committees with tyranny or propose that they be dismissed, if not proscribed? Of the deputies who had returned from their missions, more than one nursed grudges against them. The recalled terrorists, deeming themselves personally threatened, strove hard to involve their colleagues. This was particularly true of Tallien, whose mistress, Thérésia Cabarrus, had recently been arrested and was calling to him for help, and Fouché, who was infinitely more skilful. The former later claimed to have been the author of 9 Thermidor, but the latter has a better title to the role. Actually by themselves they would never have succeeded. The Plain did not like these terrorists, many of whom, as men of bad reputation, did not otherwise deserve esteem; and in due time it demonstrated its dislike. If their action was effective, it was because they became the accomplices of some of the men in power. The committees destroyed themselves by quarrelling, and thereby restored to the Convention the authority it had been coveting.

The Committee of General Security was jealous of the Committee of Public Safety, and after the Law of 22 Prairial the conflict grew more bitter. The tendency towards centralization also threatened Cambon, who controlled the Committee on Finances and the Treasury. Once again the animosity was concentrated on Robespierre. Undoubtedly the organization of a homogeneous central power that would achieve unity of action in the revolutionary government obsessed both him and Saint-Just as the indispensable complement of centralization. Moreover, the Hébertist tendency persisted among many members of the Committee of General Security, while opposition to dechristianization and the cult of the Supreme Being angered them. Robespierre probably also displeased them by his manners, which were precisely what made him popular among the revolutionary lower middle class, of which he seemed to be the prototype. Remaining poor despite his ability, he led a modest life at the home of the cabinetmaker Duplay, in the Rue St.-Honoré. The founder of the democratic party and close to the humble, he was nonetheless attentive to his appearance, and repudiated the dishevelment, 'carmagnole', and red liberty cap of the sans-culotte.

Had the Committee of Public Safety at least remained united, it would have maintained the advantage. The Plain would no more follow the Committee of General Security than it would the terrorists; but the great committee was disintegrating, and it was Robespierre whom the majority blamed. Couthon and Saint-Just alone remained loyal to him. It is not astonishing that Billaud-Varenne, who reproached him for having delayed in abandoning Danton, and Collot d'Herbois, Fouché's collaborator at Lyons, took sides against him. They served as a link to the Committee of General Security. But the others? There is no question about Prieur of Marne and Jeanbon Saint-André, who were on mission; and Barère, testing the wind as always, made up his mind only at the last moment. What of Lindet, Carnot, and Prieur of Côte-d'Or? Like Barère, all three represented that part of the Plain which rallied to the Mountain in order to assure the salvation of the Revolution, without swerving from its spirit of bourgeois conservatism.

To them the controlled economy seemed a temporary expedient, the social accomplishments of the democracy of the Year II at least open to revision; and they certainly disliked the Ventôse decrees. Lindet still held aloof, and Prieur of Côte-d'Or could be counted upon only as an auxiliary; so the moving spirit of the opposition, and finally of 9 Thermidor, was Carnot. Yet it cannot be doubted that the divergence of social ideals was tainted by personal quarrels that a violent individualism engendered. These capable and honest men were authoritarians. Carnot, in particular, was irritated by the criticisms directed at his plans by Robespierre and Saint-Just, who, exhausted by work and over-excited by the danger, restrained themselves with difficulty. Robespierre, whose health was weakening, proved irritable, and did not forgive easily. Amiable and gentle among close friends, but cold and distant elsewhere, he was unable to smile. Dispute followed dispute.

At the end of Prairial, Vadier undertook to ridicule the Supreme Being and its pontiff in connection with an old woman, Catherine Théot, who claimed to be the 'mother of God' and had acquired some inoffensive followers. Robespierre opposed her trial, and emerged victorious after a violent scene. Soon he ceased to attend the Committee, and the month of Messidor passed without his breaking silence. This delay could only favour the propaganda of his opponents and strengthen their alliance. At the beginning of Thermidor they attempted a reconciliation. Saint-Just and Couthon favoured it, but Robespierre doubted the sincerity of his enemies. It was he who brought about the fatal intervention of the Convention. On 8 Thermidor, Year II (July 26, 1794), he denounced his opponents, and demanded that 'unity of government' be realized. The Assembly voted that his speech be printed and transmitted to the municipalities. When called upon to name those whom he was accusing, however, he refused. This failure destroyed him, for it was assumed that he was demanding a blank cheque. The Plain reversed itself, and the decree was revoked. Would it not yield on the next day, however, as it had done before, when Robespierre and Saint-Just returned to the offensive?

Henceforth, to avoid their own proscription, their enemies resolved to proscribe Robespierre and Saint-Just. Foreseeing that the Commune would call the sections to arms, these enemies skilfully agreed on the tactic to follow; and it was then that the accomplices played a major role. When the session of 9 Thermidor opened at noon, they prevented Saint-Just and Robespierre from speaking. In the uproar and confusion the committees had Hanriot removed from command of the National Guard, which was turned over to the heads of the eight legions, who were to serve in rotation. The arrest of Dumas, president of the Revolutionary Tribunal, was ordered, and then an obscure Dantonist demanded and obtained the arraignment of the two Robespierres, Saint-Just, and Couthon, to whom Lebas heroically added himself. At three o'clock all was over.

The Commune declared itself in a state of insurrection. Hanriot behaved ineptly and, in attempting to free his friends, was captured. Only two legion commanders responded to his call. Thus the authority of the Convention prevailed, and the Robespierrists were now able to see where the condemnation of the Hébertists and the dispersal of those capable of insurrection had led. Nevertheless, at about seven o'clock in the evening some 3,000 men with thirty-odd cannon were assembled in the Place de Grève. This formidable force lacked leaders. Coffinhal withdrew it to release Hanriot; but since the accused had been taken to prison, he returned instead of dissolving the Convention. Recovered from its fright, the latter outlawed the accused and the rebels. Intimidated, the revolutionary committees, the sections, and the Jacobins, who were deliberating, reached no decision. The arrested deputies were in fact liberated, and between nine o'clock and one in the morning they reached the Hôtel de Ville one by one; but they did not take charge of the insurrection. They did not disavow it, but they probably felt that it was hopeless. Having always declared that they were governing in the name of the national representation, they were paralysed by the contradiction, and abandoned themselves to their fate.

Left to themselves, the sans-culottes gradually withdrew, so that by one o'clock in the morning the square was deserted. At this moment the forces of the Convention arrived. Since the National Guards from the wealthy neighbourhoods had furnished a contingent, it was entrusted to Barras, a former officer who, thus promoted as the saviour of the Thermidorians, opened a new career for himself. But the Gravilliers section, which (according to Michelet) had not forgotten Jacques Roux, dispatched a column at the same time. With all hope gone, Lebas committed suicide; and Robespierre turned a pistol on himself, but succeeded only in shattering his jaw. The Hôtel de Ville was invaded without a shot, and its occupants were arrested. Throughout Paris an enormous round-up of members of the Commune and Jacobins began.

On the evening of 10 Thermidor (July 28), Robespierre, Saint-Just, Couthon, Dumas, and 18 others were guillotined on the Place de la Révolution, where the scaffold had been moved. The next day a 'batch' of 71, the largest of the Revolution, followed, and the day after, a third one of 12. Three other 'outlaws' eventually completed the hecatomb. Throughout France the terrorists were disconcerted. Robespierre a traitor to the Republic like Hébert and Danton! At heart, most could not believe it; but the great majority of the nation appeared satisfied. It considered the revolutionary government mortally stricken; and it was not mistaken.

CHAPTER THREE

The Thermidorian Reaction and the Treaties of 1795

THE THERMIDORIANS harrassed the Jacobins and disestablished the revolutionary government. Exploiting the White Terror and the reaction against the 'drinkers of blood', they eliminated the controlled economy and social democracy at one and the same time. Such is the real significance of 9 Thermidor, the day to which the proscription of the *Enragés* and the Hébertists seemed to be the prologue. The bourgeoisie regained the dominance that the Revolution of 1789 had conferred upon them and which they would retain henceforth. Since, however, the currency was no longer sustained, it collapsed, and the Republic found itself unable to continue the war in order to impose a general peace. The liberal regime that the Thermidorians had intended to re-establish was compromised; moreover, it inherited a legacy of bankruptcy and war.

DISESTABLISHMENT OF THE REVOLUTIONARY GOVERNMENT

Saved by the Plain, Robespierre's enemies intended to retain power. Having decided to treat Jacobins and sans-culottes as it pleased, the Convention did not re-establish constitutional government; but fearing above all to fall again into bondage, it hastened to regain control of the executive power. As early as

11 Thermidor, Year II (July 29, 1794), it decreed that a fourth of each committee should be renewed each month, and that no member might be re-elected until after an interval of one month. Within a month the terrorists had disappeared from their midst, with the exception of Carnot, who was retained for some time. The members of the Convention, happy to be in power at last, took their place, and some, notably Merlin of Douai and Cambacérès, gained influence; but their authority was weakened.

On 7 Fructidor, Year II (August 24, 1794), the Committee of Public Safety, reduced to powers over war and foreign affairs, was deprived of its dominance. With the purge of administrations, control of the interior and of justice passed into the hands of the Committee on Legislation. The twelve executive commissions which had replaced the ministers were subordinated to the twelve principal committees of the Assembly. In the provinces the deputies on mission again increased, and as before, they applied the policy of the central government as they chose. Fragmentation of authority resulted in anarchy.

Finally, it was against terrorist coercion that opinion turned most violently. On the day following 9 Thermidor the Law of 22 Prairial had been repealed. The decimated Revolutionary Tribunal had ceased to function; reorganized, it could not resume its bloody work, because the 'question of intent' permitted acquittals on the pretext that the accused had not been inspired by counter-revolutionary motives. The release of suspects began, and after 7 Fructidor, following violent attacks upon them, the watch committees were reduced to one per district. Although it was still maintained in principle, the revolutionary government had lost simultaneously its three essential attributes: its stability, its centralization, and its coercive power.

The Plain, however, still feared that the reaction would benefit the counter-revolutionaries, and it summoned all republicans to its side. The Convention accorded the honours of the Panthéon to Marat. It completed the secularization of the state by separating it from the constitutional church, the budget of which disappeared on the '2nd sans-culottide' of the Year II (September 18, 1794). By the end of Thermidor, however, Montagnards and Jacobins were protesting against the release of suspects. In Marseilles the sans-culottes demonstrated against the deputies on mission. The schism burst into the open and played into the hands of the Right, where the remainder of the Girondins (and those who called themselves Girondins) sat, whose spokesmen, from the beginning, were Tallien, Fréron, and Rovère. The newspapers, almost all Thermidorian, became numerous once again, the salons reopened, and festivities resumed at the Palais Égalité. Thérésia Cabarrus, 'Our Lady of Thermidor', currently Madame Tallien, set the tone for Parisian society. Financiers and speculators resumed their lobbying. The republicans of the Plain were won over by this fashionable society, and having listened for so long to talk of virtue, they found it pleasing to indulge themselves.

They were asked not only to destroy the work of the Montagnards—the reactionaries also hoped to wreak vengeance on the Jacobins and sans-culottes by turning the Terror against them. On 12 Fructidor, Year II (August 29, 1794), and again on 12 Vendémiaire, Year III (October 3, 1794), Lecointre maintained that the members of the former committees were lying when they denied their solidarity with Robespierre, and demanded that they be indicted. The Plain would not go this far. Having permitted the committees to do as they pleased, it was loath to put itself on trial. As for the lesser terrorists, its policy had been to prosecute only those who were convicted of unlawful acts and abuses of the common law; but once again the decision was imposed upon it from outside.

The reactionaries revived the sections and organized the *jeunesse dorée* into armed bands filled with draft dodgers (*insoumis*), deserters, shop-boys, and law clerks encouraged by their employers. These bands were the law in the sections. They took over the streets and attacked the patriots with cudgels under the complacent eyes of the police. The Jacobins succumbed. They did not constitute a strictly disciplined class party, and despite purges, their clubs had never been very homogeneous. Moreover, they had been concerned primarily with discussion. Where action was involved they had resorted to the agencies of political democracy—the Commune and the revolutionary committees, the sections, and the National Guards—thanks to the impotence or with the tolerance of the government. Now these agencies were gone, and on 25 Vendémiaire, Year III (October 16,

1794), the Convention immobilized the clubs themselves (as the Constituent Assembly had done during its closing days) by forbidding them to affiliate or to present collective petitions. Finally, while their enemies could mobilize at will, the sansculottes, occupied with their work, found that mass action was possible only by means of 'days'.

The appearance before the Revolutionary Tribunal of 132 prisoners from Nantes, who had been sent to Paris by Carrier in the preceding winter, precipitated a crisis that subordinated the moderate Thermidorians to the new terrorists. They were acquitted, but since the debates had implicated Carrier, the Convention, after having regulated the procedure for the prosecution of its members, instituted his trial. In order to intimidate waverers, Fréron led the *jeunesse dorée* in an attack on the Rue St.-Honoré Club, on 21 Brumaire, Year III (November 11, 1794), and the government used the disturbance as an excuse for closing the club. Carrier, brought before the Revolutionary Tribunal, was guillotined on 26 Frimaire, Year III (December 16, 1794). A week before, the Convention had reinstated 78 deputies who had been arrested or expelled after the revolution of May 31st.

The reinforcement provided by these proscribed men, who were thirsting for vengeance, brought redoubled attacks by the Right. On 7 Nivôse, Year III (December 27, 1794), a commission began to examine the cases of Billaud-Varenne, Collot d'Herbois, Barère, and Vadier. It took its time, and the gangs resumed their offensive in the streets—destroying busts of Marat, whose remains they had removed from the Panthéon—and in the theatres, where the 'Réveil du Peuple' supplanted the 'Marseillaise', song of the 'drinkers of blood'. In the provinces the reaction was intensified. There, too, the *jeunesse dorée* moved into action, allied with returning émigrés and refractory priests. In the south there appeared 'Companies of Jesus' and 'Companies of the Sun', which attacked Jacobins, purchasers of national property, constitutional priests, and all the 'patriots of '89'. On 14 Pluviôse, Year III (February 2, 1795), a massacre marked the beginning of the White Terror in Lyons.

Since Catholics were included among the reactionaries, the Right hoped to improve their condition, and events in the west enabled it to secure from the Plain concessions which characterized the period. Charette and Stofflet still held the field in the Vendée, and even before 9 Thermidor the *chouannerie* had appeared north of the Loire. Hoche (now commander in the region) and the Thermidorians on mission considered that the insurrection could be put down only by restoring the churches and giving full liberty to the refractory clergy. On 29 Pluviôse, Year III (February 17, 1795), the pacification of La Jaunaye, concluded with Charette and ratified by the Convention, granted an amnesty, reimbursed the bonds issued by the rebels, and awarded them indemnities for war damages. The Republic even accepted insurgents in its pay and promised that they would never be sent to the frontier. Ultimately similar agreements were reached with Stofflet and the *chouans*.

How could other Frenchmen henceforth be denied the re-establishment of freedom of worship, which, in theory, had always existed? Despite the administrations, the constitutional clergy began to say mass again almost everywhere, and the nonjurors revived clandestine worship. On 3 Ventôse, Year III (February 21, 1795), on the basis of a report by Boissy d'Anglas, the Convention reiterated that the celebration of worship was not to be disturbed. But it confirmed the separation of church and state. The Republic would grant neither churches nor subsidy, ceremonies would remain strictly private, and external symbols, the ringing of bells, and clerical garb remained prohibited.

These compromises could not endure. In the Vendée, Hoche foresaw that by not being disarmed, the population was actually being provided with means of resuming the war at the first opportunity. Indeed, this is what its leaders were thinking, and on 6 Prairial, Year III (May 25, 1795), Hoche arrested the so-called Baron de Cormatin, whose correspondence he had seized and whose disloyalty had been established. On the other hand, the law of 3 Ventôse (February 21) did not satisfy the Catholics. They wanted to recover their churches and re-establish public worship. Moreover, although the refractory clergy were resuming office in the west, the laws against them remained in force. Yet by the end of spring the Thermidorians no longer refused anything, even to avowed royalists. Once more, economic crisis roused the people, and the entire bourgeoisie closed ranks against them.

FINANCIAL AND ECONOMIC CRISIS AND THE WHITE TERROR

As has been pointed out, the proscription of the terrorists constituted the spectacular side of the reaction, not its essential feature. What the bourgeoisie, great and small, rural and urban, detested above all was the controlled economy. The Convention was of the same opinion. Having restored itself, it returned to the liberty it had always cherished. In Brumaire it began to revise the Maximum and the requisitioning system; but as the Terror was turned against the Jacobins, it became more and more difficult to make these measures respected. In an oblique attack their adversaries upbraided the bureaucracy, the Commission on Commerce, and nationalized enterprise for their arbitrariness, negligence, and waste. Moreover, were not the agents of the controlled economy terrorists, who should be removed? Furthermore, famine was prevalent in the spring. It was necessary to restore to merchants and neutrals the power to import grain as they chose, in order to secure a supply and to turn to account the capital which had left France. On the basis of a report by Lindet himself, the Convention agreed to this, and attached to the commerce commission a council of businessmen, in which Perregaux held the seat of honour.

How could imports be put on sale and the Maximum be observed at the same time? Finally, on 4 Nivôse, Year III (December 24, 1794), it, too, was abolished. Within a few weeks foreign trade, exchange, and traffic in specie became free again, and the stock market reopened. The war industries ceased, and in Ventôse the government resumed dealings with contractors such as Lanchère and Cerfberr. The upper bourgeoisie obtained some satisfaction, but not enough. At home, requisitioning remained in effect in order to supply markets. A new commission 'on provisioning' retained the right of pre-emption for the service of the state, and had to be trusted, because contractors were incapable of meeting their obligations.

In effect, the abandonment of the controlled economy necessarily provoked a frightful catastrophe. Prices soared and the rate of exchange fell. The Republic was condemned to massive inflation, and its currency was ruined. In Thermidor, Year III, assignats were worth less than 3 per cent of their face value. Neither peasant nor merchant would accept anything but cash.

On 3 Messidor, Year III (June 21, 1795), the Convention itself acknowledged the fall of the assignats by reducing their nominal value according to a 'scale of proportions' based upon successive issues. On 2 Thermidor (July 20) it ordered payment in kind of half the land tax and rents. Then it re-established licences and the personal property tax, which the Montagnards had suppressed. It also had to grant civil servants a sliding scale of wages based on the price of bread. The debacle was so swift that economic life seemed to come to a standstill. Wages, of course, were unable to keep up with rising prices, and the constriction of markets, owing to reduced purchasing power, resulted in a stoppage of production. At Littry, for example, the mines suspended operations.

The crisis was greatly aggravated by famine. Market requisitions, first maintained for a month, had to be adjourned until 1 Messidor, Year III (June 19, 1795); but the peasants finally stopped bringing any produce, because they did not wish to eccept assignats. The government continued to provision Paris, but was unable to supply the promised rations. Other towns experienced great difficulty in obtaining provisions, so once again they began to buy directly from the peasants or to seek abroad. They received some subsidies and were authorized to contract loans on condition that they refrain from coercion. So municipal regulation became far more severe than in the Year II, but it did not succeed in assuring adequate distribution. The misery of rural day labourers, abandoned by everyone, was often appalling. As always, a number of peasants profited from the inflation, selling only for cash and buying with assignats. Inflation ruined creditors to the advantage of debtors. It unleashed an unprecedented speculation that created a new rich and supported the luxury of the *Merveilleuses* and *Muscadins*, who contrasted scandalously with the destitution of the lower classes.

The insurmountable obstacles raised by the premature reestablishment of economic freedom reduced the government to a state of extreme weakness. Lacking resources, it became almost incapable of administration, and the crisis generated troubles that nearly brought its collapse. At the beginning of spring, scarcity was such that more unrest appeared almost everywhere. Paris was active again. The sans-culottes, who had unprotestingly permitted the Jacobins to be proscribed, began to regret the regime of the Year II, now that they found themselves without work and without bread. The Thermidorians accused the Montagnards of pushing them to revolt in desperation.

On 2 Germinal, Year III (March 22, 1795), the Convention began to debate the indictment of four members of the former committees, and on the 8th the trial of Fouquier-Tinville and the jurors of the Revolutionary Tribunal began. The proposals of the reactionaries augured the preparation of a new constitution. No proof of the Jacobins' deeds was produced, but it is a fact that the rebels took as their slogan 'Bread and the Constitution of 1793!' Thus the crises of 1789 and 1793 were repeated. Misery and political agitation went hand in hand. But this time almost all the bourgeoisie, from republicans to partisans of the Old Regime, were solidly against the popular movement. The experience of the Year II had taught them class discipline, and now they held power.

By contrast, the disorganization of the popular party, accentuated by the departure of its youngest and most ardent elements for military service, was so advanced that the 'day' of 12 Germinal, Year III (April 1, 1795), was reduced to the disorderly gathering of an unarmed mob that invaded the Convention and was dispersed by National Guards from the prosperous neighbourhoods. The only result was to intensify the reaction. During the very night of the 12th–13th, a decree deported Billaud-Varenne, Collot d'Herbois, Barère, and Vadier to Guiana without trial. In the ensuing days the Convention ordered the arrest of a score of deputies, including Cambon. On the 21st (April 10) it prescribed the general disarming of individuals compromised by the 'horrors of tyranny', and on the 27th it named an eleven-member commission to draft a constitution. Fouquier-Tinville and fifteen of the jurors of the Revolutionary Tribunal went to the scaffold on 18 Floréal (May 7). Barère never sailed, Vadier went into hiding, and Cambon fled to Switzerland.

Disturbed, the Plain displayed new restraint; but with famine mounting, the ferment grew, and some action had to be taken. Since the amalgamation of forces and the re-establishment of discipline had returned the army to state control, it was thought possible to use it in conjunction with the National Guards from the western sections of Paris. For the first time since 1789, troops entered Paris and undertook to fight the rebellious people. The 'days' of Prairial thus marked a decisive turning point. The rising proved more violent but no less confused than that of 12 Germinal. On 1 Prairial, Year III (May 20, 1795), the mob overwhelmed the assembly and murdered the representative Féraud. The Montagnards were permitted to compromise themselves before it was driven out, and then it was dispatched without difficulty. On the 2nd the Convention went so far as to preach fraternization. On the 3rd the army surrounded the Faubourg St.-Antoine, which, starved and unarmed, surrendered the following day without a fight. This is the date which should be taken as the end of the Revolution. Its mainspring was now broken.

Henceforth the White Terror was unleashed. A military commission pronounced thirty death sentences, notably on six Montagnards, the 'Prairial martyrs'. The Convention had the members of the former committees (except Carnot and Prieur of Côte-d'Or) and a dozen deputies arrested. In the provinces terrorists—for example, the members of the commission at Orange and Lebon—were executed. Many Jacobins, persecuted, deprived of office, molested, and threatened, had to flee. In the south-east, in Lyons, Lons-le-Saunier, Bourg, Montbrison, St.-Étienne, Aix, Marseilles, Nîmes, and Tarascon, they were imprisoned and then massacred. The 'Companies of Jesus' and 'Companies of the Sun' hunted patriots as though they were partridges. The sans-culottes of Toulon took up arms, and after their defeat a popular commission dealt with them.

As always, the Right united repression with satisfaction for its friends. The Convention restored the property of those who had been sentenced to death or deported, pardoned the federalists, and suppressed the Revolutionary Tribunal and certificates of patriotism (*civisme*). On 11 Prairial, Year III (May 30, 1795), it returned the churches to the faithful; but if the re-establishment of religion increased its progress, religious peace was not yet realized. The ban on the external symbols of religion remained in effect, and in the reopened churches it was made certain that both the constitutional clergy and the Catholic priests would participate in the Tenth Day ceremonies. This caused continual conflicts. Moreover, it required clerics to take an oath of submission to the laws. The constitutional clergy obeyed and reconstituted their church under the direction of Abbé Grégoire; while some of the others followed the example of Abbé Emery, former director of St. Sulpice. But the 'submissive' clergy were opposed by the 'unsubmissive' clergy, who continued their secret proselytizing.

Once again the Plain took fright. It restored order in Lyons; and despite the sections and provincial authorities, the Committee of General Security began to liberate the Jacobins. What most frightened the Thermidorians who remained republicans was the fact that the royalists no longer concealed their hopes. They named the members of the Convention who were ready to come to terms with them. Still, they would not surrender themselves bound hand and foot, and the royalists were not agreed concerning the concessions to be offered. Some hoped to revise the work of the Constituent Assembly and to govern in the name of Louis XVII; others intended to re-establish the Old Regime. Unfortunately for the constitutional royalists, the child king died in the Temple on 20 Prairial, Year III (June 8, 1795). The count of Provence, now at Verona, took the title of Louis XVIII, and on June 24 issued a manifesto that promised punishment of the revolutionaries and a restoration of the old order.

The moderates now had no choice but to come to an agreement with the Thermidorians of the Plain in order to vote a tolerable constitution. From their point of view the absolutists could make only one more mistake. They could resort again to civil war, with foreign aid. Such, in fact, was their intention. A royalist agency existed in Paris, and in June, Pichegru, commander of the Army of the Rhine, was approached. In Franche-Comté and in the south attempts were made to instigate an uprising as a prelude to invasion. At the beginning of Prairial the *chouans* once more took up arms, relying on the aid of the count of Artois at Jersey and on the expedition that the English had finally announced. The time was poorly chosen, for the Coalition was disintegrating. The absolutists were rushing into an adventure that was to turn to the advantage of the Revolution.

THERMIDORIAN DIPLOMACY

Since France remained at war with Europe, the disestablishment of the revolutionary government, the abandonment of the controlled economy, and the ruination of the currency had their most disastrous effects upon the army. There had always been draft dodgers and deserters. In the Year II these had been sought out; in the Year III they were permitted to return to their homes, to play a part in the sections and the *jeunesse dorée*, and to join the royalist bands and the *chouans*. Certainly many found excuses. The *Patrie* was no longer in danger. The war appeared to be at a standstill. The misery of the soldiers far surpassed that in the Year II. Moreover, the anniversary of the levy *en masse* was permitted to pass without calling up unmarried men who had reached the age of eighteen. Those who had been drafted in 1793 would serve indefinitely. In short, from the month of March on, out of a nominal total of 1·1 million men only 450,000 were present; is the shortage increased in the course of the summer. So much was this the case that on the Rhine the French finally lost the advantage of numbers. The same was true of matériel and equipment, for war manufactures and transports were turned back to the contractors for want of funds.

Happily for the Thermidorians, the disorganization did not have an immediate effect. Hence they were able to take possession of Holland, and shortly thereafter of the left bank of the Rhine. Better still, even though the French had lost their fighting energy, the Coalition itself was dissolving. If they were being forced towards peace, some of their enemies desired it no less eagerly. Since November, 1794, Prussia had been negotiating at Basel. At Paris, Count Carletti seemed willing to treat in the name of Tuscany. Finally, Spain attempted to negotiate.

The Thermidorians hoped to deal with each power separately, so as to divide the Allies; a general peace would involve delays from which England and Austria might benefit. But they also intended to propose that Prussia and Spain join with the Republic. Danton's diplomacy was being revived, and with it the anti-Austrian tradition and that of the Family Compact. There was nothing wrong in this. In the spring of 1793, Danton's policy had offered no prospect of success, because France was being invaded and defeated. It was illusory, and it aggravated the danger. Now, however, victory made it acceptable. True, it was doubtful that kings could be so quickly united with regicides; but there was no harm in trying.

Whether a peace or an alliance was concluded, it was intended that the other belligerents, especially Austria, would be compelled to cease fighting. The duration of their resistance would be determined by conditions in France. Certainly England would be the last to yield, and if the Republic hoped to make important conquests, years would undoubtedly pass before England would resign herself to them. In 1793 the Convention had let itself be won over to the policy of extending French territory to the 'natural boundaries' and to annexing Savoy, Nice, Belgium, and the left bank of the Rhine as well. Perhaps the Committee of the Year II did not feel that it was bound by these resolutions until a plebiscite had declared them constitutional, but after 9 Thermidor they became party issues. The counter-revolutionaries campaigned for peace at any price (which pleased a large part of the nation) and the abandonment of conquests that their complicity with the enemy imposed upon them. The republicans, who claimed that these advocates of 'old frontiers' were guilty of treason, came to think of the acquisition of natural boundaries in terms of defence of the Revolution.

The policy of the Committee of the Year II, moreover, had opened the way for the republicans by appealing to national feeling and prescribing that peoples who were resigned to servitude should be treated as enemies. The concern for security, self-interest, and the spirit of glory was consolidated thenceforth in a belief that the natural boundaries should be kept as a reward and as a guarantee of victory. Surrender of these regions would be opposed by the army. More and more it had come to enjoy great influence in the Republic, and the revolutionary government could have disbanded it only with difficulty. Certainly in the midst of the crisis of the Year III such an understanding would have been impossible. Moreover, the army was the real repository of republican loyalty, and the Thermidorians had called upon it to defend the Convention. If the army were to be preserved, a war was necessary. Even better, at the moment it was provisioning the nation. Under its protection requisition agencies despoiled the occupied countries (not overlooking works of art), and the Committee of Public Safety had ordered that no attention be paid to desires for 'reunion', because immediate annexation would have obstructed the operation.

The Thermidorians suppressed the Jacobin agencies, which they accused of pillage. A French administration was installed in Brussels, and another at Aix-la-Chapelle for the Rhineland, which was divided into seven districts. These dealt with local authorities through requisitions, paid in assignats, and until 1795, according to the Maximum. Assignats were also made legal tender in the Batavian Republic, and in their negotiations with the latter the Thermidorians insisted chiefly upon the war indemnity. This would place at their disposal large quantities of letters of exchange on Genoa and Switzerland, and these could be used to finance the campaigns on the Rhine and in the Alps. After having drained the occupied territories, they were tempted to annex them, in order to forestall an anti-French reaction (as after the decree of December 15, 1792), and to conquer others so as to maintain the army and replenish the Treasury. Undoubtedly, future difficulties were thereby increased, but the Thermidorians had lost control of events.

At first, however, they refrained from putting the annexations of 1793 into effect. They long hesitated to decide the matter, and they became divided—not over Savoy and Nice, which, of course, were not in question, but over Belgium, and even more over the left bank of the Rhine. Between conquest and renunciation, a strategic rectification of the existing frontier offered a middle ground that commended itself to the moderates as well as to the constitutional royalists. By annexing the Sambre-Meuse region, Namur, and Luxembourg, France would be perfectly protected. Nonetheless it seemed that so far as Belgium was concerned, annexation won the general support of the republicans. In the summer of 1795, however, Merlin of Douai and Merlin of Thionville were loath to annex the Germanic population of the Rineland, because they considered it not assimilable. In direct opposition was the Alsatian Reubell, who deemed the acquisition indispensable to preserve his province from invasion, and Sieyes, who resolved to attain the Rhine in order to profit from the compensations that Prussia would receive from the reshaping of the map of Germany. The uncertainty was prolonged until the middle of the period of the Directory.

Since the Thermidorians took no stand, they were careful at the outset not to tie their own hands. But the Treaty of Basel, with Prussia, although it decided nothing, determined their course. Reasoning like the Allies, they reached an understanding with the Coalition on condition that they receive their share. The rights of man were forgotten; or rather, the advantages which the annexed peoples were supposed to have derived therefrom masked the violence about to be done them. All that was lacking was a return to the old diplomacy. Through it, by means of secret articles, embarrassment could be relieved and treason disguised. Having dealt with Tuscany, on February 19, 1795, the Committee succeeded in having the Convention ratify the *fait accompli*; and on 27 Ventôse, Year III (March 17, 1795), it was able to secure a free hand in the conclusion of secret agreements which would not be subject to ratification.

THE TREATIES OF BASEL AND THE HAGUE (APRIL–MAY, 1795)

A Prussian envoy, Meyerinck, had arrived at Basel on November 22, 1794, but the discussions dragged on. Although Frederick William II wanted peace, he did not know what kind of peace he wanted. As always, two factions among his advisers were in conflict, and he vacillated between them. The ministers, primarily concerned with the territorial interests of the kingdom, had their eyes fixed only on Poland, and they meant to conclude an immediate, and therefore separate, peace with France at all costs. They did not wish to defend Mainz, and if the French demanded the left bank of the Rhine, they saw in such action only a pretext for claiming aggrandizement in Germany for themselves. Haugwitz was now in agreement with his colleagues on these matters.

Hardenberg, on the contrary, currently in charge of administering Prussian domains in Franconia, maintained that the king could not isolate his cause from that of the Empire without losing all influence over the princes. He would accept only a general peace, or at least one for the Empire. On December 22 the Diet demanded negotiations through the mediation of Prussia. The Rhenish princes wished to negotiate. Bavaria was absolutely unwilling to permit an Austrian garrison to enter Mannheim, and she supported the city so badly that it capitulated on December 24. In defending the interests of the princes,

Hardenberg hoped to increase Prussia's influence; but in order to win their confidence he first had to avert any dismemberment of Germany. Since he was of Hanoverian origin, the ministers accused him of being more German than Prussian. The sovereign, however, loath to treat with regicides or to abandon his allies, listened to him with approval.

Nevertheless the ministers triumphed, because the motives that had prompted Frederick William to negotiate were still valid. Prussia's position in the east was deteriorating. Since the fall of Warsaw, Catherine II was once more mistress of Poland. There she permitted a reign of terror, imprisoning the patriot nobles or deporting them to Siberia, confiscating their lands and those of the émigrés to the profit of her treasury and her favourites. Determined to proceed to the third and final partition in order to reach the line of the Bug River, she had no intention of excluding Prussia from it. It would have meant a fight she was neither ready nor willing to undertake. A war with Turkey was more to her advantage. Moreover, despite the gravest disagreements, the solidarity of the three accomplices persisted. Finally, Catherine still desired to have the Revolution crushed, and in order to vanquish Prussia she would have had to permit Austria, as well as herself, to negotiate with France. She was no less determined to reduce Frederick William's share to a bare minimum, and intended that the palatinates of Cracow and Sandomierz, partly occupied by Prussia, should go to Austria. By reducing Prussia's share she would re-establish the balance between the two Germanic powers, and would once more conciliate the emperor, at no cost to herself.

Thugut, who since the beginning of the year had increased his overtures to St. Petersburg, subscribed in advance to the tsarina's decisions. In his instructions to Ludwig Cobenzl, on November 29, 1794, he once more recognized the second partition on condition that he be granted Bavaria in exchange for the Netherlands, as well as a 'bonus' taken from France; or failing that, something at the expense of Venice. As for the third partition, he insisted upon the necessity of checking Prussian ambitions and of conceding Cracow and Sandomierz, along with Lublin and Radom, to Austria. An agreement was easily reached, and on January 3, 1795, the treaty was signed in two parts. The first, of which Berlin would be informed in due course, settled the Polish question once and for all, and granted Frederick William only Warsaw, with the northern part of the country extending as far as the Niemen and Bug rivers. The other, destined to remain secret, assured Russia of an Austrian alliance in the event of a war with Turkey.

The Prussian ambassador, Tauentzien, kept in the dark since August, had left no doubt at his court as to what was taking place. Consequently on December 8, 1794, Frederick William decided to send to Basel the Count von Goltz, whose Francophile sympathies were well known. The Committee of Public Safety, before authorizing Barthélemy to negotiate, required that an agent be sent to him. It wanted to learn about Prussian proposals for itself, and above all to strengthen its prestige by showing that it was Prussia herself who wanted peace. Accordingly Harnier came to Paris, and on January 7, 1795, he was informed of the views of the Republic. Finally, about this same time, Möllendorf abandoned Mainz and withdrew to Westphalia. Barthélemy then received instructions. They called for Prussian approval of the eventual annexation of the left bank of the Rhine, and in order that she be fully committed, the Committee dangled before Harnier the prospect of compensations. Barthélemy prepared a draft treaty, and to smooth the way still further, he pointed out that the provision might remain secret, since the cession would necessarily be postponed until such time as the Empire itself had concluded peace.

Still the king hesitated. The English were intriguing at Berlin, but without promising the money that might have prompted a change of policy. At this moment Goltz died—February 5, 1795—and Hardenberg replaced him. The choice seemed favourable to the enemies of peace. Indeed, Hardenberg did his utmost to postpone peace, contrived to arrive at Basel only on March 18, and proposed a new plan in the hope of affirming the neutrality of Prussia and of associating at least some of the princes with her cause. It was a matter of drawing a line of demarcation that would close off North Germany, including Hanover, from the belligerents. The Committee of Public Safety objected vehemently. Again, on 10 Germinal, Year III (March 30, 1795), although there were still 80,000 Prussians in Westphalia, it spoke only of an ultimatum.

Hardenberg would willingly have profited from this opposition in order to gain time, but on March 31 a letter from the king ordered him to negotiate at once if the French yielded. Circumstances necessitated moving the army of Westphalia to Poland. Barthélemy refrained from communicating the Committee's ultimatum and assumed responsibility for signing on the night of 15–16 Germinal (April 4–5). It was all the better, since the 'day' of the 12th had caused the Committee to change its opinion. The joy was real—Prussia was the first great power to recognize the Republic; but soon the realities of the situation became apparent. Publicly she had granted only her neutrality, and, through the line of demarcation, she even covered Hanover. But Barthélemy pointed out, with good reason, that this line also protected Holland, and that, by a secret article, Frederick William was abandoning the Stadtholder.

In fact, if the Committee had ordered the termination of discussions at Basel, it was because it suspected the Dutch of counting on Prussia. The envoys of Daendals and the Estates General, who had arrived in Paris on 20 Ventôse, Year III (March 10, 1795), courageously resisted the ruthless demands of the Committee by invoking their fidelity to France and the generosity of the Republic, for which they would vouch before their compatriots. On 10 Germinal (March 30) they received an ultimatum, and once the Treaty of Basel became known, Reubell and Sieyes left for the Hague, where they forced the Estates General to agree to the treaty of 27 Floréal (May 16). Holland ceded Flanders, Maestricht, and Venloo, and contracted a defensive and offensive alliance with France. She increased her army and navy, and agreed to maintain an army of occupation of 25,000 men until the peace. Most important of all, she was to pay an indemnity of 100 million florins. To revitalize her monetary circulation she would have to redeem some 30 million assignats. Engaged in the war against England, she was soon stripped of part of her colonies, and her trade suffered seriously.

At the same time discussions were opening at Basel between Barthélemy and Yriarte, the Spanish envoy, and at Bayonne as well. Godoy's overtures, preceding the battle of Black Mountain, aimed at nothing less than the creation of a kingdom for Louis XVII in the south of France, and the restoration of Roman Catholicism. The Committee demanded Guipuzcoa, Santo Domingo, and Louisiana. The death of Louis XVII removed the first difficulty. Then Moncey took the offensive, broke the Spanish centre, drove the left wing back on Bilbao, occupied Vittoria, and reached Miranda on the Ebro. Finally, the Quiberon expedition moderated the Committee's demands, and an agreement was hastily concluded on 4 Thermidor, Year III (July 22, 1795). Once again France was content, or nearly so, with neutralizing the enemy. She received only the Spanish part of Santo Domingo.

It remained to be seen whether Austria could now be dealt with, but success did not seem likely. In Messidor, Thugut had just rejected the Committee's proposals, which, as usual, were exaggerated. In fact, circumstances favoured the chancellor. On hearing of the peace of Basel, Catherine showed the keenest indignation, and moved 40,000 men into Courland, which had been recently annexed. Pitt offered the Austrians (whom he had already guaranteed a loan in London) the money maladroitly denied to the Prussians. On May 20, by a new treaty of alliance, subsidy of £600,000 for the maintenance of 200,000 men was agreed upon; and on September 28 Russia added her signature. Thus encouraged, protected by his allies against Prussia, and satisfied with his share of Poland, Thugut felt that he might be able to retake Belgium. Prussia, however, had not been notified of the third partition, and, besides, Thugut coveted Venice. Perhaps he might have accepted a partition of the Netherlands. Since the Committee rejected such a solution, might it not at least try to reduce Austria to impotence by getting the princes to help close Germany to the Habsburgs?

Hardenberg, having signed the convention of demarcation on 28 Floréal, Year III (May 17, 1795), moved in this direction. On July 3 the Diet decided to accept the good offices of Prussia in concluding peace with France, on the basis of the territorial integrity of Germany. The emperor's adherence was reserved, but it could not be doubted that if he refused, the princes would ignore him, as did the landgrave of Hesse-Cassel on August 28. Everything depended upon France, said Hardenberg. It was enough that she renounce the Rhine. Barthélemy asked nothing more, and in Prairial and Messidor the Committee hesitated. Merlin of Douai thought that the annexation might cause trouble. Aubry, Henry-Larivière, Gamon, and Boissy d'Anglas, more or less involved with the constitutional royalists, were obliged to hold out for the old limits. But in Thermidor, Reubell and Sieyes returned to the committees, in which the annexationists regained a majority; and at that moment the expedition prepared by the absolutists and the English strengthened the revolutionary feeling among the members of the Plain.

QUIBERON AND 13 VENDÉMIAIRE, YEAR IV

Following Windham's accession to power in July, 1794, the project for an expedition to the Vendée or to Brittany finally found supporters in the British government. Dundas opposed it, and Pitt was unenthusiastic. He did not disdain the aid which the royalists brought to the Coalition, and since October, 1794, his agent Wickham, installed at Basel and well provided with money, had been doing his best to support the absolutists as well as the constitutionalists. Pitt wished for the success of the latter, and since the Thermidorians expected to re-establish an elected government, hope for a peaceful restoration was revived. If the absolutists were once more taking up arms, he would scarcely look with favour upon sacrificing part of his effectives to them, because he foresaw their failure. Yet he yielded to the entreaties of Puisaye, who, although reputed to be a constitutionalist, offered to recruit regiments of émigrés for a sudden death blow. Some came from Germany, and to these were added prisoners of war who consented to enlist.

The English fleet repulsed Villaret's squadron, and on 9 Messidor, Year III (June 27, 1795) d'Hervilly's division was able to land on the Quiberon Peninsula in English uniforms. Time was lost because d'Hervilly and Puisaye quarrelled over the command, and the second division, under Sombreuil, did not rejoin them until mid-July. Informed through intercepted dispatches, Hoche thwarted the plans of the *chouans*. They succeeded in only a few surprise attacks, and the population did not rise. The republicans sealed off the peninsula with an entrenchment, and then, on the night of 2–3 Thermidor (July 20–21), they invaded it. The émigrés were driven into the sea or captured. The firing squad took care of 748, of whom 428 were nobles. Another landing party seized the Île d'Yeu, where the count of Artois appeared momentarily. Charette again took the field to help him; but the prince did not venture onto the Continent, and in

December the English re-embarked the expedition. The chief outcome of the affair was a new war in the Vendée.

The danger had been great, and the royalist threat could no longer be ignored. On the anniversary of July 14 the 'Marseillaise' once more resounded, and sans-culottes and soldiers were permitted to harry the 'black collars' ('*collets noirs*'). Yet the Plain did not break with the Right, and the 'Réveil du Peuple' still held its place. On 21 and 22 Thermidor, Year III (August 8 and 9, 1795), the Convention ordered the arrest of ten more Montagnards, including Fouché. Moreover, discussion of the draft constitution, presented on 5 Messidor (June 23) by Boissy d'Anglas, continued by common agreement until 5 Fructidor (August 22). On that day it was again decided that deputies placed under indictment or arrest might not be members of future legislative bodies; and on the next day the popular societies were suppressed.

The constitution was supposed to be ratified by plebiscite, after which the elections might proceed. At this time the republican Thermidorians, spurred on by a desire for self-preservation, decided that the most dangerous royalists were not those engaged in fighting the Republic by arms, but rather those who were about to succeed the members of the Convention. It was in vain that they had proscribed the Montagnards. The Convention remained collectively responsible for all that had been done in its name, and in order to crush the terrorists, a Thermidorian regicide was not worth a royalist, even a royalist in disguise. Moreover, monetary crisis and want would have brought disaster to any majority. Inflation continued on its headlong course. When the Maximum was suppressed, the paper in circulation was estimated at 8 billions; on 1 Brumaire, Year IV (October 23, 1795), it was appraised at 20 billions! After the harvest, poor in more than one region, it had been necessary to re-establish compulsory sales in the markets, as well as requisitions to supply them. The law of 7 Vendémiaire, Year IV (September 29, 1795), which lasted until 1797, restored, so far as grain was concerned, the programme of the Year II, except for price-fixing. The Assembly became intensely unpopular.

Accordingly, on 5 and 13 Fructidor, Year III (August 22 and 30, 1795), the Assembly decided that two-thirds of the future deputies (that is, 500) should be chosen from its own members.

Since no agreement could be reached as to the manner of selecting them, the choice was left to the voters, with the proviso that if the latter did not observe the qualification, the re-elected members of the Convention would fill their ranks by co-optation. Thus, although it did not occur until the Year VIII, they already considered co-optation a suitable means of excluding democrats and royalists to the advantage of the 'notables' who were attached to the Revolution and the Republic. But in voting the constitution, the Right had justly anticipated that the elections would bring it to power, and throughout France its partisans added their vehement protests to its own.

Although the constitution re-established property qualifications for voting, where the plebiscite was concerned universal suffrage applied, and the army and navy were permitted to participate. The results favoured the constitution. Since, despite everything, the new regime at least rid them of the Convention, many opponents doubtless resigned themselves to approving or abstaining. On 1 Vendémiaire, Year IV (September 23, 1795), the Convention declared the constitution and its supplementary decrees accepted.

The ferment increased in Paris. The Lepeletier section (the area around the stock exchange), the region of banks and speculators, took the lead and carried others with it. It proposed the formation of a central committee, and invited, with a reasonable degree of success, the primary assemblies of the entire Republic to imitate the capital. On 27 Fructidor, Year III (September 17, 1795), an insurrection broke out at Châteauneuf-en-Thymerais. Thus threatened, the Plain broke with the Right. It confirmed the decrees against émigrés and refractory clergy. On 7 Vendémiaire, Year IV (September 29, 1795), it voted a law for the control of religion, a law which forced priests to recognize the sovereignty of the people; and it established penalties against persons who attacked the sale of national property or advocated the re-establishment of monarchy. It no longer disdained the support of the sans-culottes, and on 12 Vendémiaire (October 4), it revoked the disarming of terrorists. This last measure sparked an explosion. The royalists directed the insurrection of 13 Vendémiaire; but all who feared the return of revolutionary government followed them.

Once again the army intervened. Its leader, Menou, having

conciliated the opposition, Barras once more took over the defence of the Convention. Of the associates he chose, it was Bonaparte, currently on the inactive list, who directed the decisive action. He crushed the revolt, and by so doing assured his own success. The ensuing repression was mild: only two of the leaders were shot. Nevertheless the event produced important consequences. The National Guard was disarmed. Paris remained under military occupation; its revolutionary role was ended. The Plain showed its spite against the Right by having three of its members arrested; and Fréron went to Provence to stop the White Terror.

The elections, begun on 20 Vendémiaire, Year IV (October 12, 1795), returned (it was thought) only 379 members of the Convention, almost all Rightists or suspected royalists; and there was some talk of invalidating them. Tallien demanded measures for 'public safety', and at these fearsome words the ferment subsided. Only at the last minute, on 4 Brumaire (October 26), did the members of the Convention consent to an amnesty, which saved their arrested colleagues as well as a number of terrorists. Nevertheless, as on the day following 9 Thermidor, the union of all patriots against the royalists and the Roman Church was once more the order of the day. It was under these conditions that the regime of the Directory began. But the consequences of the royalist attack did not stop there. The republican revival had a profound effect upon foreign policy.

THE CAMPAIGN OF 1795 AND THE ANNEXATION OF BELGIUM

With the living conditions of soldiers growing still worse, and with supplies lacking, Jourdan, at the head of the Army of the Sambre and Meuse, and Pichegru, shifted to that of the Rhine, had remained immobilized since winter. The impotence of the Thermidorians was now aggravated by the treason of Pichegru, who accepted subsidies from the prince of Condé. The latter got nothing for his money, because the general did not dare yield Huningue. At least he helped the enemy by refraining (unlike Jourdan) from using the few means at his disposal to prepare an offensive.

In August, however, he was forced to make a decision. The

emperor had just approved the vote of the Diet in favour of a peace that would respect the territorial integrity of Germany. Hardenberg reiterated that Prussia could not ally herself with France if the latter did not renounce the Rhine. The settlement of the partition of Poland, however, set the Austrians and Prussians at odds. On August 8, Berlin was finally informed of the treaty of January 3, and the response was anything but favourable. The Committee of Public Safety might try to win over Prussia by abandoning the Rhineland, or it might deal with Austria by limiting itself to a rectification of the Netherlands border. Because the annexationist tendency prevailed, and was reinforced by the reawakening of revolutionary spirit since Quiberon, war was the only solution. Formal orders finally reached the generals.

On 20 Fructidor, Year III (September 6, 1795), Jourdan crossed the Rhine, and Clerfayt, retreating beyond the Main, left Mainz exposed. Debouching from Mannheim, Pichegru was able to take him from behind, but not having concentrated his troops, he pushed forward only two weak divisions. These were resolutely attacked and routed. After their meeting on October 4 the two generals requested instructions from the Committee, but they received no reply. Doubtless the Committee was too busy with the problem of the Paris sections. Yet it found the time to prepare for the annexation of Belgium, proposed by Merlin of Douai and supported by Carnot. The Right protested. Lesage accused the Committee of making itself the tool of brigands, implicating the Montagnards, and forgetting that the initiative for annexation came from the Gironde. The Convention adopted the proposal on 9 Vendémiaire, Year IV (October 1, 1795). Furthermore, Merlin came out in favour of the Rhine frontier, but advocated that the decision be postponed until the general peace.

Events soon indicated, however, that such a peace would not be forthcoming in the near future. At the beginning of October, Wurmser, coming from the upper Rhine, appeared before Mannheim. Clerfayt was able to drive back Jourdan, who recrossed the Rhine, and to rout the troops besieging Mainz. Pichegru stayed where he was. In November the Austrians, turning against him, invaded the Palatinate, pushed the French back to the Queich, and retook Mannheim. During this time

Russia joined the Anglo-Austrian coalition, and on October 24 the king of Prussia resigned himself to being content with his share of Poland (Warsaw and the land north of the Narew). Reassured in the east, victorious in the west, and re-established on the left bank of the Rhine, Thugut thought only of preparing for the spring campaign. The Thermidorians, incapable of imposing a general peace by force of arms, had waived it by turning towards annexation. Would the constitution that they were inaugurating survive the test of war?

THE CONSTITUTION OF THE YEAR III

The Convention was characterized by inconsistencies that loom large in the history of legislatures. It followed policies so contradictory that at first glance it seems impossible to find a common feature among them. One, however, is apparent—the will of the Third Estate to confirm the victory won over the aristocracy in 1789. Thus the gap between the Constituent Assembly and the Convention was not so great as has been thought. From this point of view, revolutionary solidarity continued up to the time of the Montagnards.

In the eyes of the Montagnards, however, civil and foreign war required an authoritarian government and so long as this lasted, the Revolution was condemned to a dictatorship. On the other hand, they planned a social democracy, and they relied upon the sans-culottes to institute it. The Third Estate dissociated itself from this policy. In the thinking of the members of the Constituent Assembly, the Revolution of 1789 established liberty and conferred political and social power on the upper middle class. Nor did the majority of the Convention think otherwise. In this guiding principle may be seen the importance of the Thermidorian Reaction. Through the medium of the Jacobins it revived the tradition of the Constituent Assembly.

Constitutional monarchists and republican Thermidorians were undoubtedly divided as to the title and attributes of the head of the executive power; but in drafting the Constitution of the Year III, they agreed on the necessity of re-establishing an elective and liberal government, as well as on the place of the 'notables'—that is, well-to-do men of property, at least—in the political and economic leadership of the country. 'We should be governed by the best,' said Boissy d'Anglas. 'The best are those who are the most educated and the most interested in maintaining the laws. With few exceptions, you will find such men only among those who, owning property, are attached to the country in which it is located, to the laws which protect it, to the peace and order which preserve it, and who owe to this property and to the affluence which it yields, the education which makes them the ones to discuss, with wisdom and accuracy, the advantages and disadvantages of the laws that determine the fate of the land. . . . A country governed by landowners is in the social order; that which is governed by nonlandowners is in the state of nature.'

This concept had had some influence on the positive work of the Thermidorians, which was considerable. Faithful to the spirit of the eighteenth century, like the Montagnards they continued the preparation of the civil code and the metric system. Likewise they proceeded with the creation or the restoration of research agencies and higher education: the Bureau of Longitudes, the Museum of Natural History, the Museum of French Monuments, the Polytechnic School, and the School of Medicine. On the eve of their dissolution they decided to establish the Institute of France. But the central schools, which they had prescribed in each department for training disciples, did not suit the young bourgeoisie. After having limited the number of primary schools in the Year III, they ruined them on 3 Brumaire, Year IV (October 25, 1795), by discontinuing the pay of the teachers. Shortage of money provided a pretext, but like Boissy d'Anglas, many felt it imprudent to favour the creation of a 'parasitic and ambitious minority' of educated poor. The financial motive also resulted in the abandonment of a 'national charity' organization. If the second project for a civil code did not materialize, at least a mortgage code was voted, the inheritance laws of the Year II were weakened, national property was no longer divided up, and there was talk of halting the partition of common lands.

The Constitution of the Year III crowned the reaction and facilitated its development. The new declaration of rights which preceded it omitted the famous article, 'Men are born and remain free and equal in rights,' because of its dangerous implications. Care was taken to specify that 'equality means that the law is the same for all men'. Also lacking were the articles of the Declaration of 1793 that justified social democracy. It goes without saying that economic liberty was expressly confirmed. Finally, a declaration of duties was added, even though some of the citizens were denied the right to participate in the making of laws that all were ordered to respect.

In effect, suffrage ceased to be universal. True, the Thermidorians proved in some respects more democratic than the members of the Constituent Assembly. If they suppressed the legislative referendum and re-established the representative system outright, at the same time they maintained popular consultation on constitutional matters, required only the payment of a nominal tax by active citizens, and even permitted a voluntary payment. But this was really superficial. Suffrage in two stages remained, and the electors designated by active citizens had to be owners of property valued at 200 days' labour in communes of 6,000 inhabitants or more; otherwise they had to be landlords of dwellings worth 150 days' labour in rent or of a rural property with a rent equal to 200 days' labour. Thus about 30,000 electors, chosen inevitably from among the 'notables', constituted the 'legal country'.

Regardless of these property qualifications, they elected a legislative body consisting of two Councils. Bicameralism was no longer a danger now that the possibility of a house of lords was not feared. The Council of Five Hundred, whose members were at least thirty years of age, were to vote 'resolutions' that the Council of Elders, numbering 250 members at least forty years of age (married or widowed), would transform into laws if they found them appropriate. The government was confided to a Directory of five members (also at least forty years of age), chosen by the Elders from a list of fifty drawn up by the Five Hundred. This Directory was to name the ministers, and they would be responsible only to it.

The Thermidorians took precautions against both Jacobins and counter-revolutionaries. The former seemed especially under fire. Instead of a mayor and a 'commune' for Paris and other large cities, there were to be several municipalities. A military guard would protect the government and the Councils, and the Elders might have the latter moved out of Paris. By once more authorizing clubs, they transformed them into simple public gatherings. The legislative body had the power to suspend freedom of the press for one year, and to permit the search of homes. The Directory might cause the arrest of anyone suspected of conspiracy, without the intervention of legal formalities. With civil war continuing, however, the counter-revolutionaries remained the most abused. The laws against émigrés and priests were still on the books. The law of 3 Brumaire, Year IV (October 25, 1795), served as more than a reminder. It barred relatives of émigrés from holding office; and the property of both émigrés and Vendémiairists remained confiscated. Furthermore, the measures directed against the Jacobins also threatened royalists, whether they were absolutists or constitutionalists.

In short, the Thermidorians imagined that the Republic continued to live, although those who had founded it were pushed aside; that it was bourgeois, although part of the bourgeoisie was denied power; that it remained authoritarian, although it was styled liberal. Their adversaries heaped sarcasm on them. How many partisans would there now be, since the Convention had bequeathed bankruptcy and war to France? Whether it was a gamble for the Thermidorians to count upon the elective regime would be determined by the Two-thirds Decree. While they were reproaching the Montagnards for having founded a dictatorship by suspending elections, they re-established elections, but were careful to make certain that they were 'rigged'. They came close to arriving at co-optation pure and simple. If they failed in future elections, they would maintain themselves through *coups d'état* that would restore dictatorship.

With war continuing at home and on the frontiers, it was another gamble for all to unite in refusing the government stability, speedy decisions, and energetic action. Elections were to be held annually to renew the Councils by one-third, the municipalities by one-half, and the Directory and the departmental administrations each by one-fifth. As a precaution against the omnipotence of the state, the bourgeoisie increased the independent powers of each of them. The danger was obvious, and the Constitution granted the Directory extensive powers: the 'regulatory power', that is, the right to issue decrees, which it extended *ad infinitum*; control of diplomacy, war, general police, and supreme authority in local administration.

If decentralization reappeared in the elective departmental

and municipal administrations, authority was nonetheless concentrated and governmental control reinforced. A single 'central administration' of five members sat in the chief town of each department, and the districts disappeared. Towns of more than 5,000 inhabitants were reduced to government by municipal officers, and other communes to an agent and his aide; and the municipalities consisted of meetings of the agents at the canton seat. The Directory might annul decisions of the local administration without appeal; it might remove their members and replace them if none remained, and in any case to the contrary, co-optation was applied; and for each administration it named a commissioner chosen from the department.

Yet this regime was a far cry from the centralization of the Jacobins or the Consulate. Taxation remained in the hands of the elected administrations, and the Directory did not have control over the Treasury. Unless it could resort to military commissions, the Directory lacked the power of coercion, for judges remained elective. The worst feature, however, was that there was no guarantee of co-operation between the Directory and the Councils. The Directory had no legislative initiative, it communicated with the Councils only through messages, and it could neither adjourn nor dissolve them. Conversely, unless they rejected the budget or impeached the holders of executive power, the Councils possessed no control over the Directory. Nor did they have any contact with the ministers. As for amending the Constitution, it could be done, but the process involved a minimum delay of six years. To modify it a new *coup d'état* would be necessary, and this it could not survive.

II

THE VICTORIOUS OFFENSIVE OF THE REVOLUTION

CHAPTER FOUR

Europe and the Revolution at the End of 1795

THE TREATIES OF BASEL marked a turning point in the conflict between the Revolution and aristocratic Europe. Up to that time the latter, virtually of one mind, had beset France on all sides. Could she defend herself? Her enemies thought her lost, but the revolutionary government proved that they were mistaken. Henceforth it was the victorious and expanded Republic that took the offensive in the midst of a divided Europe. Would it be able to conquer under Thermidorian leadership? Hope revived among those who, but yesterday, seemed vanquished.

THE NEUTRALS AND THE COALITION

Prussia, Spain, and Tuscany had reverted to the neutrality that had proved so profitable to Switzerland, the Scandinavian states, Genoa, and Venice. Grouping about her the princes behind the line of demarcation, Prussia congratulated herself on having planned a North German confederation, which, in fact, would dismember the Empire to her advantage. Holland was in the hands of the French. The Coalition, rejuvenated by the end of the summer of 1795, counted only England and Austria as serious belligerents.

England had always been the mainspring of the Coalition.

She paid the Continental Powers to continue the fight while she used her own troops and ships to secure control of the seas and possession of colonies. But Catherine II also thought primarily of her own interests, so that her support was only nominal. Although constantly preaching a crusade against the Revolution, she sent others to conduct it. Meanwhile she confined herself to giving Austria a little money and to dispatching some vessels to the North Sea and the English Channel. The princes of South Germany were ready to capitulate as soon as the invasion took place. Sardinia would follow their example if Austrian troops were removed, and the other Italian states avoided hostilities. Thus the armies of the Republic would have to deal only with those of the Habsburgs.

Vienna and London were by no means in agreement. England wished Austria to retake Belgium and Holland from France; she was welcome to whatever other territory she might acquire. But Thugut had little interest in the Low Countries, and Germany concerned him even less than Italy. By choice, his attention became focused upon the possessions of Venice. The dynastic and naturally polymorphous Habsburg state would have had no more reason than Prussia to complain of the war had she been able to substitute for distant Belgium, if not Bavaria, at least the territories of His Most Serene Highness. With the completion of the partition of Poland and the promise of subsidies, Austria would have considered peace only if the French renounced their conquests and left her a free hand.

Such was not exactly the case with England at the end of 1795. She did not feel personally threatened—such fear was to come only after Campo Formio, and then her effort gave her courage—and the war was profitable to the ruling class. Finally, Windham, Grenville, and the king wanted to hold fast, to pursue the crusade preached by Burke, to rid the world of the disturbers of the social order. But Pitt was worried. Quite apart from the disappointments of Quiberon and 13 Vendémiaire, prospects on the Continent were not bright. For the conquest of Belgium, Thugut demanded a Russian army, the promise of aggrandizement at the expense of Holland and France, and assurance that the Scheldt and Antwerp would remain open to navigation. Above all, conditions at home were not encouraging.

British commerce, relieved of French competition, had been

prospering. Even though the debt was increasing, finances seemed sound, and it was unthinkable that the Bank of England might fail. Republican conquests and the treaties of Basel, however, changed the situation; extensive markets were lost to Britain, and competition from French commerce revived among the neutrals. Moreover, the harvest of 1795 was extremely poor. The exasperated masses were stirring. Great rallies were held, and on October 29, while George III was on his way to open Parliament, his carriage was stoned. The speech from the throne indicated that the government would negotiate if France would take the initiative.

THERMIDORIAN PREDILECTIONS

The Constitution of the Year III forbade the Directory to declare in secret treaties the alienation of any specified Republican territory, including (apart from forgotten Senegal) the colonies. In the opinion of the Thermidorians this prescription was equally valid for treaties submitted to the Councils for ratification. Their thinking in this connection was like that of the Jacobins. Furthermore, they held that the law of 9 Vendémiaire, Year IV (October 1, 1795), had been implicitly ratified by plebiscite at the same time as the Constitution. Hence the nine 'Belgian' departments were considered within the 'constitutional limits'. How, therefore, could any agreement be reached with England? Ensuing events were to prove that it could be done if England were satisfied on the seas and in the colonies, and if Continental peace were securely established. The French had no intention, however, of recognizing the world empire of 'perfidious Albion'. Their ignorance of the resources of capitalism still led them to regard British power, based on credit and exports, as a colossus with feet of clay. Furthermore, already in control of Holland and the Bank of Amsterdam, they counted on gaining the support of Spain in short order.

As for the Continental peace, another concept of limits, that of 'natural boundaries', posed a potential obstacle. Thugut had no intention of ruining imperial authority by abandoning the Rhineland. Nonetheless, in this connection the opinion of the Thermidorians was by no means unanimous; the disastrous results of the autumn campaign of 1795 had discouraged many of them. Ultimately the Councils, and despite Reubell, the Directory itself, proved very cautious. In any case, nobody thought of expanding beyond the natural frontiers, or of reviving Girondin or Hébertist propaganda. For the moment, however, the Thermidorians deemed it inexpedient for the Republic, enlarged and hopeful of an alliance with Prussia (similar to the engagement with Spain), to moderate its ambitions officially.

Traditional diplomacy once more became the order of the day. Each party, desirous of peace, waited for the other to take the first step, and by so doing, manifested an inferiority complex. Semi-official attempts at negotiation produced no results. Everything depended upon the next campaign; but in the minds of the Coalition Powers it depended also upon the manner in which the Constitution of the Year III was applied in France.

CHAPTER FIVE

The First Directory

On 4 Brumaire, Year IV (October 26, 1795), the Thermidorians relinquished power and resumed it at one and the same time. Thermidorians and 'Directorials' were identical: the same men, the same objectives, the same methods. Having destroyed the revolutionary government and driven out the Jacobins, they ended with the Two-thirds Decree and the laws of disallowance. The history of the First Directory confirmed these portents.

INAUGURATION OF THE DIRECTORY

According to the decrees, the electoral assembly in each department had first drawn up a principal list of members of the Convention—those who would constitute two-thirds of the deputation. It had been anticipated that the best-known reactionaries and moderates would be nominated in several constituencies; in fact, thirty-nine departments nominated Lanjuinais, thirty-seven Henry-Larivière, and thirty-six Boissy d'Anglas. Hence, a supplementary list of three times the number was required. From this list the members of the Convention who were to fill seats left vacant by option would be chosen, in the order in which they had been elected. Then the electors would have free choice of the new third. With some four exceptions, the members seeking re-election were defeated.

On the basis of the official list of 6 Brumaire (October 28), historians have claimed that only 379 members of the Convention were chosen; but at the time, all the results were not known, and the process was so complicated that very few contemporaries could have made an accurate count. A study by J. Suratteau[1] has shown that, in fact, 413 members of the Convention entered the new Councils: 394 retained by the electoral assemblies, and the 19 representatives from Corsica and the colonies, whose terms were extended by law. Since the legislative body had to be composed of 500 men, the results still fell short of the mark. The re-elected deputies, gathered in an Electoral Assembly of France, provided for the remainder. They did this by restoring to the departmental supplementary lists those of their colleagues whom they believed eligible, without regard to imbalance in the geographic distribution of seats. Of the 105 thus chosen, 11 had already been elected; so only 94 were actually sustained. When the new third added 4 others, the Councils received 511 members of the Convention all told.

The electoral assemblies seemed generally to prefer the most colourless individuals. The quota of the Electoral Assembly of France was somewhat more to the advantage of the Left, while the new third reinforced the Right with constitutional monarchists or avowed counter-revolutionaries. All in all, more regicides remained in power than has been assumed—158—besides 37 who, after voting for the death of Louis XVI, had called for a reprieve. It may be noted, however, that some had already changed their positions. Of the deputies whose opinions may be determined with some degree of certainty, 305 were openly republican, mostly Thermidorians, and 158 royalists, mostly liberals. Between these two groups, 226 considered themselves attached to the Constitution of the Year III, provided, however, that the regime adopt a moderate policy. Hence the Thermidorians could not govern without the support of this last group. The result was that, as had been the case since 9 Thermidor, they had to conciliate them as circumstances warranted in order to stay in power. For the time being, the victory of 13 Vendémiaire disrupted the ranks of their adversaries and impressed the moderates; and they succeeded in

[1] 'Les elections de l'an IV' in *Annales historiques de la Révolution française*, XXIII (1951), 374–94, and XXIV (1952), 30–62.

dictating the choice of Directors, which was a matter of major importance.

Apart from five regicides, the list of persons presented by the Five Hundred consisted chiefly of nonentities. The importance of the five, however, was such that the Elders chose them: La Revellière-Lépeaux, Reubell, Letourneur, Barras, and Sieyes. Sieyes declined. In Thermidor he had proposed constitutional articles that would have weakened the authority of the state. Blaming the new regime for his failure, he withdrew to the side lines to become its gravedigger, and Carnot was chosen in his place. This Directory was as lacking in cohesion as the great Committee of Public Safety had been. On one side were Reubell, the most determined of the lot, and La Revellière-Lépeaux, an honest man without talent or prestige. But they were far from being in perfect agreement. The first was a former Montagnard, the second a violently anti-Jacobin Girondin. On the other side was Carnot, supported by Letourneur. Suspected of democratic sympathies, Carnot was accepted to direct the war; but in time his conservative and authoritarian character pushed him towards the Right. Between them was Vicomte Barras, the acknowledged 'saviour' of 9 Thermidor and 13 Vendémiaire; but no one trusted him. He thought only of himself, surrounded himself with disreputable men and loose women, and was considered (with good reason) to be venal.

These five men organized a secretariat (which Bonaparte inherited) and provided for six ministers, to which a seventh, that of general police, was soon added. Merlin of Douai became minister of justice, and later minister of police, which office he ultimately yielded to Cochon. Ramel-Nogaret soon became minister of finance and held the post until the Year VII. Far more difficult was the selection of the local assemblies and judges. Numerous electoral assemblies, permitted to sit for only ten days, had not fulfilled their task, and the Constitution forbade them to hold special sessions. The Councils resigned themselves to permitting the Directory to fill the vacancies. As refusals, resignations, and removals multiplied, it assumed the choice of replacements when the majority of members of a body disappeared. So the power of the Directory grew, quite apart from the fact that its decrees infringed on the competence of the Councils, which protested in vain.

The civil war continued. Hoche subdued Charette and Stofflet (who were executed), and then the *chouans*, by methodically disarming the population. In June it was possible to dissolve the Army of the West, but scattered groups of insurgents remained and turned to brigandage. For several weeks unity among republicans remained the order of the day. The government permitted the Jacobins to reopen their clubs, principally that of the Panthéon, and to publish their newspapers, notably Babeuf's *Tribune of the People*. It accorded them public offices everywhere. But the monetary crisis soon disrupted the agreement.

MONETARY CRISIS AND THE CONSPIRACY OF THE 'EQUALS'

Just as the Directory was being installed, inflation was reaching its final stages: the hundred-franc assignat was worth 15 sous, and prices rose hourly. The scale of national property had to be suspended, and creditors were saved from ruin only by the declaration of a moratorium. In four months the issue of paper money doubled to reach 39 billions. Paper was printed each night for the following day. The Councils accepted a forced loan, but to no avail. Funds came in only after a long delay. On 30 Pluviôse, Year IV (February 19, 1796), assignats were discontinued.

An immediate return to specie seemed impossible. Not more than 300 millions were in circulation (so it was said), as contrasted with some 2 billions in 1789. Financiers offered to create a bank that, by taking control of the sale of national property, would issue notes and provide advances for the Republic. They would have the advantage of a 'superbank', capable of accepting the commercial paper that they discounted for their clients, and thus they could increase the volume of their business. The attempt failed. If they had to return to paper money, the Councils wanted to retain control over it. On 28 Ventôse, Year IV (March 18, 1796), they created 2·4 billions' worth of land warrants (*mandats territoriaux*), valid for the purchase of national property by the first taker, at an estimated price and without competitive bidding. Six hundred millions' worth would redeem the assignats at 30 to 1, while the rest would go to the Treasury. No one had any confidence in the land warrants, and their exchange would have been impossible without the help of foreign credit. In July people would no longer accept them, so the government resolved to return once more to specie. The principal result of this expedient was to squander most of the remaining national property for the benefit of the bourgeoisie and the speculators.

The winter had been frightful, the more so since the peasants no longer fulfilled requisitions and markets remained deserted. In the countryside, vagabondage and the brigandage of the '*chauffeurs*' (bandits) spread to such an extent that even mobile columns of the National Guard and the establishment of the death penalty were of no avail. In Paris many would have died of hunger if the Directory had not continued the distribution of food; as it was, in the Year IV more than 10,000 deaths were recorded in the department of Seine. Poverty produced endemic agitation, which made the Jacobins' recriminations more fearsome. The Montagnards who had been declared ineligible, notably Lindet, were conducting a campaign against the bankers' plan, which was rejected on 3 Ventôse, Year IV (February 22, 1796). On the 7th the Directory retaliated by closing the clubs. It began to remove Jacobins from office and to prosecute their newspapers. Once more under the ban, they resorted to conspiracy, and the Thermidorian adventure began all over again.

This time, however, Jacobin activity took a new form, because Babeuf and Buonarroti assumed its leadership. They hoped to achieve true equality, and it is from this principle that the plot derives its name, 'The Conspiracy of the Equals'. Thus socialism, heretofore but a literary utopia, entered political history. These two men were steeped in a moralizing, often ascetic, communism, which had attracted many writers in the eighteenth century. The revolutionary proclamation of civil and political equality (which they considered ineffectual), the strong urge to own property that they saw in the peasants, and the partial nationalization of the economy in the Year II matured their thinking.

Babouvism bore the mark of its time: the peasant would continue to work his fields and would bring his harvest to the common storehouse. Aiming at distribution rather than production, in which capitalist concentration did not yet threaten individualism, the doctrine remained utopian. Still, many of its features seem indicative of things to come. The plan appealed to the self-interest of the proletariat, 'their best guide'. Nevertheless, not relying upon the subjugated people whom it was supposed to free, it vested the revolutionary mission in an intellectual minority. Thus it stated precisely the idea of popular dictatorship that came from Marat and some Hébertists. Yet most of the conspirators were not advocates of communism—they were simply bourgeois democrats and a few members of the Convention who wanted to regain power.

Warned by an informer, Carnot took charge of their suppression, and thenceforth he hunted down his former battle companions with grim relentlessness. Babeuf and Buonarroti were arrested on 21 Floréal, Year IV (May 10, 1796), and their papers facilitated the imprisonment of many others. At the end of August the accused were taken to Vendôme, where the High Court was located. On the night of 23–24 Fructidor (September 9–10) their partisans attempted to win over the soldiers of the camp at Grenelle. Carnot was aware of their plan and purposely kept silent. Surprised by cavalry, some were killed, and many others were arrested and handed over to a military commission. The Court of Cassation ultimately declared the commission incompetent—after thirty had already been shot! The trial finally began at Vendôme in February, 1797, and lasted for three months. On 8 Prairial, Year V (May 27, 1797), Babeuf and Darthé were guillotined.

THE NEW ANTI-JACOBIN REACTION

As in the Year III, the split between the Directory and the Jacobins altered the political equilibrium. The Left followed only with bad grace, and the Right took the lead. Besides, Benjamin Constant (whom Madame de Staël, just returned to France, had pushed into the arena) was urging the constitutional royalists to rally on behalf of the establishment of a solid conservative party. The Directory removed the functionaries whom the reactionaries denounced and replaced them with its own candidates. For example, it sent the royalist Willot to be commander in Provence, where he permitted the White Terror to flare up again. In the Councils the Right demanded repeal of the law of 3 Brumaire, Year IV (October 25, 1795), and even the amnesty of the 4th. It secured only an extension of the ban on office-holding by persons who had profited therefrom.

The Right was primarily interested in ameliorating the condition of priests. Carnot also wished for a reconciliation with the papacy and took advantage of the peace negotiations that Pius VI, threatened by Bonaparte's army, had just begun. Real agreement was possible, for the papal envoy had in his possession a bull inviting the clergy to recognize the government of the Republic. He did not present it to the Directory, however, and because the latter demanded that the sovereign pontiff revoke all his decisions relative to French affairs since 1789, a rupture ensued. The bull, however, reached the Directory, which published it, and by so doing it turned royalist priests and constitutional clergy against each other once more. The Right, at least, was able to obtain abrogation of the article of the law of 3 Brumaire that revived terrorist laws against the clergy; but the question remained: Were the laws themselves thereby revoked? The administrations that were still republican answered negatively. Nevertheless, on Cochon's orders, the application of the laws once again became favourable to the clergy. Regulation of religion was abandoned, émigrés and deported persons returned freely, and the sale of national property was halted.

Also, as in the Year III, the reaction benefited the royalists. Louis XVIII, who had withdrawn to Blankenburg, home of the duke of Brunswick, continued to refuse any reconciliation with the constitutionalists unless he could forbid them to prepare favourable elections; and he authorized the absolutists to resort to violence. His agency at Paris entered into dealings with the guard of the Directory, which, when exposed, brought the leader of the conspiracy (Abbé Brottier) and its chief participants to prison. One of them, Duverne de Presle, betrayed the Anglo-royalist plot, which the government kept secret until 18 Fructidor. In addition, the agency organized an association of the Friends of Order. This the constitutionalist Dandré, aided by the *chouans*, transformed into a Philanthropic Institute, which took deep root in Bordeaux. Wickham provided funds to maintain their newspapers and to organize electoral propaganda; but in each region the reactionaries themselves were busy, and they certainly did not lack arguments

Most of the nation had little love for the Old Regime, and

it cared nothing for Louis XVIII. No longer fearing their return, it thought only of paying lower taxes and of being freed from the necessity of fighting. Still, the war subsided in France and was enjoying success abroad. Public opinion considered the most important tasks to be internal pacification, the re-establishment of security, and the revival of prosperity. It was greatly concerned with religious discord. It was oblivious to the incompatibility between the Revolution and Catholicism, which many refractory clergy and republicans proclaimed. Besides, the constitutional priests denied it; and the juring clergy (*soumissionaires*), distinguishing (like Abbé Emery) between the temporal and spiritual, politics and religion, refrained from stressing it.

Faith, and still more often, habit, and the conviction that it was necessary to teach morality and to preach submission in the family and society in the name of God, bound most Frenchmen to the traditional religion. The civil religion with its Tenth Day ceremonies, which certain bourgeois discovered in Masonic lodges (now reopened) and in Theophilanthropy (founded at the beginning of 1797 by the bookseller Chemin and protected by La Revellière-Lépeaux), did not interest the masses. In any case, they preferred one day's rest in seven to one in ten. Finally the schism led to quarrels even in the home. The constitutional church lost ground; but it survived, and in 1797 it held a national council. In certain towns (Sedan, for example) it remained dominant. Among the Roman Catholics, divisions became exasperating, and the hierarchy was wavering. The attraction of peace made the secularist agitation by the men of the Directory unpopular.

They were still more widely reproached for the various evils resulting from the monetary situation and the deplorable state of public finance. The catastrophe of the land warrants had forced a new moratorium, and until their last days the Councils strove to reconcile the opposing interests of debtors and creditors. To this problem was added the uncertainty of the inheritance of relatives of émigrés. Then the miseries of deflation were added to those of inflation. Since specie remained rare, credit was scarce; and prices fell because the harvest of 1796 was so abundant that regulation was discontinued.

This combination of circumstances intensified the government's difficulty in maintaining public services and financing the war. It had informed the Councils of the necessity of balancing the regular budget and of finding additional resources for the army and navy. But the Councils never really acknowledged this problem. They granted credits desultorily, voted taxes tardily, refused to re-establish indirect taxes, and despite all this, blamed the Directory—as if it were enough to provide for expenses of the Treasury. The Right hoped to force the government into making peace by cutting off its supplies. The Left quibbled with it in order to diminish its authority. Both feared the voters. Although taxpayers were exempt to a lesser degree than has been supposed, money was still lacking. As for the war, the sale of national property—once more conducted by auction since 16 Brumaire, Year V (November 6, 1796)—was its sole and inadequate source of revenue.

As in the case of Louis XVI, the Directory was thus reduced to expedients. It persisted in making use of requisitions in redeeming bonds. Above all, it contracted with financiers of all types, munitions makers, and 'dealers in services'. It reimbursed their advances only in driblets, according to an order decreed each *décade* as funds became available. The exact amount of these funds was unknown, because the accounts of the Treasury and the collectors were so hopelessly confused. The Directory also granted them national property—diamonds, such as the Regent, and Batavian rescriptions paid by Holland under the terms of the Treaty of The Hague—in order to provide collateral. It authorized them to subscribe to accommodation bills, which the banks discounted and for which the Treasury stood surety. Finally, warrants were accepted in payment for national property, and there was a return to the 'anticipations' of the Old Regime, which delegated to creditors the timber cut in the national forests or the income from taxes in certain departments.

War contractors calculated their prices in terms of risks, and since they were ransoming the state, claimed that they were justified in countenancing dishonest exactions by impecunious officials. Nor did they refrain from corrupting the latter or making overtures to politicians. Everyone knew of the embezzlements by Barras and Talleyrand, among others, and of the unscrupulous schemes of Ouvrard and Hainguerlot. By their scandalous dealings with the Republic, the Dijon and the Flachat companies gained the Directory the discredit that is always associated with governments whose finances are unsound.

It was still more dangerously compromised by the damage suffered by private citizens, already severely affected by the monetary crisis and deflation. The lot of bondholders was pitiful. They received only 'quarter bonds', payable in specie when possible, and 'three-quarter bonds', the use of which (like the requisition bonds) was limited to the payment of taxes and the purchase of national property. To secure money, bondholders and peasants sold these bonds for next to nothing to the first bidders. The entire country suffered from the decay of public services: the constabulary sold their horses because they could not feed them; the highways were falling into ruin; courts, schools, and relief were left to the care of equally wretched local administrations. Nothing could be done without money, and it had to come from the taxpayers; but as usual the government was made responsible for these difficulties as well as for the deficiencies.

THE ELECTIONS OF THE YEAR V AND THE CONFLICT OF THE DIRECTORY AND THE COUNCILS

The Directory scarcely responded to opposition propaganda. Perhaps it may have felt that this would be offset by Bonaparte's victories; but it was mistaken. The elections of Germinal, Year V, for replacing a third of the deputies—one-half of the 'perpetuals'—brought a stunning success for the Right. Only some dozen departments remained faithful to the Republic. The choice of individuals such as Pichegru, Willot, Imbert-Colomès, and Royer-Collard was typical. The Directory was divided. Reubell recommended dictatorial measures, while Carnot advocated an understanding with the new majority. Fate deprived the latter of his friend Letourneur, whom the Councils, meeting on 1 Prairial, Year V (May 20, 1797), replaced with the diplomat Barthélemy, a constitutional monarchist who proved to be no man of action. With which side would Barras align himself? For the moment, at least, he did not disavow the royalist tempters.

The Right, which met at the Clichy Club, was unable to agree on tactics. Pichegru, elected to the presidency of the Five Hundred, never dared take the initiative by resorting to violence. The constitutional monarchists would leave the *chouans* alone, but would not help them. Those who formed what was called the 'belly' preferred to temporize. The reactionaries proved especially aggressive in the provinces. The Philanthropic Institute took root everywhere. Many administrations and courts were exceedingly harsh towards Republicans. In Paris and the south the latter tried to unite for resistance through 'constitutional circles', but the Council suppressed them.

At the outset they had repealed the law of 3 Brumaire, Year IV (October 25, 1795), which forbade relatives of émigrés to hold public office, and they ultimately abrogated the terrorist laws against priests. The still-numerous Left, however, secured several concessions. In a 'balancing act', public offices were opened to persons pardoned on 4 Brumaire, Year IV (October 26, 1795); yet a declaration of obedience to the laws remained compulsory for the clergy. In the eyes of republicans, however, the chief peril arose from the efforts of the Right to deprive the Directory of control of the government and direction of the war. Reduction of the executive power would pave the way to a restoration. Meanwhile this would be advantageous to Austria and England, which had been engaged in negotiations since the armistice of Leoben. To this end, on 30 Prairial (June 18), Gilbert-Desmolières managed to effect the transfer of all financial administration from the Directory to the Treasury, which was filled with reactionaries. The Elders rejected the recommendation. Already, however, Reubell and La Revellière-Lépeaux had decided to be done with them. Barras joined them. Having been informed by Bonaparte of the proof of Pichegru's treason(found among the papers of d'Antraigues), he undoubtedly feared that the royalists would force him out of office.

There was no question of resorting to popular force. La Revellière-Lépeaux would not even permit an appeal to the sans-culottes for help, as on 13 Vendémiaire. Thus the use of the army was the only alternative. Moreau could not be counted on; he permitted royalist propaganda to spread in the Army of the Rhine. Also, during the course of the campaign he had seized, in the baggage of an émigré, evidence which compromised Pichegru; but he kept this from the Directory until 18 Fructidor. On the other hand, Bonaparte and Hoche were favourable. Hoche, now at the head of the Army of the Sambre and Meuse, was nearer, and on 13 Messidor, Year IV (July 1, 1796), he dispatched troops to Paris. Carnot, however, was unaware of the plans of the 'triumvirs', and insisted that the Right be conciliated by a change of ministry. On 26 Messidor (July 14) he was cruelly betrayed by his three colleagues. The favourites of the reactionaries were removed, while Merlin and Ramel, whom they despised, remained in office. In the Ministry of Foreign Affairs, Barras installed Talleyrand, who had just returned from America and was indeed worthy of becoming his associate. The Ministry of War went to Hoche; but Petiet, his predecessor, hastened to inform the Councils of the troop movement.

Thus the crisis entered its decisive phase. On its solution depended not only the regime but the orientation of foreign policy as well. More than ever the Coalition Powers awaited the breakdown of the Directory, while Bonaparte turned against the Councils solely to make himself the master of both war and peace.

CHAPTER SIX

The Directory and the Coalition

WITH THE WAR CONTINUING, the Directory was forced to invade Germany and Italy in order to feed its armies, impose peace, and assure the preservation of Belgium (and perhaps the natural boundaries) by securing pawns. New dangers were to be born of these new conquests. As the armies moved farther from home their generals would become masters over them, and the Republic might fall at their discretion. On the other hand, the spirit of propaganda, the pleas of refugees, and the personal policy that any general, following Dumouriez's example, might pursue (with the support of the army contractors) would impel the abolition of the Old Regime in the occupied countries. At the same time it would incite their exploitation, as in 1792; and this likewise made their retention essential. The Thermidorians, by advancing towards the natural boundaries (even though efforts would surely be made to regain these), had condemned France to new wars in the not too distant future. At any rate, peace might last if Austria, like Prussia, were permitted to gain advantages from it. To overrun the frontiers would be to bar any reconciliation with her. The only result would be armistices in an eternal war.

NAPOLEON BONAPARTE

The Directory was aware of these dangers. Reubell was bent upon reuniting the Rhineland with France, but he resolutely opposed other annexations. Under his influence the Directory for several months affirmed its decision to make no conquests beyond the natural boundaries unless they involved an exchange of territory. As for the generals and army contractors, it did not forget that the Committee of Public Safety had kept them under control by subordinating them to the deputies on mission. It thought it could do likewise by creating 'army commissioners'—Joubert and Alexandre for the armies of the North and the Sambre and Meuse, Haussmann for that of the Rhine and Moselle, Salicetti and Garrau in Italy. If it granted them in principle merely a right of surveillance, it was not slow in giving them authority to conclude armistices, collect war taxes, and repress pillaging. Although less extensive than those of the deputies on mission, such powers were certain to bring the commissioners into conflict with the generals. In the Year II the Revolutionary Tribunal had guaranteed the obedience of the generals. Behind the commissioners lay nothing but the faltering authority of the Directory; so they were sacrificed, and the generals continued as before.

Still, chance precipitated developments. In Carnot's plan, Jourdan and Moreau, at the head of the armies of the Sambre and Meuse and the Rhine and Moselle, were to strike the decisive blow by marching upon Vienna; the weaker armies of the Alps and of Italy, under Kellermann and Schérer, would conquer Piedmont and Lombardy if possible. On 12 Ventôse, Year IV (March 2, 1796), however, the Directory substituted Bonaparte for Schérer and permitted him to take the offensive. Hoping to negotiate with the princes of South Germany, who were alarmed by revolutionary tremors, the Directory itself waited until May 20, when Austria denounced the Rhine armistice concluded in December, before opening the campaign on this front. Bonaparte's lightning victories determined the future.

Bonaparte was born in Ajaccio in 1769, just after the French had occupied Corsica. His father, rallying to the side of the French, obtained recognition as a nobleman, and was able to have his son admitted to the school at Brienne. From there he went to the École Militaire and emerged as a second lieutenant in the artillery. Poor and with no prospects, he owed everything to the Revolution; but, detesting the French, at first he saw in the Revolution only an opportunity for liberating his native land and playing some role there under the leadership of Paoli. The latter preferred the Pozzo di Borgo family to the suspect Bonapartes, and when he broke with the Convention and called in the English, the Bonapartes were expelled. It was then that Napoleon 'naturalized' himself in the service of the Montagnards.

He made a name for himself at the siege of Toulon, and later in the Army of Italy, which he inspired to perform brilliant operations at Saorgio and Dego. Arrested briefly as a Robespierrist and deprived of his post, he re-established himself on 13 Vendémiaire, and on 9 Ventôse he took it upon himself to close the Jacobin clubs. Three days later he obtained the command of an army. He left Paris after marrying Joséphine Tascher de la Pagerie, widow of the Vicomte de Beauharnais, who had been guillotined in 1794. It is difficult to believe that he knew nothing of her liaison with Barras, or that he was indifferent to the value of her political influence; but he loved her passionately, and it is beyond question that Carnot, now approving his plan, named him with full knowledge of the situation.

By creating the national army the Revolution had altered the circumstances of the war, but Carnot was unable to take full advantage of the situation. As late as 1796 he thrust into Germany two armies which eventually would be beaten separately. Napoleon's genius conceived the new strategy. Never doubting himself, and joining a rational and meticulous concern for performance with an inexhaustible fertility of imagination, he put it into effect with an unequalled mastery, which fortune served for years. The essential features of his Italian campaign had been established as early as the Year II: eliminate Piedmont, conquer Lombardy, then, neglecting the rest of the peninsula, march upon Vienna.

VICTORIES OF THE DIRECTORY, AND ENGLAND CONFOUNDED

The Army of Italy occupied a large part of the Genoese Riviera, and after Schérer's victory at Loana, it held the upper valley of the Tanaro, as well as the passes to the two branches of the Bormida. Bonaparte assembled 38,000 men to overwhelm Colli's 12,000 Piedmontese. Beaulieu commanded

35,000 Austrians: but with a French brigade threatening Genoa to extract money, he hurried to intercept it, and charged Argenteau with cutting off its retreat. Thus removed, he was unable to aid either Colli or his own lieutenant. Bonaparte began by ridding himself of the latter, who, beaten at Montenotte on April 12, 1796, and driven from Dego, lost contact with the Piedmontese. At the same time Augereau drove the Piedmontese from Millesimo, and Sérurier descended the Tanaro. Attacked at Ceva on the 16th, and at San Michele on the 18th, Colli inflicted bloody reverses upon Bonaparte; but constantly turned and finally routed at Mondovi on the 21st, he withdrew to Turin. With the revolutionaries agitating, the court took fright, and on the 28th it concluded an armistice at Cherasco.

Beaulieu had retired behind the Ticino. Bonaparte caught him from behind by a surprise crossing of the Po at Piacenza. Suspecting the danger, however, the Austrians had already retreated and escaped, leaving only a rear guard on the Adda. The bridge at Lodi was captured by assault on May 10. Retracing his steps, Bonaparte then entered Milan. The king of Sardinia signed a treaty of peace on May 15, and ceded Savoy and Nice; so the army resumed its march, reached the Mincio without hindrance, and began the siege of Mantua. Since Beaulieu had not respected Venetian neutrality, a convention gave Verona to the French, and granted them right of passage. The dukes of Parma and Modena secured armistices; the papal towns of Bologna and Ferrara threw open their gates without firing a shot; and Genoa agreed to a loan and closed her port to the English.

At Milan, Bonaparte's policy had already taken shape. He permitted a club to form, promised independence, and gave the National Guard the tricolour cockade of Italy. But he also exacted a tax of 20 millions from the rich, and the army lived off the country. The inconsistency was immediately obvious; revolt broke out and was harshly repressed, especially at Pavia. France could thus count only upon the Italian Jacobins, whose avowed intention was to revolutionize all Italy and make it a unified republic.

The Directory's attitude, however, was quite the opposite: Italian conquest would constitute merely a pawn, which should be exploited thoroughly before being restored. As has been seen, it soon negotiated with Rome, without manifesting any desire to destroy the temporal power of the pope. Booty preoccupied the Directory to the point that it ordered Bonaparte to leave Lombardy under Kellermann and proceed to collect a ransom from the rest of the peninsula. Now that the Austrians were preparing to resume the offensive, the order was absurd, but it was especially unfortunate in that it permitted Bonaparte to put his strength to the test without any risk. He offered his resignation, and the Directory capitulated at once.

True, the wishes of the Directory were partially satisfied. The dukes of Parma and Modena, as well as the pope, were subjected to heavy indemnities, in addition to the surrender of manuscripts and art objects chosen by a commission; and a division occupied Leghorn, the principal centre of British trade. Bonaparte seems to have drawn some 50 millions from Italy, and the Directory received about 10 millions. This merely hastened the emancipation of the general. On the eve of Lodi he had become aware of his destiny. 'I saw the world drop away from beneath me as if I were being carried into the air.' About him clustered a horde of army contractors and individuals seeking profit, persons such as Haller, who became the treasurer of the army, and Hamelin, who paid Joséphine for her influence. Bonaparte himself was growing rich. The army was becoming his, and he paid it half in specie—something the Directory was unable to do for the others.

Still, the Directory was not disturbed, for the summer had been a lucky one. Jourdan having crossed the Rhine on May 31, was repelled by Archduke Charles, who did not evacuate the left bank. On receiving news of events in Italy, Wurmser, who had been facing Moreau, was dispatched there with part of his troops. Charles, the one remaining leader, abandoned the Palatinate; and when Moreau finally crossed the Rhine on June 24, Jourdan returned to the attack. He advanced as far as the Naab, and Moreau reached Munich. In Italy, Wurmser's troops, descending from the Tyrol down both sides of Lake Garda, were beaten at Lonato, and on August 5 at Castiglione. Returning to Trent, Wurmser hoped to reach Mantua through the valley of the Brenta; but Bonaparte was already pursuing him, and he was forced to take refuge in the fortress.

The conqueror continued his policy, aided by the good Jacobins Saliceti and Garrau, without concern for the government. On October 16, Modena and the Legations taken from the pope were united in a Cispadane Republic. The general still desired to rid himself of the commissioners. Italy was being exhausted, and the state of the army was again deteriorating. After Saliceti was sent to Corsica, Garrau alone remained exposed to recriminations. On October 25, Bonaparte took the decisive step by charging Baraguey d'Hilliers, who commanded in Lombardy, with the entire administration of the country—without even mentioning the commissioners!

The affairs of England declined no less than those of Austria. On August 19, 1796, the Directory succeeded in contracting an alliance with Spain. The British fleet left the Mediterranean after evacuating Corsica, which the French reoccupied in October; and Bonaparte was thus protected against all English intervention. From July on, plans were being laid for an invasion of Ireland in co-operation with Wolfe Tone, who was preparing an insurrection. In September the rumour of a French landing caused panic in London. The economy was also disturbed. Since the end of 1795 the exchange rate had fallen; the Bank of England redressed it by increasing the discount rate, but business activity felt the effects. The monetary situation seemed graver still, for in February, 1796, the holdings of the Bank were reduced to £2·5 million. The horizon seemed to darken further in November. On the 17th, Catherine II died. Her son, Paul I, was fond of Prussia alone, and it was only with difficulty that his ambassadors—Vorontsov in London and Razumovski in Vienna—prevented a rupture. At any rate, the Coalition could no longer count on Russia. These extra misfortunes prompted Pitt to negotiate. The Directory agreed to a conference at Lille, and Malmesbury set out on October 15.

REVERSES OF THE AUTUMN OF 1796

At this moment, however, events had already begun to take a bad turn for the Republic. Since Jourdan and Moreau had not tried to join forces, the archduke directed the major part of his troops against the former. His slowness permitted the Army of the Sambre and Meuse to withdraw without great losses; but at the end of September it recrossed the Rhine. Charles then undertook to cut off the retreat of Moreau, who had withdrawn tardily. Again he was unable to concentrate his forces or to hurry. The Army of the Rhine and Moselle veered through the Höllental and succeeded in reaching Huningue on October 26. For the most part, the Austrians were now free to leave for Italy, but they were determined to take the bridgeheads of Kehl and Huningue, which resisted through the winter. A new commander, Alvinczy, nevertheless had some success against Bonaparte. He reached the gates of Verona and repulsed all assaults at Caldiero. By furious fighting at Arcole, on November 15–17, his adversary succeeded, however, in turning him and forcing his retreat. The French had barely escaped disaster, and their material condition and morale were pitiful.

Thugut thenceforth refused to participate with England in the discussions at Lille. Recovering himself, Pitt demanded the abandonment of Belgium and the cession of colonies. On December 19 the Directory dismissed Malmesbury. The Irish expedition under the command of Hoche had already set sail, but it was dispersed by storms, and returned in disgrace. Shortly thereafter a 'Black Legion', formed and commanded by an American named Tate, who had fought as an officer against the English during the American Revolution, landed in Wales; but it was soon captured. At the same time, on February 14, 1797, Jervis defeated the Spanish fleet off Cape St.-Vincent, and reopened access to the Mediterranean.

Bonaparte profited from the failures of others as well as from his own victories. He remained the only hope. After all, the defeated generals proved no more docile than he. Kléber and Bernadotte took the lead, in the midst of their retreat, by submitting their resignations to Jourdan and abandoning him. Beurnonville, who replaced Jourdan, came into conflict with Commissioner Alexandre. Moreau had signed an armistice with Württemberg without consulting Hausmann, and returned to France completely at odds with him. Disheartened, the Directory suppressed the commissioners, so that the generals alone remained in control. Moreover, the calamities of the autumn had given Carnot the helm. He tried to enter into secret contact with Thugut, and in November he demanded that

Clarke, head of his military bureau, be sent to Italy to negotiate an armistice and to investigate the situation. Clarke was quickly won over by Bonaparte. Furthermore, the Directory, by confirming its intention to exchange Lombardy for the Rhineland, ordered him to consult the general regarding the peace treaty.

THE SURRENDER OF AUSTRIA: PRELIMINARIES OF LEOBEN

Fortune, however, soon changed sides again. In January, 1797, Alvinczy descended the Adige, while Provera advanced upon Mantua from Friuli. This was the most dazzling exploit of the Army of Italy. On the 14th, on the plateau of Rivoli, Bonaparte routed into the mountains the Austrian columns that had attacked him, and Joubert dispersed or captured the remainder the next day. Departing immediately with Masséna's division, the general-in-chief forced Provera to capitulate on the 16th, and Mantua finally surrendered. Added to the excitement of victory was the reaction following Brottier's plot, which drew the Directory from its chosen path. Clarke was given the task of defending the Cispadane Republic, and on 15 Pluviôse, Year V (February 3, 1797), in a famous letter, Bonaparte was invited to destroy the papal government.

Redress was not long in coming. Although Bonaparte and Clarke demanded authorization to give Lombardy a constitution, they were permitted only to set up a provisional administration under one general alone, and not committing the Directory. Then the Army of the Sambre and Meuse, entrusted to Hoche, crossed the Rhine on April 17–18, and speedily arrived before Frankfurt. On the 20th, Moreau also crossed the river. Clarke received orders to postpone any armistice; Germany would once more become the principal theatre of the war. It was too late, however, because Bonaparte had already cut the Gordian knot.

After the fall of Mantua, Bonaparte marched on Rome, but with no intention of going very far. Through Clarke he knew that if he did not sign the peace himself, Lombardy would be retroceded. Thus he must reach Vienna ahead of the German armies. At Tolentino he hastily concluded a peace with Pius VI, exacting only several millions in addition to Avignon and the Legations. On March 20 he launched an offensive against the Austrians, now commanded by Archduke Charles. Thanks to reinforcements dispatched from the Rhine, Bonaparte had a larger army. Without great difficulty he reached the Tarvis Pass, whence Masséna's division advanced as far as the Semmering Pass. On April 7, at Leoben, the plenipotentiaries met to negotiate. It was Bonaparte himself who, as early as March 31, had offered to treat with the archduke.

Since the armies of the Rhine had not yet attacked, the Austrians might be able to take the time to overcome him, and his rear lines worried him. It would seem that even before launching the campaign, he judged it impossible to realize his plans if he did not appease Thugut, and he conceived the idea of offering part of the Venetian territories. In March his subordinates provoked a revolution at Brescia and Bergamo; this would not have been done without his consent. Next they attempted to stir up the Venetian mainland, but the peasants, angered by military occupation and indoctrinated by the clergy and nobles, turned against the French. On April 17 the garrison at Verona was surprised and part of it was massacred.

Bonaparte's hazardous position, as much as his eagerness to appear as the peacemaker and to retain his conquest, explains the extraordinary choice which he offered the Habsburg monarch: either Istria, Dalmatia, and the entire Venetian mainland as far as the Oglio (with the exception of Venice), if he were to cede Belgium and Lombardy; or Venice alone, and only as far as the Tagliamento, if he were to abandon the Rhineland, as well as Belgium, while recovering Lombardy. He virtually dictated the reply: exchange Lombardy for the Venetian territories, and save the emperor's prestige by retaining the Rhineland for Germany. Thugut had not hoped for so much. With no authorization, and without consulting Clarke, who had been dispatched to Turin, Bonaparte signed both the armistice and the preliminaries on April 18. So it was accomplished. The Republic expanded beyond its natural frontier of the Alps without even attaining the one that it held most dear. Imitating the scandalous partition of Poland, to suit its own needs it sacrificed an independent state and delivered the Italians over to the Germans.

Bonaparte soon dispatched couriers to the armies of the

Rhine to halt them, and took care that the news of the peace should spread before the terms were known to the Directory. Could the latter, immediately following the elections of the Year V, defy both public opinion and the general? It dared not, and despite Reubell, it ratified the agreement. Installed at Mombello (Montebello), in the palace of the Crivelli, Bonaparte now seemed a sovereign. He transformed Lombardy into the Cisalpine Republic, gave it a constitution, and united the Cispadane Republic, the Valtelline, and a part of the Venetian possessions with it. He sought to persuade Valais to concede France a route through the Simplon Pass to the new state; his failure was soon to produce the idea of intervening in Switzerland. Access to the sea was assured when the Republic of Genoa, 'revolutionized' by the Jacobins and now the Ligurian Republic, placed itself under Bonaparte's protection.

The definitive treaty with Austria still remained to be concluded. To conciliate the Directory, the general pointed out that he did, indeed, intend to retain Mantua and to obtain the Rhineland. On his own initiative he declared war on Venice on May 2; on the 12th the democrats overthrew the oligarchy and called in the French; on the 16th he negotiated with the representatives of the defunct government, which action permitted him to ignore the new one. Free to dispose of Venice itself, he expected to attain his ends; and Thugut, hoping to secure the Legations as well, was willing to parley. Conferences opened at Udine.

THE ENGLISH CRISIS

At the very moment that Austria was abandoning the struggle, England was emerging from a grave crisis, the complex causes of which had been foreshadowed earlier in 1796. It would appear that the treaties of Basel and The Hague, and the entry of Spain into the war, gave rise to trade difficulties. In 1797, exports are supposed to have declined slightly from the preceding year, although they were still above those of 1792. French privateers now captured the maximum number of prizes—700—and Parliament forbade merchant ships to sail henceforth without escort. The trouble derived, however, chiefly from the straits of the Exchequer. Pitt had scarcely resorted to taxation to finance the war. In December, 1796, he slightly increased taxes which bore on the rich. Nevertheless the increase in receipts (from £19 million in 1792 to almost £21·5 million in 1797) resulted primarily from customs duties and indirect taxes; imports and exports in 1796 had exceeded those of 1792 by 17 and 14 per cent respectively. Yet expenses mounted from £26 million in 1792 to £75 million in 1797.

Pitt had borrowed to make up the deficit. In 1797, subscriptions to the Consols provided £43 million, 57 per cent of expenditures. Since this was insufficient, he exacted advances from the Bank of England. These were secured principally by navy bills, that is, by future returns on taxes, a veritable 'anticipation' that went as high as £2 million. He also issued Exchequer bills, or short-term Treasury notes, to the extent of £15 million to £20 million. Part of these were sold and the remainder were retained by the Bank. At the end of 1795 it held almost £13 million worth, and in February, 1797, £10·5 million. The circulation of bank notes did not increase; from £14·5 million in 1795 it even fell to £9·6 million in February, 1797. If prices did increase—141 in 1797 as against a base of 100 in 1790—inflation from provincial banks alone could have contributed to the price rise; but the Bank was reducing its reserves.

It diminished these still more when the Exchequer had to secure gold to provide for the support of troops abroad and to pay subsidies to the Coalition. From 1794 to 1797 almost £21 million thus went to Europe alone, not counting two loans to Austria that amounted to at least £5 million. To this flight of gold was added the outlay for troops in the colonies, interest on Consols held by foreigners, and freight charges and insurance on neutral ships in the service of Great Britain. Finally, in 1796, £2·5 million had to be devoted to the purchase of grain overseas. Gold coin became scarce at home, and bank notes were exchanged for specie at the Bank, the cash reserves of which declined.

Confidence probably fell to its lowest level after Hoche's attempted landing. Yet the news of Tate's landing in Wales created panic in London on February 25, 1797. The Bank held no more than £1,086,000. An Order in Council suspended convertibility of bank notes from the 27th; it was not to be resumed until 1821! The economy suffered, but less than in 1793; and Pitt did not consider the offering of state loans indispensable. The Bank sufficed because of its liberal discount policy. Ultimately specie became scarcer still, and the value of bank notes declined. Yet suspension of the gold standard did not develop into a catastrophe. Businessmen showed a patriotic spirit, and since they saw the need for solidarity of capitalist interests, they pledged themselves to accept the notes at par with specie. It was unnecessary to make paper money legal tender before 1812. With the nation recovering its composure, with bank deposits and the circulation of bills resuming, and with the shipment of subsidies ceasing along with hostilities on the Continent, the Bank was able to raise its reserves to more than £4 million by August, 1797, and to pursue its recovery.

Although she had overcome this near collapse with great difficulty, England still grievously felt the defection of Austria, to which Pitt had just addressed a new proposal for general negotiations. Great Britain found herself alone at grips with France, which, sooner or later, could take advantage of the revolt that had already begun in Ireland. At this very moment the fleet, bulwark of the island, mutinied. Political agitation played no part in it. The appalling life of the sailors, who were poorly fed, paid at seventeenth-century rates, deprived of leaves, and treated with pitiless brutality, reduced them to despair. Seeing their complaints disregarded, they rose at Spithead on April 16, 1797. Within a month, however, they were forced to submit, after having obtained some satisfaction; meanwhile the North Sea fleet at the mouth of the Thames had followed their example. It was joined by part of Duncan's fleet, cruising off Holland, and land forces began to show signs of unrest. Concessions and an amnesty, which reduced the number of those hanged to twenty-three (including the leader, Richard Parker), finally restored order, but only in mid-June.

In conflict with the Councils, the Directory was unable to take advantage of this extraordinary opportunity. Nevertheless violent agitation against the government was manifested in Parliament and in public opinion. The situation in France, and the advent of Barthélemy, persuaded Pitt to seek order by offering peace. Malmesbury returned to Lille, with the mission of securing what he could but without breaking off even if he were refused everything. The negotiations began on July 7,

1797. He demanded Ceylon and the Cape of Good Hope, which the Directory refused, since it had pledged its allies not to sacrifice them. When Talleyrand became minister the atmosphere changed. In harmony with the English government, he persuaded the Directory to request Holland and Spain to give it a free hand. Agreement seemed likely, inasmuch as the representative of Portugal, England's last ally, signed the peace.

FOREIGN AFFAIRS AND THE ARMY VIS-À-VIS 18 FRUCTIDOR

Yet there was no success at either Udine or Lille—Thugut and Pitt knew what was happening at Paris. The former attempted to transfer negotiations there. A secret agent saw Carnot and Barthélemy, demanded that Bonaparte be disavowed, and offered the Rhineland in exchange for the Legations and indemnities in Germany. The two Directors declared themselves powerless; but what if the Councils were to agree? At Lille treason was called into play. In exchange for bribes Talleyrand, and probably Barras as well, promised to secure the abandonment of some colonial possession. Maret, undoubtedly in agreement with Barthélemy, handed over the text of the treaty with Portugal, which Grenville hastened to have disavowed. Moreover, like Thugut, Pitt was waiting until the fate of the Directory was determined. Thus the connection between the foreign policy of the Revolution and its internal vicissitudes, a permanent feature from its inception, suddenly became very close. If the Directory succumbed to the intrigues of the Anglo-royalist plot, the foreign powers would triumph easily.

By attacking the generals, however, the Right determined their attitude. The Venetian affair had ignited the powder. On 5 Messidor, Year V (June 23, 1797), Dumolard, in a vehement speech, directed a well-justified indictment against Bonaparte. The general replied with a threatening proclamation, which was read to the troops on the occasion of July 14. In truth, he played a double game. Continuing to correspond with Carnot, he sent Augereau to the Directory; and it was the latter who executed the *coup d'état*. But on the advice of his aide-de-camp, Lavalette, who had also come to Paris, he did not forward the three millions he had promised. Hoche was incapable of such subterfuges, and being on hand, he might have carried out the operation if the Directory had been more adroit. Would this have changed the destiny of the Republic? Perhaps. The memory of the citizen-soldier, who died shortly after 18 Fructidor, remained dear to the republican nation as the symbol of its heroic and faithful youth.

The soldiers followed their generals. The divisions of the Army of Italy sent violent addresses, and the Army of the Sambre and Meuse soon drew up similar ones. Many of the combatants preserved a keen attachment to the Revolution and to the 'Indivisible Republic' that they did not differentiate from it. Having risked their lives for these, they felt it right to protect them against the foolish citizens ('*pékins*') who elected royalists. Yet we must not be mistaken, for the armies also yielded to the influence of their leaders. This is proved by the fact that the Army of the Rhine and Moselle, under Moreau, followed the two others only after some delay.

Thus the political influence of the generals in the Republic derived largely from the ascendancy which they had gained over their troops. They owed it to a rapid transformation in the thinking of the soldiers. The change was latent in the amalgamation of forces. Volunteer and conscript both were subjected to the discipline of the regular army, which the revolutionary government further strove to restore. The Thermidorians then continued to reinforce passive obedience. Subordinates no longer participated in the choice of their superiors; juries no longer figured in military tribunals; nor were there any ordinary soldiers among the judges.

Moreover, it can be said that the soldiers of the Directory, their ranks purged by desertion, were in a sense volunteers. They remained in service because they loved war and adventure or because they did not know what might become of them once they were out of their regiments. Gradually they came to distinguish themselves from the rest of the nation. This was all the more so because no one was any longer conscripted, and because conquest had taken them far from France. As professional soldiers, camped in foreign countries, how could they fail to turn towards their commanders? But they never became a Praetorian Guard. Soldiers and generals carried out the *coup d'état* of 18 Fructidor, as they were to carry out that of 18 Brumaire, only at the call of the bourgeoisie.

CHAPTER SEVEN

18 Fructidor and the Treaty of Campo Formio

On 18 Fructidor, Year V (September 4, 1797), the Directory, aided by the army, overthrew opposition in the Councils, and returned the Revolution to dictatorship. The consequences of the *coup d'état* were as complex as its causes: it provoked a rupture with England, and permitted Bonaparte to dictate to Austria the terms of a peace that could be nothing more than a truce.

18 FRUCTIDOR, YEAR V (SEPTEMBER 4, 1797)

Learning of the dismissal of the ministers whom it supported, the movement of Hoche's troops, and the arrival of cavalry at La Ferté-Alais near Corbeil, within the 'constitutional radius' forbidden to the army, the Right was finally convinced that the Directory was preparing to resort to violence. It thought of issuing an indictment against the executive, with the co-operation of Carnot; but he, informed by Barras of Pichegru's treason, made it clear that he would have nothing to do with a restoration. On the other side, Hoche, taken to task by Carnot (whom he had believed amenable), inveighed against Barras. Moreover, when the Right denounced the accession of the general to the ministry as illegal, because he was not forty years of age, he was replaced. The Directory justified the movement of troops by saying that they were being sent to Brest as reinforcements, and claimed that their presence within the 'constitutional radius' was purely accidental.

The government profited from the interval that ensued. Hoche moved his soldiers forward, and his friend Chérin assumed command of the guard of the Directory, while Augereau took over the 17th (Paris) military division. Under various pretexts, detachments, arms, and munitions were brought into Paris, where the hunt for the 'black collars' had resumed. When the Right protested, particularly against illegal petitions from the armies, the Directory blamed the disorders on counter-revolution. La Revellière-Lépeaux declared that he would not compromise with the enemies of the Revolution. What was to be done? The Councils decided to reorganize the pick of the National Guard, in order to rearm the bourgeoisie of the rich neighbourhoods, and to prepare a new Vendémiaire; but the triumvirs paid no attention to the law, and other effective measures either remained under discussion or expired in the Council of Elders. On 17 Fructidor, Year V (September 3, 1797), it was finally resolved to impeach the Directors—but they forestalled such action.

During the night of 17–18 Fructidor (September 3–4), the city was occupied by troops. At dawn Augereau arrested Pichegru and his friends, as well as Barthélemy; but Carnot escaped. A proclamation announced that all advocates of the re-establishment of monarchy or the Constitution of 1793 would be shot without a trial. Opponents were immobilized. The Councils, dismayed because even the Left could not conceal the fact that the Constitution had received a mortal blow, voted the 'law of exception' of 19 Fructidor (September 5) proposed by the triumvirs, and then the law of the 22nd (September 8) against the press.

Forty-nine departments had their elections entirely quashed, and others had their candidates purged. Sixty-five persons were designated for deportation to Guiana; 17 were sent, and of these, 8 died in exile and several, notably Pichegru, escaped. In all, 177 deputies were eliminated without being replaced. Several others ceased to attend the sessions or took refuge in silence. Of the opposition newspapers, 42 were suppressed, and their owners and editors were condemned to deportation;

but almost all of them managed to evade the penalty. Moreover, the press was placed under police supervision for a year, as the Constitution allowed.

Émigrés who had returned to France received orders to leave the country within ten days, under penalty of death. The law of 3 Brumaire, Year IV (October 25, 1795), was revived, and was extended to deprive relatives of émigrés of the right to vote. Since the repeal of laws against priests had been annulled, the persons sentenced to deportation had to leave again; but their capital penalties were commuted to deportation to Guiana. In return, the Directory obtained the right to send any priest there on a bill of attainder. An oath of hatred of monarchy and the Constitution of 1793 was substituted for the promise to obey the laws, and as a result, a new category of recalcitrants was created.

The authority of the executive power increased. It was charged with replacing the administrators and judges who had been dismissed. The Court of Cassation was also purged. Only the Treasury was spared. The government likewise recovered the right (of which the Councils had deprived it) of proclaiming a state of siege where and when it pleased.

Violating the Constitution, the 'day' of 18 Fructidor brought an end to the liberal experiment of the Thermidorians, and forcibly established a dictatorship; but it did not organize it. Humiliated, the legislative body was no more consoled than the Convention had been after May 31, 1793. It co-operated with the Directory no better than previously, and finally destroyed it. The role of the army made the probability of a military dictatorship more apparent, and the influence of Bonaparte increased.

THE TREATY OF CAMPO FORMIO (OCTOBER 18, 1797)

Because the collusion of royalists with a foreign power was partly responsible for Fructidor, the *coup* had repercussions on foreign policy. Reubell regained the upper hand in diplomacy, and Talleyrand observed a prudent compliance. At Lille, new plenipotentiaries demanded that Malmesbury restore outright all the colonies of France and her allies, without calling into question the conquests of the Republic; and a rupture ensued.

In the Rhineland, Hoche's death ended his project for a Cisrhenane Republic, which Görres had supported enthusiastically. Thugut, resigned to the situation, sent Cobenzl to reopen conversations with Bonaparte, who was established in the castle of Passariano, near Udine. The Directory no longer wavered in the matter of natural boundaries. It retained the Cisalpine Republic, and even more important, it did not intend to sacrifice the Venetians. Insisting upon the entire left bank of the Rhine, it granted Austria only Istria and Dalmatia, and reestablished the Most Serene Republic. Plans for a winter campaign were begun.

Bonaparte knew full well that the fighting would take place in Germany, and he had no intention of letting it obscure his own activities. On his own authority he offered Thugut Venetian territory as far as the Adige, including the capital, but not the Ionian Islands, which he intended to reserve for France. In exchange, Austria would approve the cession of the left bank of the Rhine, except for the region around Cologne. Cobenzl finally accepted. The dismemberment of Germany would be concluded with the Diet at Rastatt. The treaty was signed on October 18 at Passariano; but it bears the name of the small village of Campo Formio, where the formalities had begun.

The Directory, although disappointed, ratified the treaty nonetheless. Apart from the fact that, following the *coup d'état* it would encounter a thousand difficulties, it could not break with the imperious general, who was now without a rival—Hoche had disappeared, and Moreau, more than suspect, had been cast aside. Yet, diplomatically, the Rhenish stipulations were attended with disastrous consequences. Thugut excluded the Cologne region from the cession, because Prussia had possessions there; hence Prussia could claim no indemnity. Consequently there was cause for fear lest she oppose the cession and become alienated from France. In such case, with the war against England still going on, was it not possible that the Coalition might be revived?

Nothing seemed more likely to suggest new encroachments beyond the natural frontiers than the fact that the Republic had not completely attained them. It was important that she be sure of the buffer states she protected. In time the Batavian and Cisalpine republics would become aware of this. To bind the latter to France, Bonaparte considered seizing Valais, if not Switzerland, and it was simpler still to occupy Piedmont. Everywhere the new ambassadors—Delacroix at The Hague, Ginguené at Turin, Truguet at Madrid—began to consider themselves as overlords.

Moreover, although their services had not been officially called upon, the Jacobins applauded the *coup d'état* and lent their support. By stressing the royalist peril the Directory re-animated revolutionary ardour, and revived universal propaganda and the spirit of war to the death against tyrants. In the Year VI the republicans began to take pride in belonging to the *Grande Nation* that assumed the mission of liberating the world. La Revellière-Lépeaux felt Girondin idealism reawakening; Barras was not averse to disturbances. Like them, Reubell complacently envisaged the fall of papal power, and linked to the democrats of Basel, he could not fail to be tempted to intervene in Switzerland. Finally, it went without saying that everywhere generals and contractors, out of natural inclination and self-interest, made themselves the protagonists of the propaganda that rendered them indispensable and assured them of honours and profits. Less than six months after 18 Fructidor the French entered Bern and Rome, with the approval or at the instigation of Bonaparte, whose departure for Egypt soon afterwards was to result in the formation of the Second Coalition.

CHAPTER EIGHT

The Second Directory

EIGHTEEN FRUCTIDOR marked a break in the history of the regime established by the Thermidorians; it put an end to the constitutional and relatively liberal experiment. The Second Directory, as it has come to be called, resorted to extraordinary repressive measures (long since virtually abandoned), devised new ones, and reduced its opponents to silence. With the establishment of Continental peace, it was able to devote more attention to internal administration; but it did not succeed in winning public approval.

TERROR UNDER THE DIRECTORY

If the dictatorship of the Directory maintained itself by terrorist methods, these were never as extensive as those of 1793, because the threat from abroad was temporarily removed and the civil war was reduced to brigandage. The High Court was slow and uncertain, and the regular criminal courts, which were occasionally used, seemed to suffer from the same defects; but the Revolutionary Tribunal was not revived. Military commissions, used as special jurisdictions, were increased at the time of the disorders that followed 18 Fructidor, although these were serious only in a few places in the south. The legislative body authorized the searching of homes for only a month in Messidor, Year VI, but its authorization was dispensed with, as in the rural repressions. At the beginning of the Directory, local authorities, without any right whatever, ordered the virtually indefinite imprisonment of suspects. The privacy of letters was no more respected than was personal liberty. The government repeatedly suppressed many newspapers, and those that continued became remarkably drab. Nor did books or the theatre escape the highhandedness of the police. Three categories of persons were the particular objects of attack: brigands, émigrés, and priests.

A new special law placed brigands under the jurisdiction of military commissions, and decreed the death penalty for outrages committed by more than two persons. This was reminiscent of summary justice (*prévôtale*), and foreshadowed the special courts of the Consulate.

Clear in theory, the situation of émigrés was not without problems, because the official list contained errors. The Directory always opposed the slightest moderation of this legislation. The military commissions and local administrations were cautious, but executions continued, at least during the Year VI. Relatives of émigrés remained under the disabilities of the law of 3 Brumaire, Year IV (October 25, 1795), and were unable to dispose of their property until an anticipated succession (*partage pré-successif*) had been determined. Certain members of the Directory considered going further; Sieyes, for example, proposed that all nobles be expelled. Vigorous opposition forced them, however, to be content with depriving nobles of citizenship unless they were naturalized under the same conditions as foreigners (9 Frimaire, Year VI—November 29, 1797). Those who had rendered services to the Revolution, however, were exempted, and since the list of such persons was never drawn up, the law remained a dead letter.

The situation of the priests was not so clear as that of the émigrés, for it was never decided whether the laws of 1792 and 1793 were still applicable. In any case, the minister of police remembered in the Year VII that deportees who returned would incur only deportation to Guiana. Still, many were included on the list of émigrés, and some forty are known to have perished as a consequence. The military commissions and local administrations saved others, and in the Year VII the minister specified that anyone accused could challenge the inclusion of his name on the list.

On the other hand, priests who refused the oath of hatred of monarchy, and all others, even those who obeyed the law, could be deported by order of the Directory on a bill of attainder. This was a meaningless encumbrance that was not taken into account in connection with the Belgian clerics, 9,234 of whom were condemned *en masse*. Elsewhere in the Republic, 1,700–1,800 priests seem to have been thus affected. Actually only three vessels left for Guiana. One was captured by the English; the other two carried 253 captives. More than 1,100 remained interned on the islands of Ré and Oléron, and the infirm and aged were placed in confinement. The prisoners suffered greatly, and partly because of their advanced years, many of them died.

The faithful associated the new terror with the revival of the law of 7 Vendémiaire, Year IV (September 29, 1795), which forbade public religious ceremonies and ordered the destruction of outward symbols of worship. Moreover, churches where no priest officiated regularly were put up for sale. Also vexatious to them was the consuming zeal of the members of the Directory for the revolutionary calendar and Tenth Day worship. The Directory prescribed that all administrations should observe the calendar rigorously. The laws of 17 Thermidor, Year VI (August 4, 1798), and 23 Fructidor (September 9), confirmed the Tenth Day as a day of rest and regulated the celebration of festivals. Finally, the Directory, unable to regain control over public schools, and encountering the opposition of parents who favoured religious teaching, laid the blame upon the free schools, almost all of which were Catholic. It subjected them to inspection by municipalities, forbade functionaries to send their children to them, and announced that it would select its officials only from among students at the national schools. Apparently these last two provisions had not the slightest effect, but some denominational schools closed their doors.

The 'dry guillotine', as deportation was called, left an evil memory, but the terror of the Directory was not very bloody. The military commissions had at least 160 persons shot, and the criminal tribunals added an unknown number of death sentences. With time, an increasing disapproval of the cruellest punishments developed. After August, 1798, nobody was sent to Guiana, and after March, 1799, only one émigré is known to have been executed. More adroit than the Jacobins, the men of the Directory aimed only at designated groups, so that the mass of the population felt no danger. The repression remained strictly governmental, and the watch committees (efficient because they knew local conditions, but influenced by personal animosities and pressures) were not re-established. The terror threatened to become worse again only at the end of the Year VII, when the collusion of the royalists with the foreign enemy revived passions. Since, however, many Frenchmen did not differentiate between the terror and the religious policy of the Directory, it contributed greatly to the unpopularity of the regime.

Some republicans, La Revellière-Lépeaux for example, believed that the policy of repression was too mild. Not above imitating the 'tyrant Robespierre', they wished to fight the Catholic Church with the civil religion of the Supreme Being; but the majority would have none of it. Still, certain individuals tried it, in January, 1797, by founding Theophilanthropy. This new cult never reached the people, any more than did Freemasonry, with its similar principles, which Roëttiers de Montaleau revived after 1796. The regime should have directed its major efforts towards primary education, but partly because of lack of funds, it did nothing. It contented itself with opening central schools and organizing the Institute, where the ideologues held sway. It expected to do much more for propaganda by imposing the use of the revolutionary calendar and Tenth Day worship, but it had no success. Besides antagonizing 'believers', it also annoyed the indifferent by interfering with their daily life.

If it did not win over public opinion, the Directory, by using terror, at least reduced counter-revolution to impotence for the duration of peace on the Continent. Since nothing prevented terror from being turned to other ends, it served just as well against the Jacobins when the Directory once more began to fear them.

Terror is indispensable to any dictatorship, but it cannot compensate for incompetent leaders and a defective organization of authority. Merlin counted for something in the Directory, but François de Neufchâteau was little more than an administrator. Of the ministers from the Year IV only Ramel remained in office, and except for the Belgian Lamprecht, the change had not been for the better. Several members of the Directory made it clear that a provisional suspension of the Constitution (following the example of the Montagnards) would not do; that what was needed was a modification that would reinforce the executive power permanently. It seems that Sieyes, Talleyrand, and probably Madame de Staël and Benjamin Constant contrived the most coherent of the plots.

Talleyrand warned Bonaparte that Sieyes intended to consult him, and the general's reply is known. He advised that the control of peace, war, and taxation be taken away from the legislative body. 'The power of the government, in all the latitude I give it, should be considered as the true representative of the nation.' Naturally the Councils disagreed, but twice they proposed to the Directory that elections be suspended for several years. On 18 Fructidor the triumvirs, asking the deputies to approve their initiative, had not dared request an increase in their powers as well. With the opportunity past, it would have required a new *coup d'état*, since legal revision entailed an extremely long delay. They could not agree as to whether they should risk it. La Revellière-Lépeaux affirmed that the Constitution had been violated only to preserve it. Reubell distrusted Barras, and Bonaparte even more so. Although it had become more powerful, the Directory was defenceless before the Councils and the Treasury, while the administration in the departments remained unstable.

For several months the union of republicans, at least, seemed re-established. The ineligible Montagnards were rehabilitated, the Jacobins secured their share of appointments, and their newspapers were spared. Until winter's end there was reason to believe that the Directory was most afraid of its generals. Augereau denounced its ingratitude, because he had not been made a Director. Bonaparte, ceremoniously received in Paris on 20 Frimaire, Year VI (December 10, 1797), proved cold and arrogant. Replying to Barras' speech, he let fly his famous shaft: 'When the happiness of the French people is established on the best organic laws, all Europe will become free.' Nevertheless, during the months that followed he was consulted about foreign affairs, and more than any other, he pushed the Republic along the path on which he had set it.

THE THIRD ANTI-JACOBIN REACTION: 22 FLORÉAL, YEAR VI (MAY 11, 1798)

With the electoral system as it was, the political world anxiously awaited the elections, which, by the end of spring, would once more bring the results of 18 Fructidor into question. The stakes were high, for the recent expulsions raised to 437 the number of seats that would have to be filled; and among them were those of the second half of the 'perpetuals'. This time the precautions, which had been rejected in the Year V as being incompatible with the representative principle, were adopted on 12 Pluviôse, Year VI (January 31, 1798). The legislative body took upon itself the impending verification of credentials, so that the 236 outgoing members of the Convention would participate, along with the 297 remaining deputies, in a purge of the newly elected men who were to replace them On the 24th (February 12) the Councils decided that the choice of a Director should take place on 26 Floréal (May 15)—that is, they arrogated it to themselves. On that day they replaced François de Neufchâteau with Treilhard.

Gradually, however, they came to realize that the royalists, excluded or intimidated, would not vote, and that the votes of the discontented would be diverted from the outgoing members. Would the Jacobins not benefit from this situation? They headed many 'constitutional circles', had many friends among the administrators, and their propaganda caused alarm. La Reveillière-Lépeaux was terrified—he believed that the terrorists wanted to assassinate him. Merlin, out of a real or tactical anxiety, assumed Carnot's role, and alerted the bourgeoisie against a return to the democracy of the Year II. The *Moniteur* warned the propertied class against the 'shameless anarchists who preached the levelling and equality of Robespierre, and promised to give the "have-nots" the property of the "haves".' In a more doctrinaire fashion, Benjamin Constant spoke along the same line. In fact, the neo-Jacobins no longer maintained relations with the sans-culottes, but the 'social fear' served the men of the Directory as it had the Thermidorians, and as it would serve Bonaparte at a later time.

In vain Barras protested against the division that was being incited among republicans, for his colleagues had an ulterior motive. The conflict between them and the Councils was reviving. Thus it was a question of securing a docile majority by eliminating not only the Jacobins but also independents, such as Lamarque, even though he was a Girondin. Bonaparte would say, 'No opposition is necessary.' Having made its plans, the Directory this time carefully prepared for the elections. It dismissed many officials, placed several towns in a state of siege, and sent inspectors, on pretext of investigating the application of the highway toll, but actually to take instructions and funds to the commissioners. Merlin advocated increasing the divisions (*scissions*), so there would be a choice between rival delegations.

There was nothing in the results to frighten the bourgeoisie, but it was thought that the new legislative body would probably be less docile. Since it was supposed to meet on 1 Prairial, Year VI (May 20, 1798), haste was necessary. The confidants of the Directory prepared a list of those who were to be excluded, and invited the Councils to adopt it in its entirety. The law of 22 Floréal, Year VI (May 11, 1798), barred the deputies from eight departments where there had not been a split, so that their seats remained vacant. In nineteen constituencies the rival faction was seated; elsewhere one or more representatives were excluded. Moreover, more than 60 administrators and judges were removed. In all, 106 of those elected were 'Floréalized', while some 60 opponents seem to have escaped. The governmental character of the 'day' is further confirmed by the fact that 68 commissioners and 17 other functionaries, plus 106 administrators and judges (many of whom owed their positions to the Directory) entered the Councils. The subjugation of the legislative power ran its course, and the intrusion of agents of the state was to vitiate the representative system for a long time.

Still, disillusionment was not long in coming. The majority, unhappy about the sacrifice of so many men it esteemed, secretly nursed its rancour against the authors of its own subjection. In the opposition, Lucien Bonaparte criticized the regime with demagogic violence. While the Directory was attaining the height of its power its fall was being prepared.

FINANCES AND THE NATIONAL ECONOMY

It was during the twenty months following 18 Fructidor that the Directory accomplished the greatest part of its administrative work. Although in more than one respect it prepared the work of the Consulate, this achievement has not been given adequate recognition. Financial recovery was most imperative. The Councils somewhat hastily adopted a new curtailment of the debt. One-third was retained or registered in the Great Book, and the securities were accepted in payment for taxes or for that portion of the price of national property payable in specie. The remaining two-thirds were repaid in bonds acceptable for the remainder of the price in competition with the other worthless paper (*valeurs mortes*). Such was the 'Ramel liquidation', or bankruptcy of the two-thirds, ordered on 9 Vendémiaire, Year VI (September 30, 1797), for the perpetual annuities, and on 24 Frimaire (December 14) for life annunities, pensions, and outstanding claims or floating debt.

The budget was reduced by more than 160 millions, and was relieved of payments in arrears. It remained to be balanced. To hasten the collection of direct taxes, a 'tax agency' (*agence des contributions*) was created in each department. The commissioners of the Directory established the assessment, with the assessors representing the taxpayer, and assured the preparation of the rolls. But they were busy with other things, and they lacked technical competence; hence the reform did not achieve all the anticipated results. The harsh device of quartering troops in the homes of tax delinquents proved more effective. The Councils granted some new taxes, notably the road tolls, but they persisted in voting expenses without any overall plan and taxes too tardily. They still disliked indirect taxes, and permitted them only in the form of municipal customs duties.

The deficit of the Year VI was estimated at 250 millions. During the autumn, in the first months of the Year VII, they finally approved (perhaps because of the renewed threat of Continental war) the essential laws on licences, stamps, registration fees, and land and personal property taxes, which endured for a long time or are still in force. They further instituted a new direct tax on doors and windows. The effects of the receipts would be felt only in the long run. As for extraordinary expenses, the national property was inadequate. The principal resources came from a loan of 80 millions for the war against England, and from the exploitation of the sister republics.

The penury of the Treasury was perpetuated, and the financiers remained its masters. The Directory continued to pay them back in kind and to submit to their demands. The fame of Ouvrard, Hainguerlot, Paulée, Vanlerberghe, Seguin, and Simons (the husband of Mademoiselle Lange) grew. Corruption among functionaries and politicians persisted. In August, 1798, several aides to Schérer, minister of war (including his own brother), were dismissed, and he was held responsible for their peculations. Numerous scandals revealed the fraudulent dealings of the companies of contractors. The Directory failed to break down the resistance of the Treasury, and treason infiltrated it. In Thermidor, Year VI, it contributed to the failure of the second expedition to Ireland by leaving it without money.

The Continental peace lasted but a year and a half, instead of four as under the Consulate, which, for a year, also enjoyed a maritime peace. It should not be surprising that the results were less dazzling. Furthermore, the Directory faced the damage wrought by deflation—ruin of credit and collapse of prices. Specie remained scarce. Borrowing was impossible at less than 10 per cent interest, and short-term loans went as high as 7 per cent a month. True, in 1796, Perregaux and Récamier founded the Office of Current Accounts. In 1797 a Commercial Discount Office appeared, and several banks of issue opened in the provinces. But the Councils still refused to convert their notes into currency by accepting them for the state coffers. Hence these institutions served only as discount agencies for their shareholders.

The fall in prices likewise contributed to discouraging the spirit of enterprise. The harvests of 1796 and 1798 were overabundant. In 1798 a slump in wine occurred, and a drought forced the peasants to dispose of their livestock. The government derived some advantages from this, and with life becoming easier, public order benefited; but the persistent decline in income made the Directory very unpopular among the large farmers, the well-to-do cultivators, and the large landowners, from whom the electors were chiefly recruited.

As always, the agricultural crisis reacted upon industry, at the very time that the manufacturers were painfully recouping the losses caused by price controls, requisitioning, and war. Internal transport encountered obstacles of all kinds—deteriorating roads, abandoned canals, and brigandage. Maritime commerce suffered even more, for the merchant marine gradually disappeared, the colonies maintained scarcely any ties with the homeland, and the Egyptian expedition shut off Turkey and the Levant.

These circumstances promised no great results from the efforts that the Directory was making on behalf of the economy. The chief credit for these goes to François de Neufchâteau, once again minister of the interior in the Year VI. With a mind fertile in projects, he had to confine himself to issuing information bulletins and providing encouragement. On the Third Complementary Day, Year VI (September 19, 1798), he inaugurated the first national exposition. Actually, production continued below that of 1789. France remained an essentially agricultural country, but even in farming she progressed slowly.

With the sluggishness of the economy reacting on public finance, already heavily burdened by military expenses, the projects of the *philosophes* on behalf of national education and social assistance (realized in principle by the Montagnards) seemed more and more to be only ambitious utopias. As heretofore, it was necessary to accept a limited progress, modestly conceived and painfully and slowly won. Here, too, François de Neufchâteau was the best craftsman. A Superior Council of Public Instruction was formed. A French prytaneum was projected, which, taking scholarship holders as boarders, would complement the central schools. The 'welfare board' in each commune took charge of the assistance that the receipts from *octrois* occasionally financed.

The lot of the French had improved but little. Yet the Directory was able to survive because of peace and because its troops were maintained largely at the expense of the vassal lands. With the war resuming, with defeat bringing the armies back into France, expenses would weigh heavily again and would make the rulers intolerable.

CHAPTER NINE

The Anglo-French War

ABANDONED BY THE CONTINENTAL POWERS, England considered herself in danger. To a certain degree the war assumed a national character, so that Pitt was able to increase taxes and expand recruiting. In fact, the Directory was unable to shake the maritime and commercial power of Great Britain, and finally it authorized the Egyptian expedition, which disturbed the enemy but did her the great favour of renewing the Coalition.

THE ENGLISH WAR EFFORT

Alone in the struggle against an aggrandized France that was master of Holland and allied with Spain, the British government was aware of the danger. In the Atlantic the situation did not seem alarming, but it would become serious if the Toulon squadron, meeting and joining the Spanish fleet, reinforced that of Brest. Moreover, would French expansion not reduce exports, and with them the profits that sustained loans? The best course would have been to revive the Coalition. Austria exhausted, and Prussia preoccupied with the indemnities that she hoped to obtain in Germany, turned a deaf ear, and until the Egyptian expedition, Paul I, despite his hostility towards the Revolution, waited to see what would happen. For a year England could count only on herself. Accordingly she had to intensify her war effort.

The solidarity of the governing classes, already displayed during the spring crisis, became increasingly apparent. For a time political rivalries within the government majority were put aside. Canning, hitherto suspected as a Francophile, caught the enthusiasm for the fight against the egalitarian Revolution, and undertook the publication of his magazine, the *Anti-Jacobin*. The newspapers and the caricaturists (notably Gillray), although not renouncing their right to criticize, all served the 'good cause'. The invasion of Switzerland and Geneva, the 'Calvinist Rome', outraged many and inspired Coleridge's ode against sacrilegious France.

Within the country, moreover, feelings did not subside. Heretofore a large part of the population had given no heed to the war: it was the government's business, thought the peoples of the Old Regime. Pitt's policy prudently humoured this indifference by sparing his compatriots coercion and sacrifices until, finally, aware of the danger, they demanded them. The threat of invasion hastened the occasion. The democrats, who continued to demand peace and to proclaim their fraternity with the revolutionaries, incurred the charge of treason. Even Fox and his Whig friends came under attack.

From the end of the year onward Pitt profited from the national awakening to strengthen the fiscal system. In the budget for 1798 the assessed taxes were increased—the measure is known as the 'triple assessment'—and the wealthy were called on to subscribe to a voluntary contribution. The result yielded scarcely more than two-thirds of what had been anticipated. Accordingly, for 1799 Pitt established the income tax, on the basis of two shillings per pound, or 10 per cent of income, above £200, a graduated rate below, and exemption under £60. Yet the ruling class made only a moderate sacrifice. In 1800, direct taxes still provided only £10·5 million, as against more than £21 million from indirect taxes. The assessment of the income tax was left to the gentry, under the watchful eye of a commision of the Exchequer. Moreover, Pitt authorized the redemption of the land tax in exchange for subscription to a loan, at considerable profit to the landlords.

It was more difficult to improve methods of recruiting. The regular army set no store by the militia. Since 1794, in order to avoid drawing lots for the militia, numerous volunteers had organized themselves as they pleased. They promised to fight invaders if they came within a fixed distance; until such time they would remain at home. More useful seemed the home guard (fencibles), numbering some 25,000, who were regularly raised for home service during hostilities. These formations curbed enlistments in the regular army. In 1796 it had been decided to ask the parishes to provide 15,000 conscripts, drawn by lot, under penalty of a fine. This failed completely, because they preferred to pay the fine. So in 1798 it was decided to offer men a bonus for enlisting. This system succeeded, was legalized on July 12, 1799, and operated until 1815.

From 39,000 men in 1793 the army increased to 140,000 in 1801; but a large part of it was used in the colonies. With these garrisons withdrawn, Britain could send only about 12,000 men as an expeditionary force. In 1799, for the first and only time between 1794 and 1801, she ventured on to the Continent, and in order to attack Holland, she added those fencibles who were willing to go. There was some progress in tactics. Mounted batteries appeared in 1797, and the artillery became an independent corps in 1799; but anarchy continued in military administration and the conduct of operations.

Though the war effort was incontestable, nonetheless it remained limited. In any case, military preparations did not guarantee success against invaders, and compulsory service was not even considered. The English continued to rely on their fleet, and with good reason. Nevertheless so long as a French invasion remained a possibility, and the Irish rebellion capable of assisting it was not crushed, uneasiness persisted. Wolfe Tone and his friends maintained relations with the English democrats and the Directory. On guard, the government profited from informers, and O'Connor and Fitzgerald were arrested. The Irish waited for Bonaparte. On May 19, 1798, he set sail—but for Egypt!

Poorly informed, the Irish took up arms in the south-eastern counties at the end of the month. With reinforcements arriving slowly from England, the rebels resisted until the end of June; but by the time Cornwallis took command they had succumbed. Of the two priests, Michael and John Murphy, who were exhorting the rebels, the former was killed and the latter hanged. Cornwallis had to fight only the small band of French troops that landed in August, under the command of General Humbert; and he captured it on September 8. This crisis permitted Pitt to intensify repression and to put an end to the British Jacobins. In 1798 the suspension of habeas corpus was extended, and the following year printers were made subject to a declaration, and members of illegal associations were punished with seven years' transportation.

Reassured at last, the loyalists were able to admire the exploits of their sailors. Nelson had destroyed Bonaparte's fleet. Malta was besieged. At year's end Pitt vainly attempted to save Naples, but the British fleet protected Sicily and seized Minorca; the Mediterranean was becoming an English lake. The colonial empire was growing: St. Lucia was reconquered; the Dutch lost Guiana, Ceylon, and the Cape of Good Hope, an essential way station on the route to India, where Wellesley was completing the conquest of Mysore; and the Spanish lost Trinidad, an admirable depot for contraband for use on the neighbouring coast. Moreover, Miranda, expelled by the Directory, was now soliciting the support of England and the United States to carry insurrection into the Spanish colonies on the mainland. Exports continued to increase: they exceeded those of 1792 by 23 per cent in 1798, and by 37 per cent in 1799. The Turkish alliance had opened the Levant. All colonial trade was falling under the control of Great Britain.

Undergoing the ordeal without weakening, she was unable, however, to deal with her adversary without the aid of the Continental Powers—mercenary aid if need be. By the end of 1798 everything seemed to indicate that she was about to secure it.

FRENCH PROJECTS: FOREWARNINGS OF THE CONTINENTAL BLOCKADE

For the revolutionaries, too, the war took on a new aspect once it was aimed at England alone. At sea and in the colonies France suffered grave losses. Her squadrons moved furtively, and no longer sought combat. Her commercial shipping dwindled to nothing. Her colonies had fallen, except for Guadeloupe, which Victor Hugues still held, and the Mascarene Islands, where the colonists of the Île de France (Mauritius), still refusing to free their slaves, forced the commissioner of the Directory to leave.

The same was true of Guiana and the Cape of Good Hope, both lost by the Dutch, and Trinidad, by Spain.

In principle, Santo Domingo remained; for Toussaint L'Ouverture, in collaboration with Rigaud, a mulatto who had maintained himself in the south, forced the English to evacuate the island. Soon, however, he made himself the master of the country. He sent back to France both General Lavaux and Commissioner Sonthonax, who had returned on a mission, on the pretext that they had been elected to the legislative body. General Hédouville, who replaced them, soon gave way. Toussaint L'Ouverture, who applied himself to restoring production by subjecting the Negroes to forced labour, did not break with the Directory; nevertheless the homeland no longer retained anything but nominal authority. It looked as though the French were in the last act of the 'Second Hundred Years' War', begun under Louis XIV for the domination of the seas and of the world.

The French detested the English as traditional enemies, and the republicans accused 'perfidious Albion' of financing the counter-revolutionary crusade to satisfy its selfish greed in complete safety. Already, in the Year II, Jacobins and sans-culottes had expressed the hope that the army of the Republic would soon land on the island to overthrow its mercantile oligarchy. Now that peace reigned on the Continent, the moment seemed to have come to destroy the 'modern Carthage', and in a circular of Nivôse, Year VI, the Anglophile Talleyrand burst into imprecations against the 'tyrants of the world', the 'vampires of the sea'. The Directory was able to float a loan of 80 millions for that year, and some inventors proposed dirigible balloons, even submarines. Some 50,000 men were assembled near Brest, and Bonaparte received command of the 'Army of England'.

The economic war also assumed a new character. In principle the Thermidorians had kept in force the prohibitions against English merchandise. The Councils occasionally were liberal in matters of customs, and the tariff for the Year VI was lower than that of 1791; but the bureaucracy remained mercantilist in spirit, and manufacturers, especially the fiercely protectionist cotton manufacturers, besieged the government. On 10 Brumaire, Year V (October 31, 1796), a law once more made the seeking out of British goods the order of the day. It designated numerous articles as British, regardless of their real origin, and required of others a certificate of origin visaed by French consuls. Searches of homes, seizures, and even the arrest of English subjects followed.

During the summer the Directory notified neutrals that it would confiscate their goods, even on the high seas, if they continued to submit to the demands of the enemy. Nevertheless they do not appear to have ceased trading with French ports. The Directory had to take into account the opposition of the Councils, where Pastoret protested against the harsh penalties and claimed that they would lead to a rupture with the United States. After 18 Fructidor, Year V (September 4, 1797), however, the warlike tendency moved from threat to action. The law of 29 Nivôse, Year VI (January 18, 1798), authorized the seizure of neutral vessels that submitted to English regulation, or aboard which any item whatsoever of British origin was found, whether a sailor's knife or the captain's table setting. This severity seemed unprecedented, but it was to reappear in the Milan Decrees of 1807.

The neutrals deserted France. This blockade, turned to purposes of war that Napoleon was to revive, suited neither the consumers of colonial goods nor the manufacturers, who had to obtain indispensable raw materials (primarily cotton), and who looked upon the blockade just as the English did, as essentially mercantilist and favourable to their business. Numerous exceptions to the prohibitions had to be granted. The policy weakened exports and brought France and the United States close to war, with the Americans attacking French ships in reprisal. They did not abandon negotiation, however, and Talleyrand was thus provided with an opportunity for demanding a bribe from their envoys. When the correspondence of the latter was communicated to the United States Senate and made public, it unleashed a frightful scandal in the spring of 1798. The break appeared imminent.

Thus conceived, the economic war could produce its full effect only through the co-operation of the Continent, and thus it was joined with the spirit of propaganda to favour revolutionary expansion. The conquest of Italy, and the gaining of control over the Hanseatic cities, in order to close Germany to English commerce, met with the approval of the partisans of total war.

The annexations of Mulhouse and of Geneva, which became the chief town of a department of Leman, dated from 1798. They can be explained, at least in part, by a desire to suppress two centres of smuggling. But although applied to a territory far more extensive than in 1793, the blockade by the Directory did not restrict British exports; in fact, they increased. So this was but the first step.

THE EGYPTIAN EXPEDITION

The preparations for the invasion of Great Britain soon came to an end. On October 11, 1797, Duncan defeated the Dutch at Camperdown; Jervis blockaded Cadiz, and Nelson's squadron entered the Mediterranean; and Brueys declared himself unable to bring his vessels to Brest. The military commanders had no faith in the invasion, and on 5 Ventôse, Year VI (February 23, 1798), on his return from an inspection in the west, Bonaparte decided to abandon the project. It had as its sequel only the expedition of General Humbert, which was sent to the aid of the Irish but landed two months after their disaster. There was no lack of motives to explain the failure: the navy had declared itself impotent, and the Continental peace was too insecure for the Republic to deprive itself of an army and its best general. Bonaparte added that the war had to be carried to Egypt. All arguments against the invasion of England were even more valid against such an Egyptian undertaking, and others were forthcoming.

Already, in Italy, Bonaparte's imagination, like that of Alexander the Great, had become obsessed with the fabulous Orient. He had retained the Ionian Islands, and proposed to seize Malta. He surely would have preferred the conquest of England, but once this had to be abandoned, the Orient returned to the forefront. Were he to remain idle, his prestige would suffer. If his choice finally fell upon Egypt, it was undoubtedly due to Talleyrand; but the latter's role is still uncertain. True, Egypt had held a place in French history since the Crusades, and in the commerce of Marseilles since the Capitulations.[1] Merchants complained of the Mamelukes, the merce-

[1] Commercial treaties between France and the Ottoman Empire; first concluded in 1535, and periodically renewed until 1740, when they were made permanent [trans.].

naries who exploited the country under the nominal authority of the sultan; and the consul Magallon affirmed that intervention would succeed. Furthermore, Egypt would open a route to India, where Tippoo continued to defend Mysore against Wellesley.

In Messidor, Year V, at the Institute, Talleyrand recommended the resumption of colonial expansion—and what more magnificent prey than Egypt? But he hoped for an agreement with England, and intended, contrary to legend, to retain the natural boundaries. Yet it could not have escaped him that the conquest of Egypt would make the enemy irreconcilable, and that by reopening the Eastern Question, it would compromise France's conquests by provoking a war with Turkey and Russia. It may be that he sought only to serve Bonaparte; but it is quite possible to blame him for diverting to Egypt the army that threatened England, and providing the latter with the elements of a new Coalition. A letter from his mistress, Madame Grand, affirming that he wanted to 'favour his English friends', fell into the hands of the Directory, which suppressed it. Undoubtedly, on the eve of the elections of the Year VI, Talleyrand and Bonaparte could not be thrown into the opposition. That it did adopt their rash proposal, out of weakness and a desire to remove an ambitious general, testifies against the Directory as nothing else can.

Decided upon on 15 Ventôse, Year VI (March 5, 1798), and prepared with the greatest secrecy, the expedition comprised 13 ships of the line, 7 frigates, 35 other warships, 280 transports, 16,000 sailors, 38,000 officers and soldiers, as well as a commission of 187 scientists, scholars, and artists, including Berthollet, Monge, and Geoffroy Saint-Hilaire. It left Toulon on 30 Floréal (May 19). Its progress was slow, and it did not reach Malta until June 9. The grand master of the order yielded to bribery and handed over the island without firing a shot. Continuing on its way, the fleet barely escaped Nelson. He had been searching for it everywhere; he outran it without sighting it, touched at Alexandria, and left again for the Aegean Sea. Meanwhile, behind him Bonaparte landed and seized the port. The army skirted the Nile, skirmished with the Mamelukes, and on July 21 it routed them near the Pyramids and entered Cairo. Bonaparte pursued Ibrahim, one of the two chiefs, as far as the Isthmus of Suez, while Desaix drove Murad beyond Aswan.

Nelson, however, had returned to Sicily, where the complicity of Queen Maria Carolina and her minister Acton permitted him to take on supplies. Informed at last, he appeared on the evening of July 31 off the roadstead of Abukir, where Brueys, awaiting orders to return to Corfu, was holding his squadron at anchor. On August 1 the French fleet was destroyed and its commander killed. This terrible disaster, which imprisoned Bonaparte in his conquest, without hope of escape or reinforcements, had a tremendous impact on Europe. On September 9, Turkey declared war on France. At Naples, Nelson rejoined Lady Hamilton, the adventuress who reigned at the court; and counting on the aid of British forces, the Neapolitans decided to attack the Roman Republic that the French had recently founded.

Nevertheless Bonaparte organized his conquest as though it were to endure. He left the native administration in office, but controlled it; in other words, he established a protectorate. His aims became more specific. He created a council of notables, chosen by him, for it was thus that he conceived the constitutional regime and the social hierarchy. His religious policy asserted itself: he affected a profound respect for Islam and showered its leaders with favours. His enlightened despotism undertook to modernize the country through measures against the plague, repair of canals, creation of postal and transport systems, introduction of printing and windmills, and projects to substitute irrigation for flooding, and to join the Nile with the Red Sea. The scientific commission became the Institute of Egypt and prepared the celebrated *Description of Egypt*. But the defiance of the Moslems, whom Turkey summoned to a holy war, proved irremediable. They attacked isolated soldiers and outposts, and the nomads never stopped fighting. The population might have become resigned had the French army not had to live by taxes, requisitions, and confiscations. Bonaparte exacted a declaration of landed property, and imposed taxes on land transfers and notarized and legal documents. The result was a terrible insurrection in Cairo on October 21, and its bloody repression.

Since Turkey was preparing an invasion supported by an English squadron, Bonaparte decided to invade Syria to destroy the army which was assembling there. He set out with 15,000 men in February, 1799, crossed the desert, and advanced as far as Acre without encountering great resistance. But Djezzar Pasha and the émigré Phélippeaux defended the town stubbornly, and Sidney Smith captured the vessels carrying siege artillery. Finally, on May 20, Bonaparte beat a retreat, and returned to Egypt with heavy losses. At least the Turkish attack across the Isthmus had been postponed. Another army soon landed at Abukir, and on July 25 he destroyed it. Still, the situation was indecisive, and the Directory vainly attempted to send Bruix to his aid. In August, Bonaparte abandoned his army to Kléber and left to seek adventure in France. For some time the Second Coalition, which his activity had set in motion, had been attacking the Republic; but revolutionary expansion was as responsible for this as was Bonaparte.

CHAPTER TEN

Revolutionary Expansion

IN ORDER TO HAVE SOME CHANCE OF SUCCESS in the war against England, the Directory needed Continental peace, just as Vergennes had at an earlier time. Nevertheless, from the beginning of 1798 it undertook new conquests. Austria felt that such action was contrary to the agreement of Campo Formio, because she was not expanding in a comparable fashion. Hence the war party gradually recovered its ascendancy at Vienna. If the Egyptian expedition gave rise to a new Coalition, by uniting Turkey and Russia with England, the foreign policy of the Directory led Austria into it. Only Austria's adherence could make the Coalition a serious threat to the territory of the Republic, and shield England and her empire from all attack.

By requiring the retention of Lombardy, Bonaparte had prepared the way for encroachment in Italy. He likewise contributed to provoking the invasion of Switzerland. Still, however powerful his influence in these instances, in neither case was it as great as his Egyptian adventure. On the land approaches to France other factors combined to force his government along its perilous path. At war with Great Britain, it had to secure the aid of the 'sister republics' and deprive the enemy of markets from which its own national commerce would profit. Then Bonaparte's example led the gencrals to desire the creation of other vassal states, which they would rule, while the war contractors and financiers awaited the opportunity to exploit them. Finally, the revolutionary exaltation that followed 18 Fructidor, which affected the Directory, revived propaganda. The reconstruction of regions still subject to the aristocracy and to despotism once more became the order of the day.

HOLLAND AND ITALY

The Directory got little help from Spain. Neither Godoy nor his successors, Saavedra and Urquijo, was willing to invade Portugal or to contribute to the preparations against England. The other maritime ally, the Batavian Republic, only attracted more attention. It required a stable government capable of aiding its protector, and this it did not have. The provisional rulers, in power since 1795, did indeed have a convention vote a constitution, which they submitted to popular ratification in August, 1797. But, exploiting the discontent aroused by French domination and demands for men and money, a coalition of partisans of the House of Orange and unitarist democrats secured its rejection. Thus disavowed, the moderate bourgeoisie lost favour with the Directory after 18 Fructidor. Delacroix, sent to The Hague, came to an agreement with the democrats to propose a *coup* by force. Daendels, who commanded the Dutch army, and Joubert, head of the forces of occupation, promised their co-operation. On 3 Pluviôse, Year VI (January 22, 1798), the Batavian assembly declared itself constituent, and after being purged, drew up a new constitution, which was adopted.

It seemed no less necessary to make sure of the Cisalpine Republic. On 3 Ventôse, Year VI (February 21, 1798), the Directory concluded with it a treaty of alliance, according to which the republic was to pay the cost of an army of occupation of 25,000 men. At the same time they signed a liberal commercial agreement. The Cisalpine councils, however, rejected the whole as excessively onerous. The regime in office had been instituted by Bonaparte without popular ratification or the approval of France. The Directory thus felt free to intervene to modify it. The councils were purged and arrests effected, after which the treaties were ratified.

Bonaparte's conquest, moreover, became a centre for agitation. The Cisalpine conservatives felt that their understanding with France entitled them to expand. Serbelloni and Visconti, negotiators for the republic in Paris, spoke of Piedmont, the Papal States, and Genoa. Those who dreamed of Italian unity hurried from all parts of the peninsula, and they made common cause with the generals and army contractors. Armed bands readily penetrated the Marches. It was hoped that the revolutionaries at Rome would rise. Indeed, they did attempt an uprising, on December 28, 1797, but their adversaries won out; and holding the French responsible, they threatened the embassy, which was then under Bonaparte's elder brother, Joseph. In the disorder General Duphot was killed, and Joseph left the city. The Directory, hostile towards the papacy, took advantage of the situation. Berthier, now at the head of the Army of Italy, received orders to march on Rome, and Bonaparte encouraged him.

Still, the Directory did not intend to create a new Cisalpine Republic for Berthier, and it soon sent a civil commission (including Daunou and Monge) to organize the Roman Republic. Berthier, however, disliked his assignment. Arriving at Rome, he was further embarrassed when Pius VI accepted all his conditions. Nevertheless, since a number of revolutionaries (surrounded by curious spectators) had proclaimed the republic in the Forum and called upon the French, he recognized it, occupied the city, dispatched the pope to Siena, and had himself replaced by Masséna. The commission promulgated the constitution drafted by Merlin, who instituted a tribunate, a senate, and consuls, and submitted the laws and acts of the government for ratification by the French general. Hence the Roman Republic was the least free of all.

It was soon also the most exploited. From the outset, generals and army contractors began their raids. Subaltern officers protested and mutinied at the arrival of Masséna, who had the reputation of being one of the most shameless plunderers. They had long had a grudge against him, since most of them belonged to regiments of the Army of the Rhine, which, having come as replacements at the beginning of 1797, were antagonistic to his division. The commission was unable to restore order, and finally the Directory had to replace Masséna with Gouvion Saint-Cyr, one of Moreau's lieutenants. Thus the Roman Republic began under the most unfortunate auspices.

Piedmont's hour had not yet come, but it was not far off. In

1797 the king of Sardinia severely repressed a revolutionary movement, and left a treaty of alliance with France in abeyance. After 18 Fructidor he hastened to ratify it; but Ginguené, who soon arrived in Turin, and Brune, named commander of the Army of Italy, busied themselves with aiding the Jacobins, and armed bands penetrated into Piedmont. For several months the Directory posed as a mediator. Finally, when Ginguené had succeeded in imposing on the terrorized king a convention that delivered up the citadel of Turin to the French, it decided to retain it.

SWITZERLAND

Where the confederated cantons were concerned, the Directory was not without grievances. But after having long failed, it now secured concessions: the departure of Wickham, the émigrés, and Mallet du Pan, the paid publicist of counter-revolution; and negotiations for an agreement that would abandon to her the territory in the Jura and the town of Bienne (Biel), dependencies of the bishopric of Basel, which had now become the department of Mont-Terrible. Some Swiss democrats, however (notably Ochs of Basel), looked to the Directory for aid. Wishing to transform the cantons into a unified republic and end the domination of the patricians, and not relying upon the initiative of their compatriots, they desired, not that France invade their country, but that it appear threatening enough to force the oligarchy to resign. La Harpe of Vaud went still further. He solicited intervention by invoking a sixteenth-century treaty in which the king of France, while recognizing the rights of Bern over Vaud, nonetheless guaranteed the liberties of the latter. Until 18 Fructidor these suggestions had no apparent effect.

Bonaparte had shown less forbearance. Despite the pretensions of the 'Grisons League', he annexed the Valtelline to Lombardy. Determined to establish free communication between the Cisalpine Republic and France across Valais, and unable to secure mastery of the Simplon route, he threw decisive support to the Swiss democrats. The affair was decided, on December 8, 1797, at a dinner that brought Bonaparte and Ochs together at Reubell's home. Soon Ochs strove to have the cantons accept a constitution drafted by him and Merlin. Several persons were a party to it. At the same time a division of the Army of Italy moved to the frontier of Vaud, with orders not to cross over unless it was attacked. But the Vaudois hastened to comply with the new constitution. The Bernese sent some troops against them. The French commander dispatched a flag of truce, and in the darkness the bearer was shot at by mistake. Vaud was immediately occupied. The situation was not yet irreparable. Suddenly, on the night of February 13–14, 1798, the Directory ordered a march on Bern, most likely at the urging of Bonaparte. Brune advanced from Lausanne, and Schauenbourg from the Jura. The town fell after some rather sharp fighting.

The Directory at once appointed a civil commissioner, a former member of the Convention named Lecarlier, and gave him as assistant Rapinat (brother-in-law of Reubell), whose name caused gibes as unfair as they were facile, for he was a very upright man. They seized the treasury of Bern, the riches of which had undoubtedly motivated the enterprise (at least in part), and served to finance the Egyptian expedition. Since it included foreign securities that had to be negotiated, Talleyrand likewise profited from it. The cantons had a tax of 15 millions imposed on them. An assembly, meeting at Aarau, put the constitution into effect. Neither Ochs nor La Harpe enjoyed the favour of public opinion, however, and they were not included in the Directory of the Helvetian Republic. The commissioners strove to suppress arbitrary requisitions and pillaging, but civil war broke out. The Catholic cantons—Schwyz, Uri, and Unterwalden—revolted; Valais, giving itself a constitution, intended to remain independent. Such resistance had to be broken.

More adroit, the Bernese bought off Talleyrand, and thus secured a treaty which reduced their taxes. Rapinat, who had only recently succeeded Lecarlier (named minister of police), became indignant and refused to execute the treaty. This embroiled him with the Helvetian Directory. On 28 Prairial, Year VI (June 16, 1798), without consulting Paris, he effected a *coup d'état*. Ochs and La Harpe took control of the executive. The fate of the new republic, while less harsh than the rule to which Rome was subjected, appeared very precarious from the outset. Soon, it is true, the abolition of personal feudal dues, small tithes, and tithes on new lands (*novales*), and the suspension of payment of real dues and great tithes satisfied the peasants, but the redemption of the two latter categories was prescribed. Since, however, a land tax was instituted at the same time, the benefits seemed meagre.

THE CONGRESS OF RASTATT

After Campo Formio, Austria had seemed to resign herself to the loss of Belgium and the Rhineland. The Congress of Rastatt, where the envoys of the Directory were supposed to negotiate for cession of the left bank of the Rhine by the Empire, opened on November 16, 1797. Bonaparte appeared momentarily, secured Austria's relinquishment of Mainz in exchange for the occupation of Venice, and then yielded his place to Treilhard. The Directory had applied French legislation in the nine departments into which the Austrian Netherlands, the bishopric of Liége, and the Dutch cessions were incorporated; and national property in those regions was put on sale. The principal difficulties resulted from the religious schism, and although they presented no immediate danger, they did pave the way for revolutionary disorders. The Directory entrusted administration of the Rhineland to a commissioner, Rudler, who began to introduce French rule, and divided the region into four departments. Such action, without the decision of the Empire, could give rise to disputes. But how could Austria remain indifferent in the face of the extension of French influence beyond the limits agreed upon at Campo Formio?

Thugut was not annoyed. Still thinking in terms of expansion in Italy, he was simply awaiting the opportunity to demand compensations. It is true that the creation of supposedly independent republics in Rome and Switzerland was insufficient for such purposes; but at Rastatt the Directory exceeded the letter of the treaty. Reubell regretted that the Empire retained the Cologne region. From the general political point of view, his colleagues could not deny that if they did renounce it, they would alienate themselves from Prussia, disappointed in her expectation of advantageous indemnities in Germany. Consequently Treilhard demanded the entire left bank of the Rhine, and secured the Diet's adherence in principle on 19 Ventôse, Year VI (March 9, 1798).

Cobenzl immediately demanded compensations. Treilhard's reply was as surprising as it was categorical: The Cologne region, long occupied by troops, could not be considered a new acquisition. Would war be avoided on this account? It seemed imminent when, in April, Bernadotte, ambassador to Vienna, was attacked by rioters for having hoisted the French tricolour. Failing to secure suitable reparations, he left the city. Bonaparte even temporarily postponed his departure for Egypt. The crisis abated, however, for Thugut was unready and the Directory was preoccupied with the elections. Moreover, the wind shifted once more in Paris. Since the Directory had broken with the Jacobins, was its foreign policy not about to be modified?

THE AFTERMATH OF 22 FLORÉAL, YEAR VI (MAY 11, 1798)

Indeed, the Directory began to combat the Jacobins of the sister republics, principally in Italy, in favour of the conservatives; and it showed suspicion for the generals and army contractors who favoured propaganda. The Batavian Republic suffered the first repercussions. The unitarist democrats, already embroiled with Daendels and Joubert, were denounced by the 'notables' as dangerous anarchists. Delacroix was recalled, and on 24 Prairial, Year VI (June 12, 1798) a purge purified the government, and new elections secured it a majority. In Switzerland the Directory annulled Rapinat's *coup d'état* and dismissed him. Since, however, he was not replaced, he continued to perform his duties; and it was he who signed the treaty of alliance of August 19. The counter-revolution was not disarmed. The Catholic cantons took up arms again, and suffered a bloody defeat at Stans. But in October the oligarchs got the Austrians to enter Grisons.

In the Cisalpine Republic the about-face of the Directory provoked insoluble disorder. Into Italy it sent financial agents who, while ordinarily capable, were odious to the generals whom they were coming to control, and were hostile to the Jacobins. Chosen from among the *ci-devants*, they were consequently denounced as counter-revolutionaries. Such were Faipoult de Maisoncelle, a former minister; Amelot de Chaillou, son of a minister to Louis XV and former intendant of Burgundy, then director of the Special Bank (Caisse de l'Extraordinaire) under the Constituent Assembly; Laumond, who had succeeded him in this latter post after having served in the office of controller-general of finance; and Eymar, brother of an abbé who was classed among the 'blacks' in the Constituent Assembly. To them was added, in the post of ambassador, Trouvé, a protégé of La Revellière-Lépeaux and an ambitious mediocrity.

Under the influence of the Lombard nobles, the Directory declared Bonaparte's constitution a dead letter and ordered Trouvé to draft another, which, despite Brune, was imposed upon the Cisalpines. Soon, however, the general (probably thanks to Barras) arranged for this constitution to be subjected to a plebiscite. When Trouvé and Faipoult protested, they were replaced by Fouché and Amelot. With the connivance of Fouché, Brune, on the night of October 18–19, effected a new *coup*, which drove out Trouvé's followers, and popular ratification ensued. Similarly, Ginguené and Brune's lieutenant at Turin organized a demonstration, which they undoubtedly hoped would cause disturbances that would permit the occupation of Piedmont. This time the Directory became annoyed, dismissed Ginguené, recalled Fouché, and sent Brune to Holland. Nevertheless it purged the Genoese government itself.

Just as hostilities were beginning, with the Neapolitans invading the Roman Republic, the Directory adopted the measure that best characterizes the effort sustained since Floréal with so little success. On 5 Frimaire, Year VII (November 25, 1798), it re-established the commissioners with the armies—Rapinat in Switzerland, Amelot in Milan, and Faipoult in Rome. They received no more authority than had their predecessors, and ended far worse. Joubert, Brune's successor, considered this control unbearable, and submitted his resignation. The Directory finally accepted it in January, but faithful to its vacillating policy, it replaced Amelot with Laumond. Schérer, substituted for Joubert, proved deferential towards the commissioner, and this was one of the reasons he was hated by his subordinates. It was to cost him dearly. Masséna, from the moment of his arrival in Switzerland, disregarded Rapinat, who demanded his recall. The worst befell the army charged with repelling the Neapolitans. The contention between its commander, Championnet, and the commissioner, Faipoult, resulted in a far-reaching conflict.

To a certain degree then, the Directory checked the activity of the propagandists. It prevented them from revolutionizing

Piedmont and from attacking Tuscany. To win back Austria, however, it would have had to renounce its gains; and this it had no intention of doing. After 22 Floréal the Directory and Thugut agreed to send François de Neufchâteau and Cobenzl to confer at Seltz in Alsace. The former received orders to limit discussions to the Vienna incident, and to refer the question of compensations to Rastatt. There Austria could demand only German territories, now that she had designs on Italy. For the Directory this last obviously remained a private preserve.

Thus the Directory did not really modify its foreign policy. The fear of premature hostilities inspired some moderation, but delay was not repentance. The disgrace of the Jacobins in the sister republics, which in Italy turned some of them into enemies of France, was only a logical consequence of the internal policy marked by the 'day' of 22 Floréal. The control that the Directory attempted to impose on the generals appeared mainly as the complement of its dictatorship. Without greatly retarding the war, the anti-Jacobin reaction increased disorder, compromised the prestige of the Republic, and brought the Directory new and formidable enemies.

CHAPTER ELEVEN

The Second Coalition

ENGLAND NEVER LOST SIGHT OF THE FACT that in order to defeat France she would have to renew the war on the Continent. The Germans would not agree to this, but the Egyptian expedition and the foundation of the Roman Republic revived the Coalition. Paul I, who had become the ally of Turkey, secured access to the Mediterranean, and set himself up as protector of the Order of Malta and the court of Naples. The latter, already encouraged by Nelson, began hostilities, and with the fate of Italy once more brought into question, Thugut accepted the help of the Russians.

RUSSIA IN THE MEDITERRANEAN

Like his mother, Paul I detested the French Revolution. After Campo Formio he put the army of Condé in his pay, and permitted Louis XVIII to settle at Mitau. It was reported to him that prominent Poles were included in Bonaparte's army and were well received by the French ambassador at Vienna. His entourage, which included Joseph de Maistre, stimulated his hatred. He took a liking to the Jesuits, who hoped to convert him, and in 1797 he took the Order of Malta under his protection. The fall of the island infuriated him, and he began to arm. In October, 1798, the knights elected him grand master. Deeming Naples to be in danger, he granted the king his patronage.

This orientation did not result solely from the fancy of a half-mad man. Ever since Catherine had reached the Black Sea the eyes of the Russians had been turned towards the Mediterranean. Paul opened the ports of Crimea to foreign commerce, and Greeks ships traded there; but the opening of the Straits was most desirable. This economic policy constituted only a corollary to the penetration of the Ottoman Empire, sparked by the Treaty of Kuchuk Kainarji in 1774, which had given the tsarina a vague right to intervene on behalf of the Christians. The disintegration of Turkey promised new gains to the tsar. Since 1793, Selim III had been trying hard to create a modern army, but in many provinces he retained only nominal authority. Ali Tepeleni was carving out a fief for himself in Albania and Epirus. Pasvan Oglu, seizing Vidin and marching on Adrianople, had himself named pasha. Djezzar ruled in Syria; and Abd-ul-Aziz, leader of the Wahabites, had conquered Nejd, and threatened the holy cities and the pasha of Baghdad.

The Greeks, and the Serbs even more so, were a source of concern. The former (thanks to Turkish neutrality) were taking advantage of the war to expand into the Mediterranean, and they now formed colonies in all the large ports. Koray and Rhigas told them of the Revolution, and the French tricolour waved over the Ionian Islands. The Serbs, exasperated by the depredations of the Janissaries, had lent their aid to Joseph II, and Karageorge and Nenadovic asked only to help the Russians.

The Egyptian expedition brought Muscovite expansion an unforeseen success. After declaring war on France the Turks judged it wise to conclude the alliance that Paul hastened to offer them. The treaty of December 23, 1798, opened the Straits and the Ottoman ports to the Russians for the duration of the war; and it was agreed that their army and navy, penetrating the Mediterranean, would conquer the Ionian Islands. Corfu was the last to succumb, on March 3, 1799. Established on the periphery of the Ottoman Empire in Europe, the Russians thereby acquired a privileged position that they have never recovered. If possible, Malta, Naples, and other Italian principalities would furnish additional bases, which would eventually give them control of the Mediterranean.

At Naples, however, Maria Carolina, placing confidence in the assurances of Nelson, ordered the invasion of the Roman

Republic. This so fired Paul I with enthusiasm that on December 29, 1798, he allied himself with the Neapolitans and the English, and promised to send contingents to Naples and Lombardy.

THE WAR IN ITALY: THE PARTHENOPEAN REPUBLIC

Under the leadership of the Austrian General Mack, the Neapolitans occupied Rome on November 26, 1798, and with the aid of Nelson, landed at Leghorn. Thus they facilitated a great success for the revolutionary propagandists. The Directory declared war on their king, as well as on the king of Sardinia, who was considered an accomplice, and who retired to Cagliari. Piedmont was entirely occupied. From Rome, Championnet had led his small army behind the Tiber. Attacked at Civita Castellana, he routed his opponents, re-entered Rome, took the offensive, and on January 23, 1799, occupied Naples. He affected to ignore Faipoult, the civil commissioner. En route, the army and numerous commanders indulged in pillaging. The castle of Caserta, the Neapolitan Versailles, was plundered. In Naples the generals seized all the public funds.

Championnet clearly showed that he regarded himself as the Bonaparte of southern Italy. Making common cause with the bourgeoisie and the liberal nobles, he proclaimed the Parthenopean Republic, entrusted its government to them, and promised to be content with a tax of 60 millions. Faipoult intervened on behalf of his own authority and the intentions of the Directory. The latter did not desire another republic, intended the conquest as a bargaining item, and ordered its thorough exploitation. This was a return to the policy of 1796. Faipoult demanded that war prizes be turned over to him, and that the property of the crown and of the émigrés who had followed the king to Sicily be confiscated. He subjected the country to a monthly tax. Championnet resisted, and finally expelled him. The Directory recalled both of them, and when better informed, it had the general arrested and brought before a council of war. Several of his subordinates experienced the same fate or were cashiered. For the first time the Directory endeavoured to bring the generals to their senses. They were to contribute to its overthrow.

AUSTRIA ENTERS THE WAR: CHARACTER OF THE COALITION

To attack the Republic the Coalition required the aid of the Germans. Grenville would have preferred that of Prussia, but she declined. Frederick William III no longer listened to Sieyes, whom the Directory sent to him in May, 1798. Prosperous behind the line of demarcation—'the enchanted circle'—dominating North Germany, coveting Hanover, seeking to annex Nuremberg, and patiently awaiting the indemnities that the cession of their inconsequential Rhenish possessions would bring, the Prussians persisted in their neutrality. They collaborated, without regret, in the disintegration of the Empire, the ironic death certificate of which had been drawn up by Görres.

Thugut long remained wary, the more so since Pitt seemed in no hurry to promise subsidies. Though secretly allied with the Neapolitans, the Austrian chancellor did not aid them. Lacking Prussia, he wanted to be sure of effective support from Russia. When Paul I dispatched a first army, Thugut finally made up his mind and gave it free passage. A month elapsed before the Directory invoked this as a cause for war. On 22 Ventôse, Year VII (March 12, 1799), it finally declared war on Austria, which thus was joined to the Coalition without any treaty. The French soon occupied Tuscany, and removed Pius VI to Valence, where he died in August.

A bloody drama characterized the conflict in the eyes of the revolutionaries. On the night of April 28, Austrian hussars attacked the French plenipotentiaries as they were leaving Rastatt. One of them, Jean Debry, escaped though wounded; the two others, Roberjot and Bonnier, perished. To shrieks of 'Vengeance! Vengeance!' the Directory denounced the murders as a symptom of the blind hate that the kings and aristocrats vowed for the Republic. The origins of the assassinations remain obscure, but it cannot be doubted that they were intended to involve the Empire in the war, or at least the sovereigns of South Germany, since Prussia persisted in its defection. Thugut knew that these princes had no desire whatsoever to fight. Frederick II, duke of Württemberg, had not extricated himself from his quarrels with the privileged classes, and in Bavaria, Maximilian Joseph (who succeeded Charles Theodore in 1799) feared that the Habsburgs would contest his rights.

The Second Coalition was complete. Gustavus IV added Sweden, but only in October, 1799, and he furnished no troops. Since Thugut had signed nothing, the alliance was less stable than the first. As always, England appeared as the mainspring, and had to finance at least the Russian army: £225,000 immediately, plus £75,000 per month. Its very origins once more added to the weaknesses that would ruin the Coalition. Grenville assured Paul I that Great Britain, although besieging Malta, had no intention of keeping the island. She finally did secure the opening of the Straits to her merchant ships, but it was inconceivable that she would grant subsidies to the Muscovites to permit them to dominate the Mediterranean. If Thugut accepted their aid, it was to conquer Italy. Did Paul I intend to make him a present of it? England liked the idea no better than did the tsar. She thought only of depriving France of the former Austrian Netherlands, and to this the chancellor gave scarcely any thought.

The Coalition had plenty of men. Although distance did not permit the Russians to send more than 80,000 to the West, the Allies had the advantage of numbers. Yet their organization and methods of war had made no progress at all. Archduke Charles was projecting the formation of the Austrian troops into divisions when hostilities intervened. Money was particularly scarce. During his reign Paul I increased the debt from 43 million to 132 million rubles and issued 56 millions in paper. In Austria the deficit was perpetuated: the debt rose from 370 million gulden in 1792 to 572 millions in 1798; and the war was financed only by means of bank notes (*Bankzettel*), the circulation of which increased from 27 millions in 1793 to 200 millions in 1801.

The English economy, the mainstay of the Coalition, encountered difficulties during 1799. With the gold standard suspended, specie disappeared, small bank notes increased, and inflation progressed. It is probable that the local banks, the number of which was growing, inflated their issues as well as their advances. Moreover, England suffered from the repercussions of the crisis that had broken out at Hamburg by the end of winter; at least twentybankruptcies were declared in London. Industry felt the effects when, with the price of bread increasing, the harvest proved poor. Agitation by the workers caused Pitt to intensify the repression by extending it to the proletariat. The Combination Act of July 12, 1799, confirmed the ban on strikes, as well as that on associations and the collection of funds that established or sustained them.

As the year went on, it was necessary, however, to purchase grain abroad; and this necessitated an export of £3·5 million. In spite of everything, British capitalism, which the government had sustained with such skill, successfully withstood the shock. Obliged to renounce the convertibility of bank notes, Pitt checked inflation. Nevertheless it developed sufficiently that, as prices continued to climb, business escaped the depressing influence of the deflation that afflicted the Directory. Public finance remained healthy, and the Bank of England was able to sustain it by absorbing a reasonable quantity of Exchequer bills.

PREPARATIONS OF THE DIRECTORY

Since autumn the Republic had been preparing to resist; but the war effort was not comparable with that of the Committee of Public Safety. It may be assumed that the Directory was in no hurry to begin military action; when spring began, it was still unprepared. Eighteen Fructidor had once again made general arming of the nation the order of the day. Jourdan's first project (he was now a deputy), introduced on 23 Nivôse, Year VI (January 12, 1798), had to be reframed, however, and was passed only on 19 Fructidor (September 5). The Jourdan Law, or General Conscription Law, instituted compulsory military service for men between the ages of twenty and twenty-five, except for those married before 23 Nivôse, Year VI. It thus re-established the levy of August 23, 1793, on a permanent basis. Conscripts liable for service were to be enrolled by the Ministry of War on a national list in five classes, according to their dates of birth. If a contingent became necessary, the legislative body set it, and the minister levied it, beginning with the youngest. Another law annulled the deferments and exemptions granted since 1793.

A call-up was decided upon immediately, and on 3 Vendémiaire, Year VII (September 24, 1798), it was fixed at 200,000 men. Once again considerable difficulties impeded it. The rolls were incomplete or nonexistent. Since there were no provisions governing physical examinations, the ministry placed them under the control of boards recruited from among the fathers of conscripts; and this gave rise to notorious abuses. Establishment of the national list seemed practically impossible. Of those enrolled, 143,000 were considered fit for service, and this figure meant an enormous loss. Of these only 97,000 presented themselves for duty. They were sent on to the armies in isolated detachments, and this facilitated desertion; 74,000, or only 51 per cent, finally joined their regiments. On 28 Germinal, Year VII (April 17, 1799), the legislative body ordered the completion of the quota, at the same time profoundly modifying the law. Persons liable were authorized to gather beforehand to obtain volunteers, or to draw lots among themselves. The conscripts designated were permitted to offer substitutes. This was a return to the levy of February, 1793. Nevertheless only 71,000 men responded to the summons, and of these but 57,000 reached the front.

Through this influx, which led to a new amalgamation, the army of the Directory, which had become a professional one, recovered something of the popular character of that of the Year II. Not all of these reinforcements reached it, however, before the opening of the campaign; and unlike its predecessor, it did not possess numerical superiority over the enemy. Nor could it be adequately supplied. In order to clothe, equip, and arm the conscripts, the legislative body put on sale 125 millions' worth of national property; and the great fiscal laws of the Year VII probably attest a similar effort. It was too little and too late. The conscripts set out unprepared, and the armies lived in want in vassal or enemy countries, which were already exhausted. In Italy the chief resources were drawn from Piedmont, newly occupied and thoroughly exploited.

THE SPRING CAMPAIGN, 1799

The spirit of the new war was totally lacking from the conception of the campaign. With the 45,000 men of the Army of the Danube, Jourdan was to invade South Germany, while Bernadotte covered his left on the middle Rhine with 30,000. Of the 100,000 troops in Italy, Schérer was able to assemble only 45,000 on the Adige; and, between them, Masséna would conquer Grisons and threaten the Tyrol. The French thus attacked everywhere at once, in a line, instead of grouping the main striking force in Switzerland, where it could move at will into Italy or Germany to assure a decisive action. As might be expected, the Austrians did likewise. Archduke Charles commanded 75,000 men in Bavaria, Kray had 60,000 in Venetia, and 20,000 others guarded the Tyrol. Seemingly unaware of their numerical superiority, they awaited the Russians before taking action. Thwarted by Thugut's preoccupation with diplomacy, the slow and desultory campaign manifested all the features of a war of the Old Regime.

Masséna had the greatest success. He occupied Grisons, but having entered the Vorarlberg, he failed before Feldkirch. Jourdan advanced very slowly as far as Lake Constance, and attacked the archduke at Stockach on March 25. Repulsed, he led his army back to the Rhine, and submitted his resignation. The archduke did not persist, for Thugut sent him to Switzerland. Schérer captured the fortified positions at Pastrengo and Rivoli, but his poorly planned manoeuvre against Verona tested him sorely. Attacked in turn at Magnano on April 5, he beat a retreat (although the battle was indecisive), and without attempting to make a stand anywhere, he withdrew to the Adda, and abandoned the army to Moreau. Kray did not advance, but awaited Suvorov, who, with 18,000 Russians, took command. This old man, famous for his victories over the Turks and the Poles, was a remarkable leader of men, not a strategist. From April 25 to 27 he attacked the crossings of the Adda, and forced several of them, notably at Cassano. Sérurier's division was annihilated. Moreau evacuated the Milanese, and reassembled the wreckage of his forces at Alessandria. Suvorov made a theatrical entry into Milan, dispersed a large part of his troops, and attacked Moreau only on May 12, without much success. Again the French retreated to Genoa and Cuneo.[1]

Moreau counted on Macdonald, who laboriously led the army from Naples across the insurgent peninsula. Instead of awaiting Macdonald, Moreau arranged to meet him at Ales-

[1] Both the domestic and foreign policies of the Directory had been detrimental to the French in Italy. The partisans of Italian unity, normally of Jacobin leanings but disappointed by the attitude of the Directory, had gone over to the Coalition. General Lahoz fought against the French, and in Piedmont the Jacobins, like the partisans of the Old Regime, organized an insurrection.

sandria. Macdonald crossed the Apennines and found his route blocked by Suvorov on the banks of the Trebbia. The battle lasted three days (June 17–19). Unable to force a crossing, Macdonald returned over the mountains, and skirting the coast reached Genoa. Moreau, who had advanced victoriously as far as Marengo, retreated to link up with him.

The failures in Germany and Italy led to Masséna's withdrawal. He evacuated Grisons, and when the archduke crossed the Rhine, withdrew behind the Limmat. Attacked, he won the first battle of Zurich on June 4, but he deemed it wise to recross the river and abandon the town in order to take up a position between the Rhine and the Lake of Zug, where he would be covered by the Limmat and the Lake of Zurich. Since Lecourbe had had to abandon the St. Gotthard Pass and the Reuss valley, however, Masséna might be taken from behind by an army coming from Italy.

When summer came, there was reason to expect large-scale operations; but these did not materialize. For weeks the Allied governments discussed plans for them; meanwhile their armies fought where they were. Suvorov besieged fortresses, which (including Mantua) surrendered so rapidly that cries of 'treason' arose in France. He had to smash an offensive thrust by Joubert, who had taken command of the Army of Italy, retaining Moreau as an aide. Pressed to return to Paris, where Sieyes had destined him for a political role, Joubert attacked at Novi on August 15 without having concentrated his forces. He was killed at the very beginning of the engagement. Moreau contained the enemy but lost a third of his effectives, and had to retreat by night. Master of Piedmont, Suvorov reinstated the functionaries of Charles Emmanuel, in conformity with the tsar's intentions, and planned to invade Dauphiné.

Suvorov's actions did not suit Thugut, who regarded him simply as an auxiliary and intended to determine the fate of Italy himself. His commissioner refused to recognize the agents of the king of Sardinia. The minister was scarcely less disturbed by what was happening in the south of the peninsula. Macdonald had left only weak forces there; an English squadron entered the port of Naples, Cardinal Ruffo had stirred the peasants to revolt, Russians and Turks arrived from Corfu; and in June the defenders of the capital, bottled up in their forts, capitulated.

Nelson broke the agreement and abandoned the patriots, both noble and bourgeois, to an atrocious repression. But King Ferdinand did not stop there. He wanted to seize all or part of the papal domains, and in September his troops entered them. The Austrians at once moved in from the north.

The English were inclined to approve the tsar's re-establishment of the legitimate sovereigns in Italy, but they particularly desired that the Coalition concentrate its efforts on Switzerland and the Netherlands. Hopes of a restoration of the Bourbons revived in London, and the counter-revolutionaries, as usual, offered themselves to the enemy. Wickham returned to settle in Switzerland, where he prepared an insurrection in Franche-Comté and the south, and Bourmont was ready to stir a new revolt in the west. They also counted on bribing Barras. The British government insisted, therefore, that the French be driven from Switzerland, and that France be invaded through Burgundy. Abandoning Italy to Thugut, it secured Archduke Charles's departure to fight Masséna, and it persuaded Paul I to assign the same task to a second army, of 28,000 men, entrusted to Korsakov. To take the French from behind, it suggested that Suvorov leave Italy so as to cross the St. Gotthard Pass. Nothing suited Thugut better. The tsar was told that the deliverance of the Swiss cantons would constitute an exploit worthy of the saviour of Europe, so he yielded.

Before the plans could be put into effect, another English project intervened—the reconquest of Holland and Belgium. In May the tsar had allowed himself to be convinced that he should send 18,000 men to join the expedition being prepared by the duke of York. Thugut was not greatly interested in the former Austrian domains of the Netherlands; but if they were retaken from the French, he intended to dispose of them. On July 30, Archduke Charles received orders to leave Switzerland and go to Mainz. Since the Russians were not supposed to arrive until September, he perceived the danger and did not hurry, and discussions continued during August.

As in 1793, the Coalition Powers thus gave the Republic time to consider the situation. Yet despite the pleas of the Directory, the French generals considered themselves unable to undertake anything before summer's end; and by that time the war had long since provoked decisive events in France.

CHAPTER TWELVE

The Crisis of the Year VII in France

CONTINENTAL PEACE did not make the dictatorship of the Directory popular, but it did afford it a respite. When war resumed, however, the Directory was held responsible, and its masters were the first victims. Then the succession of defeats definitively compromised the regime instituted by the Thermidorians. Civil war reappeared, and the threat of invasion provoked new measures for public safety. A last anti-Jacobin reaction prepared the advent of military dictatorship.

30 PRAIRIAL, YEAR VII (JUNE 18, 1799)

At the beginning of Germinal, Year VII (the end of March, 1799), no reverse had yet overshadowed the conquest of Naples. Nevertheless the elections augured unfavourably for the Directory. Since autumn the threatening war had intensified discontent because of business stagnation, increased taxes, and above all conscription. The unsatisfactory results of the Jourdan Law attested the fear inspired by military service; moreover, it increased disorder everywhere. In November, 1798, part of the Belgian countryside (Walloon as well as Flemish), already much disturbed by religious conflict, revolted; and this 'peasant war', which lasted for two months, left the country greatly troubled. In France a new Vendée was so feared that the government was authorized to suspend application of the Jourdan Law in the west. Nevertheless *chouannerie* recovered its strength. In March the town of Château-Gontier was taken by surprise. Everywhere draft dodgers and deserters joined the armed bands, whose outrages increased.

Public opinion generally reproached the Directory for having provoked the war. The Jacobins accused it of unpreparedness and of permitting counter-revolution to play the enemy's game once more. The majority in the Councils was not indifferent to these diverse charges, the more so because it suffered the dictatorship of the executive impatiently. As usual, the Directory denounced the combination of royalists and anarchists, aiming particularly at the latter in order to conciliate the bourgeoisie. 'Are you waiting for a new Maximum to complete your ruin?' asked a circular by François de Neufchâteau. The usual procedures were used to prepare for the elections, though with less energy than in the Year VI—probably because the functionaries felt that pressure was ineffectual. Indeed, their backing was often enough cause for the defeat of a candidate. Was it not possible at least to have another 22 Floréal? The attitude of the Councils made such an idea impracticable. Once more, electors were found to constitute schismatic electoral assemblies; but their choices were systematically rejected in favour of those of the 'mother assemblies'.

Since the Directory had chiefly fought the Jacobins, its defeat was regarded as their victory. Yet such was not the case. It soon became evident that the Thermidorians retained a majority. Greatly angered at the Directors, these latter came to an agreement with the Jacobins to overthrow them; but their political and social tendencies remained the same. The crisis thus unfolded in three acts: the fall of the Second Directory, the apparent triumph of the Left, and a violent and victorious anti-Jacobin reaction.

In the weeks that followed the elections the situation of the Republic became critical. Naples and Milan were lost, and Switzerland was invaded. At home 'everything was falling apart,' according to a police report of 19 Prairial. The animosity against the Directors increased. Were they incompetent or criminal? The charge of treason recurred. The addresses which were beginning to come in from the departments openly accused Schérer, the former minister of war. Lucien Bonaparte fulminated against the commissioners with the armies, and the generals supported him. The collusion of the latter with the opposition, obvious in the press and in their speeches, clearly derived from the preferred placement given them by the Five Hundred on their lists of candidates to the Directory during the crisis. One list of ten names included seven generals and admirals. At the end of Germinal an indispensable examination of financial measures strained the reports of the Directory and the outgoing Councils to the utmost. The rumour of a new Fructidor spread; but this was an impossibility. The government had quarrelled with its generals; and in any case, they had been defeated and had lost prestige.

Even before the new Councils had met on 1 Prairial, Year VII (May 20, 1799), fortune turned in their favour. Reubell left the Directory, and the Elders replaced him with Sieyes. He was known to be an enemy of the Directors, and quarrels began. Nor was it overlooked that he wished to change the Constitution; and Barras had aided in his election. The Trojan horse had entered the fortress. Returning from Berlin, he did not assume his seat until 20 Prairial (June 8); but ten days were enough for him to attain his ends. Thus it may be wondered if this 'mole of the Revolution' (as Robespierre called him) had not been intriguing for a long while.

Suddenly, on 28 Prairial (June 16), Poullain-Grandprey recalled that the message of the 17th, demanding an accounting from the Directory, had remained unanswered. He persuaded the Five Hundred to decide that it would remain in permanent session until the report was received, and the Elders followed suit. That evening Treilhard's election in the Year VI was attacked on the pretext that at the time he had been out of the legislative body less than a year. The objection had been brushed aside in the preceding year because the time interval was supposed to date from his departure from office to his return to authority, and not to his election. Nevertheless he was forced out of the Directory. His place was filled by Gohier, president of the Court of Cassation, who, as minister of justice in the Year II, was considered a Jacobin.

On the 30th the attack was resumed, this time against La Revellière-Lépeaux and Merlin. Since the previous day Sieyes and Barras had been pressing them to resign so as to avoid indictment, and a deputation from the Elders urged them to yield. Merlin was the first to capitulate; then La Revellière-Lépeaux resigned. They were replaced by Roger Ducos, who was designated by Sieyes, and Moulin, an obscure general and Jacobin, chosen by Barras. The ministers, including Talleyrand, also disappeared.

The 'day' of 30 Prairial, Year VII (June 18, 1799), was thus *not* a *coup d'état*: the two Directors dared not risk an indictment that was legal; but it *was* a '9 Thermidor' which restored the Councils' control over the executive. Still, it did not subordinate the latter or weaken it, as the Convention had done with the Thermidorian committees. Sieyes had his way, and in his obstinacy to prepare the ruin of the regime, he showed a skill and firmness that contrasted with his incompetence on 18 Brumaire. Thirty Prairial was, moreover, the 'day' of the generals. Bernadotte received the post of minister of war, and Joubert the command of the Army of Italy. Championnet was released from prison and was given the army being formed in the Alps against Suvorov. The commissioners with the army finally lost all their authority. Rapinat had resigned, and when Joubert arrived in Italy, he sent Laumond back to France.

Finally, 30 Prairial represented the revenge for 22 Floréal, because the three new Directors had been 'Floréalized'. The entry into the Ministry of Finance of Robert Lindet, a former member of the Committee of Public Safety, seemed symbolic. This impression was confirmed by numerous dismissals and by the nomination of prominent Jacobins. Newspapers reappeared, even before the Elders had approved the re-establishment of freedom of the press. Clubs also reopened, the most famous of them in the Manège, which the Five Hundred had vacated in the Year VI in order to move to the former Bourbon Palace, and its first 'regulator' was Drouet, who had been implicated in the Babeuf plot.

THE JACOBIN LAWS

The triumph of the Jacobins seemed to be demonstrated in the voting of laws that the Left obtained, without delay, by invoking the danger to the Republic. As in the Convention, part of the majority was responsive to it. Still agitated by the struggle against the Directors, it took several days to realize that it was once more moving towards a revolutionary government. The law of 10 Messidor, Year VII (June 28, 1799), proposed by Jourdan, achieved, as he said, 'the levy *en masse*'. The five classes of conscripts were called up in their entirety, and replacements were not allowed. There were an estimated 223,000 conscripts, 116,000 of whom (again, 51 per cent) were placed on active service. One month later a second law ordered the reorganization of the National Guard. These were not empty words, since the Guard furnished the mobile columns against the rebels.

Property, as well, underwent radical treatment. Requisitioning increased, openly generalized this time by orders of the Directory to the departmental authorities. At the same time as the levy, Jourdan had obtained the adoption of a forced loan of 100 millions. The method of its collection was established, with great difficulty, only on 19 Thermidor (August 6). Based on a progressive scale, it affected those who paid at least 300 francs in land taxes as well as personal taxes (calculated fairly by a panel of citizens not subject to the loan) over 10,000 francs, with provision that a fortune made by speculation might be taxed in its entirety.

Next came the repressive Law of Hostages on 24 Messidor, Year VII (July 12, 1799). In departments which the legislative body declared to be in a state of disturbance (in whole or in part), the central administration had to choose hostages from among the relatives of émigrés and rebels, so as to intern them. In the event of the murder of a functionary, soldier, or purchaser of national property, the Directory would deport four; moreover, all would share a fine and the full cost of damages. An amnesty was offered to the rebels, except the leaders, on condition that they surrender their arms. If they did not take advantage of this they would be brought before a military commission and executed, merely on verification of their identity.

On the same day of 24 Messidor (July 12), a report was presented on the indictments that had been demanded everywhere, and it concluded by confirming those of the four ousted Directors and Schérer. The Five Hundred approved the indictment; but the law required an investigation. This was supposed to take thirty-three days, even before it might be brought to the Elders, so that there might be time to organize resistance.

THE LAST ANTI-JACOBIN REACTION

This resistance proved to be already vigorous by the end of Messidor, Year VII, and on the 26th (July 14, 1799), Sieyes issued the first warning. He did not shrink from taking measures of public safety, nor did the majority, but only on express condition that their execution be reserved to the latter in order to ensure strict control. The Jacobins aroused fears by declaring that the recent laws would remain meaningless if the old ardour were not reawakened among the people. The inference was that they would soon claim to associate the people with the government, and that, at the very least, the revolutionary committees would reappear. The report of 19 Prairial (June 6), which has already been cited, counselled that agents be sent into the provinces to stimulate local administration, as had been done after August 10, 1792. It carefully specified that they must be chosen 'from among upright and well-to-do citizens; they must be the protectors of persons and property'. In opposition, Lamarque made some no less significant observations: 'Some want to employ popular force to repel the barbarians; others fear the use of this all-powerful force, that is to say, they fear the mass of republicans more than the hordes from the north.'

The levy *en masse* and requisitioning undeniably redoubled the fear and exasperation in the country. Nevertheless these sentiments were particularly sharp among the upper middle class, which alone was affected by the forced loan. Lindet succeeded in getting a certain number of bankers and contractors to agree to a treasury operation that mobilized part of the revenue anticipated from the loan, and Perregaux set a good example. In general, however, recriminations and passive resistance presaged failure, and hardly more than one-third of the sum expected was received. Many of the wealthy dismissed their servants and left Paris; and it was announced that factories would close.

Within the Directory and among its partisans there was particular concern over the attacks against those who had been

'Prairialized'. If these succeeded, the tumbrils would roll again. Barras, and Sieyes especially, now came under attack. It was said of the latter that he had concluded an agreement at Berlin for the abandonment of all or part of the French conquests, and the re-establishment of the monarchy in favour of the duke of Orléans or the duke of Brunswick. There is no doubt that, as in the Year III, part of the majority and some of the generals thought in terms of a restoration. In any case, the charge frightened Sieyes. Most newspapers, pamphlets, and placards inveighed against the Messidor laws. Nor did the members of the clubs shun provocative demonstrations—such as Jourdan's toast of July 14 'To the resurrection of the pikes!'—or even proposals hostile to the rich. The *jeunesse dorée* threatened the Manège, and they came to blows. In several towns—Rouen, Amiens, Caen—similar conflicts disturbed public order, and blood was spilled at Bordeaux.

Although its adversaries evoked the memory of May 31, 1793, the Left could not count on a rising by masses discouraged by a long reaction and relapsed into indifference. No means of organizing such a movement remained, and it never stirred more than a few hundred demonstrators—artisans, shopkeepers, and clerks—who had remained faithful to their memories. The government held the entire administration in its hands, and since 18 Fructidor it had maintained a garrison of some 20,000 men in Paris. The only precaution it took was to put the majority on its guard, and by a resolute attitude, prevent its being weakened. Sieyes worked at this with determination.

On 8 Thermidor, Year VII (July 26, 1799), Cornet, one of Sieyes' confederates, suddenly got the Elders to decide that no political society would be admitted henceforth within the confines of the legislative body. Since the Manège was an annex of the Tuileries, where the Elders sat, the club moved to a church in the Rue du Bac. Following Cornet, however, Courtois, the troublesome friend of Danton, had asserted that the terrorists were plotting to assassinate the Directors and convoke a convention. A commission was established to investigate the charge. On the 13th (July 31) it could report only two posters that were judged to be seditious. Nevertheless it invited the Directory to 'apply the Constitution'. Two days earlier the

Ministry of Police had been confided to Fouché, and on the 24th (August 11) General Marbot, who had been dismissed, yielded the command of the 17th army division to Lefebvre. On the same day the final discussion of the indictment of the 'Prairialized' men began. On the 26th, Fouché closed the club, and on 1 Fructidor (August 18) the indictment was rejected by a vote of 217 to 214. This indicated that it might have passed if the waverers had not been intimidated by Sieyes' *coup*. Henceforth the clubs no longer spoke for the Left, and its recriminations accomplished nothing. The break between Sieyes and the Jacobins had been completed, and Barras, compromised on both sides, found himself isolated.

Nevertheless the Left found two occasions for resuming the offensive. Royalist insurrection suddenly broke out, on 18 Thermidor, Year VII (August 5, 1799), in Haute-Garonne and the neighbouring cantons, under the leadership of former General Rougé and Count de Paulo. It was formidable, and at one point Toulouse was surrounded; but the outbreak remained isolated. In the west, Bourmont appeared only at the end of August, and set the rising for mid-October. Toulouse had been in the hands of the Jacobins since the Year IV and would not surrender. Administrators and republican officers in the vicinity held fast, and after a few successes the rebels were gradually dispersed. Those who persisted gave battle on 3 Fructidor (August 20) at Montréjeau, where they were routed.

The news reached Paris on 26 Thermidor, Year VII (August 13, 1799), at the moment the club was being closed. Emotion moved the Councils immediately to authorize the searching of homes for a month, and ultimately to declare a large number of cantons in a state of disturbance; but the Law of Hostages was never actually applied effectively in them. Sieyes, for his part, ordered the deportation of the staffs of thirty-four of the remaining royalist newspapers under the law of 19 Fructidor, Year V (September 5, 1797). He took advantage of the situation to strike a double blow. The next day, on the pretext of conspiracy, a second decree ordered the arrest of the staffs of sixteen other newspapers, and this time Jacobin publications appeared on the list.

The disaster of Novi dated from 28 Thermidor (August 15), but it made less of an impact than the landing of the English in Holland on 10 Fructidor (August 27). A new invasion was foreseen if they pressed rapidly southward, and the alarm was great. On the 27th (September 13) Jourdan proposed to the Five Hundred that France be declared 'in danger'. Tumult erupted, and the galleries took part in it. This was the last of the dramatic sessions of the Revolution. Lucien Bonaparte turned against the Jacobins, and Daunou appealed to the majority: Either the declaration was pure rhetoric, or it would be invoked to extort measures that could be foreseen all too easily from precedent. Boulay finally secured adjournment. Nevertheless the crowd assembled. The Jacobins had sounded out Bernadotte. What would he do? Despite his brave talk, he was disinclined to take chances. Sieyes finally settled the matter by having a message sent to him stating that the Directory accepted his resignation—which he had never submitted! On the 28th, Jourdan's motion was rejected. Suddenly, brilliant victories changed the situation completely and set the seal of discredit on the Left.

THE AUTUMN CAMPAIGN

Before leaving Switzerland, Archduke Charles had vainly attempted to crush Masséna on August 17; on the 30th an attack by the French failed likewise. At the beginning of September, Charles had to resign himself to obeying his orders: he descended the Rhine and was no longer useful. Still, the pleas of the English had secured Thugut's consent for Hotze, the archduke's lieutenant, to remain in position with 25,000 men. He held the Linth, while Korsakov established himself at Zurich and on the Limmat. Meanwhile, Lecourbe, aided by Turreau, who had come from Valais, had retaken the Grimsel and St. Gotthard passes, and once more held the valley of the Reuss. Molitor had advanced to Glarus. Thus this route was closed to Suvorov, who did not leave Italy until September 11. Temporarily covered in the rear, Masséna took the passage of the Limmat at Dietikon by surprise once the archduke had gone, and cutting Korsakov's army in two, repulsed the right wing towards the Rhine while he bottled up the left in Zurich. Korsakov escaped with difficulty and recrossed the Rhine with the remnants of his forces. At the same time Soult routed

Hotze's corps, and Hotze was killed. The second battle of Zurich had lasted three days (3–5 Vendémiaire, Year VIII—September 25–27, 1799).

Suvorov, however, after having crossed the St. Gotthard, drove Lecourbe back step by step to Altdorf. There, for want of a route along the lake, he had to turn obliquely across the mountains, and he encountered Mortier, whom the victorious Masséna hastened to support. Leaving Rosenberg before them, Suvorov moved against Molitor, who, driven back along the Linth, repelled all assaults at Näfels. Finally learning of Hotze's disaster, Suvorov's one thought was to withdraw across the Alps. He succeeded only because of the resistance of Rosenberg, who barred Masséna's path. On October 7, under great stress, the Russians reached the Rhine at Ilanz, whence they escaped to the Vorarlberg.

In Holland the British expedition landed at Den Helder on 10 Fructidor, Year VII (August 27, 1799). The Batavian fleet surrendered without a fight, and this was the sole English gain from the expedition. The Russians came as reinforcements, and the duke of York took command, but his offensive was halted at Bergen, on September 19, by the Franco-Batavian army under the command of Brune. On October 2 the latter had to retreat to Castricum; but there, on the 6th, he once more repelled the enemy. The Orangist insurrection did not materialize, and broken dikes, constant rain, shortage of supplies, and epidemics soon made the situation of the invaders untenable. On 26 Vendémiaire, Year VIII (October 18, 1799), the duke of York signed an evacuation agreement at Alkmaar. The Russians were transported to Jersey in the vain hope of organizing an invasion of Brittany. Paul I, who was already much annoyed by Suvorov's failure, recalled his troops on October 22 and sent a letter to Austria announcing his withdrawal. The Coalition was disintegrating.

Some seemingly miraculous news was added to the announcement of these victories. On 17 Vendémiaire, Year VIII (October 9, 1799), Bonaparte had landed at Fréjus, and was moving towards Paris, unleashing enthusiasm everywhere. The return of the 'invincible' finally gave assurance that the Republic was saved. Since the outset of the war the pattern had always been the same. Defeat produced extreme measures, and victory made them unnecessary. In times of danger the Jacobins won control because of their daring and intransigence. Once the danger was past, the moderates triumphed easily, and the reaction then was consolidated. The Five Hundred decided to modify the Law of Hostages and the legislation concerning émigrés. On 9 Brumaire (October 31), in a report on the forced loan, the Council of Elders proposed to replace it with an increase in direct taxes. 'The counter-revolution is made!' cried Lesage-Senault. The debate continued on the 16th and 17th, and was supposed to be resumed on the 18th. This was the day of the *coup d'état*.

CHAPTER THIRTEEN

18 Brumaire

THE IMMEDIATE DANGER to the Directory had vanished—but for how long? The authoritarian methods practised since 18 Fructidor were obviously ineffective; they were supposed to be associated with the liberal Constitution of the Year III, which made for instability and a conflict of powers. Because the Thermidorians, like the Montagnards, recognized that the war necessitated a revolutionary dictatorship, the latter had to be organized, but in such a way that the bourgeoisie would not suffer. Such was the object of 18 Brumaire. The bourgeoisie secured the lasting benefits that they had desired or approved; but the *coup d'état* removed them from the control of the state. In achieving it, circumstances suddenly bestowed the leading role on the army, that is, on Bonaparte.

THE REVISIONISTS

The crisis of the Year VII had been averted; but after such a severe test, would it not be folly to delay until similar causes provoked another one? True, in the spring the fighting with Austria was over; yet the war might resume with all its dangers. At home the civil war continued. On October 14, at the signal from Bourmont, the *chouans* seized Le Mans, then Nantes, and subsequently St.-Brieuc—ephemeral successes, undoubtedly. In the Vendée, Travot promptly suppressed the rebellion, and

Hédouville was soon able to negotiate peace north of the Loire. Nevertheless the counter-revolution remained a menace. Besides, now that the armies had returned to the frontiers, where would the money come from? Officials and *rentiers* complained of hard times, and public services were at a standstill. The nation demanded peace, not caring which regime secured it so long as it preserved the essentials of the social achievements of the Constituent Assembly.

The bourgeoisie looked to a more distant horizon. For the moment they were reassured. Sieyes held the rudder firmly, and the laws of Messidor were to be either repealed or weakened. But the bugbear of Jacobinism still frightened them. What kind of government would emerge from the elections of the Year VIII? For the Thermidorians this question was of prime importance. They wished to retain power so as to defend the Revolution and the Republic, to be sure, but also for personal reasons. In any case, the uncertainty became unbearable, and they were driven to despair at the prospect that this would be an annual occurrence.

Finally, what was to be done with Bonaparte? Since his arrival in Paris on October 16 he had shown a thoroughly republican discretion, and frequented the Institute, where he fraternized with the ideologues. But all eyes were focused on him. No one seemed to remember that he had been largely responsible for the new war, and had had nothing to do with the recent victories of the Republic. No one thought of reproaching him for the Egyptian adventure. Exiled by the evil Directors, he had thwarted their plans in an astonishing manner—twice miraculously escaping from Nelson! His star brought good luck. Never would he have a better opportunity to confirm his belief that it was less important for him to convince the mediocre intelligence of men than to capture their imaginations by fabulous undertakings, and to win over the most obtuse through the magic of improbable successes. After Campo Formio he had been adviser to the government, and he could be chosen to conduct the war as generalissimo. How could anyone believe that he would be satisfied with such a pittance? Legally he was too young to be named as either Director or minister.

The need for constitutional revision thus became more

urgent every day. Since 18 Fructidor this idea had constantly gained new adherents. The triumvirs, not daring to believe it feasible in France, had shown their feelings, however, by modifying the constitutions of the sister republics. They reproduced that of the Year III, only with important modifications to increase the authority of the executive power. Benjamin Constant, Madame de Staël, and the ideologue heirs of the philosophic thought of the century leaned in the same direction. The revisionist *par excellence* was Sieyes, who, since the Year III, had offered his plan in opposition to the one adopted. Since then his ideas had changed. We know them only through conversations subsequent to the *coup d'état* reported by Boulay, Daunou, and Roederer; but in part they inspired the Constitution of the Year VIII.

Immediate revision was impossible, so Sieyes had been contemplating a *coup d'état* ever since his election. Even if they thought it indispensable, the majority in the Councils would not take the initiative. Hence it would be military and antiparliamentary, as on 18 Fructidor, but much more hazardous. In the Year V the Councils had yielded to the Directory under pretext of saving the Constitution. This time it was not only a matter of violating the Constitution but also of curtailing their powers. If they resisted, they would have to be driven out. Did Sieyes fail to see the consequences? By all evidence the *coup d'état* thus executed would result in a military dictatorship. Even had he concluded an agreement with the military leaders beforehand, they would have kept their bargain only insofar as it suited them. Did he thus feel that intimidation would suffice, and that the Councils would co-operate with him in drafting a new constitution? Since he did not arrange it, it is doubtful that he cherished such an illusion. Unless it is assumed that he gave little thought to his personal safety, he directed the affair with such rashness that he became its victim.

For the army as well, circumstances were far different from those of the Year V. Then it had willingly helped drive out the royalists; this time republicans and even Jacobins were involved. It did not like the 'lawyers' (*avocats*), and it required a leader of striking prestige, with an incontestable revolutionary past, to carry it off. In both respects Bonaparte was unequalled. Chance provided him at just the right moment. He himself could do nothing that was not in agreement with the other conspirators. Having left his army without authorization, his legal status was questionable. As an unattached general he could take command at Paris only if he found accomplices within the Directory and the Councils. The difficulty was that he would not consider Barras (except, perhaps, to buy him off), and he detested Sieyes. Talleyrand intervened, and Cambacérès, minister of justice, was apparently in on the secret. Nothing seems to have been said to Fouché, but, well informed, he made himself an unofficial accomplice.

In the Council of Elders, President Lemercier and the sergeants at arms played a decisive role. Elected to the presidency of the Council of Five Hundred, Lucien could be counted on. Several generals—Jourdan, Augereau, Bernadotte—appeared hesitant; but most of them rallied to Bonaparte. Even Moreau felt enough rancour to come to his aid. Collot, the contractor, provided money, and was doubtless not alone in so doing. On 7 Brumaire, Year VIII (October 29, 1799), a law suspended the authorizations issued to the financiers until their accounts were audited. These were returned on the evening of the 19th.

18 AND 19 BRUMAIRE, YEAR VIII (NOVEMBER 9 AND 10, 1799)

To justify the undertaking, a terrorist plot was trumped up. Such a claim found many supporters, for it had filled the newspapers since Messidor. The extent to which it terrified some persons is attested by Madame de Staël. 'One of my friends, present at the meeting at St.-Cloud, sent me news every hour. He warned me that the Jacobins were about to win, and I prepared to leave France once more.'[1]

It seemed safer to operate outside Paris, and the conspiracy provided the excuse. A special session of the Elders was called, and suspect members were informed too late to be able to attend. On 18 Brumaire, Year VIII (November 9, 1799), they voted to move to St.-Cloud (which was legal), and named Bonaparte commander of the Paris troops (which was not); the Directory alone had the authority to make such appointments. Already the generals were gathered at Bonaparte's

[1] *Considérations sur la Révolution française*, Part IV, Chap. 2.

apartment on the Rue de la Victoire, and troops assembled on the pretext of a review. If the majority of the Directors refused to recognize the unconstitutional decision of the Elders, they might possibly have found a general to oppose Bonaparte. Everything depended upon Barras, but he resigned. Gohier and Moulin remained Moreau's prisoners until they had submitted their resignations.

At St.-Cloud, on the 19th, the army surrounded the palace where the councils were meeting. The affair took a bad turn because the conspirators had not drawn up a detailed plan. The Elders did not have the initiative, and those who were absent on the previous night protested. Bonaparte intervened and again denounced the Jacobins, but made no positive proposal. As he himself said, he could speak only to command, or when he was sure that no one would dare reply to him. When some voices invoked the Constitution, he flew into a rage. 'You have violated the Constitution; it no longer exists!'

The situation was worse in the Five Hundred. By what right did he enter without being summoned? Attacked by the assembled deputies, he left the chamber to the cry of 'Out-law him!' Lucien defended his brother in vain, and grenadiers had to lead him away. Bonaparte had harangued the troops without any great success. It was Lucien who, on horseback, succeeded in rallying them by denouncing the factious representatives, bought by England, who had attacked their general with daggers. The guard of the legislative body itself finally yielded, and as the charge was sounded, it forced the evacuation of the Orangerie, where the Five Hundred were still deliberating.

The Elders and, in the evening, a small number of the Five Hundred pathetically reassembled, adjourned the Councils, from which sixty-one additional members were excluded. They substituted two commissions charged with voting the laws presented by the three 'consuls' (who replaced the Directory), and with preparing, in accord with them, a new constitution. The consuls were Bonaparte, Sieyes, and Roger Ducos. Presumably they were equal, but nobody was deceived. This day of lies, with daggers added to the conspiracy, was also a day of dupes. Bonaparte put Sieyes into eclipse.

III

THE WORLD AT THE ADVENT OF NAPOLEON

ON THE EVE OF 18 BRUMAIRE the French Revolution was still far from the bourgeois goals of 1789. The new order began to assume definitive form only under the tutelage of Bonaparte. For this reason his work appears as the conclusion of the crisis, the vicissitudes of which have been described in this book. Nothing foretold, however, that peace was near between the Revolution and the Europe of the Old Regime. The struggle aroused the hostility of aristocrats, churches, and kings. The war had impelled the Directory to annex territories and to create satellite states. Hence, to the spontaneous propagation of revolutionary ideas the force of arms added the destruction of the traditional order and the introduction of French institutions into conquered territories.

Thus, becoming increasingly bitter, the conflict threatened to continue indefinitely unless exhaustion and fatigue induced the powers to reach a compromise, which, while sparing their own interests, would at least provide a temporary truce. Here also the personal role of Bonaparte exerted such an influence that the Consulate and the Empire may be considered as an episode in the history of the Revolution. Accordingly this volume does not exhaust the subject. Since, however, it terminates on the threshold of Napoleonic domination, it would seem advisable to examine the results of the crisis and the problems that it left unsolved.

CHAPTER FOURTEEN

The Results of the Revolution in France

THE PRINCIPLES that the Constituent Assembly attributed in 1789 to the order that the bourgeoisie claimed to be establishing have already been stated. They have continued to inspire most of the nation, but great difficulties developed in interpreting them and in shaping institutions and public life accordingly. This was partly because the Revolution was a civil war in which destruction increased while construction lagged, partly because the Third Estate became divided. In the Year II the controlled economy and the social laws of the Montagnards impaired the stability of the middle class. To elucidate the historical significance of 18 Brumaire it is necessary, therefore, to summarize, on the one hand, the upheaval in the structure of society and the character of the reconstructed state; on the other, the variations to which circumstances, divergent class interests, and different currents of thought subjected the reorganization of institutions and impeded it, without succeeding in stabilizing it to the satisfaction of the bourgeoisie.

DESTRUCTION OF THE OLD CORPORATE SOCIETY

Once the principles of the new order had been proclaimed, the revolutionary bourgeoisie continued to maintain that emancipation of the individual implied the ruin of the hierarchical and corporate structure of society, founded upon birth and privilege. This has been called abstract and chimerical individualism, because men soon regroup according to their interests, convictions, or tastes. Actually the bourgeoisie were by no means opposed to 'association' so long as it was to their own advantage. Once their domination was assured, they restored many organizations; but first they had to remove all obstacles. The division of Frenchmen into three orders could not survive the night of August 4; and the decree of November 7, 1789, ended it once and for all. Nevertheless a compromise solution would have shown a greater appreciation of many features of the old society. Civil war led the bourgeoisie gradually to eliminate the aristocracy entirely, without even considering the possible danger to themselves.

The clergy suffered most. With its assemblies, courts, 'free gift', autonomous financial administration, tithes, and vast property holdings, it had constituted a state within a state. It disappeared, and for this reason the 'Church', which it personified, lost its legal existence and became simply a spiritual community. Nonetheless the memory of it, constantly intensified by the increasing secularization of the state (one of the essential features of the Revolution and of the society which it created), persisted in public opinion.

Individual corporations had existed within the clergy, but on February 13, 1790, religious orders were abolished; and on July 12 the Civil Constitution disestablished chapters as well. Teaching and charitable congregations enjoyed a period of grace, but they were not to survive the 'day' of August 10. On the 18th they, too, were suppressed. Church property, now deemed ownerless, passed to the nation. Exceptions were gradually eliminated—the reservation of the property of foundations (February 10, 1791), vestry boards (August 19, 1792), the Order of Malta (September 19, 1792), *collèges* and all teaching establishments (March 8, 1793), hospitals and other charitable institutions (23 Messidor, Year II—July 11, 1794). Like the regulars, secular clerics were reduced to the status of ordinary citizens, partly pensioned by the state. Those who subscribed to the Civil Constitution became salaried public functionaries; but on the '2nd sans-culottide', Year II (September 18, 1794), they, too, were abandoned.

The French nobility had no real corporate organization. Nevertheless it constituted an order in the Estates General, in the provincial estates, and in the provincial assemblies created in 1787. Its hereditary titles, privileges, and seigneurial authority made it a special social class. As such, it likewise lost its existence; and on June 19, 1790, the Constituent Assembly, going a step further, with a view to eliminating all distinctions between nobles and commoners, abolished hereditary nobility, titles, and coats of arms. It was the disappearance of the seigneurs that was appreciated above all by the majority of Frenchmen, the peasants whom they had held in subjection. This derived in principle from the decree of August 5–11, 1789, which incorporated the decisions taken on the famous night of August 4, and immediately put an end to serfdom and personal manorial rights without compensation. In February, 1790, the formation of elective municipalities deprived the seigneurs of their administrative authority in the villages; the decrees of March 15 and June 19 took away their honorary prerogatives; and the reform of the judiciary, on August 16, eliminated their courts.

Since the nobles, like the priests, had become ordinary citizens, their property lost its special status. The distinction between noble land and that of the commoners, the hierarchy of fiefs and their customary rights, primogeniture, the right of pre-emption (*retrait*), and freehold (*franc-fief*) all disappeared along with feudalism. The wealth of numerous families dwindled, in many instances because manorial rights had provided the greater part of their revenue. True, landed dues, by far the most important, were redeemable, and the decree of March 15, 1790, regulated the indemnification; but the peasants made no allowance for this. On June 18, 1792, the Legislative Assembly suppressed redemption where 'occasional' dues (*droits casuels*) were concerned, except on presentation of original titles. Then on August 25 it extended this provision to *all* dues (*redevances*); and on the 27th it included the free tenancy domains (*congéables*) of lower Brittany among the liberated holdings. Finally, on July 17, 1793, the Convention abolished all the remaining dues outright.

The landed property of the nobility, in addition to being subject henceforth to the same fiscal charges as other property, was similarly affected. Part of it came from common lands appropriated by seigneurs through their right of eminent domain, sometimes in conformity with royal ordinances, sometimes not. The Constituent Assembly limited itself, on March 15, 1790, to nullifying all partitions of common lands authorized by the king in the preceding thirty years in violation of the ordinance of 1669. On August 28, 1792, the Legislative Assembly cancelled the thirty-year proviso, abolished Colbert's regulation, and recognized communal ownership of wasteland, as well as the right of roadside dwellers and municipalities to trees along public roads. On June 10, 1793, the Convention granted the peasants the additional privilege of submitting disputes to arbitration.

Emigration resulted in still harsher treatment of the nobility, even though only a few families were affected. The property of émigrés, confiscated by the Legislative Assembly in March, 1792, was put up for sale by the Convention: chattels in November, 1792, and real property on June 3, 1793. Moreover, the decree of March 28, 1793, which inflicted 'civil death' on the émigrés, really turned over to the Republic whatever property they might inherit. For this reason their relatives were forbidden to dispose of such property until an anticipated succession had been determined.

The future seemed equally dark to families who had escaped these penalties, because the revolutionaries were taking steps that tended to break up the large estates. Undoubtedly the bourgeoisie felt that the new economic order required mobility of property, and that social stability would be enhanced by increasing the number of owners. But the desire to diminish the influence of the aristocracy, and the passion that the civil war aroused against it (as well as against wealthy commoners who were deemed its accomplices) are factors that must be considered. On December 18, 1790, the Constituent Assembly forbade perpetual leases, which might have re-established tenures implicitly. Its rural code even suppressed the renewal of leases by tacit agreement. Of even greater significance was the decree of April 8, 1791, which required equal division of intestate inheritances. On March 7, 1793, the right to make wills and to distribute gifts during one's lifetime to relatives in direct line was abolished, but only in principle; the decisive blows came with the Convention. On October 25, 1792, it condemned entails, fiduciary trusts that secured them, and the rights of primogeniture that followed therefrom. Thus the surreptitious perpetuation of birthrights became impossible.

The inheritance laws of the Montagnards went much further. Those of 5 Brumaire and 17 Nivôse, Year II (October 26, 1793, and January 6, 1794), confirmed the equal division of inheritance among heirs, with unlimited power to protest, and permitted bequests in favour of non-heirs only to the extent of a tenth, or if there were direct or collateral beneficiaries, to the extent of a sixth. On June 4, 1793, natural children were permitted to inherit, and the law of 12 Brumaire, Year II (November 2, 1793), granted them a share equal to that of legitimate children. Moreover, these measures were made retroactive to July 14, 1789; and paternity suits were authorized for the determination of portions.

In addition to the loss of prestige resulting from the deprivation of legal or actual privileges, the nobility suffered as well from the constitutional and administrative reforms. The king ceased to exploit the Treasury for gifts and pensions. He retained the power, but since the civil list was fixed at 25 million francs, he lacked the wherewithal. As long as Louis XVI had certain appointments at his disposal the upper nobility continued to enjoy preferment in the high offices of diplomacy, the army, and the royal household. At first the bourgeoisie, as much from traditional deference as from gratitude or political acumen, gave their support to nobles who resigned themselves to the situation and agreed to serve in the new administration or to command the National Guard. The *hobereaux* (indigent country nobles) suffered no less severely from the transformation of the army—not so much from the suppression of venality, however, as from the admission, on February 28, 1790, of all persons to the ranks. They were further affected adversely by the regulation of promotion, in September, which placed considerable emphasis on seniority. No one dared demand any favours whatsoever because of birth.

Among the nobles most severely affected were those of the robe, administration, and finance, who held the highest ranks in the state. With purchase of offices made impossible, they were compensated at the current rate, in assignats; and they remained unemployed. This overwhelmed the members of the parlements, who were not retained as elected magistrates, to say nothing of the tax collectors, who, in addition to a remuneration proportional to their receipts, had always had the latter available to obtain credit for their own benefit. At the end of the Old Regime many nobles had belonged to the farmers-general, but these disappeared with the indirect taxes.

The situation of the nobles gradually became worse. Increasingly suspect, they became fewer in public office, obtaining posts only if they gave incontestable proof of loyalty to the Revolution. Even before the flight of the king, Robespierre demanded that the army be purged. Finally, in 1793, the sans-culottes determined to deprive the nobles of their civil rights. The Committee of Public Safety did not agree, and continued to employ those who were known to be reliable. Nonetheless, exclusions, imprisonments, and condemnations took their toll, and the law of 27 Germinal, Year II (April 16, 1794), expelled the nobles from Paris and from fortresses. Some (Davout, for example) prudently took refuge in abstention from public life.

The Thermidorian Reaction did not appreciably improve legislation in favour of the *ci-devants*. The law of 3 Brumaire, Year IV (October 25, 1795), barred relatives of émigrés from public office; and although it was repealed by the royalist majority of the Year V, it was re-established on 18 Fructidor. Shortly thereafter, Sieyes proposed, through Boulay de la Meurthe, the banishment of nobles who had held office or enjoyed high position under the Old Regime, and the reduction of all others to the status of foreigners. The law of 9 Frimaire, Year VI (November 29, 1797), was limited to the second of these measures, although it permitted exceptions for those who had performed services for the Revolution. Since, however, these exceptions were never defined, the proscription had no effect. Nevertheless, until 18 Brumaire the great majority of nobles either lived outside France (and even fought against the armies of the Republic) or no longer held any place in the public life of the nation.

In discussing the increasingly effective measures against the clergy and the nobility, attention must be paid to the popular massacres, the terrorist executions, and 'revolutionary vandalism'—châteaux laid waste or burned, churches despoiled and demolished, archives sacked, statues pulled down, and coats of arms destroyed. At the height of the disturbance the Legislative Assembly, and particularly the Convention, had expressed approval at every opportunity. Church bells, chains and other metal, and parchments suitable for making cartridges were seized for war purposes. The law of July 17, 1793, ordered the burning of all feudal title deeds. The decrees of October 2, 1793, and 8 Pluviôse, Year II (January 27, 1794), revoked this, and the burnings finally ceased; but the loss was irreparable.

It must be noted, however, that in this destruction of the corporate society the clergy and nobility were not (contrary to what one might tend to believe) the only ones involved. The bourgeoisie of the Old Regime were seriously affected as well. More than one of their members, possessing personal nobility or about to obtain it, saw this pleasing prospect (always exciting to the newly rich) vanish. Some, including representatives of the people, possessed fiefs, fragmentary manorial rights (*banalités*, for example), or even an entire manor. Others, yielding to vanity or self-interest (because manorial rents were redeemable only with the lessor's consent), had made use of the formulas of feudal lawyers in settling land rents, and had anticipated such items as the quitrents (*cens*). The law of July 17, 1793, dispossessed them of these.

Many officeholders were commoners; hence the redemption of their posts, and the suppression of the organized bodies on which their social rank and part of their income depended, hurt them as it did the others. The notaries became functionaries—recourse to attorneys was henceforth optional. Many bailiffs lost the employment derived from institutions that had disappeared. Even the other liberal professions that were not venal experienced some loss. With the lawyers dissolved as a body, the role of 'public defender' was open to all. Physicians ceased to be an organized group. Beginning in 1791 the artists, under the leadership of David, vigorously challenged the monopoly maintained by the academicians over the Salon, and the authority they exerted over the School of Rome. Finally, on August 8, 1793, the Convention, by suppressing the academies and universities, deprived some of the artists, scientists, men of letters, and professors of their claim to status.

During the Montagnard period the commercial middle class in turn found its future compromised. On August 24, 1793, the Convention eliminated the joint-stock companies, the most advanced form of capitalism. This was affected (far more than by the disappearance of the East India Company) by the disestablishment of the Discount Bank, which had acted as a national bank of issue and a 'superbank'. The advent of the controlled economy, taxation, and requisitioning slowed the rise of capitalism even more abruptly by regimenting business activity and limiting profits.

Nor did the 'people'—the artisans, retail merchants, and employees—emerge unscathed. Many persons of small means had to seek new ways of making a living when the collection of indirect taxes ceased, especially the salt tax (*gabelle*), *octrois*, internal customs and duties, the tithe, and the field rent (*champart*). On February 16, 1791, the Constituent Assembly suppressed the craft guilds. Such action seemed democratic, at least to the extent that the technical conditions of the time permitted wage earners to profit thereby through opening their own shops. Nonetheless it deprived masters of their monopoly. Besides harming their interests, it wounded their pride, for they had been jealous of their special privileges and their carefully controlled authority. This was specially true of surgeons, booksellers, goldsmiths, and wigmakers.

Finally, the private life of the Third Estate was affected. The inheritance laws applied to commoners as well as to nobles, and occasionally ruined their legacies. Nor should it be forgotten that many bourgeois emigrated, that in the invaded areas a host of persons from all classes left France when the Carmagnoles reappeared, and that the great majority of those harmed by terrorist repression were neither priests nor nobles. It was essential, however, for the revolutionaries to loosen the bonds that subjected child and wife to the discretionary power of the paterfamilias under the Old Regime; and this applied to the Third Estate as much as to the aristocracy. It was particularly for this reason that limitations were placed on the right to make wills. The claim was made from the rostrum of the Assemblies that heads of families should be prevented from disinheriting next of kin who were favourable to the Revolution.

Paternal authority was greatly diminished. Henceforth the family court, instituted on August 16, 1790, shared disciplinary authority with the father. At age twenty-one (or eighteen in cases of emancipation) children were 'liberated' and regained control of their property. No longer need a wife fear imprisonment by means of *lettres de cachet*; her consent was required for the marriage of her children, and like her husband, she could seek a divorce. The Convention had facilitated this last by its decrees of 8 Nivôse and 4 Floréal, Year II (December 28, 1793, and April 23, 1794). The rehabilitation of 'natural' children heralded a still more formidable disruption of family solidarity. Every social revolution tends to carry its attack to the point where it seems fitting that individuals (particularly the young) be released from traditional conformity, so that, whatever the risks, they may adapt themselves to the new order because restraints have been removed. Once the goal is attained, however, discipline must be re-established within the remodelled society.

To stop here would be to leave an inadequate impression of the social upheaval. No less far-reaching were the effects of inflation, which, despite the return to metallic currency, continued its ravages until 18 Brumaire. The Directory flooded the market with its bonds, its warrants for payment (backed by insufficient funds), and its requisition certificates. Inflation was devastating to acquired wealth. In the Year III the depreciation of assignats brought a rush of debtors, hastening to pay, at low rates, not only for public taxes or national property, but also for landed rents which were redeemable by paying the capital. But the bourgeoisie willingly invested their savings in mortgage loans, of which these rents constituted the interest. On 25 Messidor, Year III (July 13, 1795), it was necessary to forbid the repayment of funds advanced before January 1, 1792, and to pay off the rest in advance.

Throughout the greater part of France land was cultivated on a share-crop basis. At the termination of his lease (normally of a year's duration) the tenant farmer returned the outlay made by the landowner; or if that was impossible, he paid a sum agreed upon as the value of the original loan. Beginning with the Year II, however, tenants hastened to sell, at the highest prices, whatever was exempt from the Maximum (chiefly livestock), so that they could make their payments in depreciated paper. On 2 Thermidor, Year II (July 20, 1794), the Committee of Public Safety forbade this practice so far as cattle leases were concerned, and on 13 Fructidor (August 30) for other items (*garniture morte*), but without success. The decree of 15 Germinal, Year III (April 4, 1795), repeated the prohibitions, and innumerable petitions have preserved the complaints of desperate lessors. Farmers also gained at the expense of landowners, since the former paid their debts in paper. On 3 Messidor, Year III (June 21, 1795), they were ordered to pay at the rate of six for one, and on 2 Thermidor (July 20, 1795) they were directed to pay half their farm rents and their taxes in grain. Still, they retained the right to plead that their harvests were inadequate.

During the entire period of the Directory the Councils considered methods of reconciling the opposing interests. Their concern with restoring acquired wealth (which has not been recovered to this day) is one more proof that the Thermidorians were able to re-establish the pre-eminence of the bourgeoisie in their ranks. In such cases, however, the losses to the property owners could not be restored in their entirety. Building property fared even worse. For example, the decree of 3 Messidor, Year III (June 21, 1795), which brought help to landed proprietors, maintained the payment of rents in assignats at par. Then a severe housing shortage developed, especially in Paris, and at the end of the Directory the value of real estate was still declining. Finally, the bourgeoisie held the greatest part of the public debt. Thus it bore the brunt of Cambon's readjustment of perpetual and life annuities, of Ramel's liquidation of the public debt, of the continued decline of income under the Directory, and of the payment of dividends in worthless notes.

The number of these changes, and the infinite variety of their repercussions, greatly influenced men's thinking. They alienated the aristocracy from modern society, rallied some members of the bourgeoisie of the Old Regime to counter-revolution, and caused others to desire a conservative reaction. This reaction, suitable for restoring stability, was perceptible as early as 9 Thermidor; but it was still far from complete by 18 Brumaire. Only those who speculated on the purchase of national property and provisions recovered their losses; but the principal benefits of these operations did not go to the bourgeoisie of the Old Regime. As is usually the case, the war and the monetary disorder produced *nouveaux riches,* whose intrusion into the ranks of the impoverished bourgeoisie added to the social upheaval a quality that had not been anticipated.

THE STATE

At the end of the Old Regime the state, embodied in a divine-right monarch, still retained a personal character. Since the seventeenth century, however, a centralized administration had been tending to make its bureaucratic regulations prevail, and it was making the state bourgeois by rationalizing it. This trend ran afoul of provincial and urban concern with autonomy and the chaotic diversity of an expanded kingdom, governed empirically as historical circumstances permitted, but far more often according to the wishes of the corporate hierarchy. The class which dominates a society always regards the state, created to ensure respect for the positive law and to maintain order, as the bulwark of its prerogatives. The rivalry between royal power and the interests of the aristocracy engendered the Revolution, and the bourgeoisie put an end to the contradiction by seizing the state themselves.

They abolished the privileges of the provinces and the towns, as well as those of the aristocracy, and proclaimed the equality of all Frenchmen before the law. The intermediate bodies, which Montesquieu had regarded as the only means of curbing the absolutism of the state, disappeared. Traditional institutions were swept away, and national unity was achieved through administrative uniformity. It seemed henceforth that the will of the state would encounter no obstacles other than distance and the technical difficulties of communication. In this sense Tocqueville was able to say that the members of the Constituent Assembly crowned the work carried on over the centuries by the Capetian dynasty.

But this was only part of their work. In proclaiming the rights of man, with liberty foremost, the bourgeoisie intended to protect them against the state; so they transformed the latter. Substituting popular sovereignty for that of the prince, they destroyed personal power. From an attribute of a proprietary monarchy, the state was transformed into an agent of the governed, and its authority was subordinated to the rules of a constitution. Monarchy was not abolished, but Louis XVI became the first of the 'functionaries', that is, of the representatives for the nation. Heretofore his commands had been carried out through the administrative machinery. Hence the wishes of his subjects were voiced not only on behalf of liberty but equally against centralization. They desired to make themselves masters of local administration even more than of the central authority. The popular revolution drove out the royal agents, whose place was taken by elected councils established by the Constituent Assembly. This autonomy responded to a human inclination naturally antagonistic to centralization, even when the latter works to the advantage of the representatives of the people. Undoubtedly this is because bureaucracy occasionally abuses centralization or brings it into disrepute through stupid and routine sluggishness, or even negligence; also because uniformity irritates individual independence, and runs counter to the infinite variety of interests and peculiar habits of each of the small communities that comprise the nation.

Thus the Revolution of 1789 did not reinforce the power of the state. On the contrary, it weakened it by associating the elected representatives of the nation with the king, by requiring them to respect individual rights, and by diluting authority through decentralization extended as far as the localizing of tax collection and the maintenance of public order. Many citizens went further still. In the name of popular sovereignty and of Article 6 of the Declaration of the Rights of Man (which did not prohibit direct democracy) they claimed the right to subject the decisions of their representatives to review, and even to authorize their revocation. This tendency toward libertarian anarchy appeared as much among the counter-revolutionaries and moderates as it did among the sans-culottes. Its conflict with the indispensable predominance of a central authority thus reveals one of the eternal contradictions of every society—that of freedom and authority, the individual and the state.

The bourgeoisie were by no means unaware of the difficulty. They were willing to run the risk, and, in truth, a triumphant class is never embarrassed by so doing. The violent convulsions that the structure of the state underwent throughout the decade are not testimony to the incompetence or rashness of the Constituent Assembly. They stemmed from the struggle of the Third Estate with the aristocracy, from the support which Louis XVI accorded the latter, and from collusion with foreign powers. As had happened so often in the past, the nation had to reawaken to the fact that its power at home and its security abroad necessitated a government with sufficient power to meet the full extent of the danger.

Establishing themselves in power by denying the poor the right to vote, and by granting the well-to-do only the option of choosing from among the 'notables', the bourgeoisie did not doubt that they could maintain their position. Since the new state was supposed to protect their economic and social dominance, they did not think that the political and administrative organization should paralyse it; but the rigorous separation of powers and excessive decentralization threatened the executive with this fate. A parliamentary system would have corrected the first error, a relatively strict control the second; but the members of the Constituent Assembly adopted neither. Unable to put their confidence in Louis XVI, and daring neither to replace him nor to establish a republic, they did not succeed in establishing a true government. For a long time most Frenchmen did not regret this, because they could ignore those decrees of the Assembly that did not please them. Even public disorders, so long as they appeared to be only transitory, did not trouble them greatly. It required the aggravation of civil war and the threat of invasion to force them to choose between compromise (if not surrender) and restoration of the authority of the state.

But the bourgeoisie were soon divided: first the monarchists, and then the Feuillants, chose the first solution; the intransigents made the second one prevail. They succeeded only by altering the social foundation of the state. Since many of the 'notables' who had assumed power refused to follow them, they depended upon the 'people', and extolled political equality. August 10 appeared to cut the Gordian knot. It eliminated monarchy, and thus nothing seemed left to impede the organization of an effective executive. At the same time the advent of universal suffrage appeared to remove control over the state from the 'notables'. Actually the republicans, in turn, became divided. The first Terror frightened the Girondins, and thenceforth they repudiated dictatorship. Economic freedom in particular was a dogma to them. The Montagnards, on the contrary, by joining with the sans-culottes, compelled the Convention to create the revolutionary government, endowed it with control over the economy, shared the administration with their allies, and acknowledged that the popular classes, too, should derive advantages from the Revolution.

Thus, in the hands of the Jacobins the state once more became authoritarian, but its personnel was democratized to a certain degree. Moreover, it displayed some of the features of a social democracy. During the brief existence of the revolutionary government there could be seen, as in a flash of lightning, the boundless horizon presented by this equality of rights, which the bourgeoisie had proclaimed in 1789 to condemn the privileges of the nobility. The Montagnards made no promise to suppress inequality of wealth, but they undertook to reduce it. They did not expect that equal rights would benefit everyone fully, but they did assign to the democratic republic the responsibility of giving at least some reality to the principle.

This was but an interlude. A number of those in control saw it merely as an expedient for public safety. It would have required much time and money for social democracy to bear fruit. For the moment everything had to be sacrificed to victory. The Jacobin state refused to deprive itself of the help of those who agreed to aid it, even if they were nobles. It disapproved of dechristianization. It subordinated the controlled economy to the needs of the army, although the sans-culottes had intended it for their own benefit. By ceaselessly accentuating centralization, suspending elections, and imposing a ruthless discipline, it antagonized libertarian independence and disappointed the ambitions of the popular leaders. Then, when they balked, it broke them.

Moreover, neither Jacobins nor sans-culottes organized anything resembling a true party for imposing their dictatorship. They acted within the framework of political democracy—the sections, the National Guard, the clubs—and despite purges, the other citizens were represented. They claimed to command in the name of the Convention; yet if it were to escape from their yoke, and if they lost control of the machinery of state, they would be reduced to impotence. Nor did they represent any one class. They were recruited from all elements of the Third Estate, from the rich bourgeois to the proletarian. For this reason the Maximum sowed division in their ranks; landowning peasants, artisans, and merchants clashed with their workers and with the consumers.

After 9 Thermidor the bourgeoisie (who were more or less sincerely republican) recovered complete power and hastened to remove state control of the economy. The Constitution of the Year III re-established the elective and liberal system inaugurated by the Constituent Assembly. Disavowing universal suffrage, the Thermidorians intended to establish a property-owners' republic, a republic of landowners, as Boissy d'Anglas indicated; but it bore the mark of the trials that had left them with bitter memories. Hence they continued the special measures affecting the partisans of the Old Regime, the constitutional royalists, and the Catholic priests, on the one hand, and the democrats on the other. Even the suspension of the rights of the citizen remained a possibility.

The need for a vigorous executive, at a time when the war was continuing and the assignats were collapsing, did not escape the Thermidorians. Not only was the salvation of the Revolution and of their republic at stake, but also their own security. Driven from the government, they risked suffering the same fate as the Montagnards. They believed that they had strengthened the Directory sufficiently; but, ignoring the inconsistency, they arranged a balance of authority between it and the Councils that was ingeniously devised to prevent the state from interfering with the freedom of action of the bourgeoisie within the country. Rectifying the doctrine that he had directed against the nobility in 1789, Sieyes explained that popular sovereignty by no means possessed the absolutism that the king had arrogated to himself, and it had to respect the natural rights that existed before society, especially property. From this point of view, he declared, the precautions of his colleagues were insufficient.

The Thermidorians paralysed the state by setting the executive and legislative powers at odds. Owing to circumstances, the

Directory increased its authority. Besides its commissioners it named a great number of administrators and judges. Through its decrees it ceaselessly expanded its regulatory power (as the Committee of Public Safety had done), with the reluctant assent, or despite the protests, of the Councils, which took their revenge on 30 Prairial, Year VII (June 18, 1799). Nevertheless it sustained the war only by means of expedients, and it succeeded neither in crushing the counter-revolution in France nor in imposing a general peace. Further, the social basis of the regime was too narrow. The Republic henceforth rejected the aid of those who had founded it, while the class it claimed to represent remained largely hostile.

The men in power maintained themselves solely by tampering with election results or by openly violating their own constitution. The legislative power was moving towards the subservience which came with the Consulate; yet the Directory failed to acquire the prerogatives it deemed indispensable, as evidenced by the institutions that it set up in the vassal republics. Last of all, the failures of the Year VII and the final upsurge of the Jacobins prompted the property-owning bourgeoisie to look to Bonaparte in the hope of reinvigorating the executive without damaging their own social supremacy.

The war had committed the Revolution to dictatorship, and the bourgeoisie, terrified by the experience of the Year II, were willing to let it be a military dictatorship. The day had not yet dawned for the government they had dreamed of in 1789, and it would be long in coming.

SECULARIZATION OF THE STATE

Whatever interest the political transformation of the state may arouse, its secularization seems no less important today. Since the *philosophes* had inveighed against the intolerance of the church, it would seem that freedom of conscience should have been inscribed most prominently in the Declaration of the Rights of Man of 1789, beside that of inquiry or of criticism; and the secularization of the state would emanate therefrom as one of the essential features of the Revolution. Yet the members of the Constituent Assembly contented themselves with an allusion, as brief as it was timid, to religious toleration. It was only at the end of the year and the beginning of 1790 that they advanced a bit further by conferring civil rights upon Protestants and the Jews of the south. Still, they did not create a lay state. Hence, even though every man became free to choose his religion, or even to change it, he had to espouse one.

By refusing, on April 13, 1790, to retain Catholicism as the state religion, the Assembly implicitly indicated that its legislation would henceforth be free from ecclesiastical censure. Nevertheless, far from proving indifferent in this regard, it accorded a monopoly of public worship to that faith. Only Catholic priests were paid and housed. Until 1792, vestry boards remained intact. The parish priests continued to register births, marriages, and deaths. Education and charity were left to the church, and its teaching and hospital congregations continued. The members of the Constituent Assembly were obviously conciliating the patriotic priests, and recognizing the prestige of the clergy, they did not wish to alarm the populace. Moreover, they considered that religion was necessary, at least for the people. Apparently they had not yet developed a clear idea of secularism. On the contrary, the representatives of the Third Estate, mostly jurists, held that the church is in the state, and that the latter might regulate it so long as it did not disturb the dogma universally accepted by the faithful. In this regard, even the Gallicans allotted the state a rather large role.

This legacy from the Old Regime inspired the Civil Constitution of the clergy, in itself radically at variance with the secularization of the state. Yet this became the leaven in the development of the latter. The schism it produced, after having led the revolutionaries to treat refractory priests as enemies, gradually detached them from the constitutional clergy, and finally from Christianity itself. As early as 1791, while the Constituent Assembly was granting the refractory clergy access to the churches, some departments were spontaneously taking coercive measures against them. The war extended these, and after August 10 the refractory clergy were proscribed. It seemed that at least those priests who had compromised themselves for the Revolution would remain respected. On the contrary, the hostility provoked by the non-jurors spread to their religion, bringing suffering to the constitutional clergy who professed it. On September 20, 1792, the Legislative Assembly finally created the civil state and instituted divorce; it was a decisive step towards secularism.

The situation of the constitutional clergy became more difficult. Politically, they were soon suspected of being attached to monarchy, then to the Girondins. In October, 1793, the Convention permitted the deportation of those who were denounced as unpatriotic, and it created new difficulties for them in the revolutionary calendar and the observation of the Tenth Day. Then the sans-culottes undertook to close the churches. The Convention and the Committee of Public Safety did not approve the use of violence, and the decree of December 6 confirmed freedom of worship; but this decree remained a dead letter, and 9 Thermidor brought no immediate change. It was not until the '2nd sans-culottide', Year II (September 18, 1794), that Cambon secured the suppression of the clerical budget, so that the Civil Constitution was implicitly abolished, and the separation of church and state consummated.

With the reaction in full swing, Catholicism revived. Then the Thermidorians regulated it strictly and restored its churches. Thermidorians and constitutional clergy both profited from this, while the refractory priests developed their clandestine ministry. Until 18 Brumaire the Directory conciliated or ill-treated one group or the other as circumstances warranted. Similarly, the suppression of the teaching and charitable congregations after August 10, and the sale of the property of the *collèges*, universities, and hospitals led to the secularization of education and welfare. The former remained free, but the Convention decreed the organization of an educational system in which religious precepts would have no place. Through the Register of National Charity the Montagnards assigned public relief to the Republic. The Directory returned it to the municipalities and created welfare boards, but it made no change in principle.

Thus the secularization of the state seemed complete. Actually it was not, in the sense that the majority of republicans deemed it necessary to provide a metaphysical foundation for utilitarian and civic morality. Nourishing the illusion that deism would satisfy the believers and that Tenth Day worship and national festivals would at least be effective in replacing Catholic ceremonies, they strove to impose this kind of national religion (which had developed spontaneously during the first years of the Revolution) in opposition to the traditional forms of worship. In this respect secularism, gradually realized under the pressure of civil war, did not abandon its aggressiveness. As constituted, it was in harmony neither with freedom of conscience and worship nor with positive rationalism, which was indifferent to metaphysics. It simply proves that the thought of the eighteenth century was not familiar with the latter.

The torment did not uproot Christian tradition, but to a certain degree it detached some Frenchmen from it. Once the state had ceased to compel attendance at Sunday mass and Easter communion, conformity was immediately weakened in many departments, particularly the Paris region and central France. On the eve of 18 Brumaire the clergy were in no position to reverse the tide. Deprived of resources and partially driven underground, they could gather but few recruits. Already undermanned, they included many aged priests who would have no successors. They were deeply divided, and the hierarchy had been shaken. Some refractory clergy proved extremely independent towards their bishops, and the constitutional parish priests contested the authority of theirs.

Observance of the sacraments became less frequent among the faithful, and religious instruction of children was often impossible. Habits were being worn away, and much effort would be required to restore them during the first half of the nineteenth century; but the sans-culottes continued their hostility and bequeathed it to their descendants. Unbelief, limited to the nobility and bourgeosie before 1789, was thus established among the common people, and to this very significant innovation was added the no less important rupture between the Revolution and the church. The revolutionary bourgeoisie came to think that the principles of 1789 and Catholicism were irreconcilable, while the church reached the same conclusion. As early as 1790, Pius VI had condemned the Declaration of the Rights of Man. The French clergy at first accepted the Declaration, or (in large part at least) refrained from repudiating it. Now, however, with the schism a reality, persecution increasing, and secularization growing more serious, it became (apart from the constitutional clergy) the enemy of the Revolution.

The majority of the nation cared very little. Principles were of no interest to them, and still less the conflict between principles.

Daily experience had shown that life condemned thought to oscillate between contradictions. The achievements of the Revolution of 1789, especially its social results, remained the principal source of popular satisfaction. At the same time, however, the populace clung to its religion out of conviction, out of the conservative interest that it attached to faith, and more generally still, out of habit and a concern for tranquillity. With religious quarrels dividing families and disturbing domestic peace, many wished that the state would contrive to put an end to them, so that there would be only one mass. Such a peaceful solution did not appear imminent, because part of the clergy, obeying the émigré bishops, supported royalist plots financed by England. An immediate solution required an agreement with the pope, which would reduce his priests to submission or to political neutrality. The Directory had foreseen this in 1796, but it remained for Bonaparte to take advantage of it.

PUBLIC SERVICES

No matter to what extent circumstances may have been responsible for diversity in the central government, no one has ever been able to deny that the bourgeoisie found a place in it for capable men, whose use of power enriched their ability, and from whom Napoleon drew the best elements of his personnel. In the life of the governed, however, the decisions of the legislative authority and the regulations of the executive power were not the sole questions at issue. It was just as important (if not more so) that the administrative apparatus prove efficient, and, moreover, that its directors have effective and conscientious associates. Dealing directly with the public as they do, minor officials count for a great deal in the reputation of a regime.

Like the Assemblies, the departmental and district administrations were recruited from the bourgeoisie and were not democratized to any extent (especially the districts) until 1793. In towns, the artisan class, retail merchants, and members of the liberal arts entered the general council of the commune, if not the town government, in relatively large numbers; and in 1793 they predominated. Men of lower professions and of more modest means—clerks and even some small numbers of journeymen—joined them. This 'contamination' was one of the bitterest complaints voiced by the 'notables'; but the Directory was unable to put a complete stop to it, because the complaints came largely from royalists. In these elective bodies the citizens became accustomed to the management of public affairs; and to a certain degree, ability marked those suitable for promotion to higher posts. For this reason some thought was given in the Constituent Assembly and the Convention of the Year III to the introduction of a system of progression; but in point of fact most political careers began with some apprenticeship of this kind.

In the rural areas, on the contrary, the formation of town governments frequently brought disillusionment. The peasants who ran them were completely illiterate or did not even know the French language. Foreseeing this difficulty, Condorcet, among others, proposed, as early as 1789, the formation of 'great communes'. These were not resorted to until the Year III, when municipal administration of cantons was created. These borrowed only an 'agent' and his aide from each commune. This attempt offended the still-vital spirit of local autonomy, and it was unsuccessful.

The local councils sat neither very often nor very long, so that their members did not assume heavy obligations until the revolutionary government required them to meet in permanent session. From the outset such permanence became a necessity for the town governments and district and departmental directories, which were compelled to direct and supervise the daily course of events and to exercise judicial powers. The administrative jurisdiction, which the administration and sale of national property, the preparation of lists of émigrés, and the application of innumerable revolutionary laws made extraordinarily active, devolved upon the directories. The town governments retained judgment over minor offences, and beginning in 1793, they took cognizance of infractions of the Maximum. In such stormy times the administrators' diligence did them great honour. Furthermore, the revolutionary bourgeoisie (despite property qualifications for voting) and the democratic republicans (for better reasons still) never admitted that, because of these absorbing duties, only the rich could be elected. The 'functionaries', whose tasks monopolized their time, were paid in the same way as the deputies; nevertheless more than one had to decline office because of the pressure of private business.

On the other hand, some of the newcomers lacked ability and character. Some degree of stability was needed to permit them to become familiar with their functions, but elections were frequent. The Constituent Assembly replaced half the departmental and district administrations every two years, and the town governments annually, while the Constitution of the Year III changed one out of five members of the central administration of a department and half the municipal administration each year. Purges had increased the instability between 1793 and 1795. Frequent elections harmonized with the democratic concept and corrected the representative system. They increased the number of citizens who hoped to be called to public administration, and interested them in it. They also reminded the elected that they were not irremovable. Still, their frequency, in addition to increasing the number of abstentions, threatened to diminish the experience of the elected officials. The disadvantage was particularly apparent because the civic education of the nation had only begun.

Under any regime the continuity and perfecting of administrative methods depend in part on the subordinate personnel, on the 'civil servants'. At first the personnel of the Old Regime remained in office; then the 'parties' succeeded one another in power and filled the bureaux with their followers. The multiplication of 'bureaucrats' was one of the features of the revolutionary government, because of the functions it assumed. The education and professional ethics of many of the recruits left much to be desired. After the Year III the situation improved in one sense: the commissioners of the Directory, more stable than the elective bodies, assumed the supervision of minor officials. Unhappily, the monetary disorder and financial penury spread corruption, a feature by no means unknown before 1789. Complaints of the fabulous corruption of the war commissioners and their quartermasters were without end.

One of the aims of the men of Brumaire was to stabilize administrative authority by eliminating elections, and to reconstitute professional services, undoubtedly with the aim of reestablishing the omnipotence of the state, but also to assure competence and efficiency at all levels. It cannot be denied that, for example, the suppression of the controllers of the 'twentieth' (*vingtième*) had done great harm to the establishment of the rolls of direct taxes; or that the administrators of the revolutionary era neglected the use of statistics, one of the remarkable innovations of their predecessors. The controlled economy forced the Committee of Public Safety to resort to it briefly, but at the end of the Directory, François de Neufchâteau was still advocating it.

The elective principle was also maintained in the judicial organization until the Consulate, and it did not give rise to as many difficulties. Indeed, if no technical qualifications were required of the justices of the peace (who were never included in the magistrature), the law of August 16, 1790, required that members of courts have previous experience, either as judges for five years or as lawyers regularly attached to a jurisdiction. This stipulation disappeared on September 22, 1792, but the electoral assemblies continued to determine their choices in a similar manner. They named justices of the peace for two years only. The mandate of magistrates lasted far longer: six years, according to the law of 1790, and five in the Constitution of the Year III. All were re-eligible and, in short, less exposed to insecurity. The institution of justices of the peace continued to be favourably received—at least their election ordinarily attracted as many voters as that of municipal officers—and Napoleon did not suppress them until 1804. Nor did district courts appear to cause any complaints.

Criticism derived rather from the procedural complications created by the gradual standardization of the law and the variations of revolutionary legislation. It goes without saying that, as always, the special repressive jurisdictions provoked furious anger and undying hatred; but it does not seem that criminal courts of common law and the juries associated with them aroused disapproval. In suppressing elections the men of Brumaire thought primarily of reinforcing the authority of the state and of guaranteeing the bourgeoisie a monopoly over judicial posts, as much to strengthen its own prestige as out of a concern for social preservation.

The effort of the Constituent Assembly to make it unnecessary for litigants to resort to judges and lawyers, by permitting them to resolve their disputes at the least expense, had scant success. Under the Directory the arbitration and family courts disappeared. The private citizens called on to judge were poorly trained in law, inspired no confidence, and lacked self-assurance. They really served as a screen for professionals, whom they called on to pass judgment. Attorneys, or 'advocates' (*avoués*), and lawyers, or 'official defenders', were still being resorted to (although they had become optional), so justice continued to be costly. Moreover, the Constitution of the Year III permitted only one civil court and from three to six correctional courts in each department; and by suppressing the districts, all litigation was directed to the central administration of the department. Delays and expense of travel increased. Besides, the men of Brumaire officially provided that court costs go to the 'ministerial officials', who were re-established for the benefit of the bourgeoisie.

At the time of 18 Brumaire criticism was aimed primarily at the lack of repressive prosecution. Discontinued by the Constituent Assembly, the office of the public prosecutor (*parquet*) had not actually been re-established. Examination remained entrusted, in the first instance, to officers of the constabulary and justices of the peace; next, to the presidents of the civil courts acting as the foremen of grand juries. The elected public prosecutor demanded a hearing. The national commissioner (whose post was abolished in October, 1792, and restored by the Constitution of the Year III) controlled only observance of the law and the execution of sentences. The restoration of the office of public prosecutor, furthermore, was realized only gradually during the following decade.

The reform of criminal procedure had engrossed the Constituent Assembly from the beginning, and it remains one of its memorable achievements. The introduction of trial by jury was never challenged, although the selection of jurors caused discussion, because the conservative interests were bent on controlling it. The regular courts seem to have respected the new rules. Again the Assembly strove to protect the accused before the jurisdictions that it retained in the army and navy. Here it introduced juries of soldiers or sailors. Although it finally created a National High Court for crimes against the nation, nonetheless it regulated its operation in a similar manner.

Civil war, however, contributed to the restraint, abandonment, and violation of the guarantees of the common law. The Committee of Inquiry, the watch committees, the Committee of

General Security, and the Committee of Public Safety obtained the power to order searches and arrests without intervention by the magistrates. The local authorities imitated them whenever circumstances seemed to demand it, and from 1793 to 1795 the terrorist laws gave them discretionary power. In fact, the Directory inherited this, and its commissioners even used preventive arrests to assure favourable elections. As for the special courts, procedures were simplified, and the Convention eventually prescribed the death sentence on mere verification of identity for émigrés, deported persons, armed rebels, and individuals whom it had declared 'outlaws'. The Directory also resorted to military commissions, and did not worry about judicial scruples where the Babouvists were concerned. Public opinion did not nourish the illusion that those who governed (whoever they might be) and their political police would ever experience such scruples so long as the war continued. Nor did it really expect to see the government abandon its administrative authority to independent professionals.

There were complaints that the codification of civil legislation, so new and so constantly changing since 1789, was still unfinished. The Constituent Assembly adopted a rural code only in September, 1791. The Convention, in 1793 and again after 9 Thermidor, began discussion of a civil code, but did not complete one. The project presented in 1796 by Cambacérès remained in abeyance, and the Councils contented themselves with voting a tardy code on mortgages. The enormity of the work and the unsettled conditions do not in themselves explain the delay. It is also accounted for by the intervening Montagnard laws (filled with retroactive provisions), the vacillation of the reactionaries, and the interminable readjustments of obligations necessitated by the monetary castastrophe. Nevertheless it was still incomplete.

The organization of public taxes established by the Constituent Assembly underwent continual change. This was not astonishing in view of the discontent aroused by the assessment of the land tax, and the even greater resentment of the personal property tax, among the territorial circumscriptions. It is also necessary to note the mediocre success of the *patente* (business-licence tax), based on declarations of those who were liable to it. The Convention abolished the *patente* on March 21, 1793, then did away with the personal property tax, and altered the land tax on 23 Nivôse, Year III (January 12, 1795). During the civil war the collection of taxes declined, and the Montagnards secured revenue through the forced loan, revolutionary assessments, the payment of taxes in grain, requisitioning, and inflation. In Thermidor, Year III, with the assignats ruined, their opponents re-established the personal property tax and the *patente* on a new basis. They imposed the payment in kind of half the land tax, and before it was repealed on 3 Vendémiaire, Year V (September 24, 1796), their measure was of great value to the Directory.

Having thus returned to the system of the Constituent Assembly, the Thermidorian Republic did not put an end to recriminations. It modified the assessment of the personal tax twice, and that of the *patente* far more often. Finally, in the Year VII, the Councils proceeded to a general revision of the three taxes, the registration fees, and the stamp tax; and at the same time they instituted a fourth direct tax on doors and windows. This arrangement was fairly successful, and the laws of the Year VII remained fundamental for more than a century; but they did not satisfy the taxpayers.

True, the demands of the state diminished from 1791 to the Year VII. The land tax fell from 240 millions to 210 millions. It tended to become stabilized in a kind of contract, as the farmers had wished. The personal property tax dropped from 60 millions to 30 millions, a reduction that gratified private citizens so far as their own shares were concerned; but it did not remove all grievances, because it was of particular benefit to the rich town dwellers. Furthermore, the character of a progressive tax on income, which was to some extent conferred on the personal property tax by the Constituent Assembly, and strongly accentuated by the reform of 14 Thermidor, Year V (August 1, 1797), disappeared in that of 3 Nivôse, Year VII (December 23, 1798). The latter made taxation more proportional to rent, and thus prepared the way for the regulation that the Consulate established, which was to endure for many years to come. But since the land tax was still the principal source of revenue for the regular budget, its assessment continued to be the chief cause of discontent.

The allocation was carried out in a fairly equitable manner

within the commune; but despite constant modifications, it was impossible to achieve the same result between communes and departments. It depended on the preparation of a land survey, which had been demanded in 1789 without the realization that it required a trained personnel and much time and money. Only the re-establishment of internal peace would permit Napoleon to begin this work, which was to go on for almost a half-century.

The prime concerns of the state were collecting taxes, financing the war, and replenishing the Treasury. The Constituent Assembly left the establishment of fiscal documents—tax registers and rolls—as well as collection, to the town governments. This showed a continued respect for a feature of the Old Regime; and the popular revolution would never have tolerated the diminution of communal autonomy on this fundamental point. Before 1789, however, the royal government, besides having available assessors of the *vingtième*, who strove methodically to draw up tax registers with the aid of registries and the taxpayers, relied on office-holding collectors to exact payment. These last were compelled to hasten collection because they subscribed to rescriptions for the profit of the Treasury. They were interested in collecting because their commissions depended on the total of their receipts, and because they were authorized to use force against delinquents by quartering troops and by seizure.

Such motives did not animate the salaried civil servants who were instituted by the Revolution, and who had neither force, nor even independence, at their disposal. It was only after 18 Fructidor that a 'tax agency' was created in each department to supervise the preparation of tax rolls, but, entrusted to commissioners from the Directory and not to professionals, these agencies did not achieve the anticipated success; and the dispatch of troops to communal tax collectors and taxpayers was reinstituted. The collection of taxes increased more appreciably than some have admitted; but the first concern of the Consulate was to be the establishment of a specialized administration, independent of local authorities, to assure the preparation of tax rolls and the collection of taxes.

Slow and irregular, direct taxes were of less value to the Treasury than the daily receipts it derived from indirect taxes on consumers' goods. One of the first concerns of the popular revolution had been to do away with these, and the Constituent Assembly had no choice but to sanction their disappearance. The unpopularity of indirect taxes prevented the Councils of the Directory from consenting to a tax on salt, and it was only with reluctance that they agreed to a small tax on tobacco. Napoleon himself was not to adopt the policy until 1804. Moreover, the Treasury was deprived of rescriptions, and could rely on no loans unless they were compulsory. It was necessary, however, to provide for the liquidation of the debt, and then for the extraordinary expense of war. The situation became still worse when the Montagnards, justly outraged at the greed and peculation of the financiers, as well as at their corrupt collusion with civil servants and representatives of the people, forbade recourse to them; although they had long helped the Treasury by short-term loans, and had provided for the maintenance of the armed forces by advances.

The Treasury guaranteed regular services and supported the war only by the assignats and the sale of national property; and it is not without reason that these are credited with saving the Revolution. Having returned to free enterprise, the Thermidorians permitted contractors to operate without restrictions. Deprived of a paper money that the financiers demanded only for use in creating a national bank that would have a monopoly—something the Councils never accepted—the Directory was reduced to expedients that the Old Regime had used more than once: the squandering of the national domain, the proliferation of worthless notes, and bankruptcies.

Inflation and then the deplorable penury of the Treasury produced social consequences that will be discussed later. They constituted a further revolution, and alienated or discouraged those who suffered from them. These persons, for diverse reasons, constituted almost the entire nation. Financial recovery was the first concern of the Consulate, and with the power of the state, Bonaparte's popularity drew great strength from it. But this is not all. For want of money the work of the revolutionaries was partly abortive. The Constituent Assembly, and then the Montagnards themselves, did not (as they might have liked) dare to use the national property to increase the number of small landowners. Of the two great public services, education and relief, which had been promised in the preamble to the Constitution of 1791 and which the Montagnards regarded as the vital organs of the democratic Republic, one was only half realized, and the other failed completely.

No one expressed better than Condorcet the hopes that, in the eyes of the disciples of the Encyclopedists, exalted the goal assigned to national education. The Revolution owed it to itself to organize education so that the 'ever-increasing progress of enlightenment may open an inexhaustible source of aid according to our needs, of remedies according to our ills, of means to individual happiness and of common prosperity' in order to 'contribute to this general and gradual improvement of the human race . . . the ultimate aim towards which every social institution must be directed'. As the interpreter of a humanism that was generous enough to repudiate propertied egotism, the democratic Condorcet, by thus taking up the message of Descartes, had singularly amplified its significance. He assigned national education the aim of 'assuring every individual the opportunity of developing to the fullest extent the talents with which nature has endowed him; and thereby to establish among citizens an actual equality and to effect the realization of the political equality recognized by law'. It was thus a matter of providing all with the means of attaining the enjoyment of rights within the framework of bourgeois society.

The character of the system remained to be determined. Would the state direct it? Would its administration be left to local authorities or to the heads of families? Or would it be granted autonomy? Would it not require compulsory, free attendance to secure its ends? If so, who would bear the expense? Open to all, the national schools could not be denominational; but would their monopoly not be substituted for that of the church? Circumstances left no doubts about their secular nature, but opinion was still divided over the other problems. The Constituent Assembly contented itself with hearing Talleyrand's report on September 10, 1791. The Legislative Assembly listened to Condorcet present his famous plan on April 20–21, 1792, and ordered that it be printed; but took no further action. The Girondin Convention heard reports from its Committee on Public Instruction, began discussion in December, 1792 (during the king's trial), and resumed it, but reached no conclusion.

Condorcet, although not mentioning compulsory attendance,

seemed to imply it; but recalling that every citizen might establish a school, he excluded governmental monopoly. For national education he proposed primary instruction, destined for girls as well as boys, which would include an elementary section and secondary schools, then an intermediate level provided by 'institutes', and finally a higher stage composed of nine *lycées*. A certain number of selected young people would pass from one grade to another as 'national scholars', at the expense of the state. As for the rest, lectures and national festivals would extend the education begun in their youth. A National Society, divided into four classes and recruited by co-optation, would assume the direction of national education and research. The choice and supervision of teachers at each level would be made by those of the highest section. Condorcet thereby created (and he was reproached for it) an independent corporation to remove education from political fluctuations, family interference, and clerical censure.

The Montagnards were no less interested in large institutions for scientific research. The reorganization of the 'Royal Garden', which became the Museum of Natural History, began on June 10, 1793. Yet they felt that the establishment of primary education was urgent. They undoubtedly counted on it to prepare future citizens. Also, because they desired it to be practical and utilitarian, they intended to prepare the youth for positive activity through professional education. Out of an egalitarian spirit, the most radical advocated further that there should be only one school. On July 13, 1793, Robespierre informed the Convention of the plan prepared by Lepeletier de Saint-Fargeau, and on the 29th, in the name of the Committee on Public Instruction, he proposed its adoption. It instituted a state monopoly. The Republic would take charge of children—girls between the ages of five and eleven, boys between five and twelve; but it put the school under the direction of a council of fathers of families, and made it a kind of co-operative. The pupils were to provide for their own needs as far as possible, and would sell part of the product of their labours. They would be inculcated far less with intellectual learning than with moral and professional principles. The influence of *Émile* is obvious. Lepeletier approved the higher levels of education foreseen by Condorcet, but he said nothing about their organization.

In the decree of 29 Frimaire, Year II (December 19, 1793), the Convention accepted neither the plan of Condorcet nor that of Lepeletier. Like the latter, it concerned itself only with 'primary schools'. Education was to be free, and no technical probation was imposed on the 'schoolmaster'. The fathers of families sent their children, for at least three years, to the school of their preference. The Republic paid the schoolmasters in proportion to the number of pupils. If there was no private citizen to teach in the commune, the town government might select a schoolmaster, whom the state would provide with a fixed salary. The text of the decree did not stipulate that the schools be secular, or that the clergy be forbidden to have schools; but a certificate of patriotism was required of all teachers. Supervision was shared by the section or town government and the heads of families. The Committee of Public Safety was to publish the books that the schoolmasters would have to use, and in these books the Declaration of the Rights of Man was to receive the greatest emphasis.

This education, strictly controlled by the state, but decentralized to an extreme, was in harmony with the sans-culotte mentality. In the midst of the war the Montagnards occasionally even accentuated the utilitarian character they bestowed on education, and the assistance they demanded of the research done for its benefit. Pressed for time, as always they made revolutionary haste the order of the day. They called from the provinces those citizens chosen to prepare saltpetre, and put them under the tutelage of noted chemists for several *décades*. They drew young men from the levy *en masse*, gathering them in a War College (*École de Mars*) to provide for officers.

At first the Thermidorians did not repudiate the work of the Montagnards. On 9 Brumaire, Year III (October 30, 1794), they even decreed the opening of a 'normal school', where masters of high repute would train as teachers 1,300 persons sent by their districts. They were also interested in small schools. Their law of 27 Brumaire, Year III (November 17, 1794), really created public education by deciding that the Republic would open a school, if not in every commune, at least for every group of 1,000 inhabitants, and would pay its schoolmaster. He would be appointed and inspected by a board of education designated and controlled by the district. Freedom of choice in schools continued to exist nonetheless, and some persons made no attempt to conceal their intention of having private schools available for the children of the bourgeoisie.

From the outset the Thermidorians displayed a great interest in institutions of higher learning. The Conservatory of Arts and Crafts dates from 19 Vendémiaire, Year III (October 10, 1794); the School of Public Services, for the army, navy, and civil engineering, from 30 Vendémiaire, Year IV (October 22, 1795). The latter became the Central School of Public Works, and was the forerunner of the modern Polytechnic School (École Polytechnique). A School of Mines completed the structure. On 14 Frimaire, Year III (December 4, 1795), three schools of medicine were created, and shortly thereafter, an Institute for Deaf-Mutes. New veterinary schools were also established. On 7 Messidor, Year III (June 25, 1795), appeared the Bureau of Longitudes, with which a course in astronomy at the Paris Observatory was associated.

Languages, archaeology, and the arts also received their share of attention. The School of Oriental Languages was formed on 10 Germinal, Year III (March 30, 1795), the Museum of French Monuments had already been established on 15 Fructidor, Year III (September 1, 1795), and the Conservatory of Music dates from the same period. On the eve of its dissolution, on 3 Brumaire, Year IV (October 25, 1795), the Convention finally proposed a National Institute to direct all intellectual activity. Thus it realized Condorcet's National Society, but without granting it the administrative authority that he had attributed to it.

The organization of secondary education seemed no less urgent a task. The sons of the bourgeoisie could not do without *collèges* to prepare themselves for liberal careers; nor could the scientific world, since it needed to recruit members and assure itself of a public. Therefore the Convention, on the basis of Lakanal's report of 7 Ventôse, Year III (February 25, 1795), decided that each department should have a 'central school'; the department would bear its expenses and name its teachers from among candidates certified by a board of education. In principle these schools would not be free. Obviously, then, the Thermidorians did not share the democratic intentions that Condorcet displayed in 1792. This change can be explained by the monetary disaster, as well as by the conservative reaction. Nor was popular education long in feeling the effect. On 3 Brumaire, Year IV (October 25, 1795), the Convention ceased paying schoolmasters' salaries, leaving them only their lodgings. It was necessary to return to salaries determined by town governments and paid by parents. No further mention was made of compulsory attendance.

Having become the men of the Directory, the Thermidorians changed nothing in their laws. Henceforth it was the application of the laws that mattered. Higher education was virtually terminated. Above all, the Directory had to establish the Institute, where, in addition to the class in the mathematical and physical sciences, there was one in the moral and political sciences (a great novelty), and a third for arts and letters. The central schools opened, and a few prospered. Classes, which were divided into three successive series of two years each, remained optional. These schools have been criticized for not initiating a course of study and for resembling universities more than *collèges*, especially since they had neither preparatory classes nor boarding students. Some corrected this on their own, but overall reform appeared necessary. This was discussed without any conclusions being reached.

As for the primary schools, the predictable effects became apparent: recruiting of teachers grew worse, but since there was a lack of normal schools, how could it be improved? Schools would have returned outright to the Old Regime if the Directory, in its conflict with the church, had not maintained their lay status. For this reason the private schools, which were usually denominational, recovered their students. The government subjected them to inspection by the town administrations, forbade functionaries to send their children to them, and decided to choose its agents only from among the former pupils of the public schools. It does not appear that these last provisions were applied; but inspections and required attendance at Tenth Day worship provoked the voluntary or compulsory closing of more than one private school, without improving national education.

These developments, then, bear traces of the democratic medium. War and insufficient resources, as well as the brevity of experience, limited achievement severely. Nevertheless the system that the greatest part of the bourgeoisie regarded as tolerable or satisfying had been approached. It differed profoundly from the traditional one. The Revolution put an end to the church's monopoly and inaugurated public, secular education. It gave priority to the exact and experimental sciences, at the same time not forgetting that knowledge of nature cannot be separated from that of man and society. It modernized classical humanism by granting primacy to the national language and literature. It laid down the principle that schoolmasters would combine research, technical application, and teaching the youth; this was one of its most original features. Though the system remained far from perfect, the Encyclopedists would have recognized it as their offspring.

The fate of public relief was worse. The disappearance of alms (insufficient though these may have been), of tithe owners, and convents, and the sale of the property of foundations, hospitals, and almshouses dealt it a terrible blow. The Assemblies countered this to a certain extent by granting occasional subsidies, which the town governments distributed or devoted to charitable workshops. By 9 Thermidor this form of social security, decreed by the Montagnards on 22 Floréal, Year II (May 11, 1794), was gone. The Thermidorians confined themselves to restoring the property of hospitals and almshouses that still remained unsold. Then the Directory created charity boards (*bureaux de bienfaisance*), and authorized the town governments to establish *octrois* to support them; but the receipts were, in fact, ordinarily absorbed into their budgets. Here again the Revolution had left its mark: relief was secularized. But if the Declaration of 1793 recognized the rights of the disinherited, the bourgeoisie of the time preferred to limit it to relief, and to rely on charity if possible.

THE ARMY

In 1799 the creation of the national army seemed to be the most successful part of the constructive work of the Revolution. The Frenchmen of 1789 had not expected it to be, for they detested the drawing of lots for the militia, and their taste for equality did not extend to desiring military service for all. War was the affair of princes; besides, would the new order not offer peace to the world? The Constituent Assembly abolished the militia, and despite Dubois-Crancé, maintained recruiting through voluntary enlistments. In February, 1790, it forbade the purchase of commissions and declared them available to all. Then, in September, it set aside one vacant second lieutenancy out of four for non-commissioned officers, and placed great emphasis on seniority for promotions. Beyond these reforms, which satisfied the lower officers and the bourgeoisie, the old order changed but little. Louis XVI remained the head of the army, and noble officers retained their posts so long as they did not emigrate. The conflict between the Third Estate and the aristocracy spread to the regiments, without the Constituent Assembly's ever deciding on a purge. The troops of the line deteriorated, and their number declined.

The popular revolution, however, had set up the National Guard against the nobility and the 'brigands'. The Assembly legalized and regulated it. Territorial, stationary, uniting all citizens able to bear arms, electing its leaders, and dressed in blue instead of white, it regarded itself as radically different from the army. Distrusting the latter, the Assemblies considered the National Guard as the bulwark of the Revolution, and would not consent to subordinating it to the military leaders. When, however, the king's flight augured invasion, the Constituent Assembly drew from this revolutionary militia 100,000 volunteers, who were organized in departmental battalions. When the war began, the Legislative Assembly increased this number, and finally, on February 24, 1793, the Convention called for 300,000 more. The National Guard continued, and although it was similarly mobilized here and there in 1792 and 1793, and later furnished the Directory with mobile columns, it preserved its character.

The Revolution thus had two kinds of defenders who were normally combatants. After August 10 the king no longer commanded them, and the Swiss regiments were dismissed. In the Year II a serious purge eliminated suspect elements. Nonetheless it would take the achievement of national unity and a summons to all Frenchmen for service to make the army truly French. This was done only with difficulty.

In February, 1793, the Convention decreed the union (*amalgame*) of the army of the line with the volunteers. In principle their regulations became the same, but the amalgamation of regiments was realized only slowly, and was not completed until the beginning of the Directory. Meanwhile compulsory military service (except for married men) made its appearance in the levy *en masse* of August 23, 1793, but only on an exceptional basis. The following year the Thermidorians failed to prescribe the enrolment of young men who had reached eighteen, and no summons was issued. Perhaps the search for absentees without leave was henceforth extended to men newly liable; in this case, however, most of them certainly escaped, while those 'requisitioned' in 1793 remained in the ranks at least until the Consulate.

It was the Jourdan Law of 19 Fructidor, Year VI (September 5, 1798), that transformed compulsory service for men between the ages of eighteen and twenty-four into a permanent institution. It exempted only men married before 23 Nivôse, Year VI (January 12, 1798), the date on which the Council of Five Hundred had taken up the proposal, but it did authorize substitutes. When the latter were forbidden on 10 Messidor, Year VII (June 28, 1799), the development seemed complete. Actually, liability did not necessarily involve service. The Jourdan Law simply endowed the Councils, which were judges of circumstances, with the right to complete or to increase the number of effectives. In Messidor, Year VII, they called up all classes. This return to the levy *en masse* aroused such sharp discontent that Bonaparte, not satisfied with re-establishing the practice of substitutions so as to please the 'notables', limited his demands until the wars of the Empire.

By the unification the Montagnards hoped to diffuse the popular character of the volunteer battalions throughout the entire army. Actually, as always happens following such a fusion, it disappeared in part. Nonetheless the stamp of the Revolution remained profound. Hostile to aristocrats and priests, the army remained the part of the nation most generally attached to the Revolution, even after Napoleon had inherited it. Democracy survived within it, for to rise in the hierarchy, knowledge counted for little—intelligence and, above all, bravery were enough. Unity remained one of its essential features. The army never lived in barracks. Hardly were the recruits clothed and armed before they left for the front and merged with the fighting men.

As a result of these original features of its army the Revolution transformed the methods of warfare. First, tactics, because of the volunteers' spontaneous initiative, some of which was always to remain. True, the cavalry could not afford recruits a long apprenticeship; and despite its progress during the Directory, it continued to be inferior to that of the Austrians until the Empire. Strategy was in even greater need of renovation, but as has been seen, after the imperfect plan of Carnot and the phenomenon of Bonaparte in Italy, progress halted. The campaign of 1799 failed to show any. Here again the final outcome was delayed, and Napoleonic genius was required for the formidable army forged by the Revolution to strike the famous blows that marked the imperial campaigns.

NATIONAL UNITY

Destructive or constructive, the French Revolution completed national unity in several respects; and on this basis, too, it fits into the historical continuity of the country. The barriers that separated the various parts of the country were broken down. Equal before the law, all inhabitants obeyed both the state and a uniform administration. No longer were there either internal customs duties or tolls—the national market was realized, insofar as means of communication permitted it. The nation was strictly defined vis-à-vis foreigners, so that manorial lords and bishops of neighbouring countries lost their feudal rights and their jurisdiction in France. The 'removal of barriers' to the political frontiers joined Alsace and Lorraine to the French economy and closed them to Germany. No less effective psychologically were the solidarity of the Third Estate with the National Assembly, and its union in the federations. But nothing equalled the creation of the national army, the war it waged, and the victories it won. Materially, numerous individuals, who had become soldiers, or who had been displaced by circumstances, came to know the diverse aspects of the community about which they had hitherto been ignorant.

Yet for the moment it had to be admitted that the task was far from complete. The co-ordination of the central government and the local administrations remained to be perfected; the codification of most of the law was still incomplete; and primary education, so essential for civic education, had not yet been established. Even where the unity of the national market was concerned, the institution of a uniform system of weights and measures, demanded by the *cahiers*, was unfinished. The Constituent Assembly had entrusted this latter task to a commission, which explained the dual basis of the new order on March 19, 1791: it would be decimal and founded on scientific observation. In conformity with the second principle, the unit of length would be equal to an exact fraction of a quarter of the terrestrial meridian—one ten-millionth part—and would be called a 'metre'. Hence the name 'metric system'. The unit of weight (the 'gram') would be supplied by a cubic centimeter of distilled water weighed under specified conditions.

Actually, resorting to nature and utilizing measures that were necessarily approximate could lead only to conventional units. The use of decimals constituted the truly rational innovation and was of undeniable convenience. The measurement of the meridian began in 1792, and in the same year the Academy of Sciences decreed the nomenclature. Ultimately, however, decimalization encountered difficulties. On August 1, 1793, the Convention had defined the monetary unit, the franc, as equal to the value of 10 grams of silver. But on 28 Thermidor, Year III (August 15, 1795), it reduced this by one-half, in order to identify it approximately with the livre of the Old Regime, the obvious intention being to placate habit by perpetuating the traditional money value. When the Directory disappeared the system had not yet been finished, and once again the work was completed by the Consulate.

On another point, the extension of the French language, the attempt was abandoned once and for all. Neither the cosmopolitanism of the century nor the concept of the nation as a voluntary association led the revolutionaries to become engrossed with it. Nor were they prompted to do so by their libertarian taste for local autonomy. On the contrary, the Constituent Assembly, on January 14, 1790, ordered that its decrees be translated into all the tongues spoken in the kingdom. In nationalizing the war the Convention changed opinion; moreover, foreign languages and dialects (to which the clergy were the chief adherents) were charged with fomenting counterrevolution, and the deputies on mission, particularly Saint-Just in Alsace, proved hostile to them.

On 8 Pluviôse, Year II (January 27, 1794), Barère obtained the enactment of a law providing that public and notarized acts would henceforth be drawn up in French exclusively, that the same condition would apply to the registration of private contracts—a reform that has persisted—and that within ten days a teacher of French would settle in each commune of those departments designated as using a foreign tongue. On 16 Prairial (June 4) Grégoire, going further, begged the Assembly to invite the authorities and popular societies to strive to eliminate dialects; but his proposal was not accepted. The fate of the article of the decree of 8 Pluviôse (January 27) on schoolmasters obviously depended on the decree concerning primary schools, and after 9 Thermidor it was given no more thought. The progress of French, like that of the national mentality, henceforth derived either from the central schools (and ultimately the *lycées* and *collèges*) or from the administrative and economic unification of the country.

While national unity was being improved, however, the civil war tended to split off an important minority: the émigrés and their relatives, refractory priests, and even most nobles, if the law of the Year VI were enforced. Amnesties might reinstate them, but it was forseeable that those who might profit therefrom would only pretend to be reconciled with the new order, and would plan their revenge. A glance into the more distant future might easily have shown that, inflamed as they were by events, special interests produced emotional responses. Hence religious, political, and social antagonism between tradition and rationalism would divide the new France morally even more than it had the old.

INTELLECTUAL LIFE

The revolutionaries remained more or less faithful to rationalism. On October 2, 1793, the Convention accorded the honours of the Panthéon to Descartes. In 1794, Condorcet wrote his *Sketch of the Progress of the Human Mind*, the supreme expression of eighteenth-century thought, which, although proscribed, attested his heroic confidence in the destinies of the human race. Deist metaphysics, in the guise of a pragmatism concerned with founding a morality, to which many, such as Robespierre, added a sentimental effusion or the hope implicit in action, lost none of its prestige. Volney, in *The Ruins* (1791), ascribed the destruction of empires to an abandonment of natural religion imposed by despotism and theocracy. Then, in 1793, he published a *Citizen's Catechism*, which should have been appropriate for the cult of the Supreme Being, Tenth Day worship, and Theophilanthropy.

Still, in the period of the Directory the ideologues, who reigned at the Institute and were in agreement with experimental science (whatever the personal sentiments of its practitioners), brought knowledge to the edge of the perceptible world, in order to make it exclusively positive. Destutt de Tracy proposed to determine, through observation, how ideas were formed; hence the name of the school. Dr. Cabanis foreshadowed experimental psychology, and Pinel, who had studied mental illness at the Salpêtrière prison, in 1798 published a work that inaugurated abnormal psychology. To them, morality became a science of morals. Ginguené and Fauriel introduced historical criticism into the study of literature and the arts. Madame de Staël was to publish *Literature Considered in Its Relation to Social Institutions* (*De la littérature*) in 1800. In 1794, Dupuis, in his *Origins of All Religions*, had seemed to try to extend the method to religion.

Always advancing, the sciences served as a rampart for rationalism. Mathematics—algebra, geometry, mechanics, astronomy—continued to shine in France. Lagrange, Legendre, and Laplace extended the development of analysis through the study of functions. Monge's treatise on descriptive geometry dates from 1799. And in 1796, Laplace had published his *System of the World*, the crowning achievement of classical mechanics, unrivalled until the twentieth century. For the moment there were no great names in physics. If chemistry mourned the loss of its creator, Lavoisier, it still had Berthollet and several others. Cuvier, Geoffroy Saint-Hilaire, and Lamarck were now teaching at the Museum of Natural History, but their controversy over evolution had not yet begun.

Those who detested the Revolution generally repudiated the rationalism of the eighteenth century (even when it remained spiritualist and deist) as being responsible for the catastrophe. A return to tradition and revealed religion was urged by the deserters from that philosophy—La Harpe, who had become a fideist, and Fontanes, who invoked social utility. A similar development was taking shape in émigré circles, and Bonald and Maistre published their first works outside France in 1796. Following Burke's example by using experimental rationalism to justify tradition, they were to become masters of counterrevolution in the nineteenth century; but contemporaries of the Directory ignored them. More immediate was the success of the *Memoirs Illustrating the History of Jacobinism* (1797), in which Abbé Barruel sought to reduce the Revolution to a Masonic plot.

What thwarted rationalism in the world of ideas was primarily the influence of Rousseau, greater than ever (despite his discredited political theories) because his sensual sentimentalism was relished. It opposed the supremacy of the intellect and favoured intuition. Yet speculative philosophy was of no importance to most of those who deplored the Revolution or who reproached rationalism for not bringing them the emotional consolation that the harshness of the time made them desire. They turned to traditional religion or to heterodox mysticism.

The Catholic clergy worked hard to restore its seriously weakened influence. Its divisions frustrated its efforts. The old constitutional church remained, retaining forty-four bishops, the most famous of whom was Grégoire. It held a national council in 1797, and published a periodical, the *Annals of Religion*. The Roman Catholic priests fought them to the bitter end, yet without maintaining accord among themselves. In the name of the intransigents the *Ecclesiastical Annals*, journal of the abbé of Boulogne, condemned the constitutional clergy (the best known of whom was Abbé Emery), who also possessed a gazette, the *Religious Annals* of Abbé Sicard. It particularly attacked the 'haters', those who had taken the oath of hatred to monarchy after 18 Fructidor.

Nevertheless those who escaped Catholic discipline did not necessarily become rationalists. Attached to a magical conception of the universe, they had recourse to confused and esoteric doctrines that were mistakenly lumped together under the name of Illuminism. Saint-Martin was still alive, and Alsace and Lyons remained two strongholds of mysticism. Furthermore, prophets or seers appeared from time to time: Suzanne Labrousse recruited the credulous during the first years of the

Revolution, as did Catherine Théot in Paris at the height of the Terror. Still, it is important to observe that the two ways of thinking cannot be said to correspond exactly to opinions concerning the Revolution. Since the French were (as Cournot noted) generally incapable of understanding the vicissitudes and complex subtleties of party struggles, they divided into two opposing camps, with summary and fixed views. They decided for or against the Revolution; and family tradition, reinforced by the schools, and personal (and sometimes professional) relationships, tended to harden the hostility. Moreover, continuity was affirmed, since the ideological conflict antedated 1789.

It asserted itself in speech as well. In the first years the language underwent an apparently profound transformation. Invariably associated with ideas of regeneration, progress, social utility, and happiness, the meaning of certain words, amplified and impassioned by hope and ardent enthusiasm, acquired a temporary emotional power: 'aristocrats', 'despots', 'tyrants' or 'feudalism', 'Old Regime', 'revolution'; or assumed a majestic quality that soon lost its force: 'law', 'constitution', 'citizen'; but occasionally retained it: 'nation', '*Patrie*'. Carried away by excitement, excesses in vocabulary, hyperbole, and grandiloquence overly encumbered style, at the same time spawning phrases of unforgettable power: 'Have you made a pact with victory?' 'We have made one with death.'

Popular speech briefly contaminated the classical language. Perhaps it contributed to the decay of the simple past tense and the imperfect subjunctive, although the orators in the Assemblies used them fluently. In general, there was little change. With a few exceptions, the revolutionaries, who had been pupils in the *collèges*, observed correct speech and a respect for good taste. They turned the vocabulary of the catechism and Freemasonry to their profit; made use of periphrase, allegory, and fable; quoted the writers of antiquity extensively; and conformed to the sentimentality that had been the fashion for several decades. In addition, on the eve of Brumaire, digressions, spurned as signs of Jacobinism and sans-culottism, became increasingly rare.

The Revolution created literary styles—political eloquence and journalism—and suggested or supplied themes to authors: the Tennis Court Oath to André Chénier, Charles IX to his brother (Marie-Joseph), and Philinte to Fabre d'Églantine. Propagandists made use of gazettes, pamphlets, processions, and festivals, along with the theatre. Timely plays, violently hostile to the nobility, then to kings, at times anticlerical, and after 9 Thermidor, anti-Jacobin, showed little merit. The *Offering to Liberty*, which enjoyed great popularity, was undoubtedly the most important. By the end of the Directory the great orators were dead, no journalist even approached Camille Desmoulins, and conformist subjects and classical styles predominated.

Distinguished but uninspired writers, such as Ducis, Arnault, Andrieux, Delille, and Lebrun-Pindare, maintained the tradition; but since the society that had seen its birth had disappeared and its effects were wearing off, the tradition was dying. The *nouveaux riches* and the petty bourgeoisie, who had not gone through the *collèges*, were unable to savour its inspiration or the allusions to Greek and Latin sources. They were far more taken by the melodramas of Pixérécourt and Ducray-Duminil, which were at the origins of romantic drama. *Paul and Virginia*, the work of Bernardin de Saint-Pierre, which dated from 1787, was still being read with the same enthusiasm. The 'troubador style', made fashionable by the Count de Tressan and popularized by romance and prints, foreshadowed the romantics' infatuation with a conventionalized Middle Age.

Foreign romantics also began to seduce readers, and during the Directory nothing equalled the extraordinary fame of the poems of Ossian, fabricated by Macpherson thirty years earlier. The return to antiquity that marked the end of the Old Regime did not reinvigorate literature—the Hellenistic poems of André Chénier were still unpublished—but it had intensified the influence of the *collèges* among the orators and journalists of the Revolution, a fact continually perceptible under the Directory.

The tradition persisted for painters and sculptors. Some may say that continuity in artistic education and creation must have been impaired by vandalism. Actually, even though the Assemblies occasionally indulged in such iconoclasm, they also took measures to counteract it. The Commission on Monuments, charged with their preservation by the Constituent Assembly, then the Temporary Commission on the Arts, with which the Convention replaced it on December 18, 1793, and the later reports of Grégoire strove to halt destruction and defacement.

Reorganized or created, the National Library, the National Archives, the Louvre, and Alexandre Lenoir's Museum of French Monuments collected and preserved documents and works of art.

The emancipation of the artists under David's direction, officially consecrated by the disappearance of the Academy and the School of Rome, would also suggest a reinvigoration of inspiration and technique. Painters, sketchers, and engravers did in fact draw on contemporary events, as David's masterpieces, the 'Tennis Court Oath' and the 'Assassination of Marat', attest. Under the influence of this same David they also arranged the republican festivals; those of Regeneration (August 10, 1793) and of the Supreme Being (20 Prairial, Year II—June 8, 1794) figure among the most remarkable expressions of the revolutionary mentality. It may be added that the historical canvases exhibited by David before and after 1789—the 'Oath of the Horatii' and 'Brutus'—were in harmony with this mentality in their exaltation of civic virtue in the service of public safety.

Tradition did not, however lose it authority. Fragonard, Houdon, Clodion, and Pajou remained faithful to the art of the eighteenth century. The rebirth of antiquity and the predominance of design over colour, which had characterized the school of David even before 1789, retained their attraction. A place of importance was always accorded Roman archaeology in the decoration of festivals. Under the Directory, historical painting, which classicism set in the forefront, once again harked back to earlier works: in 1799 David exhibited his 'Sabine Women'. The originality of Gérard, Girodet, and Gros had not yet been revealed, and the fame of Prud'hon himself was yet to come. The vogue of the antique also continued to benefit from 'Alexandrian' art (that is, alleged Etruscan or Egyptian motifs), so that in decoration and furnishings the tradition of the Old Regime eventually was perpetuated along with it, and foreshadowed the 'Empire' style. Like 'Louis Sixteenth', 'Directory' was a composite style.

Revolutionary enthusiasm had penetrated music far more readily than it had literature and the plastic arts. Gossec, Méhul, and Grétry composed hymns for public festivals; and such songs were still being written in the time of the Directory. The republicans always opposed the 'Réveil du Peuple' with their own famous songs—Rouget de Lisle's 'Marseillaise' and Méhul's 'Chant du Départ' with words by Marie-Joseph Chénier—which survived the Revolution. But tradition persisted in song writing, chamber music, and light opera, for Grétry and Delayrac were still alive.

THE NEW SOCIETY

Compared with the old, one obvious feature of the new society on the eve of 18 Brumaire derived from the disappearance of the Catholic clergy. Until about this time they had been numerous, honoured, rich, and supported by the secular arm; now they were decimated, poor and in part errant, treated as suspects, even as enemies, by the Directory, and reduced by the secularized state to a purely spiritual authority recognized by the piety of the faithful.

For the moment the fate of the nobility seemed no better. Yet apart from the prestige that birth and invalidated titles retained clandestinely, the aristocrats had not been despoiled of the material sources of their influence to the same extent. More often than is believed families (such as that of the Marquis de Ferrières) lived peacefully among their former tenants and under their tacit protection; or, at worst, they suffered only imprisonment and passing difficulties that left their landed property intact. Wives of émigrés even saved their dowries or widow's portions through fictitious divorces. Some returning émigrés, amnestied or not, had already enjoyed a degree of success during the White Terror in forcing purchasers of national property to make restoration. More numerous still were those who repurchased such lands through intermediaries. Finally, many nobles remained in the service of the Republic.

It goes without saying that the Revolution benefited the bourgeoisie, but not all to the same extent. Those who formerly had boasted of 'living nobly from their own property' had been humbled. The time was coming when they would be satisfied with the title of *rentier*, or landowner, which corresponded more precisely with their origins and with the new principles of social classification. Some Old Regime bourgeois, hostile to the Revolution or the men of 1789 who had remained monarchists, had eventually been treated as nobles. Of those who survived, some emigrated, lost their property, and compromised their relatives; after 18 Fructidor others remained suspect to those of their kind who had become republicans. The fortunes of those whose prudence had kept them in the background were ruined by the abolition of corporate bodies and by revolutionary taxes, forced loans, and inflation.

Likewise affected in part, businessmen further suffered from the controlled economy, and could not regain their former prosperity so long as the war continued and credit remained scarce and expensive. As for maritime trade, the British blockade, the capture of merchant vessels, and above all, the loss of colonies meant decline and (sooner or later) ruin. Nevertheless the bourgeoisie retained their pre-eminence. The monetary disaster did not lead to consequences as serious as those of modern times, because personal property constituted only a modest part of an inheritance. Landowners retained their property, and when specie reappeared, they recovered their income. By the end of the Directory the fall in prices had sorely tried them, but such losses occur in every era. Besides, there was no doubt that more than one had compensated for his losses by purchasing national property, and particularly by participating in the spoils provided by the law of 28 Ventôse, Year IV (March 18, 1796).[1]

Far more favourable opportunities were offered to the businessmen, since their daily practices equipped them for speculation. Their capital, sent or left abroad, returned intact and was used profitably in revictualing the country or in helping the Directory. It might have been expected that the bankers Perregaux and Récamier and the manufacturers Périer and Chaptal would know full well how to turn a loss into a profit, and even better. Another Périer, called 'Milord', who at the end of the Old Regime figured among the leaders of commerce and industry of Dauphiné, and who in 1788 opened his château at Vizille to promoters of revolutionary emancipation, was equal to the occasion and founded a family destined for notoriety in the rise of capitalism and in political life.

The only conclusions, then, are that the bourgeoisie cut off a number of their representatives, sometimes the eminent ones, and that their internal equilibrium was modified. The group that depended on acquired property or that exercised functions

[1] It created the *mandats territoriaux*, or land warrants [trans.].

alien to production—*rentiers*, former officeholders, magistrates, lawyers—without actually losing its established position, was (so far as can be determined) hardly better off than before. Having prepared the Revolution intellectually, formulated its principles, and assumed its direction, this section of the populace deemed its prestige to have been damaged by the rise of managers of the economy who were getting rich, investing their assets in land, and increasing their influence and esteem among the 'notables'. Further, the bourgeoisie were strengthening themselves by incorporating these new men.

Distinctions should be made among these parvenus. The most numerous, sprung from what the Old Regime bourgeoisie called the 'people', were artisans and merchants who took advantage of circumstances to purchase their homes as well as other buildings in town, and plots of land in the vicinity. As always, speculation particularly favoured those who played (at least to some extent) the role of middlemen, especially grain merchants and millers. A few of these men swelled the ranks of trade and industry, but most of them followed the usual path. Having expanded their businesses and increased their property, they were satisfied; whereas their sons, having been sent to the *collèges*, crowded into public administration and the liberal professions if they did not succeed their fathers. They would strive to penetrate more and more effectively into the new order through marriage, connections, and manners, and would not disdain the property-based regime, from which they intended to profit.

To a lesser, though real, extent writers, journalists, actors, artists, and professors, whom the Revolution had given new stature in the eyes of the public, would feel the same way when success reconciled them to serving the governing class. The latter, it may be said, became slightly more democratic, but this trend did not fundamentally alter its character; it was merely a stage in the gradual tendency towards middle-class living that constitutes an essential feature of the social history of France.

Those who were styled the *nouveaux riches* were generally of a different type. They were individuals who, disdaining patient work, daily economies, and slow and measured progress, threw themselves as conquistadors into society in order to attain immoderate wealth in a very short time. This temperament is universal, but an age of social or economic upheaval provides adventure for those who, ordinarily, are deterred from risk either by prudence or their own mediocrity. They proliferated after Thermidor. Avid for pleasure, and more diligent still in satisfying their vanity through a display of brazen luxury, they served as a target in drama, satire, and song. Henceforth they were caricatured in *Madame Angot*.[1] Most of them, owing everything to chance, rapidly dissipated their gains or came to a bad end.

Such was not the case for all: of the pirates who ransomed the Directory (the most famous was Ouvrard), a few remained prominent for a long time. The most gifted of these audacious men eventually invigorated trade and industry by investing their capital. They differed from the older bourgeoisie in their lack of culture, felt no taste for disinterested knowledge, and were totally without revolutionary idealism. A narrow, and occasionally limited, utilitarianism was their lot, and they long retained a fierce, unscrupulous, almost naïve appetite for profit. Still, those who despised them should have recognized that such recruits always bring strength and new blood to their class. Without them it would have withered. After several generations the descendants of parvenus ceased working in order to be accepted into the aristocracy, as the rich families of the Third Estate continually managed to do.

A similar but even more important development was manifested in rural society, since the peasants constituted the majority of the population and their rebellion had dealt the death blow to the Old Regime. Fiscal equality and the abolition of the tithe and manorial dues ended the revolutionary ferment so far as rural landowners were concerned. The gap widened between them and the disinherited, whose benefits were reduced to the elimination of serfdom and personal services; and the dissolution of the peasant community was accelerated. The division of common lands popularized very small property holdings in villages that adopted it; but most of them refused, either because the property was insufficient or because they preferred to keep it as pasture land.

As for the sale of national property, it increased the number of cultivators and the extent of their possessions, chiefly during the second period, that of the Montagnard laws. For, under the Directory the predominance of bourgeois purchasers (already

[1]A parvenu fishwife in a play of 1797 [trans.].

generally undeniable because, besides part of the land, town dwellings, châteaux, abbeys, and forests passed into their hands) became really excessive. Even when circumstances were most favourable for the peasant, sale by auction was greatly to the advantage of the well-to-do small landowner and the large farmer. Thus the ascendancy of what might be called the peasant bourgeoisie was strengthened. These same people were favoured by freedom of commerce, both before and after the Maximum. Furthermore, tenants of the clergy had rejoiced at escaping the *Emptorem* law (which declared a lease void when the benefice changed incumbents) and at learning that the Constituent Assembly had compelled the purchaser to maintain the lease. The Montagnard Convention proved harsher: it authorized the cancellation of leases by the highest bidder for national property, and the controlled economy weighed heavily on the agricultural producer. He was only more inclined to believe that the same conservative interest henceforth united him with the rest of the bourgeoisie.

If the new order was thus attached to a powerful minority, whose support was to consolidate it more and more during the next century, it cannot be denied that for the moment the situation of most Frenchmen had not altered greatly. Below the bourgeoisie there still remained the host of artisans and retail merchants, whose way of life remained unchanged. It is probable that this group increased somewhat, at least in those places and trades where guilds had hitherto limited growth, and where the security of those in high positions might benefit from it. The outlook in the countryside appeared far less satisfying, because the agrarian crisis had by no means been resolved. Peasants who did not own enough land to support themselves, and who were unable to rent any, remained very numerous. As has been seen, sharecroppers (*métayers*) secured no satisfaction from the law.

As for the proletariat, it profited, like the rest, from the suppression of indirect taxes, at least insofar as *octrois* were no longer collected in the towns. In the villages it also escaped personal manorial dues. Wages withstood the fall in prices, and remained from one-fourth to one-third higher than those of 1790. The abundant harvests of the last years of the Directory brought temporary relief to the poor. Nonetheless the threat of unemployment continued unabated, particularly for rural day labourers; and insecurity was intensified by the decline in relief. Finally, the legal status of workers had not been improved. *Compagnonnages* were re-established, and a few mutual-benefit associations (which occasionally changed into centres of resistance) were founded; but the ban on unions (*coalitions*) and strikes was perpetuated without interruption.

On the eve of 18 Brumaire the upper strata of this society still seemed to be a melting pot. The 'notables', who desired to recover the reins so as to effect a regrouping and re-establish their primacy (which was as useful as it was honorific), were thus not mistaken in their intention to rely on the persistence of national conditions and habits. The nation had no choice but to tolerate the blows dealt the old corporate order so as to be done with the aristocracy. Hence it also tolerated the striking success of a small number of persons it did not respect, and saw nothing but temporary expedients and regrettable exceptions in so doing. It is quite true that alongside the salons of Madame de Staël, Madame Récamier, and Madame de Condorcet at Auteuil, others were opened. There persons of every background and culture could be seen rubbing elbows with Barras and Ouvrard, or the women of easy virtue—Madame Tallien, Fortunée Hamelin, Joséphine Beauharnais—with whom they associated, and whose scanty attire and profligacy became the subject of anecdotes to characterize the period of the Directory.

But the demoralizing spectacle of what was called 'society' (that is, a few hundred persons) did not affect the French people. If pessimists considered moral conformity disrupted, it was because of the lapses always provoked by the uprooting of many individuals and by monetary disorder. It is undeniable that the desire to reduce these lapses explains in part the attachment to Catholicism and church schools, because moral education seemed inseparable from them. Divorce itself, although it regularized situations that the Old Regime had condemned to secrecy or scandal, did not find favour in small towns and villages. It was resorted to only in the cities, and more than once it was used as an expedient to escape confiscation of property. The revolutionaries who were most enthusiastic in demanding liberty and equality in public life for themselves exercised marital and paternal authority at home, as well as authority over those they employed, with as much resolve as before 1789. Nor did they perceive any contradiction in this. The Jacobins, hostile to immorality in private life and pitiless towards profligate women, had no intention of dissolving the family or even of emancipating women. Although women played a role in certain 'days', they were kept out of politics and their clubs were closed.

ECONOMIC FREEDOM AND EQUAL RIGHTS

Thus there proves to be greater continuity than might be believed from a logical analysis (based on pure speculation) of the principles proclaimed by the Constituent Assembly. Ultimately the progress of capitalist concentration altered the social structure, while the technical innovations of experimental science increased individual independence by transforming the material conditions of life. As a consequence, economic freedom appears as a basic feature of the new order; businessmen subordinated all others to it.

By the end of the eighteenth century, however, the most daring minds had not calculated its scope, and its immediate effects had not even gained general acceptance. Undeniably, it did attract the French in one respect. Each man was satisfied that henceforth he might try his luck if he secured the necessary means to go into business; and the wage earner clung to the right to sell his services where and when he pleased. It goes without saying that the Revolution did not engender these ambitions—they are inherent in human existence—but it did legitimatize them by liberating them. In this way economic freedom became inseparable from the other freedoms; indeed it was the most precious and symbolic.

Opinion proved less favourable towards technical innovations, which were now free of all hindrance. Out of caution, routine, pride, or lack of capital, artisans appeared no more disposed than before to adopt them without serious consideration. Dislike changed to hostility when the adoption of new processes, especially machines and steam, obviously were leading to capitalist concentration. The craftsman was afraid of being transformed into a wage earner; the worker knew that mechanization began by spreading unemployment; and the peasant foresaw that, with his collective rights suppressed, he would have to abandon the land. As for agricultural methods, the bourgeoisie desired their improvement, since landed wealth remained the most highly valued, and agricultural production supplied the bulk of national revenue.

Such was not the case, however, where industrial capitalism was concerned. The bourgeoisie of the liberal professions, indoctrinated by the economists and Encyclopedists, valued large-scale enterprise, because it associated science with production and offered the advantage of absorbing some of the indigent. Nevertheless its expansion worried them. They saw in it the hand of the financiers (whom the bourgeoisie continued to defy), an appeal to rapid enrichment (which was not in keeping with their tradition), and an eventual dominance over the economy (which would weaken the role of the spiritual life that they cherished) and over politics (in which they claimed a monopoly). Even among businessmen initiative remained limited, and the inadequacy of the banking structure attests their timidity. Nothing better demonstrates the lack of the spirit of industrial enterprise than the virtually universal prejudice of the nation against the English economy, and the conviction that the latter, based on credit and committed by machines to overproduction that only exports could absorb, would collapse if Europe were closed to it.

The psychological shock of the Revolution would have expanded these horizons if France had possessed the abundant coal of Great Britain, or at least if the introduction of British machinery and technicians had been accelerated. The war, however, interrupted the impact of foreign developments. It resumed slowly towards the end of the Directory, but cotton spinning was almost the only industry to benefit from it. Steam was not yet employed, and even water power was often lacking. Such was the case in Paris, which long remained the most important centre.

Taking possession of nationalized buildings, and employing a wretched labour force (notably foundlings brought together by public relief), several great capitalist entrepreneurs now became prominent—Richard and Lenoir in Paris, Bauwens in Paris and Ghent, and Boyer-Fonfrède in Toulouse. As in England, they were far from being strictly specialized, and they continued the tradition of commercial capitalism (Ternaux, for example), directing cottage workers and a rural labour force in addition to their factories, at the same time engaging in trade, commissions, transport, and banking as well. Contrary to the impression that their very real success has made on more than one historian, they did not let it be forgotten that manufacturing enterprise remained on a small scale and widely dispersed, that the artisans alone held sway in the greater part of the country, and that France still remained primarily agricultural.

The stagnation of farming technique also attests particularly the weakness in the rise of capitalism. Whatever their sympathies for British methods, the revolutionary assemblies dared not resort to enclosure, which would have permitted improvements to spread. To lessen popular hostility, the Constituent Assembly did authorize enclosure, but stipulated that the landowners (who would be exempt from common pasture), would forego sending their cattle elsewhere. It decided that artificial meadows would remain intact, without need of enclosure; and it discontinued all crop controls, thereby doing away with 'compulsory fallow'—required crop rotation—without which common pasturing was no longer possible except on common lands.

Without arbitrary land redistribution, however, the effect of these provisions became apparent so slowly that contemporaries scarcely noticed them. When the Convention permitted the division of common lands, the sole result was an increase in small holdings. Poverty encouraged the raising of potatoes, chicory, and oil-bearing plants, just as the disappearance of the *aides* stimulated a considerable expansion of vineyards. These changes did not break the continuity of habit, however, and they by no means signified the advent of modern agriculture.

The progress of capitalism, then, was not accelerated during the decade; on the contrary, circumstances rather diminished it. Large-scale enterprise continued to disturb artisans and peasants, but there is no evidence that it caused them any more harm than heretofore. Nor did it concentrate the labour force or bring forth a strictly proletarian class. In any case, the distinction between the host of small employers and their workmen remained hazy in the minds of the men of the time.

The eventual contradictions between economic freedom and equal rights had not yet become fully apparent. The bourgeoisie saw none at all, because in their eyes equality meant simply that henceforth the law was the same for all. Yet by proclaiming this principle in order to eliminate the privileges of noble birth, it brought into the open the conflict of interests among the different social categories within the Third Estate; and it particularly accentuated the disintegration of the rural community. In other words, inequality came to the fore. Thus even in July, 1789, as it was expressing satisfaction at the popular revolution that saved the National Assembly, the bourgeoisie harboured the fear that the 'people' and the 'populace' always inspired in them. Even before the Declaration of the Rights of Man proclaimed the right of every citizen to participate in the making of laws, the Constituent Assembly followed Sieyes by making the franchise, and above all, eligibility for public office, dependent on the qualities associated with wealth.

Since a regime based on the ownership of property gave the bourgeoisie control over the state, they resolved to give priority to the problem of equal rights. Political democracy seemed to provide the answer, but from the outset some democrats went much further. They denounced the omnipotence of the 'haves' over the wage earners, and their virulent criticisms were a prelude to those of future socialist theoreticians. They showed the emptiness of equal rights, and even of freedom, to those who lacked the ability to enjoy them.

Still, their thought remained overshadowed by the traditional opposition between rich and poor. They pleaded the cause of the 'indigent' skilfully, but they never defined it precisely. Their analysis (the weakness of which is explained by the persistence of the old economy) did not extend to an emphasis on private appropriation of the means of production and on their technical development; and under pressure of food shortages they abandoned generalities. This led them, on one hand, to defend the consumer against the producer—actually the town dweller against the peasant—and on the other, to claim ownership of the soil for the people—not to remove it from the cultivator, but to legitimatize the nationalization of produce, that is, requisition.

It is characteristic that Momoro, supporting this thesis in September, 1792, should have added that industrial and commercial property, on the contrary, continued to be guaranteed by the nation. This, along with the all-powerful influence of circumstances, testifies to the essentially agricultural nature of the economy of the time. Finally, the Montagnards meant to impose arbitration by the democratic Republic on the 'haves' and the wage earners. They protected the former by pronouncing the death penalty against partisans of the 'agrarian law', but attempted to limit their wealth by inheritance laws. They placed public education at the disposal of the latter, and offered the most disinherited a rudimentary form of security. This social democracy constituted a second solution of the problem of equal rights, the memory of which was not lost, but which the bourgeoisie long and uncompromisingly countered with their own.

Nevertheless it is evident that the Montagnards contested neither the principle of hereditary property, as Saint-Simon was soon to do, nor economic freedom, for they accepted the Maximum only as a war expedient. The artisans and retail merchants were of the same opinion: they did not like the rich, but because of a basic contradiction, they did not abhor the idea of raising themselves to the same height. Countless petitioners among the peasants complained that not even a part of the national property was being reserved for them; they wished only to acquire property.

True, the sans-culottes attached more importance to regulation than did the Montagnards, but their immediate needs, aggravated by high prices and unemployment, counted for far more in the popular movements than ideological views and projects for the future. It even seems probable that the remedies they imposed lost prestige when put to the test, because scarcity and the annoyances of bureaucratic rationing came to be associated with them. Besides, the proletariat rebelled against the Maximum on wages; and for this reason those whom the liberal order favoured the least rallied to it involuntarily.

Whether political or social, democracy had already expired when Babeuf and Buonarroti proposed communism as the indispensable condition for equal rights. Yet their preaching bore the mark of the age. Advocating the 'agrarian law', they proposed in effect to divide up the land among those who cultivated it. They had no thought of establishing collective production. Their communism was limited to socializing produce, which amounted to a generalizing of the controlled economy of the Year II. For the moment they remained the only advocates of this third solution.

Already, however, the Jacobin experiment had sufficed to alienate the greater part of the bourgeoisie from the fraternity that charity, based on 'feeling' and optimism, had enjoined before 1789 and that the necessary solidarity of the Third Estate had counselled in the first months of the Revolution. The 'notables' had taken fright, and they did not forget. Nine Thermidor inaugurated a long period of political and social reaction. The Constitution of the Year III re-established the regime based on the ownership of property, and it was careful to define equality and property as the bourgeoisie conceived them. Under the Directory the greatest part of what remained of the national property fell into their hands. When, on 14 Ventôse, Year VII (March 4, 1799), the Republic surrendered to their holders the estates pledged by the monarchy—without charge or for a modest price—it was the bourgeoisie who once more profited the most. They would also have found advantages in reviving the law of July 17, 1793, in order to recover land rents that had been voided when the contract contained expressions borrowed from feudal vocabulary. The matter was considered, but they dared take no action. At least the obligation of redemption (*rachat*) was reimposed on the Breton tenants at will (*domaines congéables*), and it is significant that the new law on precarious tenure (*tenure convenancière*) was voted by the Council of Five Hundred before, and by the Elders after, 18 Fructidor.

In such matters the bourgeoisie were again of one mind. Once more the peasants found their collective rights contested (at least in the forests), and the division of common lands suspended. The judicial reform was altered: the family courts disappeared; arbitration proceedings were reduced in scope; and court clerks' fees were revived. The family also attracted attention: voices were raised against divorce, and the laws of the Year II that facilitated it were abrogated. Cambacérès explained that paternity suits had been authorized in 1793 only for the past, and his project for a code to some degree restored paternal and marital authority, at the same time that it reduced the rights of natural children. Nonetheless the reaction did not go very far, because, in spite of everything, the 'notables' remained divided. Those who lamented the Old Regime did not forgive the others. The champions of the Revolution of 1789 who had remained monarchists disapproved of the republicans and execrated the regicides. The men of the Directory feared the neo-Jacobins. The aggressive anticlericalism common to so many revolutionaries further increased the confusion.

IMPOVERISHMENT AND WAR

In the twilight of the eighteenth century the great majority of the nation, deeming the Old Regime to have vanished forever, no longer attached much importance to political life and social rivalries. So the bourgeoisie had their chance. The young retained none of the impassioned enthusiasm of 1789. Raised by chance amid unrest, and full of bitterness at the memory of the ordeals that had darkened their childhood, the growing generation felt more inclined than ordinarily to go counter to their elders. They thought only of enjoying life. Weariness dulled the spirits of mature men—they wished to grow old in peace, and if possible, to see prosperity return.

The Revolution had cost them dear, and France emerged from it impoverished. The vexatious state of public services, and the disrepair of buildings and roads, even in Paris, all attested it. The death rate had increased; it is believed that the army alone lost 600,000 men, dead or missing. True, the Republic now extended to the natural boundaries, but it had lost its colonies, and with the sea closed, it exported less than half of what it had in 1789. Moreover, it was necessary to fight again to preserve its conquests; but during the last campaign Italy and half of Switzerland had been lost, and invasion was narrowly avoided.

Now it was generally hoped that the foreign war would come to an end, and with it the civil war. Only war contractors and those manufacturers who feared English competition stood to gain from hostilities. Among the men of the Directory themselves, who several times found their last resort in the army, there were many who would have agreed to renounce all or part of the annexations in order to make peace. On 2 Brumaire,

Year VIII (October 24, 1799), the Elders rejected the resolution of the Five Hundred establishing the death penalty for anyone who proposed or favoured dismemberment of French territory, or even consented to consider offers that would involve such action. In opposing it, Porcher had shown plainly that he regarded as mad those who, in order to negotiate, refused to yield some of their compatriots to foreign domination. On 10 Brumaire (November 1) an article, attributed to Daunou (one of the men of Brumaire), appeared in the *Décade Philosophique.* It reproached the Convention for proclaiming the limits of the Republic to be intangible, and thereby declaring 'eternal war and the annihilation of all Frenchmen'. To these weary Frenchmen the heroism of the republicans of 1793 now seemed little more than a ridiculous exaggeration.

THE SIGNIFICANCE OF 18 BRUMAIRE

Apart from the army the constructive work of the Revolution remained incomplete. Even the work of the Constituent Assembly was being contested on more than one point. The reaction that had been in progress since 9 Thermidor had not yet imprinted on it the character that the bourgeoisie now desired. On the other hand, the liberal experiment of the Constitution of the Year III had turned out badly, and had been corrected by dictatorial expedients, yet without conferring the necessary effectiveness on the regime. And every year elections threatened the men of the Directory with being forced out of office by the counter-revolutionaries or the democrats. In organizing the new *coup d'état* they were thinking above all of assuring their control by substituting co-optation for election. The critics of the 'perpetuals' had a fine opportunity to reproach them for this new subterfuge. Actually, this rather narrow group did not serve its own interest alone; the entire bourgeoisie would have suffered from the triumph of either counter-revolutionaries or democrats. So in historical perspective, whatever brilliance the advent of Bonaparte may have conferred on it, the 'day' of 18 (more accurately of 19) Brumaire takes on wider meaning, more in harmony with the social development of France.

By turning the *coup d'état* into a military dictatorship, circumstances enabled Bonaparte to gain the upper hand, and this was of great value to the bourgeoisie. He was unable to consolidate or to organize his power without the aid of the men of Brumaire; but to raise himself to the throne he had to free himself from dependence on them. So he became reconciled with the church, pardoned the émigrés, and took into his service all those—aristocrats and bourgeois, royalists and republicans—who were willing to support him. Thus he arranged a temporary reconciliation between the diverse elements of the modern dominant class. This permitted it (under the tutelage of its protector) to shape institutions and codify legislation in its own way, to establish itself in the high positions of the state and the administration, and to accelerate the revival of the economy: in short, to consolidate its supremacy and thus to complete the work of the Revolution in terms of its professed aims of 1789.

The civil war came to an end, and for a moment even European peace was realized—so much did Bonaparte's popularity depend upon it—without the loss of any French conquests or colonies. Yet the men of Brumaire did not fully appreciate the imperious temperament of Bonaparte, and still less the incorrigible romanticism of his imagination. They expected that he would govern in collaboration with them—but he did not consult them; that freedom at least for the bourgeoisie would continue—but he deprived them of it. Their greatest disappointment came, however, when he crossed the natural boundaries to resume the war of conquest, to perpetuate it beyond all discretion, and to lead the nation to catastrophe.

CHAPTER FIFTEEN

Revolutionary Expansion and Its Effects

STIMULATED BY THE HOSTILITIES, the ambitions of the powers obscured the essential nature of the struggle between the Revolution and the Europe of the Old Regime. Yet contemporaries were by no means unaware of this. Above all, it was a social conflict, between the aristocracy and the bourgeoisie supported by the rest of the Third Estate, particularly the peasants. It was also a political conflict. The kings felt that their despotism was threatened, while they themselves, by taking the aristocracy under their protection, were in danger of perishing along with it. Finally, it was an intellectual conflict. The enemies of the Revolution portrayed it as the daughter of rationalism, whose impious criticism dispelled the mysteries and destroyed the traditional supports of the old order.

It has been wrongly maintained that the rulers fought merely to increase their power. Selfishness might divide them, but Burke's crusade, which their publicists—most notably Mallet du Pan and Friedrich von Gentz—continued to promote, was never a matter of indifference to them. Besides, the aristocracy would have reminded them, if necessary, that they were fighting an 'ideological' war, in defence of society and civilization. Even as Pitt and Grenville declared that they would negotiate only when the European equilibrium had been re-established and the interests of Great Britain safeguarded, they never failed to stigmatize the spectacle of destruction presented by France, and to invite the enemy to restore the monarchy, which would re-establish the indispensable foundations of the social hierarchy. Already the spirit of the Holy Alliance was guiding the Coalition, just as it was to unite it against Napoleon.

REVOLUTIONARY EXPANSION

The Old Regime no longer existed in Belgium or in the territory of Liége, which had been annexed to France, divided into departments, and subjected to all the laws of the Republic. It was not quite the same in the Rhineland. Although the cession of the left bank by the Empire was incomplete, it remained in abeyance, and administrative assimilation was only beginning. Nevertheless the aristocracy there had vanished. In the new Batavian and Helvetian republics, founded under the protection of the French armies, change was taking place. It had gone quite far in the Cisalpine Republic, but in reconquering Italy, the Austrians and Russians had neutralized its effects, had checked it in the Ligurian Republic, and had prevented it at Rome and Naples.

It was by arms, however, at the cost of even more unparalleled efforts and tragic convulsions, that the Revolution extended its sway. In the conquered countries the sympathy it might have aroused was impaired by the ravages of war, the burdens of occupation, and the arbitrary authority of soldiers and officials who too frequently were unscrupulous. In addition, events spread fear among the population, and sadness and discouragement among the partisans of the new order. Not all of these disavowed its principles: in Germany, Kant and Fichte remained faithful, and in England, the Whigs, led by Fox, continued to plead their cause. But the number of those who took refuge in silence, or who admitted their disillusionment, was increasing, even if they did not change sides.

Moreover, there were very few persons who believed that kings could be dispensed with, and the Republic was seen only as a short-lived monster. Its interpretation of equal rights and its popular character roused indignation. Democracy horrified the bourgeoisie everywhere, even more than in France; and in Great Britain and the United States, where a constitutional regime satisfied this class and, in any case, seemed to permit peaceful reforms, the bogy played particularly into the hands of the oligarchy. Washington and the Federalists used it against Jefferson and the republicans, all the more since Genêt's activities had had their impact on the people. On the Continent, however, the argument was still valid.

The advent of the Directory and its military and diplomatic successes restored some confidence among the partisans of the new France. The Republic, with its bourgeois Constitution of the Year III, once more became acceptable. Its victories and conquests proved that a state did not necessarily collapse when it repudiated monarchy. Bourgeoisie and liberal nobles in the annexed regions co-operated in their assimilation; and those in the vassal republics aided in the inauguration of regimes similar to that of France.

If the Revolution thus regained some prestige, it should not be credited entirely with the diffusion of liberal ideas. British influence did not diminish, for many followers of the principles of 1789 still remained Anglophiles. To them the government of Great Britain seemed to moderate the application of democracy so well that it need not be feared. Even more, the nobles and functionaries persisted in turning their gaze complacently towards a country where the former saw a pre-eminent aristocracy and the latter a model for the renovation of the economy. Nor did the example of the United States lose its prestige. The Creoles of Latin America were inspired by it as well as by that of France. The development and consequences of the war, above all, were responsible for currents of opinion in which revolutionary infiltration undoubtedly appeared occasionally; but this cannot be said to have been the guiding principle, even though the Old Regime governments naturally held it responsible.

In Prussia the Treaty of Basel encouraged among leaders of the Enlightenment (*Aufklärung*) an understanding with France. Pastor Riem, for example, expressed it openly. This opinion persisted among office-holders, and even at the court, but its appeal was to the interests of the kingdom. In 1796 the Directory momentarily hoped that agitation in South Germany would increase. The prospect of an invasion aroused discontent. The Bavarian nobility and the upper class of Württemberg continued their opposition, but the thought of renouncing their privileges never occurred to them. Hamburg remained a centre of French influence, because businessmen were annoyed at seeing the war continue if there were no government contracts for them.

Petitions in favour of peace increased in England for the same reason. In January, 1797, Erskine published his *Summary of the Causes and Consequences of the Present War With France*, which enjoyed an extraordinary success. The burden of taxes, economic difficulties, and especially scarcity also aroused the common people. The revolt of the Silesian weavers in 1794 and the serious outbreaks that occurred in London during the autumn of 1795 have already been mentioned, and they had some bearing on Pitt's decision to negotiate. We should not be misled by the war effort that the latter imposed on the country, beginning in 1797, when the danger reached its height. His unpopularity grew, and he deemed it prudent to send Malmesbury to France again.

In England, unlike the Continent, the influence of the French Revolution could lead only to democracy. So the British government, in contrast to the others, was disturbed by the discontent of the artisans and the sporadic agitation that high prices provoked among the working class. These circumstances favoured propaganda hostile to the oligarchy. At a London banquet on May 18, 1797, toasts were drunk to electoral reform, Irish freedom, and the French alliance. The societies continued, secretly or otherwise, and a pamphlet claimed to be the voice of 80,000 indomitable Jacobins. Even assuming that this assertion was not exaggerated, it does not follow that an insurrection was imminent; and the alarming reports that flooded the Home Office do not agree in their evidence. But the government exaggerated its fears in order to justify repression.

No longer could anyone doubt that the rise of the bourgeoisie constituted a dominant feature of European civilization. The English revolutions were proof of it. Their advent in France had demonstrated the power of this class in a far more radical way, since they had eliminated the nobility. Thus endless repercussions of the French Revolution were ensured for the future. On the eve of 18 Brumaire, however, nothing remained of the hopes cherished by the Girondins, for no other people had yet followed the example of the French. Everywhere the selfish partisans of the Old Regime held a tight grip on the machinery of repression, and they had long given adequate proof of this fact.

THE EUROPEAN REACTION

Sovereigns and publicists vilified the revolutionary government for invoking the relativity of individual rights, in order to justify their suspension in case of revolution or civil and foreign war. The British governments seemed particularly justified in becoming indignant, because eighteenth-century England was one of the few countries where the individual was respected. Actually, in practice the individual was disregarded when public safety required it, and the reaction proved this again. With habeas corpus suspended, the arbitrary power of the police was unlimited. The loyalists and their associations, through surveillance and denunciations, assumed a mission similar to that of the clubs and revolutionary committees. In 1799, measures against assemblies and seditious publications were intensified, and printers were subjected to declarations. Since Great Britain had no Vendée, the repression was limited to what was known in France under the Directory as the 'dry guillotine'. By use of the press gang suspects were shipped aboard His Majesty's vessels, and their leaders were condemned to transportation to Australia; but no special courts were created. The terror became bloody only in Ireland, where insurrection led to massacres and executions.

The Continental despots were not hampered by constitutional scruples. Their arsenal of coercion was always ready, and it sufficed for them to use it with the severity that circumstances demanded. In the Iberian states and the papal domain the Inquisition had only to open new trials. In Latin America, Nariño was sentenced to ten years in prison, and following a conspiracy that cost numerous lives, Rodríguez deemed it prudent to flee his country in 1797. His disciple Bolívar followed his example two years later. Tsar Paul I acted in a similar manner. At first he liberated Novikov, Radishchev, and Kosciusko; but nourishing his mother's hatred of the Revolution, he was not long in restoring the harshness of the oppressive regime when he took over the army of Condé and installed Louis XVIII at Mitau. In the Hapsburg Empire, Colloredo, the secretary of state (*Kabinettsminister*), improved the police methods of Joseph II, and perfected the system for which Metternich later claimed credit: the all-powerful police, the 'black cabinet' and censorship, widespread espionage, particularly at the expense of the functionaries, and arbitrary imprisonment. After the executions in Hungary, silence prevailed in the hereditary domains.

The other states of the Holy Roman Empire copied this system more or less closely, depending upon the inclinations of their rulers. Even at Jena, Fichte, accused of atheism, had to abandon his professorship in 1799. The most stubborn liberals emigrated—thus Rebmann reached Paris in 1796. In Prussia, to be sure, the leaders of the Enlightenment continued to resist. Frederick William II died in 1797, and his son Frederick William III put an end to the persecution of Wöllner, who was dismissed. Kant nonetheless was extremely prudent. It goes without saying that once the French were driven from Italy, the White Terror knew no bounds at Rome, and especially at Naples, where it was witnessed by Nelson.

The maintenance of authority did not necessarily mean that all reforms had to be renounced. Pitt could not deny that the improvements advocated by the Whigs had formerly won his approval. On the Continent the renovation of agriculture on the English model commended itself to the attention of the governing classes and the intelligent nobles, with its natural consequences—abolition of serfdom, redemption of manorial rights, redistribution of lands, and suppression of collective rights. Some elements in the constructive work of the Constituent Assembly, even of the Committee of Public Safety, were suited to enlightened despotism, and the war pointed up the defects of an administrative apparatus inherited from the past.

The great majority of the privileged few, however, detested any change as a Jacobin contamination that would lead to others. The common people, declared the Anglican bishop Horsley in 1795, had nothing to do with the laws except to obey them. The governing classes were of the same opinion. Pitt believed that any reform would encourage the popular movement, and even had he felt differently, his pact with George III would have tied his hands. Little or no improvement was made in the agencies and methods of government, because the bureaucrats and their superiors secretly opposed it.

In Austria, Francis persisted in running everything himself, communicating with his ministers only in writing or through Colloredo. He systematically reserved all high offices for nobles. He put an end to agrarian reform, and in 1798 left the commutation of *corvées* to be arranged by agreements between landlords and tenant farmers, with the approval of the administration.

Nothing better could be expected of Paul I. He was reputed, however, to be favourably inclined towards the serfs; in fact, in Little Russia he forbade their sale apart from the land, and fixed *corvées* at three days per week. In practice, however, all this was ignored. In Livonia he was content with exacting from the Diet a few modifications in serfdom, and Kiselev, his commissioner in the Danubian principalities, did no more. Moreover, Paul also apportioned (to his nobles) many royal serfs, whose lot had been considered less severe and was now thus destined to become worse. His inclination towards administrative reform remained unfulfilled, and his reign is marked by passing infatuations and sudden dismissals that did not spare even devoted servants such as Panin, Rostopchin, or Suvorov. A 'magic lantern', which threatened everyone at the same time that it paralysed the government, he was to bring about a palace revolution through assassination.

In Prussia, reforming opinion survived among high functionaries such as Schön and Schrötter, educated at Königsberg in the school of Kant and Kraus, who taught liberal economics. It was likewise represented by immigrants from western Germany, such as the Rhinelander Stein and the Hanoverian Hardenberg, or from Denmark—Struensee, for example. Frederick William III at first seemed disposed to grant fiscal equality, but upon reflection he did nothing. Stein was able to effect only some technical modifications in the financial administration, but failed to abolish internal customs duties. The nobility retained the high offices and army posts: in 1800, of 6,000–7,000 officials only 695 were commoners. The rumour spread that the new king desired to put an end to serfdom (*Untertänigkeit*), and petitions poured in. Agrarian reform did indeed continue in the royal domain, but that of the Junkers remained untouched.

No more than in Austria was any progress realized in the organization of Prussia. On the contrary, the recent acquisitions made at the expense of Poland, and administered separately by a 'lord lieutenant' (*Oberpräsident*) because of the difficulties of assimilation, escaped the General Directory (*Generaldirektorium*), as in Silesia. The Polish insurrection of 1794 resulted in confiscation of the lands of the clergy and the *starosty* (royal lands which had been yielded to noble families). The ecclesiastical benefices were left with only 35 per cent of their revenues on a salaried basis, and those *starostes* that were not included among the rebels, with 61 per cent. The king thus became the greatest landowner in the annexed territories, with 1,500 square kilometres. The farmer-general of this domain rented it out for dues that were so small that Zerboni, assessor for the Treasury (*Kammer*) accused him of graft; whereupon Zerboni was charged with participating in a secret society, and sentenced to life imprisonment.

Two countries alone deserve mention as exceptions. In Bavaria, Montgelas came to power in 1799, and began the administrative reorganization that was to mark the reign of Maximilian Joseph, the new elector and future king. He substituted ministers for groups of advisers (*collèges*), and created the Privy Council (*Geheimrat*). In Denmark the agrarian transformation was continuing, particularly in Schleswig and Holstein. There the redemption of *corvées* was regulated, and land redistribution was accelerated, with consequences similar to those of enclosure in Britain, notably the transformation of tenant farmers into day labourers in the service of noble landowners.

Thus the reformers were almost as powerless as the friends of the Revolution. It was the armies of the Republic that had begun the rejuvenation of the world, but since the French desired peace, what would be the outcome? By bringing Bonaparte to power the men of Brumaire made the decision: the Grand Army would strike down the Old Regime everywhere in its path.

THE UNITED STATES

Although they remained neutral, the conservative 'rulers' of the United States, now called the Federalist party, continued to deplore the turn taken by the Revolution. The execution of Louis XVI, the flight of Lafayette, and the stories of émigrés—Talleyrand, for example, and later Dupont de Nemours—outraged them. The momentary triumph of democracy irritated them particularly because popular ferment continued in their own nation. Numerous clubs had opened, and the influence of events in France on them was perceptible. The excise tax on alcohol increased fears, for it provoked sharp opposition in rural areas, where small distilleries numbered in the thousands. Washington had to dispatch an armed force to the frontier region of western Pennsylvania in 1794 to break the resistance. It should be no source of astonishment that Genêt, sent by the Girondins to secure anticipated payments on account on the American debt, or credits for the purchase of supplies (if not the aid that the treaty of alliance seemed to promise), acquired a following when he called on public opinion after being ousted by Washington. The president blamed the excise tax disorders on the clubs, and spoke of doing away with them, just as the Feuillants, Lafayette, and the Thermidorians had done in France.

The Federalists did not succeed in maintaining unanimity within their own class and among the ranks of their party. Jefferson, a planter himself, did not approve of Hamilton's policy, and resigned as secretary of state. He reproached the government for using the Constitution to benefit the capitalism of businessmen at the expense of the farmers, especially the host of small cultivators. Madison also broke away. The Jay Treaty permitted them to invoke national honour, and to accuse Hamilton of slavishly embracing the British cause. Thus an opposition party took form in the Republicans, who claimed to be democratic.

When Washington left office in 1797, John Adams replaced him, but he defeated Jefferson only by a small margin. He, too, disagreed with Hamilton, who retired. Also very hostile to the popular movement, as well as to the French Republic, Adams profited from the rupture with the Directory. It enabled him to enact an alien act to expel suspect Frenchmen, and a sedition act that permitted attacks on clubs and 'dangerous' writings. Virginia and Kentucky protested in vain. Thus the way was being paved to the election of 1800, which brought Jefferson to the presidency.

If the natural conditions and extraordinarily different historical circumstances that distinguished the New World from the old are disregarded, it may be seen that the fears of the privileged classes, aggravated by pessimism or moderated by optimism according to temperament, here, as elsewhere, were the motivating force of the general trend of history. The Federalists sympathized with the ideas of Burke. Having neither a king, nor lords, nor established church to defend, they might have been far closer to the French bourgeoisie, who had become conservative, and to Sieyes, their final interpreter; but the vicissitudes of the Revolution and its anti-religious measures had frightened them.

Nor did Jefferson's democratic spirit carry him as far as has been thought. He did not believe in universal suffrage, and his ideal, which harked back to a republic of small, independent rural producers, did not differ greatly from that of the Montagnards and certain members of the Constituent Assembly. A landed proprietor, he distrusted industrial capitalism. He feared it would produce a numerous proletariat, which seemed to him, as it had to Rousseau, Robespierre, and Saint-Just, incompatible with political democracy. He believed this could be avoided if the United States would leave industry to Europe and remain an agricultural country. It was a chimera; and the businessmen, entirely concerned with the profits of the moment and unconcerned with the future, unconsciously established themselves as the motivating force of history. At least Jefferson nourished the hope that the small rural landowners would increase, and in this connection his optimism was more justified than that of the most generous French revolutionary.

In the Old World arable land could be extended only at the cost of reclamation that was both difficult and increasingly less profitable; while in America the vast extent of virgin land and unexploited natural resources provided an opportunity for the daring and independent, and deferred social tension. This was why the small farmers of the Atlantic region, although hostile to the larger ones, were to bring Jefferson to power; and if the harsh and dangerous life of the frontier oriented people more strongly towards political democracy, the domination of the bourgeoisie could nonetheless establish itself in the United States in the most thorough and least contested fashion.

THE CONFLICT OF IDEAS

The political and social conflict continued to be reflected in the world of ideas. Within the dominant classes the authority of tradition came back into fashion; and whether out of conviction or to satisfy their readers, a growing number of writers displayed reserve or hostility towards the Revolution. In England, Canning had founded his *Anti-Jacobin*, and Cobbett, who later became a leading radical, now fulminated against the innovators. Appreciating the importance of propaganda, the governing class devoted much money to it. Pitt pensioned Gillray, the most famous of the caricaturists. The Genevan refugees Joseph des Arts, d'Ivernois, and Mallet du Pan took an important part in the campaign. The recriminations of the Viennese Hoffman, the Swiss Girtanner, and the Hanoverian Zimmermann against the conspiracy of the Illuminati and the Freemasons established a pattern in Germany, and in 1797 an official named Robison took up the theme at Edinburgh.

French émigrés participated in the enterprise, although they were by no means in perfect agreement: Mounier soon undertook the defence of Freemasonry, and the constitutionalists opposed the absolutists. In London, Boisgelin conceived a plan of propaganda. Chateaubriand's *Genius of Christianity*, which he began to write in 1799 (he had already published his *Essay on Revolution* in 1796), was probably connected with this. Villiers, on the other hand, became enthusiastic over Kantianism. The great majority, however, damned the Revolution, and Barruel's work, published in 1798–99, enjoyed a success that time was not to diminish.

It was in England that the new order still found its best defenders. Paine's *Rights of Man*, the second part of which dated from early 1792, remained the most ardent expression of the sympathies aroused by the Revolution. In 1793, Godwin published his *Enquiry Concerning Political Justice*, and the following year, in his *Adventures of Caleb Williams*, he satirized contemporary 'society'. In his eyes social inequality represented the supreme injustice, and traditional property the stumbling block. Like Babeuf, he aimed principally at land, but as a libertarian democrat, he expected nothing from the governing class or the political parties. He counted only on individual betterment and peaceful and legal development to attain communism. It is doubtful whether he had a following; and his wife, Mary Wollstonecraft, who for the first time demanded rights for women, had even less success.

On the other hand, the lawyers and orators who leaned towards the democrats in a more or less explicit fashion, reached the general public, and despite the police, clandestine publications continued. Yet a retreat had been perceptible ever since Great Britain considered herself threatened with invasion. Burns died in 1796, and the other poets fell silent. On the news of the French entry into Switzerland, Coleridge had made amends, and in a palinode (*France: An Ode*) he rejected the impious and perfidious enemy, the cruel and fickle race. The numerous caricatures reveal that the counter-revolutionary cartoonists attacked the court and the ministry because of their internal policy or their manner of conducting the war; but hardly any seem to have come from the democrats; these probably would not have found either purchasers or printers.

On the Continent the friends of the Revolution could participate in the daily polemic only by clandestine means and at considerable risk. Hegel did not publish his violent philippic against the tyranny of the duke of Württemberg. The great thinkers (of which Germany still retained a virtual monopoly) who came out in favour of the new principles usually presented philosophical and timeless propositions. Herder, Kant, and Fichte at least remained faithful to the Enlightenment, but not without arousing disapproval.

In 1793, Fichte had published his *Appeal to the Princes for the Return of Freedom of Thought* and his *Contribution Designed to Correct Public Opinion on the French Revolution*. He showed himself to be profoundly influenced by Rousseau, based the state on a contract, protested against privilege, and sanctioned property only if it were the result of labour. In short, he appeared as an individual violently hostile to the state. Yet in 1796, in his

Bases of Natural Law According to the Theory of Knowledge, in which he laid the foundations for transcendental idealism, he no longer spoke of the French Revolution. He oriented his political conception in a different direction: men live only in society; from their relations law is born; the state guarantees it through compulsion; and thus, thanks to the state, the individual may fulfil himself. By 1800, Fichte, to assure a man's right to life, was granting control of the economy to his 'closed commercial state'.

The *Letters on the Progress of Humanity*, which Herder issued from 1793 to 1797, remained closer to the Enlightenment. Kant, in his *Perpetual Peace* (1795), *Metaphysics of Morals* (1797), and *Conflict of the Senses* (1798), developed the principles of a 'state of law' and of juridical relations between nations, which remained in harmony with the ideal envisioned by the men of 1789. Wilhelm von Humboldt himself, in his 'Essay on the Limits of the State', which he did not publish, proved to be a partisan of an unlimited individualism that undoubtedly would not have displeased the Sieyes of 18 Brumaire.

Still, there was nothing in these speculative exercises that produced action. German thought was characterized by its insistence on subordinating the liberation of mankind to intellectual progress and, even more, to individual morality. Liberty resulted above all from a personal act of submission to the 'categorical imperative' of Kant. Men who became involved in political life to a point where they compromised themselves in the service of France—Forster, Rebmann, Görres—by inveighing against the moral inferiority of the French who compromised their Revolution, echoed the teachings of the *philosophes*, the conclusion of which was not long in coming. As for Kant, if the head of the state became a tyrant, revolt would remain no less reprehensible. And Fichte gave assurance that the people could not govern by itself; if it violated the law, who would interpose his veto?

Other thinkers, not concerned with defending the Old Regime, were nonetheless associated with the reaction insofar as they violently condemned what was happening in France. Such were the men of Weimar, most notably Goethe and Schiller, who, after a tumultuous youth, had settled down, the former as minister to Charles Augustus of Weimar, the latter as a professor at Jena. Thanks to Greek antiquity, they claimed to have discovered how the divergent tendencies of a being might be harmonized in art, the vital spirit (*élan vital*) and passions reconciled with reason. This new humanism, which advised the individual to isolate himself so as to develop in his 'totality', and which inclined philosophically towards pantheism, exerted a great attraction for some time. Goethe's *Wilhelm Meister* (published in 1794–96), and Schiller's *Wallenstein* trilogy and *Song of the Bell* (1798 and 1799) were read with enchantment. Wilhelm von Humboldt joined this classicism, and Hölderlin was not alien to it. Insisting on intellectual and artistic culture, they did not deviate from political conservatism.

The work of these writers leaves one with an impression of having listened to discussions among persons who were comfortably settled in the Old Regime. They had no illusions about it, but they feared, more than anything else, that their own well-being might be disturbed. Their tacit admission of impotence indicates a lack of awareness, and their teachings are less original than they believed. It had been said many times since Aristotle that liberty and democracy are inconceivable without the civic morality that is not easily separated from private morality. The Germans might have demonstrated that they were familiar with Montesquieu, Rousseau, even Robespierre. But the French knew also that 'virtue' could flourish only in the shelter of institutions that preserve freedom and place man in a position to elevate his mind.

Is it not tragicomic that the German writers, recommending to their compatriots an intellectual and moral effort, did not even think of delivering them from serfdom? The ancients, on the other hand, knew full well that man is not reducible to intellect alone, and that his conduct depends equally on his emotions, his senses, and his body. Had the 'libertines' not striven to repeat this since the Renaissance? Each time in history that circumstances remove all hope of curbing tyrannical domination, a philosophy or religion always appears to prove again to the oppressed that inner freedom and spiritual salvation alone are important. In this sense the Germans, although they disapproved of asceticism and ignorance, nonetheless imitated the Stoics and Christians, who had been divested of all earthly hope by the pitiless yoke of the Roman legions.

The sway of rationalism appeared less solidly established outside France. First of all, the sciences had not supported it to the same degree, for in this respect French primacy was for the moment uncontested. In mathematics, the German Gauss was just beginning. Cavendish and Priestley, the English chemists who had taken refuge in America, were ageing. Nicholson, although very respected, had not yet decomposed water. Davy and Dalton were only at the beginning of their careers, and the same was true of the Swede Berzelius. French physicists had no rivals apart from Wollaston and Rumford in England. True, a revolution in the knowledge of electricity was brewing in Italy. The experiments of Galvani, professor of anatomy at Bologna, dated from 1790. Volta, who was teaching at Pavia, and whose electrophorus and eudiometer were already recognized, was on the point of discovering electric current; but his battery dates only from 1807. Among the naturalists, Alexander von Humboldt was still travelling in Latin America, and Pallas, another German, in the Russian Empire.

Despite their great merit, these observers and experimenters lacked the synthetic genius that distinguished Lavoisier, and the speculative penetration that was now leading the ideologues to a positive conception of science. Until his death, Priestley, ingenious collector of new data, obstinately subscribed to Stahl's 'phlogiston theory', and never really grasped modern chemistry.

On the other hand, English empiricism, which (as has been said) had long since become conservative with Hume, and even more so with Bentham, contested the claim of the French *philosophes* to recognize man's control over his destiny. It strove to restore authority and moral standards, not by metaphysical considerations, but through historical observation and political experience. Just as the experimental method seeks out the constants of the physical world in order to control it by conforming to these constants, so, likewise, it would enable us to realize, through observation of social life, that customary institutions, by the very fact of their enduring, are in harmony with 'the nature of things', and that they constitute a 'truth', both factual and wholly relative, because they prove to be useful.

In Burke this pragmatism was complicated by a social vitalism (*vitalisme*) borrowed from medicine, the type of thing that had been taught in France at the school of Montpellier in the eighteenth century, and by Bichat even in the time of the Directory; experimental physiology, begun by Lavoisier, had not yet gained acceptance. The human being was considered the fruit of a spontaneous and progressive germination, caused by an irrational and mysterious force called 'life'. Similarly, Burke spoke of society as if it were a plant or an animal, with the individual only one of its organs; so that social authority was imposed on him as a condition of his existence, which he could no more repudiate than any bodily need.

From England this experimental rationalism, a blend of mysticism and romanticism, passed into Germany through Hanover. Rehberg and Brandes were steeped in it. Fichte's new doctrine, which recognized the state's primacy over the citizen, was oriented in the same philosophical direction. Friedrich von Gentz, who translated Burke in 1793, rid himself of this mystical apparatus in order to justify conformity through utilitarian observation. It has been maintained that this prepared the way for the political philosophy (if such it can be called) that Metternich ultimately brought to the service of the Habsburgs.

Even political economy was occasionally bent on reducing the pretensions of reason. In 1798, Malthus, observing the England of his day, maintained that the indefinite progress of humanity was but an illusion. Despite technical progress, population increased more rapidly than the means of subsistence. Any social betterment, by assisting the species to multiply, could only aggravate the evil; it was disease, vice, famine, and war that restored the balance. Being a liberal, Malthus found a way out: he advised the poor man to become resigned to chastity. The traditionalists nonetheless believed that he had dealt a fatal blow to the hopes of Condorcet and Godwin.

Among the émigrés, Bonald and Joseph de Maistre, who in 1796 published, respectively, *Theory of Political and Religious Power* and *Considerations on France*, were not unrelated to the experimental conservatives. Bonald often invoked the 'nature of things'. They also subordinated the individual to society, and in this sense they have been classified as 'socialists'; but they substituted the action of Providence for the operation of the 'vital force'. According to Bonald, a dogmatic and authoritarian spirit who cherished the royalist tradition as much as he did Catholicism, the limits imposed by God on society remain immutable. First in importance, the family sinks its roots into the very existence of the human race, and the king appears as the father of a family expanded into a society. To Joseph de Maistre, who had a sense of history and who, as a good ultramontane, proved rather indifferent to the form of temporal government, the Creator limits himself to preserving the social state through the infinitely supple action inspired by His wisdom, so that we must bow before the fact.

Whatever their orientation, positivism and rationalism were facing opposition, far more powerful than in France, from the anti-intellectualism (*mouvement hostile à la primauté de l'intelligence*) that had inspired Rousseau and the 'Storm and Stress' (*Sturm und Drang*) before 1789. It was now being reinforced by events that spread the taste for the dangerous and the morbid, as the success of the novels of Ann Radcliffe attests; while the spectacle of so many misfortunes revived the sense of tragedy, of the struggle of man against the forces of nature and of fate. Yet the power of this trend appears fully only if the temperament and social condition of those whom it swept along are taken into account. Most were incapable of adapting to conditions. They were sick or unstable persons, whose feebleness destined them for melancholy, even suicide—young people avid for independence and pleasure, irritated by social restrictions, or seeking their way of life—who ran afoul of the privileges of rank, wealth, or hallowed reputation. It is not astonishing that they sympathized with the 'brigand' who redressed wrongs, that with age or success many of them became wiser. There have always been romantics, but they multiplied when the rise of the bourgeoisie dislocated the social structure, and many young men became indignant or desperate.

Nowhere was this state of mind better displayed than in Germany. It dissipated the prestige of the Enlightenment and the brief attraction of Goethe's humanism. This was not accidental, for in no other country did mysticism hold such sway. It animated Lutheranism, and through the pietism of the

Moravian Brethren there was a link between Böhme, the theosophist shoemaker of the seventeenth century, and the romantics. Savants—Werner, Ritter, and Baader—gave the most unexpected symbolic interpretations to their experimental knowledge. In a similar fashion, heterodox occultism, which had infiltrated Freemasonry and Illuminism, claimed to be founded on scientific opinions or discoveries. It borrowed vitalism from medicine, and magnetism (which was also envisaged as an irrational force) from physics. Somnambulism brought the spirit to an ecstatic unconsciousness, in which it entered into contact with the supernatural world. In their fashion these cultivated individuals became reconciled to the magical conception of the universe, which interpreted the crude popular superstitions always alien to the Enlightenment.

Mysticism also penetrated philosophy. Having destroyed metaphysics, Kant reconstructed a substitute founded on moral conscience, which, in essence, meant (to him) a return to divine intuition. In this way later Germans arrived at transcendental idealism. In his *Doctrine of Knowledge*, published in 1794, Fichte, in a spiritual vision, had seized upon the 'self' as the sole reality, which is pure activity, and constructed the 'non-self' in order to give the former a reason for acting by trying to absorb the latter. Then Schelling restored to the 'non-self' its own, also purely ideal, existence. Nature and the 'self' became two aspects of the absolute, the unity of which in the unconscious is dissociated by reflection, but which artistic genius can attain by intuition and can express in its works. Finally, this trend profited from progress in instrumental music, a modern art, which took its rules only from itself, was supremely romantic, suggesting rather than describing, and was essentially devoted to moving the senses and emotions. It shone with incomparable brilliance in Germany.

Before the decade had ended, a group, detaching itself from Goethe and even more from Schiller, took as its rallying cry the words 'romantic' and 'romanticism', which it made famous. In 1798, in Berlin, Friedrich Schlegel, with the aid of his brother August, issued a magazine called the *Athenaeum*, which lasted three years. First at Dresden, then at Jena in 1799, they joined with Novalis (whose real name was Baron von Hardenberg), Schelling, and Tieck, who had just published the *Effusions of an*

Art-loving Lay Brother (left by his friend Wackenroder, who had died prematurely). They outlined a philosophy that never took a coherent and systematic form.

Disciples of the classics, they first conceived of the world as an inexhaustible and perpetually changing flow of the creations of the 'vital force'. Under the influence of scientists and of Schelling they introduced into this a 'universal sympathy', which was displayed, for example, in chemical attraction, magnetism, and human love. Touched by the religious effusions of Schleiermacher, they eventually borrowed from Böhme the idea of the *centrum*, the soul of the world and divine principle. It is always the artist of genius who, alone, through intuition, or even dreams or magic, enters into contact with true reality, and in him this mysterious experience is transmuted into a work of art. The poet is a priest, and this philosophy relies on miracles. Like the poor for whom they had scant concern, these esthetes expected miracles; unhappily for them it cannot be said that any were forthcoming. They left no great works. The best were those of Novalis, principally his *Hymns to the Night*, which dates from 1798–99.

The plastic arts emancipated themselves to about the same extent as in France. Neo-classical architecture continued to serve as a guide, and Canova's sculpture united the voluptuous tradition of the eighteenth century with the inspiration of the academy. In England, however, landscape art tended to transform painting, and the supernatural visions of Blake were allied with romantic reveries. German music likewise developed. The inspiration of Haydn, who was producing his greatest works, the *Seasons* and the *Creation*, still recalled the smiling and confident optimism of the eighteenth century; but the tragic soul of Beethoven was already stirring in his first sonatas.

Romanticism did not affirm itself as a political doctrine, but since it relied upon feeling in this realm as well, its followers acted according to circumstances. The reaction triumphed, and having their careers ahead of them, they soon became ardent counter-revolutionaries. Moreover, dissatisfied with the present, they sought refuge in a visionary past. Discovering the Holy Roman Empire and the medieval papacy, Novalis, as early as 1799, sang the praises of Christian unity, which did honour to preceding centuries. Catholicism moved them by its liturgy and music; this same Novalis dedicated a hymn to the Virgin. He remained a Protestant, but ultimately, with more positions available in Austria, several of his friends went into Habsburg service and became converts.

Whatever the interest of these novelties, their influence over opinion must not be exaggerated. Most of those who detested the Revolution were not inspired by philosophical motives, and if they felt the need for such, they sought them in the churches. Everywhere else, more than in France, the last years of the eighteenth century witnessed a religious renaissance that conservative pragmatism and intuitionism favoured, but that sprang up spontaneously. Just as it had become reconciled with the throne, the aristocracy felt bound up with state religions, and all agreed that Lucifer had been the first Jacobin. Besides, great catastrophes and long wars always bring the disturbed or frightened throng back to the altar.

Catholicism had great need of this return, for it had been the principal sufferer. France and the countries she occupied were now merely 'mission lands'. A new disaster threatened in Germany, where the treaties of Basel and of Campo Formio heralded a general secularization; and the Protestants, even those who were counter-revolutionaries, enthusiastically looked forward to 'pushing the black army away from the Rhine'. Furthermore, enlightened despotism maintained its hold. Bavaria exacted a tax from the clergy, and in Spain, Saavedra and Urquijo, Godoy's successors since 1798, posed as *philosophes*. In 1799 they forbade appeals to the court of Rome, and needing funds, they considered seizing ecclesiastical property. Pius VI had recently died, a prisoner of the Directory, and Austria scarcely concealed her desire to share the temporal domain of the Holy See with the Kingdom of Naples.

The sufferings of the church were nonetheless salutory. In the face of attack from its enemies it gained new sympathy. England had given a warm welcome to deported French priests, and owed to them the beginnings of her Catholic renaissance. Let it be added that to appease the Irish, Burke continued to advocate that they be granted religious liberty, and Pitt thought likewise. In Germany a small, ardent group, the 'Holy Family', formed at Münster around Fürstenberg and Overberg, and the Princess Galitzin and the Marquise de Montagu (the sister of Madame de Lafayette) were among its leaders. In 1800 the conversion of Stolberg seemed to give great promise. Paul I also aroused great hopes. He authorized Catholic worship in Poland; Joseph de Maistre and Father Gruber persuaded him to demand the re-establishment of the Jesuits; he took under his protection the Order of Malta, which elected him grand master.

To Protestantism, which had not benefited greatly from the Revolution, the religious renaissance was decidedly advantageous. In Germany, Schleiermacher revitalized its mystic fervour through his *Speeches on Religion*, which appeared in 1799, while Wackenroder and the romantics returned to religion through esthetic intuition. In England, Wesley had died in 1791. By creating alongside the lay preachers a hierarchy recruited through co-optation, he had brought Methodism closer to the Established Church, and in 1797 a first schism resulted; but by exciting popular mysticism, the sect nonetheless continued its conquests. It exercised a profound influence on dissent. By adopting its methods the Baptists progressed, while the rationalist Socinian Presbyterianism of Priestley and Price rapidly disappeared. Within the Anglican Church there developed a nucleus of Evangelicals, the most notable being Wilberforce, who attempted (unsuccessfully) to revitalize it.

Reinvigorated, dissent abandoned its sympathies for the Revolution; and if the conservative influence it exerted over the popular masses has been exaggerated, it appears to have been nonetheless real. In Germany the Münster circle found its match at Emkendorf in Holstein, where Reventlow fostered Protestant piety. Stolberg frequented it before his conversion, likewise Portalis, future director of religion under Bonaparte. Reventlow further extended his zeal to the entire duchy, particularly by purging the University of Kiel. It is not astonishing that at the same time he stoutly defended the autonomy of the province against the Danish government, so that the omnipotence of the German aristocracy might be protected against even the slightest risk.

Among rulers and reactionaries of all types the national idea proudly flaunted by the revolutionaries aroused unreserved hostility or sharp dislike. To the former it represented popular sovereignty, in which they perceived danger to their composite states. For the others it was associated with equality: 'Nation—

a Jacobin term' (*das klingt jakobinisch*). In the Netherlands the nobility and the clergy preferred to return to the Austrian yoke rather than lose their privileges. Similar fears weakened national resistance in Poland. In Hungary the magnates remained faithful to the Habsburgs, and allowed themselves to be partly Germanized so long as the peasants were left to them. Sovereigns continued to follow their own whims. They completed the partition of Poland. The Hungarian Diet vainly demanded concessions from Vienna: the use of Magyar as the official language, customs advantages, and access to the sea by the annexation of Dalmatia and Fiume. Despite the recommendations of the regent, Archduke Joseph, Francis turned a deaf ear. After the insurrection in Ireland, Pitt determined to destroy what remained of the island's autonomy by suppressing the government and Parliament of Dublin; and the Union was realized in 1800.

The war gradually replaced cosmopolitanism with nationalism, however, and once again the revolutionaries set the example. By fighting them England likewise became affected by it. In alliance with the common people, the remnants of the Whig party, under Fox's banner, long pretended to regard the conflict as the affair of Pitt and the Tories. After Campo Formio, however, when England was isolated and revolt was spreading in Ireland, and particularly when the landing of a French army was anticipated, fear gripped public opinion and the war became nationalized. On the other hand, in Holland, the Cisalpine Republic, and Switzerland, France contributed to the awakening or progress of nationalism by uprooting the Old Regime and introducing the territorial unity of the state. Her intervention was most beneficial to Italy, where the unificationists, more numerous than is often believed, counted on her aid. Yielding to the necessities of war, she treated these countries as conquests, and used them to feed her soldiers. Thus she made them aware of the price of independence; and in the fatal reversal, which Robespierre had predicted, she turned them against herself; in 1799 the Italians welcomed the Austrians and Russians as liberators.

But the contagion was only beginning, and Germany had not been touched. If the magnificent flowering of arts and letters, the return to the past, stimulated by romanticism, and the attachment to the Holy Roman Empire, preserved by historical memories, exalted national feeling among the literati, it had not yet taken a political form. It contrasted Germany, the 'culture nation' (*Kulturnation*), with peoples gathered in states and their barbaric struggles. The proof of its superiority and its divine mission were drawn from its very weakness. Haughty submission to this intellectual imperialism would not survive invasion.

CHAPTER SIXTEEN

The Results of the War: International Politics

THE ALLIED POWERS still dreamed of crushing the Revolution. On one hand, however, they conducted the war in the traditional manner, and the military achievement of the Committee of Public Safety disconcerted them. On the other, they never lost sight of 'aggrandizement' any more than they did of their long-standing rivalries. Hence, failing to concert their efforts, they became divided and finally parted company. England won on the seas and in the colonies, but only a land war could subdue France, which was expanding on the Continent. True, Italy had just been snatched from her, but the Second Coalition was already disintegrating. Just as within France the outcome of the Revolution was still somewhat uncertain, so the new balance of power remained to be determined.

THE ANGLO-FRENCH WAR

As has been pointed out, Great Britain conducted her part of the war according to precedent. She was primarily concerned with augmenting her navy, and gradually she increased the number of frigates for hunting down privateers, escorting merchant vessels, and keeping watch on enemy ports. Not until the end of the decade had any perceptible increase in army effectives been achieved. To conciliate public opinion Pitt refrained from introducing conscription, and even his tax increases were moderate. The special budget was financed through loans, and the Bank of England aided with the floating debt. As usual, the greatest effort was directed towards sweeping the enemy from the seas, conquering her colonies, and blockading her coasts. Except at the outset, and again in Holland in 1799, England left the Continental war to her subsidized allies. Grenville did not hesitate to justify this traditional policy by claiming that it was better to pay the Coalition than to send reinforcements that would deprive industry of workers. Moreover, the money would not be lost, for it paid for necessary supplies for the mercenary forces.

Important results proved Grenville to be correct. The colonial empires of the French, the Dutch, and even the Spanish were invaded. Since 1798, Jervis, earl of St. Vincent, had been organizing permanent squadrons in the vicinity of enemy ports, supported by a supply service and relief vessels, with orders to rally at the entrance to the Channel if enemy ships broke through the blockade. In the same year the British returned to the Mediterranean, seized Minorca, landed in Sicily, and joined with Portuguese and Neapolitan vessels. In 1799 the Dutch fleet was captured, and Nelson destroyed that of Brueys at Abukir, blockaded the Army of Egypt, and besieged Malta. Unless Paul I were to offer opposition, the Mediterranean would become a British sea.

Lines of communication were relatively assured by trade in escorted convoys. Great Britain had lost only 500 ships a year (3 per cent of her total), and this was hardly more than ordinary hazards at sea. From 1793 to 1800, insurance, which had risen to 50 per cent during the American Revolution, did not exceed 25 per cent, and in 1802, after the Peace of Amiens, it was to fall to 12 per cent. Seven hundred and forty-three privateers were captured, and by 1798, 22,000 sailors were held prisoner. Finally, the blockade made neutral ships dependent on the British government, which thereby acquired the long-sought monopoly of colonial goods, and increased its exports considerably.

Nevertheless the end seemed far distant. The French were still allied with Spain, and they held Holland. They continued to control the sea; in 1799 Bruix left Brest, reached Toulon, and returned safely. They had by no means lost all their colonies, and their friends had lost even fewer. Although their merchant marine declined, their coastal trade continued. Despite serious economic damage, they could live (and even prosper) if they retained their conquests and re-established Continental peace. Moreover, such a peace would enable them to devote their entire resources to the maritime war. Far from considering capitulation, they still held hope of one day landing an army in Great Britain or Ireland. Despising the economy of 'perfidious Albion', they counted on breaking it by keeping its trade out of France. English merchandise was banned in French territory, and following the decree adopted by the Directory on 29 Nivôse, Year VI (January 18, 1798), the break with the neutrals put an end to smuggling.

This 'Continental blockade' revealed a fighting spirit. What is more, the industrial bourgeoisie, decidedly protectionist and still vexed with the treaty of 1786, rejoiced at being able to eliminate British competition. Above all, the cotton manufacturers adhered tenaciously to the prohibition of textiles, and if they could not ban fine threads at the moment, at least they could keep out all others. Fontenay, the great merchant of Rouen, was their advocate, and after 18 Brumaire they were to guide Bonaparte. This policy was double-edged. It deprived France of raw materials and of consumer goods from the colonies. In addition, it led to recognition of the necessity for making the policy Europe-wide; if it were limited to the Republic alone it could not be really effective. It was imposed on occupied territories, and Spain supported it in principle; but it was pointed out that seizure of the Hanse cities would enable France to keep the enemy out of German markets.

England could triumph only if her allies were victorious on land. France could succeed only by securing the support of Europe, whether by conciliation or by subjugation. In this respect the war threatened to continue indefinitely. The end of the 'Second Hundred Years' War' depended on Continental policy.

THE WAR ON THE CONTINENT

On the Continent (as in England) the enemies of the Revolution continued to fight in their customary manner. They had plenty of men. From 1792 to 1799 it is estimated that they lost 140,000 dead, 200,000 wounded, and 150,000 taken prisoner; nevertheless they were not yet exhausted. What they really lacked was money. In Austria, despite increased taxation, the deficit mounted. Recourse was had to loans, sometimes 'forced loans', and England, in addition to her subsidies, had to authorize or even guarantee issues in London. In spite of everything, paper money alone provided the necessary staying power. This took the form of bank notes, forced acceptance of which was required to support the campaign of 1800. The florin began to decline on the exchanges, and in 1801 it was discounted at 16 per cent in Augsburg.

The ruble proved even weaker, and at Leipzig it was accepted at only 60 per cent of its face value. Under Paul I the debt, contracted chiefly in Holland, rose from 43 million to 132 million florins, and annually 14 million in paper rubles were added to it. Sweden also printed notes, which declined by more than one-quarter in 1798. Without Pitt's subsidies the Allies could continue the war only with difficulty. But would a coalition still exist?

Paul I had just recalled Suvorov's army, and it could not be counted on to return to the war. Rostopchin, opposed to intervention in France, had triumphed over Panin and was now chancellor. The break with Austria threatened to embroil Russia with England. Since the Straits were open to him, the tsar now enjoyed in Turkey and the Mediterranean an influence that his successors were never to regain. He established the Ionian Islands as a republic under his protection, participated in the occupation of Naples, supported the king of Sardinia against Thugut, and cast covetous eyes on Corsica. Paul even hoped to install himself in Malta as grand master of the order, for on November 3, 1799, Grenville promised that England, having conquered the island, did not intend to remain there. Was it not possible, however, that this situation might change, now that Paul had stopped fighting the Revolution? Consequences of great significance might result. It would be enough for Russia to revive the neutral league and close the Baltic to strike a dreadful blow at the exports and provisioning of Great Britain.

In any case, for the moment Austria alone remained arrayed

against France. Officially the Diet supported her, but after the Peace of Basel, the Holy Roman Empire was little more than a shadow. Prussia continued to guarantee the neutrality of North Germany, including Hanover. Behind the line of demarcation, the 'magic circle' as the Austrian Hudelist called it, this region enjoyed perfect peace and great commercial profit. The prestige of Prussia grew, and Frederick William became a 'polestar', an 'anti-emperor'. He counted on being able to place himself at the head of a North German confederation. Of course he did not lose sight of increasing his own territories; and he waited impatiently for the secularizations, coveted Hanover, and manoeuvred to annex Nuremberg.

Driven from the north, Austria found herself ignored in the south by the abandonment of the left bank of the Rhine, and disregarded in the claims she still maintained over Bavaria. Maximilian Joseph, who succeeded Charles Theodore in 1799, was for a short time afraid of losing his throne. As for Württemberg, its Diet was in chronic conflict with Duke Frederick II, and sent agents to Paris. Under these circumstances the princes of South Germany followed Austria only because they were afraid. They simply awaited a chance to come to terms with France.

A union of Germans against the Republic thus proved to be an impossibility, and even the disintegration of the Empire seemed probable. Chancellor Thugut did not give it much concern, and showed even less regret for the loss of the Netherlands. He found compensations in Poland, and had absorbed the Venetian states; and with the French driven out of Italy, he hoped to succeed them in dominating that area. In such case he calculated (and not without reason) that his master would have little cause for complaint.

The Republic must wage a new campaign against Austria. Partly because he had been so successful on their behalf, the men of Brumaire yielded power to Bonaparte. Victory won, France found herself at the crossroads. If she renounced the so-called natural frontier of the Rhine, Continental peace would present no problems. If, on the contrary, she refused to do so, peace would be unattainable until that frontier had been crossed. By thus reverting to the policy of the Old Regime she would be granting similar advantage to the other powers. In this case

England, isolated and war-weary, might also resign herself to a compromise. France would keep her conquests and her colonies; England would retain mastery of the seas, and would have the option of conquering India. The other end result would be to cross the natural frontier and to condemn herself to subjugating Europe, in the hope that the 'Continental blockade' would force Britain to capitulate.

French public opinion undoubtedly supported the first of these choices. Even though the majority of Republicans disliked renouncing the natural-frontier idea, which they deemed inseparable from the cause of the Revolution, they knew full well that national interest required them to do so. But by this time the decision was out of their hands. It rested with Bonaparte alone.

CHAPTER SEVENTEEN

The Results of the War: The Rise of Capitalism in Great Britain; European Expansion in the World

AS ALWAYS, the war altered the course of international trade. It also interfered with the rise of capitalism on the Continent. Nevertheless England derived appreciable profit from the conflict, and extended her empire. European expansion, however, was hindered. The shock to the colonial system increased as Latin America moved towards emancipation, and France even abolished slavery.

INTERNATIONAL TRADE

Deprived of the markets that France controlled, but rid of French competition, Great Britain compensated herself at the expense of her allies and the neutrals. Through the Hanseatic ports she rushed into the conquest of Germany. In 1800 she cleared 500 vessels for Hamburg, as contrasted with 49 in 1789. At the fairs of Frankfurt and Leipzig she came into contact with the Swiss, the Austrians, the Poles, and the Russians. Her cotton goods, and particularly her threads, drove out Swiss and Saxon products. Her trade with Germany rose from £2 million in 1789 to £13·5 million in 1801. Since Amsterdam had fallen into the hands of the republicans, finance turned towards London. The elector of Hesse invested his funds there, and it was in helping him that Meyer Amschel Rothschild of Frankfurt developed his business; in 1798 his son Nathan settled in England, and soon became rich.

The Baltic became increasingly important in British commerce. At the beginning of the nineteenth century 72 per cent of British imports came from Prussia and Russia—three-fourths of the grain from the port of Danzig alone. The vessels of the Hanseatic towns and the Scandinavian lands entered her service, and with or without licences, continued to touch at French ports so long as the Directory did not break with the neutrals. On the other hand, Holland was declining rapidly, and Amsterdam yielded its pre-eminence to Hamburg; the reserves of its bank, which had risen to 13 million florins in 1793, fell to 1·5 million in 1799.

In the Atlantic the preponderance of the British navy became more pronounced each year. Joining with the navies of the neutrals, it took over the triangular trade of Europe, the African coasts (from which Negro slaves were drawn), and tropical America. Still, the expansion of the United States to some extent counterbalanced this ascendancy; her vessels also developed a triangular route between her own ports, the West Indies or Latin America, and Europe. Having secured the Jay Treaty, the British accommodated themselves to this, especially since the attitude of the Directory led John Adams to break with the French. In the South Atlantic the alliance of Spain with France enabled the English to reduce relations with her colonies to almost nothing, and the Cape route saw hardly anything but British convoys. In Asian waters they no longer encountered anyone but a few Americans. The French East India Company disappeared in 1791, the Dutch Company in 1798. In the Mediterranean, France's position was better. Genoa, Leghorn, the Barbary States, and the Greeks came to her aid. Conquering Italy, she hindered her enemy without eliminating her; but she lost it in 1799, and as early as 1798 was driven from the Levant.

The naval war increased the importance of the Continental link between the Mediterranean and the northern seas. Heretofore largely assured across France, Italy, Switzerland, and Holland, it was compromised by the closing of the Rhenish route. Since 1790 France interrupted traffic along the left bank by extending her customs offices to the river, and the occupation of the Rhineland and Holland affected this route still further. In 1798 the Directory applied its tariff to the crossing of the Rhine. With the closing of the mouth of the river the trade of Cologne had already declined, and by 1800 it was reduced to less than a third. Only a part of the traffic slipped through Emden to Frankfurt to supply contraband or reach Switzerland. Moreover, the latter was separated from Genoa. The route across Europe thus retreated to the East, as in the time of Louis XIV, and henceforth it passed through Hamburg and Leipzig to Venice and preferably Trieste.

PRODUCTION

In 1800, English commerce exceeded £30 million in imports and £38 million in exports.[1] This was 53 per cent more than in 1792, and the balance of payments was almost double. The tonnage of outgoing ships had increased by a third, and rose to almost two million tons. It was during the war that the docks of London were built and endowed with the bonded-warehouse system. The expansion of markets partly explains this progress, especially as shipments to France and her satellites did not diminish greatly, thanks to the neutrals and contraband. This was to hasten the advance of England in the direction of rationalized or mechanized production and of capitalist concentration.

The price rise also remained a favourable factor. The war accentuated it everywhere, and contributed to it indirectly by the increase in the issue of paper money in almost every country. France was not alone in suffering from it. In Spain the Bank of St. Charles staved off bankruptcy only with great difficulty in 1799. In England, on the contrary, it seemed that the monetary crisis and the extension of banking organization would benefit business. Foreign capital flowed in. In 1794 the Bank of England bought £3·75 million of precious metals. After the occupation of Holland it became the safest refuge,

[1] These are 'official' figures. The research of A. H. Imlah has shown that the true figures are £66·5 million in imports, £52·3 million in exports, with a deficit of £14 million.

and the favourable balance of foreign trade had the same result. Coining of gold could be resumed: £2 million in 1797, almost £3 million in 1798.

After the crisis of 1793 the county banks again increased. In 1800 their number is said to have risen to 386; they continued to issue notes without controls, and probably added some credit inflation to the paper inflation. The Bank of England gradually extended its operations; it dealt with 1,340 clients in 1800. The suspension of convertibility of bank notes in 1797 might have struck the economy a terrible blow, but as has been seen, it did not precipitate a panic. Inflation remained sufficiently moderate that it did not ruin the currency, and it spared the English the deflation that the Directory suffered. Moreover, a fall in the pound favoured exports, since the leading businessmen took in specie, but paid their workers in notes. In its empiricism the financial policy of Great Britain attested a mastery of which no other country was then capable.

Prices increased almost continuously; taking those of 1790 as a base of 100, they rose to 109 in 1793, and reached 156 in 1799. A quarter of wheat, which was worth an average of 45 shillings from 1780 to 1789, jumped to 55 during the following decade. According to Lord Beveridge, however, the index of industrial activity, which had been in the midst of an upsurge until the war (112 in 1792 in relation to a base of 100 in 1785), appears to have dipped thereafter to 85 in 1797, eventually to recover to 107 only in 1802. It must be recognized that the expansion of exports resulted in large part from the resale of colonial products. The war assured Great Britain a virtual monopoly of these, to such an extent that the planters lamented the fall in sugar prices, although home consumption was increasing uninterruptedly. Nevertheless the needs of the army and navy sustained the demand. The disappearance of German steel was also an advantage to the metal industry (which expanded the use of coal in smelting), and mining developed. In 1800, England exported, in addition, two million tons of coal and one-and-one-half million tons of wrought and cast iron. The cotton industry prospered more than any other. Its exports rose from £1·5 million to £6 million in 1800. Even in 1797, England imported £734,000 worth of cotton; and three years later it had risen to £1,663,000 worth.

In any case, there is no doubt that the Industrial Revolution was continuing to advance. Yet it must be emphasized that it was not progressing as quickly as is sometimes believed. Cotton spinning held the lead, but weaving was still done by hand. Cartwright's loom was first adopted only in 1801, at Glasgow, and its use became widespread only after Radcliffe invented the dressing machine about 1804. The woollen industry remained in an experimental state. Even the spinning jenny was used very little, and Cartwright's frame for the spinning of cardings was perfected only in 1803. Coal mining remained backward, despite the growing use of the rail and the introduction of the steam engine. This last did not penetrate industry except in some cotton mills, the others being content with water frames.

As for communications, the canals remained the centre of attention, and there were few good roads. Owing to the slowness of transport and the increasingly low wages, the traditional industries defended themselves energetically, and capital continued to be concentrated in trade rather than in the creation of factories. Of the captains of industry of the time, Robert Owen's father-in-law, David Dale, and Radcliffe of Stockport began by 'putting out'. Even though the spinning mule was not adopted everywhere, it gave cotton spinning an irresistible superiority. Hosiery and lace made by looms prospered. Metallurgy became largely modernized, and engineers, the most famous being Bramah, inventor of the hydraulic press, increased the number of machine tools.

The rise in prices also benefited agriculture. England no longer produced enough grain to feed herself, and the war made purchases costly. Wheat had become so expensive that the Corn Laws no longer operated; and it was so much more profitable than stock raising that more was planted. Hence enclosure was further extended; so this was a golden age for landlords as well as for farmers. Techniques continued to improve, and in 1793, John Sinclair and Arthur Young were placed at the head of a Board of Agriculture. The agrarian revolution spread in Scotland. There the heads of the clans (recognized as landlords), in order to devote themselves to stock raising, evicted their tenants, who were reduced to emigration. This agricultural prosperity reinforced the might of the country, because it rendered it less vulnerable in its food supply. It also aided the small landowners to maintain themselves, and even to increase in numbers in some counties. Actually very few remained; at least they felt satisfied with their lot, and, with the farmers, they constituted an element of stability.

Despite its advances, English capitalism still did not think in terms of free trade. Far from renouncing the Corn Laws, landowners and farmers demanded that they be reinforced. Industrialists remained faithful to mercantilism to the extent of forbidding the exportation of machinery. At home, however, they increasingly evaded regulations that limited the number of apprentices and authorized the setting of a minimum wage. The workers, on the contrary, continued to invoke the Statutes of Labourers, and backed up their demands through the use of blacklists and strikes. These were forbidden in principle, but justices of the peace hesitated to condemn them when employers themselves set the example of violating the law. Also, it is worth remembering the Combination Act of July 12, 1799, which renewed penalties against strikers and workers' associations, at the same time that the authorities allowed the regulations favourable to the wage earners to fall into disuse. Depressed by the influx of foundlings, women, and uprooted farmers, wages lagged far behind the rise in the price of goods. They were further reduced by the truck system, or payment in kind, and by arbitrary fines; but since 1795 they had been complemented, at the expense of the poor tax, by assistance based on the price of bread. This was the reason for the relative resignation of the common people.

The economic supremacy of Great Britain asserted itself all the more as the war retarded the development of industry elsewhere on the Continent even more than in France. To meet competition Switzerland and Saxony considered modifying their cotton machinery. The knitting machine appeared at Chemnitz in 1797, and the water frame in 1798; and the concentration of spinning there became obvious. In general, capitalism remained in its commercial form. Moreover, traditional products suffered from unfavourable circumstances; in Silesia the cloth industry was ruined. In agriculture, Denmark alone seriously imitated England, which could not but congratulate itself, since it imported grain.

England took a similar view of the progress of the United

States, particularly in sea-island cotton, brought from the Bahamas in 1786, offered in Glasgow for the first time in 1792, and immediately appreciated by the spinners. When the difficulties of ginning had been resolved by Whitney's machine in 1793, exports soon attained a level of 8 million pounds and rose to almost 20 million in 1800, worth about $5 million. It was an event of great significance for the United States, because from that time on, slavery became a fundamental institution for the South, and the planters began to covet Florida and Louisiana. For the moment, however, the North saw in it only an occasion for using its capital and ships. English machines were just beginning to be introduced there. In 1790, Slater established the first spinning mill using Arkwright's system. The country remained primarily agricultural, and British industry doubled its shipments to it. The great fortunes of the Astors and the Girards were built on commerce and speculation in land.

At the moment of the advent of Bonaparte, however, the situation in England was critical. The war was raging on the Continent, and scarcity made the purchase of grain necessary at a cost of almost £3.5 million. The reserves of the Bank of England declined, and the exchange rate fell: the pound sterling lost 8 per cent of its value at Hamburg, and 5 per cent at Cadiz. At home the small bank notes of one or two pounds became widespread. By year's end they represented a tenth of the issue. Specie became scarce and was at a premium. The illicit practice of double prices became commonplace. Pitt realized that he would have to increase taxes. The evil had worsened, because London suffered the repercussions of the catastrophe that struck Hamburg.

The conditions of international commerce were not entirely healthy, because of the war. London, Hamburg, and Amsterdam speculated in colonial goods by conceding each other credits, and by immobilizing their capital in order to constitute stocks. During the winter of 1799 the rise was staggering at Hamburg, because the Elbe was frozen and navigation was suspended. When the ice broke up before the spring fairs, ships poured in, and a tremendous decline ensued; the price of sugar fell 72 per cent just as the war resumed, and in August, on the eve of the Anglo-Russian invasion, the bankers of Amsterdam cut off their advances. One hundred and thirty-six houses of

Hamburg failed, and the Parish family lost more than a million marks. Every financial centre in Europe was affected, but especially London. The cotton industry dismissed workers or reduced wages, while the price of bread soared. A quarter of wheat, which had been 49 shillings at the beginning of 1799, reached 101 shillings in February, 1800. This crisis was soon to weaken the morale of the nation. It strengthened the French in their conviction that the British economy was artificial and fragile.

EUROPEAN EXPANSION

As mistress of the seas, England alone was capable of imposing the authority of the white man throughout the world; but she did not seem greatly inclined to do so. Mercantile opinion did not adopt Bentham's hostility towards colonies, but the emancipation of the United States did not encourage her to multiply them. True, Canada had remained undisturbed since the Act of 1791, which (except for Nova Scotia, New Brunswick, and Prince Edward Island) had organized two provinces, one French, the other English, each provided with an elected assembly, but without parliamentary government. The Catholic clergy, moreover, had displayed no sympathy for revolutionary France. Yet this country did not interest British merchants. They were concerned only with the sugar islands, and thinking of profit alone, valued the expansion of trade most of all. Their imperialism therefore assumed a commercial character.

Yet the empire grew. The French West Indies were ripe for the taking, as were Curaçao and Trinidad. Enormous amounts of capital were invested in Dutch Guiana, which was occupied from 1796 to 1800, and production there multiplied tenfold. The navy needed ports of call, like the Cape of Good Hope, which it seized in 1795. The colonial leaders, sons of the aristocracy, satisfied their taste for action by pressing for conquest on their own. In Africa the colony of Sierra Leone had been founded in 1792. Mungo Park explored the Niger as far as Timbuktu. In Australia, Phillip landed the first convoy of convicts at Sydney in 1788.

The English expanded particularly in India. Cornwallis was not enterprising, but he had to support the Nizam against Tippoo, who reopened the campaign at the end of 1789. In 1791 the governor finally took charge of these operations, and the next year imposed on his adversary the cession of a third of his domain and the payment of an indemnity of £3 million. Then the European war permitted the occupation of the remaining French territory. It encumbered the East India Company with debts. With a revenue that rose to £8 million in 1797, it sustained itself only through loans; and its debt, which had mounted to £10 million, was doubled by 1805. Cornwallis applied himself chiefly to making reforms. He provided Bengal with courts composed of English judges and Hindu assistants. In 1793 the 'permanent settlement' of Bengal still remained the most familiar feature of its government, and constituted a good example of colonial exploitation. It was assured at the expense of the native population by the collusion of the conquerors with its own dominant class. The zamindars, who traditionally farmed out the collection of dues from their estates and taxes, were recognized as the landowners, so that the peasants were reduced to holding their lands on lease.

Cornwallis left India in 1793, and his successor remained at peace; but the situation darkened. Tippoo maintained relations with the Île de France, and the presence of Bonaparte in Egypt provided cause for concern. India and the Mahrattas became restless, and the Nizam could not be trusted. But in 1798, Richard Colley, earl of Mornington (later Marquis Wellesley), arrived. He imposed his alliance on the Nizam, and occupied Hyderabad. Then in 1799, he attacked the ruler of Mysore, who perished in his capital, Seringapatam, which was captured on May 4. Colley partitioned his conquest between the East India Company and the Nizam. Afterwards he attacked the Mahrattas. He also watched Punjab, where Ranjit Singh had been ceded Lahore by the Afghans in 1794. In Persia, in 1801, Malcolm was to obtain a treaty that opened the coast of the Persian Gulf to English commerce. Perim in the Red Sea was occupied in 1798. To the east, Malacca and the Muluccas likewise succumbed.

Without the European war the Far East would probably have been beset. In Indochina, Nguyen-Anh slowly reconquered Annam and Tonkin, but French influence had fallen to nothing. In Peking the Englishman Macartney, who had been sent there in 1793, secured no concessions; but after the death of Ch'ien

Lung, his son Chia Ch'ing (1796–1820), a cruel drunkard, threatened by revolts of secret societies, was not of a stature to resist any serious attack. Weaker yet, Japan nervously watched the English, and particularly the Russian ships that landed at Sakhalin, the Kuriles, and even Yezo in 1792.

Missionaries continued to occupy themselves primarily with America. In China, Ch'ien Lung had persecuted the Lazarists, the successors to the Jesuits; and their mission, recruitment for which had been halted by the Revolution, disappeared in 1800. A novelty was the entry into the lists of the Protestants, who, except for Anglo-Saxon America, had until now been represented overseas only by a few Moravian Brethren. In this domain, too, England reversed the situation. In 1792 the Baptists took the initiative; in 1795 the Anglicans founded the London Missionary Society; and in 1799, Marshman landed in Bengal, where the East India Company, which was little concerned with proselytism that might anger the natives, gave him a bad welcome.

White colonization remained almost nil. The population of North America increased by births and spread into the interior, warring against the Indians. Kentucky and Tennessee were admitted to the United States in 1791 and 1796 respectively, and Ohio was incorporated in 1803. But in 1800 the West still numbered only 370,000 inhabitants out of more than 5 million. Between the Atlantic and the Pacific, where Vancouver explored the coast from 1790 to 1795, and the Russians had just appeared, there was no link other than the posts of the Hudson's Bay Company, which had reached the Columbia River. To the north, Mackenzie explored the Arctic wilderness in 1793.

THE SHOCK TO COLONIAL EMPIRES

Europe's colonial domain, which had grown insignificantly, was about to undergo a new dismemberment, this time at the expense of the Latin powers. As has been seen, the convocation of the Estates General encouraged the hopes for self-rule among the Creoles in the French empire. The course taken by the Revolution then added to the planters' desire to escape the *exclusif*, the intention to maintain the men of colour in their inferior condition and to prevent any attempt to free the slaves. The planters eventually made common cause with England; and later the Île de France, refusing to recognize the Constitution of the Year III, expelled the representative of the Directory.

For the time being, Spain's American possessions remained within her grasp, but a storm was brewing. The influence of the French Revolution, reinforcing the philosophy of the Enlightenment and the emancipation of the United States, could only increase the spirit of independence among certain Creoles, and encourage the planters to shake off the yoke of the homeland to secure freedom of trade. Belgrano, initiated in the new ideas in 1789 during his stay in Spain, made himself their apostle at Buenos Aires, where he became secretary of the 'Consulate' (the chamber of commerce) in 1795. The alliance of Charles IV with the Directory stimulated the ferment still more. The British blockade reduced the exports from the ports of Spanish America to almost nothing. Those of Buenos Aires fell from 5·47 million piastres in 1796 to 335,000 in 1797. Neutral and Allied vessels received permission to enter, but the remedy was of little help, and it was discontinued in 1800. This crisis, which was to be prolonged, was one of the principal causes of the movement for independence.

Some adventurous persons had begun to conspire early. In Venezuela, in 1796, a plot brought about executions and the departure first of Rodríguez and then of Bolívar. Three plots were discovered in Mexico between 1794 and 1799. Others, who were more prudent, hoped to profit from England's century-old designs on Spanish America, and from the commercial interests of the United States, as well as from the conflict of the European powers. Had not Brissot, as early as 1792, thought of charging Miranda, who was then serving in the army commanded by Dumouriez, with bringing about revolt in his country? After the Peace of Basel, and particularly when Spain had passed into the republican camp, the Venezuelan turned towards England, with which he had never lost contact. In 1795, with the collaboration of Olavide, he formed a junta for South America in Madrid. At Cadiz another group formed, to which the Chilean O'Higgins belonged in 1799.

When the Directory expelled Miranda after 18 Fructidor, the latter went as the 'general agent' for the colonies to ask aid from Pitt. The English had occupied Curaçao and Trinidad, and these islands, already centres of contraband, would be excellent support points for the revolutionary expeditions. London became the headquarters for the refugee Creoles, and Nariño finally made his way there. They supposedly founded an association, the 'Lautaro Lodge', to prepare the liberation. Pitt received Miranda only after Abukir, and directed him towards the United States, which, having just broken with France, would probably play his game. This country likewise declined to aid him. The affair was still in doubt on 18 Brumaire.

At the outset of the Revolution the Europeans, both white and Creole, had no expectation that the native populations would one day also aspire to independence. The new ideas inspired only a few rare defenders of the Indians in Latin America, and it was in France that the rights of men of colour first found defenders. The 'friends of the Negro' deplored slavery, but as in England, they attacked only the slave trade. The Constituent Assembly suspended the payment of the premiums that had favoured it under the Old Regime, and which were abolished by the Legislative Assembly after August 10, 1792. The revolt of the Negroes in Santo Domingo in 1791 had not widened the debate, for the only thought was to put it down. This attempt was unsuccessful, and the situation changed when the English, in collaboration with the planters, undertook the conquest of the island. Sonthonax offered liberty to the rebels who would take the side of France.

Then the Convention abolished slavery on 16 Pluviôse, Year II (February 4, 1794), not only to conform at last to the Declaration of the Rights of Man, but also in the obvious hope of rallying the Negroes to the cause of the Republic, and of stirring the revolt of slaves in British colonies. As a result the English finally abandoned Santo Domingo, where Toussaint L'Ouverture, having become master of the colony, recognized only the nominal authority of France. Neither Sonthonax nor Hugues on Guadeloupe, nor Toussaint L'Ouverture himself completely freed the slaves, for they subjected them to forced labour. In the Mascarene Islands the decree of the Convention remained a dead letter. Nevertheless the Revolution had resulted not only in extending equal rights to men of colour and to Negroes, but also in inciting for the first time the creation of a native state outside the control of Europeans.

Conclusion

BONAPARTE would soon announce that the Revolution had ended, that its destructive work was over. But the new order, as the bourgeoisie had conceived it in 1789, was far from perfect. Moreover, the democratic experiment of the Year II required serious modification. This is one of the reasons why the Napoleonic period became the complement of the revolutionary decade. In agreement with the master, the 'notables' reorganized the administration and re-established the social hierarchy as they saw fit; but they were unable to get control of the government. In 1814 the Charter led them to believe that they would achieve their goal, but they encountered a contest with the aristocracy. In this sense the Restoration was the epilogue to the drama. The Revolution of 1789 was not really completed until 1830, when, having brought to the throne a prince who accepted its principles, the 'notables' gained control of France. Previously Napoleon had led the Grand Army to the conquest of Europe. Although nothing remained of the Continental empire that he dreamed of founding, yet he had annihilated the Old Regime wherever he found time to do so. Here again his reign prolonged the Revolution, and he was its soldier, as his enemies never tired of declaring.

The prestige of the principles of 1789 did not disappear with Napoleon. Social evolution, the awakening of nationalism, and the lure of ideology were not its only supports. A romantic emotion of great force attached itself, outside as well as inside France, to the memory of popular insurrections and the wars of liberty, enhanced by the Napoleonic legend. Nevertheless, if the bourgeoisie gradually progressed throughout the world, it was not because of the French Revolution alone. It had been preceded by the English revolutions, which were no less reassuring in the conservative compromises they provided. Moreover, capitalism, gradually extending its sway, imposed, to a degree that coincided with the interests of its representatives, a regime considered as the pattern most favourable to production.

An episode in the general rise of the bourgeoisie, the French Revolution still remains, among all others, the most striking. This was not because of its tragic events alone; it also contained for future generations the germs of conflict, as the events of 1793 had presaged. Opposing equality of rights to the nobility, and simultaneously, through economic freedom, opening the way for capitalism, the French bourgeoisie themselves had begun a movement of ideas and a social transformation, the denial of which ultimately characterized a new epoch in the dialectical progress of history. In addition to the bourgeois interpretation of equality of rights, the Revolution had witnessed the birth of two other versions—social democracy and communism. At the time of 18 Brumaire it was thought that these were gone for all time; yet they reappeared during the course of the nineteenth century. They have continued to serve as arguments for those who detest the Revolution, as well as for those who admire it. For both it is the Revolution of Equality, and for this reason, even though the passing of time may push it further back into the past, its name is still a watchword for mankind.

BIBLIOGRAPHY

Note

THE FOLLOWING BIBLIOGRAPHY was prepared by Georges Lefebvre for the 1951 edition of *La Révolution française*, and subsequently was brought up to date by him for the 1957 reprinting of the work. The first part of the bibliography has already appeared in Elizabeth Moss Evanson's translation of the first three 'Books'. A few recent items have been added, and several corrections have been made. Readers should note that a new edition of Lefebvre's *Les paysans du Nord pendant la Révolution française* appeared in one volume, minus the notes and tables, in 1959.

The twenty-five titles listed below constitute a representative selection of recent useful works on the French Revolution, most of them published since 1957, and some of them omitted from Lefebvre's bibliography.

BIRO, S. S. *The German Policy of Revolutionary France: A Study in French Diplomacy During the War of the First Coalition, 1792–1797*. 2 vols. Cambridge, Mass., 1957.

DURAND, ABBÉ ALBERT. *Une paroisse mayennaise: Fougerolles sous la Révolution, 1789–1800*. Laval, 1960.

ELLIOTT, JOHN. *The Way of the Tumbrils*. New York, 1958.

FAYET, JOSEPH. *La Révolution française et la science, 1789–1795*. Paris, 1959.

FESTY, OCTAVE. *Les mouvements de la population française du début de la Révolution au Consulat*. Paris, 1954.

GERSHOY, LEO. *Bertrand Barère: A Reluctant Terrorist*. Princeton, N.J., 1961.

GODECHOT, JACQUES. *La Contre-révolution: Doctrine et action, 1789–1804*. Paris, 1961.

—— *La grande nation: L'expansion révolutionnaire de la France dans le monde, 1789–1799*. 2 vols. Paris, 1956.

GOOCH, R. K. *Parliamentary Government in France: Revolutionary Origins, 1789–1791*. Ithaca, N.Y., 1960.

HAMPSON, NORMAN. *A Social History of the French Revolution*. London, 1963. Studies in Social History, ed. by Harold Perkin.

HERIOT, A. *The French in Italy, 1796–1799*. London, 1957.

JACOB, LOUIS. *Hébert, le Père Duchesne, chef des sans-culottes*. Paris, 1960.

LAUERMA, MATTI. *L'artillerie de campagne française pendant les guerres de la Révolution: Evolution de l'organisation et de la tactique*. Helsinki, 1956.

PALMER, R. R. *The Age of the Democratic Revolution: A Political History of Europe and America, 1760–1800*. Vol. I, *The Challenge*. Princeton, N.J., 1959.

POLAND, B. C. *French Protestantism and the French Revolution: A Study in Church and State, Thought and Religion, 1685–1815.* Princeton, N.J., 1957.

REINHARD, MARCEL. *La France du Directoire.* 2 vols. Paris, 1956.

RÉMOND, A. *Les prix des transports marchands de la Révolution au Ier Empire.* Paris, 1956.

RUDÉ, GEORGE. *The Crowd in the French Revolution.* Oxford, 1959.

SEARS, L. M. *George Washington and the French Revolution.* Detroit, 1960.

SHEPARD, W. F. *Price Control and the Reign of Terror in France, 1793–1795.* Berkeley, Calif., 1953.

SOBOUL, ALBERT. *Précis d'histoire de la Révolution française.* Paris, 1962; a revision and extension of his smaller work, *La Révolution française*, Paris, 1948.

—— *Les soldats de l'an II.* Paris, 1959.

SYDENHAM, M. J. *The Girondins.* London, 1961.

THOMPSON, ERIC. *Popular Sovereignty and the French Constituent Assembly, 1789–1791.* Manchester, 1952.

TØNNESON, KARE. *La défaite des sans-culottes. . . .* Paris, 1959.

WEINER, MARGERY. *The French Exiles, 1789–1815.* London, 1960.

Bibliography

SEE THE GENERAL REFERENCES at the beginning of the Bibliography in the translation of the first three 'Books' of this work by Elizabeth Moss Evanson, henceforth cited as Evanson.

PART ONE. THE COALITION AND THE REVOLUTION TO THE TREATIES OF 1795

Chapter 1. The European Coalition (1793–1795)

General works: H. von Sybel, *Geschichte der Revolutionszeit*, 5 vols. (Düsseldorf, 1853–79), English trans. W. C. Perry, *History of the French Revolution*, 4 vols. (London, 1867–69); A. Sorel, *L'Europe et la Révolution française*, 8 vols. (Paris, 1885, 12th ed., 1908), Vols. III, IV; A. W. Ward and G. P. Gooch, eds. *The Cambridge History of British Foreign Policy*, 3 vols. (Cambridge, 1922), Vol. I; R. W. Seton-Watson, *Britain in Europe, 1789–1914* (Cambridge, 1927); K. von Heigel, *Deutsche Geschichte vom Tode Friedrichs des Grossen bis zur Auflösung des alten Reiches*, 2 vols. (Stuttgart, 1899–1911), Vols. X and XI in 'Bibliothek deutscher Geschichte', pub. under direction of H. von Zwiedineck-Südenhorst; J. H. Rose, *William Pitt and the Great War* (London, 1911).

FORMATION OF THE COALITION

See general references above.

WAR AIMS OF THE ALLIES

See general references above.

On Poland, R. H. Lord, *The Second Partition of Poland* (Cambridge, Mass., 1915), Harvard Historical Studies, No. 23, which studies the partition and its consequences to the end of the summer of 1794.

On the restoration of the Old Regime in the north of France, see G. Lefebvre, *Les paysans du Nord pendant la Révolution française*, 2 vols. (Lille, 1924), pp. 548–64; J. Peter, *L'occupation étrangère dans le département du Nord* (Lille, 1927).

THE COALITION AND POLAND (APRIL, 1793–OCTOBER, 1794)

On the Polish insurrection, in addition to the general works cited above, see Count Ferrand, *Les trois démembrements de la Pologne pour faire suite aux révolutions de Pologne de Rulhière*, 3 vols. (Paris, 1820; 2d ed., annot. C. Ostrowski, 1865).

On Rulhière, Alice Chevalier, *Claude-Carloman de Rulhière, premier historien de la Pologne: Sa vie et son œuvre historique* (Paris, 1939), includes a remarkable letter from Talleyrand not found in the biographies.

See also A. von Treskow, *Beitrag zur Geschichte des polnischen Revolutionskrieges: Feldzug der Preussen im Jahre 1794* (Danzig, 1836, 2d ed., Berlin, 1937); and the collection dedicated to Kosciusko by the Committee of Rapperschwyl in 1894, *Kosciuszko: Biographia z Documentów Wysnuta* (Cracow, 1894), an anonymous work in Polish, actually written by T. Korzon.

THE WAR AGAINST FRANCE: VICTORIES AND DEFEATS OF THE ALLIED ARMIES (1793–1794)

For military operations, see Evanson, p. 331.

For the British army, see Sir J. W. Fortescue, *History of the British Army*, 12 vols. (London, 1899–1938), Vol. IV (1906).

Since the publication of the Austrian General Staff does not go beyond the end of 1792, it is necessary to consult works that present the operations from the French point of view, particularly A. Chuquet, *Les guerres de la Révolution*, 11 vols. (Paris, n.d.).

For the siege of Mainz, see K. G. Bockenheimer, *Die Wiedereroberung von Mainz durch die Deutschen in Sommer 1793* (Mainz, 1893).

For the influence of politics on military affairs, see the general works at the beginning of this chapter.

MARITIME AND COLONIAL WARFARE

See H. W. Wilson in the *Cambridge Modern History*, Vol. VIII (1904), Chap. 15, for general survey and bibliography; the celebrated work of A. T. Mahan, *The Influence of Sea Power upon the French Revolution and Empire*, 2 vols. (London, 1892), Vol. I, Chaps. 2–5; W. James, *The Naval History of Great Britain, 1793–1820*, 5 vols. (London, 1824, 2d ed., 6 vols., 1886) is still useful.

The chief French works are J. Tramond, *Manuel d'histoire maritime de la France des origines à 1815* (Paris, 1916, 3d ed., 1947); E. Chevalier, *Histoire de la marine française sous la première République* (Paris, 1886); E. Desbrière, *Le blocus de Brest de 1793 à 1805* (Paris, 1903); M. Jollivet, *Les Anglais dans la Méditerranée: Un royaume anglo-corse, 1794–1797* (Paris, 1896).

For the colonies, J. Saintoyant, *La colonisation française pendant la Révolution*, 2 vols. (Paris, 1930); H. de Poyen-Bellisle, *Les guerres des Antilles de 1793 à 1815* (Paris, 1896); Dr. Magnac, *La perte de Saint-Domingue* (Paris, 1907).

ECONOMIC WARFARE

This is the part of the history least studied, and little is known concerning the influence of the war on commercial trends. Suggestions are given in W. Cunningham, *The Growth of English Industry and Commerce in Modern Times*, 2 vols. (London, 1890, 6th ed., 1915–19); J. H. Rose, *William Pitt and the Great War* (London, 1911); A. Wohlwill, *Neuere Geschichte der Freien- und Hansestadt Hamburg, insbesondere von 1789 bis 1815* (Gotha, 1914), Chap. 3.

On prices and exchange, Evanson, pp. 291–92.

On the blockade, G. Lefebvre, *Napoléon* (Paris, 1935, 4th ed., 1953), Book I, Chap. 2, sec. 4.

On the difficulties in diplomacy created by the blockade, S. F. Bemis, *A Diplomatic History of the United States* (New York, 1936, new eds., 1946, 1950, 1955), and the same author's article, 'The United States and the Abortive Armed Neutrality of 1794', in the *American Historical Review*, XXIV (1918), 26–47.

Some texts are included in J. Brown Scott, *Armed Neutralities of 1700 and 1800* (New York, 1918), in Publications of the Carnegie Endowment for International Peace.

THE WAR GOVERNMENTS OF THE ALLIES

See general references at beginning of this chapter.

On England, J. H. Rose, *William Pitt and the Great War* (London, 1911); D. G. Barnes, *George III and William Pitt, 1783–1806* (Stanford, Cal., 1939); E. D. Adams, *The Influence of Grenville on Pitt's Foreign Policy, 1787–1798* (Washington, D.C., 1904); D. A. Chart, 'The Irish Levies During the Great French War', in the *English Historical Review*, XXXII (1917), 497–651; Sir H. McAnally, *The Irish Militia* (Dublin and London, 1949).

On Prussia, M. Philippson, *Geschichte des preussischen Staatswesens vom Tode Friedrichs des Grossen bis zu den Freiheitskriegen*, 2 vols. (Leipzig, 1880–82), which ends with the death of Frederick William II.

On Austria, I. Beidtel, *Geschichte des oesterreichtschen Staatsverwaltung*, 2 vols. (Innsbruck, 1896–98), Vol. I; and the publication of the historical section of the Austrian General Staff, *Geschichte der Kämpfe Oesterreichs: Krieg gegen die französische Revolution*, Vol. I, *Einleitung* (Vienna, 1905).

On national armament in Germany, W. Wendland, *Versuche einer allgemeinen Volkesbewaffnung in Süd-Deutschland* (Berlin, 1901), fasc. 24 of 'Historische Studien', ed. E. Ebering; R. Lorenz, *Volkesbewaffnung und Staatsidee in Oesterreich, 1792–1797* (Vienna, 1926).

BIBLIOGRAPHY

THE EUROPEAN REACTION

For England, J. H. Rose, *William Pitt and the Great War* (London, 1911), and *Pitt and Napoleon* (London, 1912); W. P. Hall, *British Radicalism, 1791–1797* (New York, 1912); P. A. Brown, *The French Revolution in English History* (London, 1918); H. W. Meikle, *Scotland and the French Revolution* (Glasgow, 1912); G. Cole and R. Postgate, *The British Common People, 1746–1938* (New York, 1939) and *The Common People, 1746–1946* (London, 1946); G. Cole, *A Short History of the Working Class Movement, 1784–1827* (London, 1949); and for counter-revolutionary caricatures, Mary D. George, *Catalogue of Political and Personal Satires Preserved in the Department of Prints and Drawings in the British Museum*, Vol. VIII, *1792–1800* (London, 1942).

For Germany, K. von Heigel, *Deutsche Geschichte vom Tode Friedrichs des Grossen bis zur Auflösung des alten Reiches*, 2 vols. (Stuttgart, 1899–1911), Vols. X and XI in 'Bibliothek deutscher Geschichte', pub. under direction of H. von Zwiedineck-Südenhorst; M. Philippson, *Geschichte des preussischen Staatswesens vom Tode Friedrichs des Grossen bis zu den Freiheitskriegen*, 2 vols. (Leipzig, 1880–82), stops with death of Frederick William II; X. Léon, *Fichte et son temps*, Vol. I (Paris, 1922); W. Behrendts, *Reformstrebungen in Kursachsen im Zeitalter der französischen Revolution* (Leipzig, 1914); J. Droz, *L'Allemagne et la Révolution française* (Paris, 1949).

For Hungary, H. Marczali, *Magyarorsgág Története II József Korálan*, 3 vols. (Budapest, 1882–88), in Hungarian, Vol. I trans. into English, with introd., by Harold Temperley, *Hungary in the XVIIIth Century* (New York, 1932); Elemér Mályusz, *Sandor Lipôt föherceg nádor iratai* (*Writings of the Archduke Palatine Alexander-Leopold*) (Budapest, 1926), in 'Fontes historiae Hungaricae aevi recentioris', with introd. in Hungarian but most of the texts in French or German.

For Italy, N. Bianchi, *Storia della monarchia piemontese dal 1773 al 1861*, 4 vols. (Rome, 1877); C. Tivaroni, *L'Italia prima della Rivoluzione francese, 1755–1789* (Turin, 1888); P. Sirven, *Vittorio Alfieri*, 8 vols. (Paris, 1934–51).

For Spain, Evanson, p. 308.

For Russia, Evanson, p. 309.

On the movement of ideas, O. Karmin, *Sir Francis d'Ivernois* (Geneva and Paris, 1920); G. Rudler, *La jeunesse de Benjamin Constant* (Paris, 1909); F. Descostes, *La Révolution française vue de l'étranger: Mallet du Pan à Berne et à Londres* (Tours, 1897); L. Pingaud, *Le comte d'Antraigues* (Paris, 1893); F. Baldensperger, *Le mouvement des idées dans l'émigration française*, 2 vols. (Paris, 1925).

On the falsification of documents, A. Mathiez, 'Un faux rapport de Saint-Just', in *Annales révolutionnaires*, VIII (1916), 599–611 (this document was used as authentic by H. von Sybel and A. Sorel); A.-C. Bruun, 'Une traduction anglaise du faux rapport de Saint-Just rédigée par d'Antraigues', in *Annales historiques de la Révolution française*, IV (1927), 275–77. See also the controversies aroused by the publication of *The Manuscripts of J. B. Fortescue Preserved at Dropmore*, more commonly known as the *Dropmore Papers*, 3 vols. (London, 1894), pub. by the Historical Manuscripts Commission; Vol. II contains bulletins on the activity of the Committee of Public Safety, which d'Antraigues had drafted on the basis of reports from Paris. These discussions are summarized by A. Mathiez in 'L'histoire secrète du Comité de salut public', in *Revue des questions historiques* (Jan. 1914), and reprinted in *Études Robespierristes*, Vol. II (Paris, 1918).

Chapter 2. The Revolutionary Government (1793–1794)

General works: General works cited in Evanson, pp. 313–14; works on the Convention cited in Evanson, pp. 334–35; D. Guérin, *La lutte de classes sous la première République: Bourgeois et 'bras nus', 1793–1797*, 2 vols. (Paris, 1946).

FALL OF THE GIRONDINS: THE REVOLUTION OF MAY 31 AND JUNE 2, 1793

In addition to the works cited in Evanson, pp. 329–30, see L. Mortimer-Ternaux, *Histoire de la Terreur, 1792–1794 . . .*, 8 vols. (Paris, 1868–81), Vol. VI of which deals with the troubles of February and March and the treason of Dumouriez; on the latter see A. Chuquet, *Les guerres de la Révolution*, Vol. V, *La trahison de Dumouriez* (1890), and the same author's *Dumouriez* (Paris, 1914), as well as A. Mathiez, *Danton et la paix* (Paris, 1919).

On the democratic movement and economic history, A. Mathiez, *La vie chère et le mouvement social sous la Terreur* (Paris, 1927); the works cited by Evanson, pp. 321–23; and on financial history, M. Marion, *Histoire financière de la France depuis 1715*, 6 vols. (Paris, 1914–31), Vol. III.

For the history of the provinces, which was very important during this period, the chief sources of information are local studies, which are too numerous to list here; see Evanson, pp. 313–14.

Of the numerous works on the Vendée, the documentary studies by C. L. Chassin are basic: *Études documentaires sur la Révolution française: La préparation de la guerre de Vendée, 1789–1793*, 3 vols. (Paris, 1892), *La Vendée patriote, 1793–1800*, 4 vols. (Paris, 1893–95), and *Les pacifications de l'Ouest, 1794–1800*, 3 vols. (Paris, 1896–99). See the general survey given by L. Dubreuil, *Histoire des insurrections de l'Ouest*, 2 vols. (Paris, 1929), and the somewhat pro-Vendée study by E. Gabory, *La Révolution et la Vendée*, 3 vols. (Paris, 1925–28). See also Marquis de Roux, *Histoire religieuse de la Révolution à Poitiers et dans la Vienne* (Lyons, 1952), concerning the origins of the Vendéan troubles; this work attributes the insurrection partly to counter-revolutionary leaders, and shows Guillot de Folleville as an agent of the nobles connected with the emigration.

On the Commune, F. Braesch, *La Commune du 10 août: Étude sur l'histoire de Paris du 20 juin au 2 décembre 1792* (Paris, 1911) has not been continued, and there is no general study of the activity of the sections.

For the revolution of May 31–June 2, L. Mortimer-Ternaux, *Histoire de la Terreur*, Vol. VII (1869); A. Tuetey, *Répertoire général des sources manuscrites de l'histoire de Paris pendant la Révolution*, Vol. IX (Paris, 1910), introd.; the study in G. Pariset, *La Révolution, 1792–1799* (Paris, 1920), Vol. II of

Histoire de France contemporaine, ed. E. Lavisse; P. Sainte-Claire Deville, *La Commune de l'an II* (Paris, 1946); H. Wallon, *La révolution du 31 mai et le fédéralisme en 1793*, Vol. I (Paris, 1886) adds little.

REVOLUTIONARY CRISIS DURING THE SUMMER OF 1793

In addition to the works cited in the two preceding sections on this chapter, see, concerning Danton's diplomacy, A. Aulard, 'La diplomatie du premier Comité de salut public', in his *Études et leçons*, Vol. III (1901).

On the outcome of the revolution of June 2 in Paris, H. Calvet, *Un instrument de la Terreur à Paris: Le Comité de salut public ou de surveillance du département de Paris* (Paris, 1941).

On the Constitution of 1793, A. Aulard, *Histoire politique de la Révolution française* (Paris, 1901, 5th ed., 1921), Part II, Chap. 4; A. Mathiez, 'La Constitution de 1793', in *Annales historiques de la Révolution française*, V (1928), 498–521; M. Fridieff, *Les origines du référendum dans la Constitution de 1793* (Paris, 1931); J. Godechot, *Les institutions de la France sous la Révolution et l'Empire* (Paris, 1951), Book III, Chap. 1.

On the social movement and the agitation of the *Enragés*, see particularly A. Mathiez, *La vie chère et le mouvement social sous la Terreur* (Paris, 1927); see also M. Dommanget, *Jacques Roux, le curé rouge* (Paris, 1948).

On the application of the Law of the Maximum, G. Lefebvre, *Documents relatifs à l'histoire des subsistances dans le district de Bergues, 1789–an V*, 2 vols. (Lille, 1913, 1921), introd., pub. by Commission d'Histoire Économique de la Révolution.

On federalism, see Vol. II of H. Wallon, *La révolution du 31 mai et le fédéralisme en 1793* (Paris, 1886) for a general survey. On this subject the local studies are superior: C. Riffaterre, *Le mouvement anti-jacobin et anti-parisien à Lyon et dans le Rhône-et-Loire en 1793 (29 mai–15 août)*, of which Vol. I is the second volume of a new series, 'Annales de la Faculté des Lettres de Lyon', 1912, while Vol. II was published in Lyons and Paris in 1928; E. Herriot, *Lyon n'est plus*, 4 vols. (Paris, 1937–40); P. Nicolle, 'Le mouvement fédéraliste dans l'Orne en 1793', in *Annales historiques de la Révolution française*, XIII (1936), 481–512; XIV (1937), 215–33; XV (1938), 12–53, 289–313, 385–410; G. Guibal, *Le mouvement fédéraliste en Provence en 1793* (Paris, 1908); P.-A. Robert, *Le tribunal populaire de Marseille* (Paris, 1913); J. Parès, *Le tribunal populaire martial de Toulon* (pp. 75–130), Vol. XI of *Notices, inventaires et documents*, pub. by Comité des Travaux Historiques (1925).

On the fate of the Girondins, C. Perroud, *La proscription des Girondins* (Paris, 1917).

On the Vendée, see preceding section of this chapter.

See also P. Caron, *Rapports des agents du ministre de l'intérieur dans les départements, 1793–an II* (Paris, 1951), the first volume of which appeared in 1913, 'Collection des documents inédits de l'histoire de France'.

ORGANIZATION OF THE MONTAGNARD DICTATORSHIP (JULY–DECEMBER, 1793)

See two preceding sections of this chapter. The work of Mortimer-Ternaux ends with Vol. VIII, which was edited (1881) by Baron de Layre from the author's notes, and it deals with the period from June 2 to the end of October. C. Vatel, *Charlotte de Corday et les Girondins*, 3 vols. (Paris, 1864–72), is chiefly a collection of documents.

For the formation of the revolutionary government, P. Mautouchet, *Le gouvernement révolutionnaire* (Paris, 1912), introd., documents, and bibliography.

For the Great Committee of Public Safety, R. R. Palmer, *Twelve Who Ruled* (Princeton, 1941), a general work that deals with general politics, developments in Paris, and several 'typical' missions, e.g., those of Couthon in Auvergne and Saint-André in Brittany.

For the Revolutionary Tribunal, E. Campardon, *Le tribunal révolutionnaire de Paris*, 2 vols. (Paris, 1866); H. Wallon, *Histoire du tribunal révolutionnaire de Paris avec le journal de ses actes*, 6 vols. (Paris, 1880–82), Vol. I of which goes up to the trial of the Girondins, and Vol. II to Ventôse, Year II.

For the revolutionary government in the provinces, H. Wallon, *Les représentants en mission et la justice révolutionnaire dans les départements en l'an II*, 5 vols. (Paris, 1889–90); also the general histories of the Catholic Church during the Revolution, cited in Evanson, pp. 323–24. Again, local studies are indispensable: A. Troux, *La vie politique dans le département de la Meurthe d'août 1792 à octobre 1795*, 2 vols. (Paris, 1936); A. Lallié, *La justice révolutionnaire à Nantes et dans la Loire-Inférieure* (Nantes, 1896); M. Gaston-Martin, *La mission de Carrier à Nantes* (Paris, 1924).

On opposition to the Committee in the Convention, A. Mathiez, *Études Robespierristes*, Vol. II (Paris, 1918), 'La conspiration de l'étranger', 'Fabre d'Églantine et la Compagnie des Indes'; and the same author's *L'affaire de la Compagnie des Indes* (Paris, 1921); J. Conan, *La dernière Compagnie des Indes* (Paris, 1942).

A study that presents Baron de Batz as the 'hero' of counter-revolutionary intrigue is Baron de Batz, *La vie, la conspiration et la fin de Jean, baron de Batz*, 2 vols. (Paris, 1908); while an opposing view is held by G. Bord, *La fin de deux légendes . . . Le baron de Batz* (Paris, 1909) and C. de Batz-Tranquelléon, *Le vrai baron de Batz* (Bordeaux, 1908).

On the sans-culotte movement, traditionally known as Hébertist, in addition to the work by Guérin cited at the beginning of this chapter (Guérin calls them 'proletarians'), see A. Soboul, *Les sans-culottes Parisiens en l'an II: Mouvement populaire et gouvernement révolutionnaire 2 juin 1793–9 thermidor an II* (Paris, 1958); the influence of Vincent and the Hébertists is examined in Gen. Herlaut, *Le colonel Bouchotte, ministre de la Guerre de l'an II*, 2 vols. (Paris, 1946).

On Paris opinion, see P. Caron, *Paris pendant la Terreur: Rapports des agents secrets du ministre de l'Intérieur*, in course of publication: begins with August 27, 1793, and has reached 10 Ventôse, Year II (Feb. 28, 1794), 5 vols. (Paris, 1910, 1914, 1943, 1949, 1958), see also Caron's *Rapports des agents du ministre de l'Intérieur dans les départements, 1793–an II* (Paris, 1951).

DECHRISTIANIZATION

L. Madelin, *Fouché*, 2 vols. (Paris, 1901, latest repr., 1955), Vol. I, Chap. 4; E. Campagnac, 'Les débuts de la déchristianisation dans le Cher', in *Annales révolutionnaires*, IV (1911), 626–57; V (1912), 41–49, 206–11, 359–73, 511–20; M. Dommanget, *La déchristianisation à Beauvais et dans l'Oise* (Paris, 1918); A. Aulard, *Le culte de la Raison et de l'Être suprême* (Paris, 1892) and his *Histoire politique de la Révolution*, Part II, Chap. 9; A. Mathiez, *La Révolution et l'Église* (Paris, 1901), Chap. 3, 'Robespierre et la déchristianisation', and *Origines des cultes révolutionnaires* (Paris, 1904).

See also general histories of the church, Evanson, pp. 323–24. Local studies are of great importance, e.g., J. Gallerand, *Les cultes sous la Terreur en Loir-et-Cher* (Blois, 1929).

FIRST VICTORIES OF THE REVOLUTIONARY GOVERNMENT (SEPTEMBER–DECEMBER, 1793)

See general works cited in Evanson, p. 331, especially A. Chuquet, *Les guerres de la Révolution*, Vol. VII, *Mayence* (1891), Vol. VIII, *Wissembourg* (1893), Vol. IX, *Hoche et la lutte pour l'Alsace* (1893), Vol. X, *Valenciennes* (1894), Vol. XI, *Hondschoote* (1895).

See also V. Dupuis, *La campagne de 1793 à l'armée du Nord et des Ardennes, de Valenciennes à Hondschoote*, 2 vols. (Paris, 1906–9), pub. by French General Staff; J. Colin, *La campagne de 1793 en Alsace et dans le Palatinat* (Paris, 1902); J. Ferval, *Campagne de la Révolution française dans les Pyrénées orientales*, 2 vols. (Paris, 1851–53, 2d ed., 1861); E. Ducéré, *L'armée des Pyrénées occidentales* (Bayonne, 1882); L. Krebs and H. Morris, *Campagnes dans les Alpes pendant la Révolution*, 2 vols. (Paris, 1891–95).

See also M. Reinhard, *Le Grand Carnot*, 2 vols. (Paris, 1950, 1952), Vol. II.

TRIUMPH OF THE COMMITTEE OF PUBLIC SAFETY (DECEMBER, 1793–MAY, 1794)

General works: See section of this chapter above, under 'Organization of the Montagnard Dictatorship'.

See also A. Mathiez, *La vie chère et le mouvement social sous la Terreur* (Paris, 1927), *L'affaire de la Compagnie des Indes* (Paris, 1921), and *Robespierre terroriste* (Paris, 1921), the last of which contains the critical text of Robespierre's notes against the Dantonists and a study of the trial of the Hébertists. The edition of *Le vieux Cordelier* by H. Calvet, with notes by A. Mathiez (Paris, 1936), is in 'Les classiques de la Révolution'. See also M. Eude, 'La commune robespierriste', in *Annales historiques de la Révolution française*, X (1933), 412–25; XI (1934), 323–47, 528–56; XII (1935), 132–61, 495–518; XIII (1936), 289–316.

See also P. Caron, *Rapports*, cited above, under 'Organization of the Montagnard Dictatorship'; Gen. Herlaut, *Le colonel Bouchotte, ministre de la Guerre de l'an II*, 2 vols. (Paris, 1946); Norman Hampson, *La marine de l'an II: La mobilisation de la flotte de l'Ocean 1793–1794* (Paris, 1959) and his complementary study, *La stratégie française et britannique pendant la campagne navale du printemps de l'an II;* R. Werner, *L'approvisionnement en pain de la population et l'armée du Rhine pendant la Révolution* (Strasbourg, 1951).

BIBLIOGRAPHY

CHARACTER AND ORGANIZATION OF THE REVOLUTIONARY GOVERNMENT

General works: A. Aulard, *Histoire politique de la Révolution française*, Part II, Chap. 5; P. Mautouchet, *Le gouvernement révolutionnaire* (Paris, 1912); G. Pariset, *La Révolution, 1792–1799* (Paris, 1920), Vol. II of *Histoire de France contemporaine*, ed. E. Lavisse, pp. 165–85; R. R. Palmer, *Twelve Who Ruled* (Princeton, N.J., 1941).

For the functioning of the regime, one must use the *Recueil des actes du Comité de salut public avec la correspondance officielle des représentants en mission et le registre du conseil exécutif provisoire*, ed. A. Aulard, 28 vols. (Paris, 1889 ff.) in 'Collection des documents inédits sur l'histoire de France'.

On Paris, H. Calvet, *Le comité de salut public du département de Paris* (Paris, 1941).

On the provinces, H. Wallon, *Les représentants en mission et la justice révolutionnaire dans les départements en l'an II*, 5 vols. (Paris, 1889–90); L. Dubreuil, *Le district de Redon: Ier juillet 1790–18 ventôse an IV* (Rennes, 1903) and *Le régime révolutionnaire dans le district de Dinan, 25 nivôse an II–30 floréal an III* (Paris, 1912)—documents, with introd. and notes; A. Richard, *Le gouvernement révolutionnaire dans les Basses-Pyrénées* (Paris, 1922); H. Labroue, *La mission du conventionnel Lakanal dans la Dordogne en l'an II* (Paris, 1915); E. Campagnac, 'Le comité révolutionnaire de Melun', in *Annales révolutionnaires*, I (1908), 467–82; J. B. Sirich, *The Revolutionary Committees in the Departments of France* (Cambridge, Mass., 1943).

On the clubs, C. Brinton, *The Jacobins* (New York, 1930), and L. de Cardenal, *La province pendant la Révolution: Histoire des clubs jacobins, 1789–1795* (Paris, 1929).

THE ARMY OF THE YEAR II

On Carnot, M. Reinhard, *Le Grand Carnot*, 2 vols. (Paris, 1950, 1952); R. Warschauer, *Studien zur Entwicklung der Gedanken Lazare Carnots über Kriegsführung* (Berlin, 1937), No. 7 in 'Historische Abhandlungen', pub. by E. Ebering, stops with Hondschoote.

See also the works by J. Colin, Evanson, p. 331; Gen. Jung, *L'armée et la Révolution: Dubois-Crancé*, 2 vols. (Paris, 1884); Gen. Herlaut, *Le colonel Bouchotte, ministre de la Guerre de l'an II*, 2 vols. (Paris, 1946).

On Prieur of Côte-d'Or, G. Bouchard, *Un organisateur de la victoire, Prieur de la Côte-d'Or, membre du Comité de salut public* (Paris, 1946).

On the deputies on mission, H. Wallon, *Les représentants en mission et la justice révolutionnaire dans les départements en l'an II*, 5 vols. (Paris, 1889–90), and the other works relative to the armies.

On military justice, L. Hennequin, *La justice militaire et la discipline dans l'armée du Rhin et à l'armée de Rhin-et-Moselle (1792–1796): Notes historiques du chef de bataillon du génie Legrand* (Paris, 1909); G. Michon, 'La justice militaire sous la Révolution', in *Annales révolutionnaires*, XIV (1922), 1–26, 99–130, 197–222 (rev. and enl. as book, Paris, 1922); A. Chuquet, *L'École de Mars* (Paris, 1899).

See also Evanson, p. 331, and the section below, under 'Revolutionary

Victory'; Capt. Gervais, *A la conquête de l'Europe*, ed. Mme. H. Coulet (Paris, 1939); and R. Werner in the following section.

On the navy, L. Lévy-Schneider, *Jeanbon Saint-André*, 2 vols. (Paris, 1901); and Norman Hampson, *La marine de l'an II: La mobilisation de la flotte de l'Océan 1793–1794* (Paris, 1959) and his complementary study, *La stratégie française et britannique pendant la campagne navale du printemps de l'an II*. Also see the works in Chapter 1, above, under 'Maritime and Colonial Warfare'.

ECONOMIC GOVERNMENT

A. Mathiez, *La vie chère et le mouvement social sous la Terreur* (Paris, 1927); C. Richard, *Le Comité de salut public et les fabrications de guerre sous la Terreur* (Paris, 1922).

On the repression of hoarding, H. Calvet, *L'accaparement à Paris sous la Terreur: Essai sur l'application de la loi du 26 juillet 1793* (Paris, 1933), Vol. V of *Mémoires et documents*, pub. by Commission d'Histoire Économique de la Révolution.

On the Maximum, G. Lefebvre, *Les paysans du Nord pendant la Révolution française*, 2 vols. (Lille, 1924), and the following articles: 'L'application du maximum général dans le district de Bergues', in *Bulletin de la Commission d'histoire économique de la Révolution* (1913), pp. 415–46, and 'Les mines de Littry sous l'Ancien Régime et pendant la Révolution', in *Annales historiques de la Révolution française*, III (1926), 16–35, 117–35.

On foreign trade, G. Lefebvre, 'Le commerce extérieur en l'an II', in *La Révolution française*, LXXVIII (1925), 132–55, 214–43; P. Caron, ed. *Procès-verbaux de la commission des subsistances*, 2 vols. (Paris, 1924–25), pub. by Commission d'Histoire Économique de la Révolution; and bibliography cited under 'Economic Warfare' in Chapter 1, above.

On Perregaux, see Vol. III of J. Bouchary, *Les manieurs d'argent à la fin du XVIIIe siècle*, 3 vols. (Paris, 1939–43).

See also R. Werner, *L'approvisionnement en pain de la population et l'armée du Rhin pendant la Révolution* (Strasbourg, 1951).

SOCIAL POLICY

A. Mathiez, *La vie chère et le mouvement social sous la Terreur* (Paris, 1927) and 'La Terreur, instrument de la politique sociale des robespierristes; les décrets de ventôse sur le séquestre des suspects et leur application', in *Annales historiques de la Révolution française*, V (1928), 193–219; these decrees are discussed also in G. Lefebvre, *Questions agraires au temps de la Terreur* (Strasbourg, 1932, 2d ed., La Roche-sur-Yon, 1954).

For the national property (*biens nationaux*), M. Bouloiseau, *Le séquestre et la vente des biens des émigrés dans le district de Rouen* (Paris, 1927), and the numerous studies by Lefebvre cited in Evanson, pp. 321–22.

On the agricultural crisis, G. Lefebvre, *Les paysans du Nord pendant la Révolution française*, 2 vols. (Lille, 1924), pp. 698–713; A. Mathiez, *La vie chère* (cited in this section above), pp. 437–60; O. Festy, *L'agriculture pendant la Révolution*, 3 vols. (Paris, 1947–50).

BIBLIOGRAPHY

THE TERROR

See section of this chapter above, under 'Character and Organization of the Revolutionary Government'; E. Campardon, *Le tribunal révolutionnaire de Paris*, 2 vols. (Paris, 1866); H. Wallon, *Histoire du tribunal révolutionnaire de Paris avec le journal de ses actes*, 6 vols. (Paris, 1880–82); Arne Ording, *Le bureau de police du Comité de salut public: Étude sur la Terreur* (Oslo, 1930), in *Norske Videnskaps-Akademie i Oslo* (*Skrifter*) with comments of A. Mathiez in *Annales historiques de la Révolution française*, VII (1930), 563–73, and of Georges Lefebvre, 'La rivalité du Comité de salut public et du Comité de surêté générale', in *Revue historique*, CLVII (1931), 336–43; H. Calvet, 'Une interprétation nouvelle de la loi de prairial', in *Annales historiques de la Révolution française*, XXII (1950), 305–19; and in the same journal, Vol. XXIII, No. 3 (1951), 225–56, G. Lefebvre, 'Sur la loi de prairial'.

The statistical method is introduced by D. Greer, *The Incidence of the Terror* (Cambridge, Mass., 1935); and for the first time an analysis of the suspects has been made in G. Sangnier, *La Terreur dans le district de Saint-Pol*, 2 vols. (Blangermont, 1938).

For biographical and local studies, see L. Jacob, *Joseph Lebon*, 2 vols. (Paris, 1933); V. de Baumefort, *Le tribunal révolutionnaire d'Orange* (Avignon, 1875); Abbé S. Bonnel, *Les 332 victimes de la commission populaire d'Orange* (Avignon, 1888).

On the role of Robespierre, A. Mathiez, *Robespierre terroriste* (Paris, 1921).

Concerning religious policy, see the section of this chapter above, under 'Dechristianization'.

See also J. L. Godfrey, *Revolutionary Justice: A Study of the Organization, Personnel, and Procedure of the Paris Tribunal, 1793–1795* (Chapel Hill, N.C., 1951); L. Jacob, *Les suspects pendant la Révolution, 1789–1794* (Paris, 1952).

REVOLUTIONARY VICTORY (MAY–JULY, 1794)

For diplomacy, in addition to the general works (principally Sorel, very hostile to the Committee), see P. Mantoux, 'Le Comité de salut public et la mission de Genet aux États-Unis', in *Revue d'histoire moderne et contemporaine*, XIII (1909), 5–35; R. Petiet, *Gustave IV Adolphe et la Révolution française: Relations diplomatiques de la France et de la Suède de 1792 à 1800 d'après des documents inédits* (Paris, 1914); Martine Rémusat, 'Un sans-culotte à la cour de Danemark' [Grouvelle], in *Revue de Paris*, IV (1912), 538–78; A. Lods, *Bernard de Saintes et la réunion de la principauté de Montbéliard* (Paris, 1888); J. Grossbart, 'La politique polonaise de la Révolution jusqu'aux traités de Bâle', in *Annales historiques de la Révolution française*, VI (1929), 34–55, 242–55, 476–85; VII (1930), 129–51.

There is no adequate work on the relations with Switzerland, especially from the economic point of view. See *Papiers de Barthélemy*, eds. J. Kaulek and A. Tausserat-Radel, 6 vols. (Paris, 1886–1910); G. Steiner, ed. *Korrespondenz des Peter Ochs*, 3 vols. (Basel, 1927–38). On Geneva, A. Mazon, *Histoire de Soulavie*, 2 vols. (Paris, 1893); E. Chapuisat, *Genève et la Révolution française* (Geneva, 1912); M. Peter, *Genève et la Révolution* (Geneva, 1921).

On military operations, see Evanson, p. 331, and the preceding sections for this chapter. See also H. Coutanceau, *La campagne de 1794 à l'armée du Nord*, 2 parts in 4 vols. (Paris, 1903–8), dealing with 'Opérations', and stopping with the battle of Tourcoing; V. Dupuis, *Les opérations militaires de la Sambre en 1794; bataille de Fleurus* (Paris, 1907), publication of the French General Staff; L. Jouan, *La campagne de 1794–95 dans les Pays-Bas*, Vol. I, *La conquête de la Belgique; mai–juillet 1794* (Paris, 1914), publication of the French General Staff, no more published; L. Hennequin, *La campagne de 1794 entre Rhin et Moselle* (Paris, 1909), also by the French General Staff; G. Fabry, *Histoire de la campagne de 1794 en Italie*, 2 vols. (Paris, 1905); J. Ferval, *Campagne de la Révolution française dans les Pyrénées orientales*, 2 vols. (Paris, 1851–53, 2d ed., 1861); E. Ducéré, *L'armée des Pyrénées occidentales* (Bayonne, 1882); L. Krebs and H. Morris, *Campagnes dans les Alpes pendant la Révolution*, 2 vols. (Paris, 1891–95); A. Chuquet, *Dugommier* (Paris, 1904).

9 THERMIDOR (JULY 27, 1794)

E. Hamel, *Thermidor* (Paris, 1891); A. Godard, *Le procès du 9 thermidor* (Paris, 1912); L. Barthou, *Le 9 thermidor* (Paris, 1926); Arne Ording, *Le bureau de police du Comité de salut public: Étude sur la Terreur* (Oslo, 1930); A. Mathiez, 'Les divisions dans les Comités à la veille de thermidor', in *Revue historique*, CXVIII (1915), 70–87, and 'Les séances des 4 et 5 thermidor aux deux Comités de salut public et de surêté générale', in *Annales historiques de la Révolution française*, IV (1927), 193–222; A. Mathiez and H. Chobaut, 'Trois lettres inédites de Voulland sur la crise de thermidor', *ibid.*, pp. 67–77. See also 'Lettres du conventionnel d'Yzez', in *Revue de France*, VI (1926), 517–21; G. Rudé and A. Soboul, 'Le maximum des salaires et le 9 thermidor', in *Annales historiques de la Révolution française*, XXVI (1954), 1–22.

Chapter 3. The Thermidorian Reaction and the Treaties of 1795

General works: See Evanson, pp. 312–13, especially G. Pariset, *La Révolution* (Vol. II of Lavisse); G. Deville, *Thermidor et Directoire* (Vol. V. of Jaurès); G. Lefebvre, *Les thermidoriens* (Paris, 1937, 2d ed., 1946), No. 196 in Collection A. Colin; J. Godechot, *Les institutions de la France sous la Révolution et l'Empire* (Paris, 1951).

On religion, Evanson, pp. 323–24; A. Mathiez, 'Le régime des cultes sous la première séparation', in *La Révolution et l'Église* (Paris, 1910); Abbé J. Boussoulade, *L'Église de Paris du 9 thermidor au Concordat* (Paris, 1950).

For diplomacy and war, see the section above, under 'Revolutionary Victory'; L. Sciout, *Le Directoire*, 4 vols. (Paris, 1895–97), Vol. I.

Excerpts from police reports and newspapers are in A. Aulard, *Paris pendant la réaction thermidorienne et sous le Directoire*, 5 vols. (Paris, 1898–1902), 'Documents relatifs à l'histoire de Paris pendant la Révolution'.

DISESTABLISHMENT OF THE REVOLUTIONARY GOVERNMENT

A. Aulard, *Histoire politique de la Révolution française* (Paris, 1901, 5th ed., 1921), Part II, Chaps. 11, 12; P. Mautouchet, *Le gouvernement révolutionnaire*

(Paris, 1912); A. Mathiez, *La réaction thermidorienne* (Paris, 1929); C. de Lacretelle, *Dix années d'épreuves pendant la Révolution* (Paris, 1842), Chaps. 10, 11; M. Bouloiseau, 'Les comités de surveillance d'arrondissement de Paris sous la réaction thermidorienne', in *Annales historiques de la Révolution française*, X (1933), 317–37, 441–53; XI (1934), 233–49; XIII (1936), 42–60, 204–17; J. Turquan, *La citoyenne Tallien* (Paris, 1898); J. Stern, *Le mari de Mademoiselle Lange: M.-J. Simons* (Paris, 1933).

On the Vendée, see references for the first section of the present chapter; also L. de La Sicotière, *L. de Frotté et l'insurrection normande*, 3 vols. (Paris, 1888).

FINANCIAL AND ECONOMIC CRISIS AND THE WHITE TERROR

M. Marion, *Histoire financière de la France depuis 1715*, 6 vols. (Paris, 1914–31), Vol. III; S. E. Harris, *The Assignats* (Cambridge, Mass., 1930); A. Mathiez, *La réaction thermidorienne* (Paris, 1929), Chaps. 8, 9; G. Lefebvre, *Les thermidoriens* (Paris, 1937, 2d ed., 1946), Chap. 6; G. Lefebvre, *Documents relatifs à l'histoire des subsistances dans le district de Bergues 1789–an V*, 2 vols. (Lille, 1913, 1921), introd.; M. Gaston-Martin, 'La vie bourgeoise à Nantes sous la Convention d'après le livre de comptes de Madame Hummel', in *La Révolution française*, LXXXVI (1933), 236–58.

On the army, H. Bourdeau, *Les armées du Rhin au début du Directoire* (Paris, 1902); F. Vermale, 'La désertion dans l'armée des Alpes après le 9 thermidor', in *Annales révolutionnaires*, VI (1913), 506–16, 643–57.

The day of 1 Prairial (but not the 2d, 3d, and 4th) is studied by F. Thénard and R. Guyot, *Le conventionnel Goujon* (Paris, 1908), first published in *Revue historique*, Vol. LXXXVIII (1905) ff.

On the White Terror, one must study local histories and special works: S. Blum, 'La mission d'Albert dans la Marne en l'an III', in *La Révolution française*, XLV (1903), 193–231; G. Laurent, 'J.-B. Armonville', in *Annales historiques de la Révolution française*, I (1924), 217–49, 315–55, and 'L'insurrection du ler prairial an III et la situation économique de la ville de Reims', *ibid.*, IV (1927), 237–54; E. Poupé, *La répression de la révolte terroriste de Toulon*, being Vol. X (1924) of *Notes, inventaires et documents*, pub. by the Comité des Travaux Historiques, Section d'Histoire Moderne; P. Vaillandet, 'Les débuts de la Terreur blanche en Vaucluse', in *Annales historiques de la Révolution française*, V (1928), 109–27, and 'Le procès des juges de la commission populaire d'Orange', *ibid.*, VI (1929), 137–63; E. Courcelle, 'La réaction thermidorienne dans le district de Melun', *ibid.*, VII (1930), 112–28, 252–61, 329–50, 443–53; E. Sarot, *Les tribunaux répressifs de la Manche en matière politique pendant la Révolution*, 4 vols. (Paris, 1881–82), Vol. IV; R. Cobb, 'Note sur la répression contre le personnel sans-culotte de 1795 à 1801', in *Annales historiques de la Révolution française*, XXVI (1954), 23–49.

On Louis XVII there is a vast literature, much of it uncritical. See particularly A. de Beauchesne, *Louis XVII*, 2 vols. (Brussels and Leipzig, 1853); R. Chantelauze, *Louis XVII* (Paris, 1884, 2d ed., 1895); G. Bord, *Autour du Temple*, 3 vols. (Paris, 1913). In one of his studies published under the title *Énigmes du temps passé*, Vol. I (Paris, 1944), L. Hastier has elucidated the drafting of the death sentence, and in a recent volume, *La double mort de Louis XVII* (Paris, 1951), he concludes that the prince died in January, 1794. See also M. Garçon, *Louis XVII ou la fausse énigme* (Paris, 1952); L. Hastier, *Nouvelles révélations sur Louis XVII* (Paris, 1954).

THERMIDORIAN DIPLOMACY

See the works cited in Evanson, p. 325, especially Sorel, Vol. IV, and Vivenot, *Quellen*, Vol. IV (on the period January–September, 1795). See also P. Bailleu, *Preussen und Frankreich von 1795 bis 1807: Diplomatische Correspondenz*, 2 vols. (Leipzig, 1881–87).

On the financial terms of the peace with Holland, J. B. Manger, *Recherches sur les relations économiques de la France et de la Hollande pendant la Révolution française* (Paris, 1923).

THE TREATIES OF BASEL AND THE HAGUE (APRIL–MAY, 1795)

See preceding note; Vol. V of Vivenot (Evanson, p. 325) deals with the Peace of Basel and the third partition of Poland.

The evacuation of Belgium and the conclusion of peace by Prussia constitute the second point debated by historians of the two great German powers (for the first point, see Evanson, p. 330). A good bibliographical summary is given in A. Wahl, *Geschichte des europäischen Staatensystems in Zeitalter der französischen Revolution und der Freiheitskriege* (Munich and Berlin, 1912), pp. 66, 67.

For the negotiations with Spain, see A. Sorel, 'La diplomatie française et l'Espagne, 1792–1797', in *Revue historique*, XI (1879), 298–330; XII (1880), 279–313; XIII (1880), 41–80, 241–78.

QUIBERON AND 13 VENDÉMIAIRE, YEAR IV

L. Dubreuil, *Histoire des insurrections de l'Ouest*, 2 vols. (Paris, 1929); E. Gabory, *La Révolution et la Vendée*, 3 vols. (Paris, 1925–28); T. de Closmadeuc, *Quiberon* (Paris, 1898). The counter-revolutionary point of view is presented by P. C. Robert, *Expédition des émigrés à Quiberon: Le comte d'Artois à l'Île d'Yeu* (Paris, 1899); see also E. Gabory, *L'Angleterre et la Vendée*, 2 vols. (Paris, 1930–31).

On the insurrection of 13 Vendémiaire, H. Zivy, *Le 13 vendémiaire an IV* (Paris, 1898), No. 6 of Bibliothèque de la Faculté des Lettres de l'Université de Paris.

THE CAMPAIGN OF 1795 AND THE ANNEXATION OF BELGIUM

In addition to the general works on military operations cited in Evanson, p. 331, see H. Bourdeau, *Les armées du Rhin au début du Directoire* (Paris, 1902); E. Caudrillier, *La trahison de Pichegru et les intrigues royalistes dans l'est avant Fructidor* (Paris, 1908); R. Bittard des Portes, *L'armée de Condé* (Paris, 1896).

On diplomacy, see Evanson, pp. 325–29.

For the third partition of Poland, Count Ferrand, *Les trois démembrements de la Pologne pour faire suite aux révolutions de Pologne de Rulhière*, 3 vols. (Paris, 1820; 2d ed., annot. C. Ostrowski, 1865); and Vol. V of Vivenot's *Quellen* (Evanson, p. 325).

THE CONSTITUTION OF THE YEAR III

A. Aulard, *Histoire politique de la Révolution française* (Paris, 1901, 5th ed., 1921), Part III, Chap. 1; M. Deslandres, *Histoire constitutionnelle de la France de 1789 à 1870*, Vol. I (Paris, 1932); A. Lajusan, 'Le plébiscite de l'an III', in *La Révolution française,* LX (1911), 5–37, 106–32, 237–63; J. Godechot, *Les institutions de la France sous la Révolution et l'Empire* (Paris, 1951).

PART TWO. THE VICTORIOUS OFFENSIVE OF THE REVOLUTION

Chapter 4. Europe and the Revolution at the End of 1795

General works: For the diplomatic history of the period, to which this part of the book is devoted, the basic work, particularly from the point of view of France, is R. Guyot, *Le Directoire et la paix de l'Europe* (Paris, 1911). See also Evanson, pp. 325–29, especially Vols. IV–VI of Sybel, Vol. V of Sorel, and J. H. Rose.

For Prussia, P. Bailleu, *Preussen und Frankreich von 1795 bis 1807: Diplomatische Correspondenz*, 2 vols. (Leipzig, 1881–87); W. Trummel, *Der norddeutsche Neutralitätsverband, 1795–1801* (Hildesheim, 1918), Vol. VII, Part XLI of 'Beiträge für die Geschichte Niedersachsens und Westfalens'; G. S. Ford, *Hanover and Prussia, 1795–1803* (New York, 1903); O. Tschirch, *Geschichte der öffentlichen Meinung in Preussen Friedensjahrzehnt vom Basler Frieden bis zum Zusammenbruch des Staates*, 2 vols. (Weimar, 1933).

On the predilections of the Thermidorians, see the general histories of the Directory under Chapter 5 below; also H. Bourdeau, *Les armées du Rhin au début du Directoire* (Paris, 1902); A. Sorel, 'La frontière constitutionnelle', in *Revue historique,* XIX (1882), 24–59.

THE NEUTRALS AND THE COALITION

See preceding note.

THERMIDORIAN PREDILECTIONS

See note at beginning of this chapter.

Chapter 5. The First Directory

General works: There is no adequate study of the Directory as a whole. L. Sciout, *Le Directoire*, 4 vols. (Paris, 1895–97), has used the memoirs of La Revellière-Lépeaux, 3 vols. (Paris, 1895), and those of Barras, ed. G. Duruy, 4 vols. (Paris, 1895–96), as well as some of the documents in the National Archives. Very hostile to the Directory, his work tends to be polemical. Occasionally one may refer to older works, e.g., *Histoire secrète du Directoire*, the work of Fabre de l'Aude, published anonymously, 4 vols. (Paris, 1834). The principal collections of documents are A. Aulard, *Paris pendant la réaction thermidorienne et sous le Directoire*, 5 vols. (Paris, 1898–1902), and A. Debidour, *Recueil des actes du Directoire exécutif*, 4 vols. (Paris, 1910–17), in the collection Documents Inédits sur l'Histoire de France; but the latter is incomplete and does not go beyond Pluviôse, Year V.

G. Lefebvre has published a brief summary, *Le Directoire* (Paris, 1946, 2d ed., 1950), No. 245 in the Collection A. Colin; see also G. Pariset, *La Révolution, 1792–1799* (Paris, 1920), which has extensive bibliographies. And for internal history, A. Aulard, *Histoire politique de la Révolution française* (Paris, 1901, 5th ed., 1921), Part III; A Mathiez, *Le Directoire* (Paris, 1934), a posthumous work brought out by J. Godechot, who assembled articles previously published in journals—but it stops at 18 Fructidor. The first two volumes of L. Madelin, *Histoire du Consulat et de l'Empire* (Paris, 1937) deal with the youth and rise of Bonaparte, and the second volume deals with the Directory from the point of view of Bonaparte.

For institutions, P. Poullet, *Les institutions françaises de 1795 à 1814* (Paris, 1907), and J. Godechot, *Les institutions de la France sous la Révolution et l'Empire* (Paris, 1951). The outstanding scholarly work of recent years is J. Godechot, *Les commissaires aux armées sous le Directoire*, 2 vols. (Paris, 1937). See also J. Bourdon, 'Le mécontentement public et les craintes des dirigeants sous le Directoire', in *Annales historiques de la Révolution française*, XVIII (1946), 218–37, and J. Godechot, 'Le Directoire vu de Londres', *ibid.*, XXI (1949), 311–66 and XXII (1950), 1–27. A. Goodwin has made a critical summary of research on the Directory, 'The French Executive Directory: A Revaluation', in *History*, XXII (1937), 201–18.

M. Reinhard has written a biography of Carnot, 2 vols. (Paris, 1950, 1952); on Reubell, documents have been edited by R. Guyot, *Documents biographiques sur J.-F. Reubell, membre du Directoire exécutif* (Paris, 1911), and B. Nabonne has published the 'Mémoire justificatif de Reubell écrit en 1799', in *Revue d'histoire diplomatique* (1950), pp. 75–103. There is a study by Georgia Robison of *Revellière-Lépaux, Citizen Director* (New York, 1938); but there is no biography of Barras.

On religious history, see Evanson, pp. 323–24; J. Boussoulade, 'Le presbytérianisme dans les conciles de 1797 à 1801', in *Annales historiques de la Révolution française*, XXIII (1951), 17–37; A. Mathiez, *La théophilanthropie et le culte décadaire* (Paris, 1904); D. Bernard, *Documents et notes sur l'histoire religieuse du Finistère sous le Directoire* (Quimper, 1936); Abbé J. Ladame, 'Les registres de catholicité de l'église cathedrale Saint-Charles de Sedan', in *Annales historiques de la Révolution française*, XVI (1939), 97–109.

On education, see bibliography for Chapter 14 below.

For local history, see Evanson, pp. 312–13; M. Reinhard, *Le département de la Sarthe sous le régime directorial* (Saint-Brieuc, 1935); J. Brelot, *La vie politique en Côte-d'Or sous le Directoire* (Dijon, 1932), in collection 'La Révolution en Côte-d'Or'; G. Caudrillier, 'Bordeaux sous le Directoire', in *La Révolution française* LXX (1917), 19–54; J. Beyssi, 'Le parti jacobin à Toulouse sous le Directoire', in *Annales historiques de la Révolution française*, XXII (1950), 28–54, 109–33; E. Delcambre, *La période du Directoire dans la Haute-Loire* (Rodez, 1940), and *La vie dans la Haute-Loire sous le Directoire* (Rodez, 1943).

On the Belgian departments, L. de Lanzac de Laborie, *La domination française en Belgique*, 2 vols. (Paris, 1895); P. Verhaegen, *La Belgique sous la domination française, 1792–1814*, 5 vols. (Brussels, 1922–29), Vols. II, III; both of these authors are hostile. H. Pirenne, *Histoire de Belgique*, 5 vols. (Brussels, 1921), Vol. V; L. Leclère, 'L'esprit public en Belgique de 1795 à 1800', in *Revue d'histoire moderne*, XIV (1940), 32–43; I. Delatte, 'La vente des biens nationaux dans l'arrondissement de Namur', in *Annales de la Société archéologique de Namur*, XL (1934), 119–39, 'La vente des biens nationaux dans le département de Jemappes', in *Mémoires de l'Académie royale de Bruxelles*, XXXIX, *Lettres*, Part II (1938), p. 136, and 'La vente des biens nationaux en Belgique', in *Revue d'histoire moderne*, XIV (1940), 44–51.

On the Rhineland, see Evanson, pp. 336–37; and J. Godechot, *Les commissaires aux armées sous le Directoire*, 2 vols. (Paris, 1937).

See also R. Cobb, 'Note sur la répression contre le personnel sansculotte de 1795 à 1801', in *Annales historiques de la Révolution française* (1954), pp. 23–49.

INAUGURATION OF THE DIRECTORY

See bibliography for preceding section. The researches of J. Suratteau have corrected much of the statistical information on the results of the elections and the composition of the Assemblies. See his articles, 'Les élections de l'an IV', in *Annales historiques de la Révolution française*, XXIII (1951), 374–94, and XXIV (1952), 30–62.

MONETARY CRISIS AND THE CONSPIRACY OF THE 'EQUALS'

For money and finance, see M. Marion, *Histoire financière de la France depuis 1715*, 6 vols. (Paris, 1914–31), Vol. III; S. E. Harris, *The Assignats* (Cambridge, Mass., 1930); R. Schnerb, *Les contributions directes à l'époque de la Révolution dans le département du Puy-de-Dôme* (Paris, 1933); G. Lefebvre, *Le Directoire* (Paris, 1946, 2d ed., 1950), Chaps. 3, 4.

On the contractors and speculators, J. Stern, *Le mari de Mademoiselle Lange: M.-J. Simons* (Paris, 1933); A.-R. Hamelin, 'Douze ans de ma vie, 1796–1808', in *Revue de Paris*, V (1926), 5–24, 281–309, 544–66, 811–39; I (1927), 46–71; J. Godechot, 'Les aventures d'un fournisseur aux armées sous le Directoire: Hanet-Cléry', in *Annales historiques de la Révolution française*, XIII (1936), 30–41, based on the man's memoirs, published in 2 vols. (Paris, 1825).

On the disorders created by inflation, E. and J. de Goncourt, *Histoire de la société française sous le Directoire* (Paris, 1855), an anecdotal collection on Paris and daily life; J. Turquan, *La citoyenne Tallien* (Paris, 1898); A. Marquiset, *Une merveilleuse: Madame Hamelin* (Paris, 1909) and *Quand Barras était roi* (Paris, 1911).

On Babeuf, Buonarroti, and the conspiracy of the 'Equals', A. Mathiez, *Le Directoire* (Paris, 1934), Chaps. 8, 9, 10; G. Bourgin has given a good statement of the matter in *Cahiers de la Révolution française*, No. 1 (1934), pp. 77–106; M. Dommanget, *Pages choisies de Babeuf* (Paris, 1935) in 'Les classiques de la Révolution'; D. Cantimori, *Utopisti e reformatori italiani* (Florence, 1943), on Buonarroti; A. Galante Garrone, *Babeuf e Buonarroti*

(Turin, 1948); A. Saitta, *Filippo Buonarroti*, 2 vols. (Rome, 1950–51); G. Lefebvre, 'Les origines du communisme de Babeuf', in Vol. I, *Rapports*, of Ninth International Congress of Historical Sciences (Paris, 1950), pp. 561–71.

THE NEW ANTI-JACOBIN REACTION

See first section on this chapter above.

THE ELECTIONS OF THE YEAR V AND THE CONFLICT OF THE DIRECTORY AND THE COUNCILS

See first section on this chapter above.

A. Meynier, *Les coups d'État du Directoire*, Vol. I, *Le 18 fructidor an V* (Paris, 1928); Thérèse Aubin, 'Le rôle politique de Carnot depuis les élections de germinal an V jusqu'au coup d'État du 18 fructidor', in *Annales historiques de la Révolution française*, IX (1932), 37–51; G. Lacour-Gayet, *Talleyrand* (Paris, 1928–34, new ed., 1946), Vol. I.

On the counter-revolutionary action and the Anglo-royalist conspiracy, which Meynier denies, G. Caudrillier, *La trahison de Pichegru et les intrigues royalistes dans l'est avant fructidor* (Paris, 1908) and *L'association royaliste de l'Institut philanthropique à Bordeaux et la conspiration anglaise en France pendant la seconde coalition* (Paris, 1908); A. Lebon, *L'Angleterre et l'émigration française de 1794 à 1801* (Paris, 1882); J. Godechot, 'Les insurrections militaires sous le Directoire', in *Annales historiques de la Révolution française*, X (1933), 129–52, 193–221; Abbé C. Jolivet, *L'agitation contre-révolutionnaire dans l'Ardèche sous le Directoire* (Lyons, 1930).

Chapter 6. The Directory and the Coalition

General works: The outstanding work is R. Guyot, *Le Directoire et la paix de l'Europe* (Paris, 1911). A. Sorel, *L'Europe et la Révolution française*, Vol. V, should be viewed in the light of P. Muret, 'Étude critique sur Bonaparte et le Directoire de Monsieur A. Sorel', in *Revue d'histoire moderne et contemporaine*, V (1907), 243–64, 313–39. See also Evanson, pp. 325–29; the section of Chapter 3 above, under 'The Treaties of Basel and The Hague'; and the general works for Chapter 4 above; A. Dry, *Soldats et ambassadeurs sous le Directoire: An IV–an VIII* (Paris, 1906).

For Austria, *Quellen zur Geschichte des Zeitalters der französischen Revolution*, pub. by H. Hüffer, Part II, *Quellen zur Geschichte der diplomatischen Verhandlungen*: Vol. I, F. Luckwaldt, *Der Friede von Campo-Formio, 1795–1797* (Innsbruck, 1907); O. Criste, *Erzherzog Karl*, 3 vols. (Vienna and Leipzig, 1912); M. von Angeli, *Erzherzog Karl als Feldherr und Heeresorganisator*, 6 vols. (Vienna, 1895–97).

For Russia, F. Golovkine, *La cour et le règne de Paul Ier* (Paris, 1905); K. Waliszewski, *Le fils de la grande Catherine: Paul Ier* (Paris, 1912); A. Brückner, *Die Razumovski*, 6 vols. (Halle, 1882–88)—Andrei Razumovski was ambassador at Vienna from 1793 to 1809.

For Italy, R. Guyot, 'Le Directoire et la République de Gênes', in *La Révolution française*, XLIV (1903), 402–34, 518–50, and XLV (1903), 39–65;

J. du Teil, *Rome, Naples et le Directoire* (Paris, 1902); and the works on Naples cited below in the section of Chapter 11 under 'The War in Italy'.

For Spain, A. Sorel, 'La diplomatie française et l'Espagne, 1792–97', Part IV, *Revue historique*, XIII (1880), 241–78. The treaty of alliance between the Republic and Spain is given in the *Revue historique*, XIII (1880), 241–78.

NAPOLEON BONAPARTE

On the origins and advent of Bonaparte, see the bibliography in G. Lefebvre, *Napoléon* (Paris, 1935, 4th ed., 1953), Book I, Chap. 2, sec. 2. See also L. Madelin, *Histoire du Consulat et de l'Empire*, Vols. I and II (Paris, 1937); S. Wilkinson, *The Rise of General Bonaparte* (Oxford, 1930).

VICTORIES OF THE DIRECTORY, AND ENGLAND CONFOUNDED

J. Fabry, *Campagne d'Italie, 1796–1797*, 3 vols. (Paris, 1901–4), publication of the 'État-major'; F. Bouvier, *Bonaparte en Italie, 1796* (Paris, 1899), up to Lodi; S. Wilkinson, *The Rise of General Bonaparte* (Oxford, 1930), up to Lodi; N. Bianchi, *Storia della monarchia piemontese dal 1773 al 1861*, 4 vols. (Rome, 1877), Vol. I; G. Ferrero, *Aventure: Bonaparte en Italie* (Paris, 1936), concerning which see P. Muret, 'G. Ferrero, historien de Bonaparte', in *La Révolution française*, XC (1937), 221–43, as well as Ferrero's reply and Muret's rejoinder, *ibid.*, XCI (1938), 1–20, 21–29; F. Bouvier, 'L'Italie de 1794 à 1796 d'après les papiers de Paul Greppi (correspondance publiée à Milan en 1902)', in *La Révolution française*, XLV (1903), 161–69; M. Reinhard, *Avec Bonaparte en Italie, d'après les lettres inédites de son aide de camp Sulkowski* (Paris, 1946).

There is no study of the campaign in Germany. See the works on Archduke Charles at the beginning of this chapter.

For Ireland, see Chapter 9 below; and the second section of that chapter deals with the attempted landings. See also G. Escaude, *Hoche en Irlande* (Paris, 1888); Commander E. H. Stuart Jones, *An Invasion That Failed: The French Expedition to Ireland of 1796* (Oxford, 1950) and *The Last Invasion of Britain* (Cardiff, 1950), the latter concerning Tate's expedition to Pembrokeshire in 1797.

REVERSES OF THE AUTUMN OF 1796

See general works cited for Chapter 5 above, and titles listed in the first section of the present chapter.

THE SURRENDER OF AUSTRIA: PRELIMINARIES OF LEOBEN

F. Luckwaldt, *Der Friede von Campo-Formio, 1795–1797* (Innsbruck, 1907), cited in full under general works above.

For Venice, M. Kovalevski, *La fin d'une aristocratie* (Turin, 1902); A. Bonnefons, *Un État neutre sous la Révolution: La chute de la République de Venise* (Paris, 1908); R. Bratti, *La fine della Serenissima* (Milan, 1917); G. MacClellan, *Venice and Bonaparte* (Princeton, N.J., 1931); *Mémoires de l'adjutant général Jean Landrieux*, ed. L. Grasillier (Paris, 1893); E. Rodocanacchi, *Bonaparte et les îles Ioniennes, 1797–1816* (Paris, 1899).

For Genoa, P. Nurra, *Genova nel Risorgimento* (Milan, 1948).

On the organization of the republics, A. Pingaud, *Bonaparte président de la République italienne*, 2 vols. (Paris, 1914), Vol. I; G. Sabini, *I primi esperimenti costituzionali in Italia, 1797–1815* (Turin, 1911); A. Sorel, *Hoche et Bonaparte en 1797* (Paris, 1896); M. Romani, *Milano capitale napoleonica: La formazione di un stato moderno, 1796–1814*, 3 vols. (Milan, 1946–47); A. de Stefano, *Rivoluzione e religione nelle prime esperienze costituzionali italiane, 1796-1797* (Milan, 1954).

THE ENGLISH CRISIS

See works cited in Evanson, pp. 309–10, 326–27, especially J. H. Rose, *William Pitt and the Great War* (London, 1911). See also Mary D. George, *Catalogue of Political and Personal Satires Preserved in the Department of Prints and Drawings in the British Museum*, Vol. VII, *1792–1800* (London, 1942); H. W. Temperley, *Life of George Canning* (London, 1905); C. Ballot, *Les négociations de Lille, 1797* (Paris, 1910).

For the monetary crisis and finances, R. G. Hawtrey, *Currency and Credit* (London, 1919); Sir J. H. Clapham, *The Bank of England*, 2 vols. (London, 1944).

On prices, J. E. Thorold Rogers, *Six Centuries of Work and Wages: The History of English Labour*, 2 vols. (London, 1884, new ed., 1949); V. J. Silberling, 'British Prices and Business Cycles, 1779–1850', in *Review of Economic Statistics*, V (1923), 223–61; Lord W. Beveridge, *Prices and Wages in England from the 12th to the 19th Century*, Vol. I (London, 1939); A. Hope-Jones, *Income Tax in the Napoleonic Wars* (Cambridge, 1939).

On the mutinies, C. Gill, *The Naval Mutinies of 1797* (Manchester, 1913); E. Manwaring and B. Dobree, *The Floating Republic* (London, 1935).

FOREIGN AFFAIRS AND THE ARMY VIS-À-VIS 18 FRUCTIDOR

See section of preceding chapter under 'Elections of the Year V'.

Chapter 7. 18 Fructidor and the Treaty of Campo Formio

General works: See last section of preceding chapter and first section of the present one.

18 FRUCTIDOR, YEAR V (SEPTEMBER 4, 1797)

See last section of Chapter 6; C. Ballot, *Le coup d'État du 18 fructidor: Rapports de police et documents divers* (Paris, 1900), publication of the Société de l'Histoire de la Révolution; V. Pierre, *Le 18 fructidor* (Paris, 1893), publication of the Société d'Histoire Contemporaine; A. Mathiez, *Le Directoire* (Paris, 1934), Chap. 14, which appeared previously in *Annales historiques de la Révolution française*, VI (1929), 521–50.

THE TREATY OF CAMPO FORMIO (OCTOBER 18, 1797)

See general works cited at the beginning of Chapter 6 above, particularly R. Guyot, *Le Directoire et la paix de l'Europe* (Paris, 1911), and F.

Luckwaldt, *Der Friede von Campo-Formio, 1795–1797* (Innsbruck, 1907). See also A. Aulard, 'Hoche et la République rhénane', in *Revue de Paris*, IV (1919), 46–62; J. Droz, *La pensée politique et morale des Cisrhénans* (Paris, 1940).

Chapter 8. The Second Directory

For general works, see those cited at the beginning of Chapter 5 above.

TERROR UNDER THE DIRECTORY

G. Lefebvre, *Le Directoire* (Paris, 1946, 2d ed., 1950), Chap. 8; V. Pierre, *Le 18 fructidor* (Paris, 1893) and *La déportation ecclésiastique sous le Directoire: Documents inédits* (Paris, 1896); D. Bernard, *Documents et notes sur l'histoire religieuse du Finistère sous la Révolution* (Quimper, 1936); C. Vuillame, *Quinze jours de Révolution à Aix* (Aix, 1892), on the royalist sedition of 22 Fructidor; A. Bernard, 'Le 18 fructidor à Marseille et dans les Bouches-du-Rhône', in *La Révolution française*, XLI (1901), 193–215; E. Delcambre, *Le coup d'État du 18 fructidor et ses répercussions dans la Haute-Loire* (Rodez, 1942); A. Mathiez, 'Saint-Simon, Lauraguais, Barras, Benjamin Constant et la réforme de la Constitution de l'an III après le coup d'État du 18 fructidor an V', in *Annales historiques de la Révolution française*, V (1929), 5–23—this constitutes Chap. 15 of his *Le Directoire*.

THE THIRD ANTI-JACOBIN REACTION: 22 FLOREAL, YEAR VI (MAY 11, 1798)

For general works, see those cited at the beginning of Chapter 5 above. See also A. Meynier, *Les coups d'État du Directoire*, Vol. II, *Le 22 floréal an VI et le 30 prairial an VII* (Paris, 1928).

FINANCES AND THE NATIONAL ECONOMY

For general works, see beginning of Chapter 5 above.

R. Schnerb, 'La dépression économique sous le Directoire après la disparition du papier-monnaie', in *Annales historiques de la Révolution française*, XI (1934), 27–40; A. Chabert, *Essai sur le mouvement des prix et des revenues en France de 1798 à 1820*, 2 vols. (Paris, 1945, 1949).

Chapter 9. The Anglo-French War

For general works, see beginnings of Chapters 5 and 6 above.

THE ENGLISH WAR EFFORT

See the section under 'Maritime and Colonial Warfare' in Chapter 1 above.

W. Anson, *The Life of John Jervis, Earl of Saint-Vincent, Admiral of the Fleet* (London, 1911); R. G. Albion, *Forests and Sea Power: The Timber Power of the Royal Navy, 1652–1862* (Cambridge, Mass., 1926), in Harvard Economic Studies, No. 29.

For Ireland, W. E. H. Lecky, *History of England in the Eighteenth Century*, 8 vols. (London, 1878–90, new ed., 1918–25), Vol. VIII; J. H. Rose, *William Pitt and the Great War* (London, 1911), Chap. 16; Sir H. McAnally, *The Irish Militia* (Dublin and London, 1949). See also the following section.

FRENCH PROJECTS: FOREWARNINGS OF THE CONTINENTAL BLOCKADE

See preceding section; G. Pallain, *Le ministère de Talleyrand sous le Directoire* (Paris, 1891)—documents; E. Desbrière, *Projets et tentatives de débarquement aux Îles britanniques*, 5 vols. (Paris, 1900–2), publication of the French General Staff; J. Tramond, *Manuel d'histoire maritime de la France des origines à 1815* (Paris, 1912, 3d ed., 1947); E. Guillon, *La France et l'Irlande pendant la Révolution* (Paris, 1888); Lieut. G. Douin, *La campagne de Bruix en Méditerranée* (Paris, 1923); Admiral Castex, *Théories stratégiques*, Vol. II (Paris, 1930).

On the blockade, see section of Chapter 1 above, under 'Economic Warfare'; C. Schmidt, *Une conquête douanière: Mulhouse* (Paris, 1910).

THE EGYPTIAN EXPEDITION

A. de La Jonquière, *L'expédition d'Égypte*, 5 vols. (Paris, 1900–7), publication of the French General Staff; Fr. Charles-Roux, *Les origines de l'expédition d'Égypte* (Paris, 1910), *L'Angleterre et l'expédition française en Égypte*, 2 vols. (Cairo, 1925), publication of the Société Royale de Géographie d'Égypte, and *Bonaparte gouverneur de l'Égypte* (Paris, 1936); H. Dehérain, *L'Égypte turque. Pachas et Mameluks du XIVe au XVIIIe siècles. L'expédition du général Bonaparte* (Paris, 1931), being part of *Histoire de la nation égyptienne*, ed. G. Hanotaux; C. Lacour-Gayet, *Talleyrand et l'expédition d'Égypte* (Paris, 1917); J. H. Rose, 'The Political Reactions of Bonaparte's Eastern Expedition', in *English Historical Review*, XLIV (1929), 48–58; A. T. Mahan, *The Life of Nelson*, 2 vols. (London, 1897). One of the most recent studies is J. C. Herold, *Bonaparte in Egypt* (New York, 1962).

Chapter 10. Revolutionary Expansion

General works: See items at beginning of Chapters 5 and 6 above.

HOLLAND AND ITALY

For Holland, P. Blok, *Geschiedenis van het nederlandische volk*, 8 vols. (Gronigen, 1892–1908), and in English trans., *History of the People of the Netherlands*, 5 vols. (New York, 1898–1912); J. B. Manger, *Recherches sur les relations économiques de la France et de la Hollande pendant la Révolution française* (Paris, 1923); H. F. Colenbrander, *Die bataafsche Republik* (Amsterdam, 1908); P. Mendels, *H. W. Daendels, 1762–1807* (The Hague, 1890); R. R. Palmer, 'Much in Little: The Dutch Revolution of 1795', in *Journal of Modern History*, XXVI (1954), 15–35.

For Italy, Evanson, p. 308; P. Gaffarel, 'L'annexation du Piémont à la France en 1798', in *La Révolution française*, XIX (1890), 289–315, 507–37; R. Guyot, 'Ginguené à Turin', in *Feuilles d'histoire*, VII (1912), 117–34; L. Madelin, *Fouché, 1759–1820*, 2 vols. (Paris, 1901); J. Godechot, *Les commissaires aux armées sous le Directoire*, 2 vols. (Paris, 1937); W. Lang, 'Karl Friedrich Reinhard in Florenz, 1797–1798', in *Historische Zeitschrift*, LIV (1885), 414–58, and *Graf Reinhard, 1761–1837* (Bamberg, 1896); P. Boulot, *Le général Duphot* (Paris, 1909); A. Dufourcq, *Le régime jacobin en Italie: Étude sur la République romaine* (Paris, 1900); V. E. Giuntella, *La giacobina reppublicana romana, 1798–1799* (Rome, 1950); C. Zaghi, *Bonaparte e il Direttorio dopo Campoformio* (Naples, 1956). For Naples in particular see Chapter 11 below, the section under 'The War in Italy'.

SWITZERLAND

For Geneva, E. Chapuisat, *De la Terreur à l'annexion* (Paris and Geneva, 1913); F. Barbey, *Félix Desportes et l'annexion de Genève à la France* (Paris, 1916).

For Switzerland, E. His, *Geschichte der neueren schweizerischen Staatsrechtes*, Vol. I, *1798–1803* (Basel, 1920); W. Oeschli, *Geschichte der Schweiz im XIXten Jahrhundert*, Vol. I (Leipzig, 1903); G. Steiner, *Korrespondenz des Peter Ochs*, 3 vols. (Basel, 1927–38); E. Dunant, *Relations diplomatiques de la France et de la République helvétique* (Basel, 1901), Vol. XIV of 'Quellen zur schweizerischen Geschichte'; J. Godechot, *Les commissaires aux armées sous le Directoire*, 2 vols. (Paris, 1937); G. Gugenbühl, *Bürgermeister Paul Usteri, 1768–1801*, Vol. I (Aarau, 1925); A. Rufer, *Pestalozzi, die französische Republik und die Helvetik* (Bern, 1928); A. Schenkel, *Die Bemühungen der helvetischen Regierung um die Ablösung der Grundlasten, 1798–1803* (Affoltern a. A., 1931); H. Wyss, *Alois Reding, Landeshauptmann von Schwyz und erster Landamman der Helvetik, 1765–1818* (Stans, 1930), the second part of which deals with Talleyrand's peculation; H. Büchi, *Vorgeschichte der helvetischen Republik mit besonderer Berücksichtung des Kantons Soleures*, Vol. I (Soleure, 1925).

THE CONGRESS OF RASTATT

A. von Vivenot, *Zur Geschichte des Rastatter Congresses* (Vienna, 1871); H. Hüffer, *Diplomatische Verhandlungen aus der Zeit der französischen Revolution*, 2 vols. (Vienna, 1878–79), Vol. II; P. Montarlot and L. Pingaud, *Le Congrès de Rastatt*, 3 vols. (Paris, 1912–13), publication of Société d'Histoire Contemporaine, and *Jean de Bry* (Paris, 1909).

THE AFTERMATH OF 22 FLORÉAL, YEAR VI (MAY 11, 1798)

See Chapter 8 above, under the section, 'The Third Anti-Jacobin Reaction'; G. Lefebvre, *Le Directoire* (Paris, 1946, 2d ed., 1950), pp. 129–32; K. Mendelsson-Bartholdy, 'Die Konferenzen von Seltz', in *Historische Zeitschrift*, XXIII (1870), 27–53.

Chapter 11. The Second Coalition

See general works for Chapter 6 above; H. Hüffer, *Der Rastatter Congress und die zweite Koalition* (Vienna, 1879) and *Der Krieg des Jahres 1799 und die zweite Koalition*, 2 vols. (Gotha, 1904); H. Weill, *Un agent inconnu de la coalition: Le général de Stamford d'après sa correspondance inédite* (Paris, 1920).

BIBLIOGRAPHY

RUSSIA IN THE MEDITERRANEAN

A. Trachevskii, *Diplomaticheskiia snosheniia Rossi s Frantsiei v epochu Napoleona I* (*Diplomatic Relations Between Russia and France in the Time of Napoleon I*), Vol. I, *Introduction* (St. Petersburg, 1890), Vol. LXX of Publications of the Imperial Society of Russia; *Archiv kniazia Vorontsova* (*Archives of the Princes Vorontsov*), ed. P. Bartenev, Vols. VIII–XIII (Moscow, 1884–1902); K. Waliszewski, *Le fils de la grande Catherine: Paul Ier* (Paris, 1912); M. de Taube, 'Le tsar Paul Ier et l'ordre de Malte en Russie', in *Revue d'histoire moderne*, VI (1930), 161–77; E. Rodocanacchi, *Bonaparte et les Îles Ioniennes, 1797–1816* (Paris, 1899); L. Pisani, *La Dalmatie de 1797 à 1815* (Paris, 1893); G. Remérand, *Ali de Tebelen, pacha de Janina* (Paris, 1928).

THE WAR IN ITALY: THE PARTHENOPEAN REPUBLIC

Capt. P. Mahon, *Études sur les armées du Directoire*, Part I (Paris, 1905), publication of the French General Staff; J. Godechot, *Les commissaires aux armées sous le Directoire*, 2 vols (Paris, 1937); B. Croce, *La Rivoluzione napolitana del 1799* (Bari, 1912); J. A. von Helfert, *Maria-Carolina von Oesterreich, Königin von Neapel und Sizilien* (Vienna, 1884); A. Bonnefous, *Marie-Caroline, reine des Deux-Siciles* (Paris, 1905); M. Leli, *La Santa Fede, 1799* (Milan, 1936); O. A. Sherrard, *A Life of Emma Hamilton* (London, 1927); A. Franchier-Magnan, *Lady Hamilton* (Paris, 1910).

AUSTRIA ENTERS THE WAR: CHARACTER OF THE COALITION

See general works for Chapters 6 and 11 above.

PREPARATIONS OF THE DIRECTORY

See general works for Chapter 6 above; G. Vallée, *La conscription dans la Charente* (Paris, 1937), on the application of the Jourdan Law.

For the financial reforms, see the documents in C. Bloch, *Les contributions directes* (Paris, 1914), pub. by the Commission d'Histoire Économique de la Révolution.

THE SPRING CAMPAIGN, 1799

Capt. L. Hennequin, *Zurich: Masséna en Suisse* (Paris, 1911), publication of the French General Staff; Archduke Charles, *Geschichte des Feldzugs von 1799 in Deutschland und in der Schweiz*, 3 vols. (Vienna, 1819); K. von Clausewitz, *Hinterlassene Werke*, Vols. V and VI (Berlin, 1883–84), French trans. Commandant Niessel, *La campagne de 1799 en Italie et en Suisse*, 2 vols. (Paris, 1906); D. A. Miliutin, *Istoriia voiny 1799 goda mezhdu Rossiei i Frantsiei v tsarstvovanie imperatora Pavla I* (*History of the War of 1799 Between Russia and France in the Reign of Emperor Paul I*), 3 vols. (St. Petersburg, 1853), in Russian; trans. into German as *Geschichte des Krieges Russlands mit Frankreich im Jahre 1799*, 3 vols. (Munich, 1856–58); H. Hüffer, *Der Krieg des Jahres 1799 und die zweite Koalition*, 2 vols. (Gotha, 1904).

Neither the domestic policy nor the foreign policy of the Directory had been to the advantage of the French in Italy. See G. Vaccarino, *Crisi giacobina e cospirazione anti-francese nell'anno VII in Piemonte* (Turin, 1952), and *I giacobini 'anarchisi' e l'idea dell'unità italiana* (Turin, 1953, 2d ed., 1955). See also G. Lumbroso, *I moti populari contre i Francese alla fine del seculo XVIII, 1798–1800* (Florence, 1932); R. Mori, 'Il popolo toscano durante la Rivoluzione e l'occupazione francese', in *Archivo storico italiano*, CV (1947), 127–52.

Chapter 12. The Crisis of the Year VII in France

For general works, see Chapter 5 above.

30 PRAIRIAL, YEAR VII (JUNE 18, 1799)

A. Meynier, *Les coups d'État du Directoire*, Vol. II (Paris, 1928); J. Godechot, *Les commissaires aux armées sous le Directoire*, 2 vols. (Paris, 1937), explains the role of the generals in opposing the Directory.

THE JACOBIN LAWS

See general works for Chapter 5 above; A. Meynier, *Les coups d'État du Directoire*, Vol. III (Paris, 1928).

THE LAST ANTI-JACOBIN REACTION

See general works for Chapter 5 above, and section above, under '30 Prairial'. E. Daudet, *Histoire de l'émigration: Les émigrés et la seconde coalition, 1797–1800* (Paris, 1887); G. Caudrillier, *L'association royaliste de l'Institut philanthropique de Bordeaux et la conspiration anglaise en France pendant la seconde coalition* (Paris, 1908); B. Lavigne, *Histoire de l'insurrection royaliste de l'an VII* (Paris, 1887); Abbé J. Lacouture, *Le mouvement royaliste dans le Sud-Ouest* (Hosségor, 1933); L. Dubreuil, *Histoire des insurrections de l'Ouest*, 2 vols. (Paris, 1929).

THE AUTUMN CAMPAIGN

See section under 'The Spring Campaign', Chapter 11 above.

For Holland, see section on that country in Chapter 9 above; P. Vermeil de Conchard, *Études historiques sur le maréchal Brune* (Brive and Paris, 1918).

Chapter 13. 18 Brumaire

General works: A. Vandal, *L'avènement de Bonaparte*, Vol. I (Paris, 1903); L. Madelin, *Histoire du Consulat et de l'Empire*, Vol. II (Paris, 1937); A. Meynier, *Les coups d'État du Directoire*, Vol. III (Paris, 1928).

THE REVISIONISTS

A. Mathiez, 'Saint-Simon, Lauraguais, Barras, Benjamin Constant et la réforme de la Constitution de l'an III après le coup d'État du 18 fructidor an V', in *Annales historiques de la Révolution française*, V (1929), 5–23 (the same as Chapter 15 of his *Le Directoire*); R. Guyot, 'Du Directoire au Consulat: Les transitions', in *Revue historique*, CXI (1912), 1–31; B. Munteano, *Les idées politiques de Madame de Staël* (Paris, 1931); Lady Blennerhasset, *Frau von Staël, ihre Freunde und ihre Bedeutung in Politik und Literatur*, 2 vols. (Berlin, 1887–89), French trans. A. Dietrich, *Madame de Staël et son temps*, 3 vols. (Paris, 1890); D.-G. Lang, *Madame de Staël: La vie dans l'œuvre* (Paris, 1924). See also the posthumous publications of the works of Mme de Staël: *Considérations sur les principaux événements de la Révolution française*, 2 vols. (Paris, 1818); *Des circonstances actuelles qui peuvent terminer la Révolution et des principes qui doivent fonder la République en France* (Paris, 1906), written in 1799, and treated by E. Herriot in *Un ouvrage inédit de Madame de Staël: Les fragments d'écrits politiques (1799)* (Paris, 1904).

18 AND 19 BRUMAIRE, YEAR VIII (NOVEMBER 9 AND 10, 1799)

See general works at beginning of Chapter 5 above, and works cited in two preceding sections of the present chapter.

A. Aulard, *Études et leçons sur la Révolution française*, 9 vols. (Paris, 1907–24): 'Les causes et le lendemain du 18 brumaire', II (Paris, 1898), 187–252; 'Bonaparte et les poignards des Cinq-Cents', III (1901), 271–89; 'Les derniers Jacobins', VII (1913), 84–112.

PART THREE. THE WORLD AT THE ADVENT OF NAPOLEON

Chapter 14. The Results of the Revolution in France

For Part III, see all the general works previously cited, especially J. Godechot, *Les institutions de la France sous la Révolution et l'Empire* (Paris, 1951).

For the present chapter, the basic work remains P. Sagnac, *La législation civile de la Révolution française (1789–1804): Étude d'histoire sociale* (Paris, 1898). The only recent publications on the subject are by P. Viard, 'L'œuvre juridique de la Convention', in *Annales historiques de la Révolution française*, VII (1930), 525–48, and *Histoire générale du droit privé français, 1789–1830* (Paris, 1931). M. Garaud, *Histoire générale du droit privé français (de 1789 à 1804)*, Vol. I, *La Révolution et l'égalité civile* (Paris, 1953), Vol. II, *La Révolution et la propriété foncière* (Paris, 1958); A. Mater, 'L'histoire juridique de la Révolution', in *Annales révolutionnaires*, XI (1919), 429–58, which has an important bibliography, and the plan for an organic study by jurists and historians, which has not materialized.

On the extent of the emigration see D. Greer, *The Incidence of the Emigration during the French Revolution* (Cambridge, Mass., 1951), Harvard Historical Monographs, No. 24.

DESTRUCTION OF THE OLD CORPORATE SOCIETY

In addition to the works by Sagnac and Mater, cited in the preceding section, see all the relevant general and special works already mentioned. See also E. Despois, *Le vandalisme révolutionnaire* (Paris, 1868), an ironic title; Crane Brinton, *French Revolutionary Legislation on Illegitimacy, 1789–1804* (Cambridge, Mass., 1936), Harvard Historical Monographs, No. 9 (cf. G. Lefebvre in *Annales historiques de la Révolution française*, XV (1938), 561–64;

G. Thibaut-Laurent, *La première introduction du divorce pendant la Révolution et l'Empire* (Clermont-Ferrand, 1938); J. de La Monneraye, 'Le mariage dans la bourgeoisie parisienne, 1789–1801', in Vol. I (Besançon, 1942) of *L'Assemblée générale de la Commission centrale des Comités départementaux* [d'histoire économique de la Révolution française], *1939*, pp. 195–208.

THE STATE

See works cited at beginning of present chapter.

SECULARIZATION OF THE STATE

See works cited at beginning of present chapter, works on religion cited in Evanson, pp. 323–24, and, on education, the following section of the present chapter.

PUBLIC SERVICES

For administration and finances, see works already cited; and for the former, add Gen. Herlaut, *Le colonel Bouchotte, ministre de la Guerre de l'an II*, 2 vols. (Paris, 1946); A. Cochin and C. Charpentier, *Les actes du gouvernement révolutionnaire*, 3 vols. (Paris, 1920), Vol. I, *Introduction* (on the bureaux of the Committee of Public Safety); P. Caron, 'Conseil exécutif provisoire et pouvoir ministériel, 1792–1794', in *Annales historiques de la Révolution française*, XIV (1937), 4–16; C. E. Labrousse, *La crise de l'économie française à la fin de l'Ancien Régime et au début de la Révolution*, Vol. I, *La crise viticole* (Paris, 1943), pp. 26–42, on the decline of statistical documentation.

On modifications in the organization of the ministry of foreign relations, A. Outrey, *L'administration en France des Affaires étrangères* (Paris, 1954).

On public relief, J. Imbert, *Le droit hospitalier de la Révolution et de l'Empire* (Paris, 1954), in Publications of the University of the Saar.

On education, G. Pariset, *Le Consulat et l'Empire (1799–1815)* (Paris, 1921), Vol. III of *Histoire de France contemporaine*, ed. E. Lavisse (see Book III, Chap. 5); and the bibliography in P. Sagnac, *La fin de l'Ancien Régime et la Révolution américaine (1763–1789)* (Paris, 1941), Vol. XII in the same series as the present work. See also James Guillaume, *Procès-verbaux du Comité d'instruction publique de l'Assemblée législative* (Paris, 1889), in Documents Inédits sur l'Histoire de France, and *Procès-verbaux du Comité d'instruction publique de la Convention nationale*, 6 vols. (Paris, 1891–1907), in the same collection; Abbé E. Allain, *L'œuvre scolaire de la Révolution, 1789–1802* (Paris, 1891); A. Leaud and E. Glay, *L'enseignement primaire en France*, 2 vols. (Paris, 1935); F. Lennel, *L'instruction primaire dans le département du Nord pendant la Révolution* (Paris, 1909); G. Lefebvre, *Les paysans du Nord pendant la Révolution française*, 2 vols. (Lille, 1924), pp. 760–73; F. B. Artz, 'L'enseignement technique en France pendant l'époque révolutionnaire, 1789–1815', in *Revue historique*, CXCVI (1946), 257–86, 387–402. On the central schools, see the bibliography in A. Troux, *L'école centrale du Doubs à Besançon, an IV–an XI* (Paris, 1926); G. Coirault, *Les écoles centrales dans le Centre-Ouest, an IV–an XII* (Tours, 1940); E. Vial, *L'enseignement secondaire en France* (Paris, 1936); Abbé J. Peter, *L'enseignement secondaire dans le département du Nord pendant la Révolution, 1789–1802* (Lille, 1912); B. Bois, *La vie scolaire et les créations intellectuelles en Anjou pendant la Révolution* (Paris, 1929); J. Liard, *L'enseignement supérieur en France*, 2 vols. (Paris, 1888–94); E. Hamy, *Les derniers jours du Jardin du Roi et la fondation du Muséum d'histoire naturelle* (Paris, 1893); G. Pinet, *Histoire de l'École polytechnique* (Paris, 1887); G. Boissier and G. Darboux, *L'Institut de France*, (Paris, 1907); *Le centenaire de la fondation du Muséum d'histoire naturelle, 19 juin 1793* (Paris, 1893); *Le livre du centenaire de l'École des langues orientales vivantes* (Paris, 1895). For bibliography on the central schools, see also J. Spekkens, *L'école centrale du département de la Meuse-Inférieure* (Maestricht, 1951).

THE ARMY

See Evanson, pp. 318, 331; Chap. 2 above, the section under 'The Army of the Year II'; Chap. 11 above, the section under 'Preparations of the Directory'.

NATIONAL UNITY

F. Brunot, *Histoire de la langue française*, Vol. IX, *La Révolution et l'Empire*, Part I, *Le français, langue nationale* (Paris, 1927), Part II, *Les événements, les institutions et la langue* (Paris, 1937), and Vol. X, *La langue classique dans la tourmente*, Part I, *Contact avec la langue populaire et la langue rurale* (Paris, 1939), Part II, *Le retour à l'ordre et à la discipline* (Paris, 1943); C. Pierre, *Les hymnes et chants de la Révolution* (Paris, 1904), in Documents Inédits sur l'Histoire de France, and cf. critical appendix in C. Rogers, *The Spirit of Revolution in 1789* (Princeton, N.J., 1949); J. Tiersot, *Les fêtes et les chants de la Révolution* (Paris, 1908); D. L. Dowd, *Pageant-Master of the Republic: Jacques-Louis David and the French Revolution* (Lincoln, Nebr., 1948); J.-A. Rivoire, *Le patriotisme dans le théâtre sérieux de la Révolution, 1789–1799* (Paris, 1950); A. Favre, *Les origines du système métrique* (Toulouse and Paris, 1931); G. Bigourdan, *Le Système métrique des poids et mesures: Son établissement et sa propagation graduelle* (Paris, 1901).

On the franc, F. Braesch, *Finances et monnaie révolutionnaire*, fasc. 5, *La livre tournois et le franc de germinal* (Paris, 1936).

INTELLECTUAL LIFE

F. Brunot (cited in preceding section); F. Picavet, *Les idéologues* (Paris, 1890); C. Van Duzer, *The Contribution of the Ideologues to French Revolutionary Thought* (Baltimore, Md., 1935).

For science, Evanson, pp. 302–3, especially, R. Guyenot, *L'évolution de la pensée scientifique: Les sciences de la vie* (Paris, 1941), No. 68 in collection L'Évolution de l'Humanité; G. Pouchet, *Les sciences pendant la Terreur* (Paris, 1896), in collection of Société de l'Histoire de la Révolution Française; H. Daudin, *Les classes zoologiques et l'idée de série animale en France à l'époque de Lamarck et de Cuvier, 1790–1830* (Paris, 1926).

For literature, Evanson, pp. 305–6.

For the plastic arts and music, Evanson, pp. 305–6; A. Tuetey and J. Guiffrey, 'La Commission du Muséum et la création du Musée du Louvre', in *Nouvelles archives de l'art français* (Paris, 1909); H. Lapauze, *Procès-verbaux de la Commission générale des arts de peinture, sculpture, architecture et gravure (18 juillet 1793–tridi de la première décade du deuxième mois de l'an II) et de la Société populaire et républicaine des arts (3 nivôse an II–28 floréal an III)* (Paris, 1903); L. Tuetey, *Procès-verbaux de la Commission temporaire des arts* (Paris, 1912), Documents Inédits sur l'Histoire de France; J. Renouvier, *Histoire de l'art pendant la Révolution* (Paris, 1863); F. Benoit, *L'art français pendant la Révolution et l'Empire* (Paris, 1897); L. Hautecoeur, *Histoire de l'architecture classique en France,* Vol. V, *Révolution et Empire, 1792–1815* (Paris, 1953). See also the works by Pierre, Tiersot, and Dowd in the preceding section.

THE NEW SOCIETY

See Evanson, pp. 321–23, the general works on economic history and the peasants, and G. Six, *Les généraux de la Révolution et de l'Empire* (Paris, 1948); J. and E. de Goncourt, *La société française pendant la Révolution* (Paris, 1854, repr., 1880, 1888), is anecdotal and deals largely with daily life in Paris.

A Gain, *La Restauration et les biens des émigrés,* 2 vols. (Nancy, 1929), considers the extent to which the émigrés were able to recover their property; see also G. Lefebvre, *Les paysans du Nord pendant la Révolution française,* 2 vols. (Lille, 1924), p. 504.

G. Thibaut-Laurent, *La première introduction du divorce pendant la Révolution et l'Empire* (Clermont-Ferrand, 1938); J. de La Monneraye, 'Le mariage dans la bourgeoisie parisienne, 1789–1801', in Vol. I of *Assemblée générale de la Commission centrale et des Comités départementaux, 1939* (Besançon, 1942), pp. 195–208; J. Turquan, *La citoyenne Tallien* (Paris, 1898); A. Marquiset, *Une merveilleuse: Madame Hamelin* (Paris, 1909).

On emigration, D. Greer, *The Incidence of the Emigration During the French Revolution* (Cambridge, Mass., 1951), Harvard Historical Monographs, No. 24.

ECONOMIC FREEDOM AND EQUAL RIGHTS

See Evanson, pp. 300–1, and Chap. 2 above, under the section, 'Social Policy'.

A. Mathiez, 'La Révolution française et les prolétaires', in *Annales historiques de la Révolution française,* VIII (1931), 479–95; H. Laski, *The Socialist Tradition in the French Revolution* (London, 1929); A. Lichtenberger, *Le socialisme au XVIIIe siècle* (Paris, 1899); A. Espinas, *La philosophie du XVIIIe siècle et la Révolution française* (Paris, 1898); the works on Babeuf and Buonarroti cited above in the section of Chap. 5, under 'Monetary Crisis and the Conspiracy of the "Equals" '; G. Lefebvre, 'La place de la Révolution dans l'histoire du monde', in *Annales: Économies—Sociétés—Civilisations,* III (1948), 257–66.

IMPOVERISHMENT AND WAR

J. and E. de Goncourt, *La société française pendant la Révolution* (Paris, 1854, repr., 1880, 1888); J. de La Monneraye, 'La crise du logement a Paris pendant la Révolution', in *Revue des questions historiques,* CVIII (1928), 298–343 (published as a book, Paris, 1928); A. Meynier, 'Levées et pertes d'hommes en France et en Europe pendant la Révolution', in *La Révolution française*, LXXXIII (1930), 143–59; and, particularly concerning military levies and losses, *Bulletin de la Société d'histoire moderne* (Jan., 1938), 3–8.

THE SIGNIFICANCE OF 18 BRUMAIRE

G. Lefebvre, *Le Directoire* (Paris, 1946, 2d ed., 1950), Chap. 15.

Chapter 15. Revolutionary Expansion and Its Effects

General works: Evanson, pp. 326–27; section of Chap. 1 above, under 'The European Reaction'.

REVOLUTIONARY EXPANSION

Evanson, pp. 326–27, and the section of Chap. 6 above, under 'Reverses of the Autumn of 1796'.

On Belgium and the Rhineland, Evanson, pp. 336–37.

On Holland and Switzerland, Chap. 10 above; see also A. Rufer, *Pestalozzi* (Bern, 1929); A. Pinloche, *Pestalozzi et l'éducation populaire moderne* (Paris, 1902).

On England, Marthe S. Storr, *Mary Wollstonecraft et le mouvement feministe dans la littérature anglaise* (Paris, 1931); H. Roussin, *William Godwin, 1756–1836* (Paris, 1913).

On Greece, A. Dascalakis, *Rhigas Velestinlis: La Révolution française et les préludes de l'indépendance hellénique* (Paris, 1937).

On America, H. M. Jones, *America and French Culture, 1750–1848* (Chapel Hill, N.C., 1927); E. P. Link, *Democratic Republican Societies, 1790–1800* (New York, 1942); G. A. Koch, *Republican Religion* (New York, 1933).

THE EUROPEAN REACTION

See Chap. 1 above, the section under 'The European Reaction'.

For Prussia, O. Hintze, 'Preussische Reformbestrebungen vor 1806', in *Historische Zeitschrift*, LXXVI (1896), 413–43.

See also G. Lumbroso, *I moti popolari contre i Francese alla fine del seculo XVIII, 1798–1800* (Florence, 1932); R. Mori, 'Il popolo toscano durante la Rivoluzione e l'occupazione francese', in *Archivo storico italiano*, CV (1947), 127–52; F. Battaglia, *L'opera di Vicenzo Cuoco e la formazione dello spirito nationale in Italia* (Florence, 1925); S. Canzio, *La prima reppublica cisalpina et il sentimento nazionale italiano* (Modena, 1944), No. 33 of Collezione Storica del Risorgimento Italiano; G. Vaccarino, *Crisi giacobina e cospirazione anti-francese nell'anno VII in Piemonte* (Turin, 1952), and *I giacobini 'anarchisi' e l'idea dell'unità italiana* (Turin, 1953; 2d ed., *I patrioti 'anarchistes' e l'idea dell'unità italiana [1796–1799]*, 1955).

THE UNITED STATES

Evanson, pp. 310–11, especially the works by Krout and Turner; J. F. Jameson, *The American Revolution Considered as a Social Movement* (Princeton, N.J., 1926, repr., 1940); N. Schachner, *Alexander Hamilton* (New York, 1946); G. Chinard, *Honest John Adams* (Boston, 1933); C. A. Beard, *Economic Origins of Jeffersonian Democracy* (New York, 1915); G. Chinard,

Jefferson, Apostle of Americanism (Boston, 1929, new ed., 1939); A. P. Whitaker, *The Spanish-American Frontier, 1783–1815* (Boston and New York, 1927) and *The Mississippi Question, 1795–1803* (New York, 1934); W. B. Smith and A. H. Cole, *Fluctuations in American Business, 1790–1860* (Cambridge, Mass., 1935), No. 50 in Harvard Economic Studies.

Wholesale commodity prices, 1795–1824, in the *Review of Economic Statistics* (1927), pp. 171–83; G. W. Danich, 'The Cotton Trade During the Revolutionary and Napoleonic Wars', in *Transactions of the Manchester Statistical Society* (Feb., 1916); A. E. Sayous, 'L'introduction du capitalisme européen aux États-Unis: Les valeurs et leur trafic de bourse à New York entre 1792 et 1873', in *Revue historique*, CXCII (1941), 249–75; CXCII, 46–67; L. C. Gray, *History of Agriculture in the Southern United States to 1860*, 2 vols. (Washington, 1933).

THE CONFLICT OF IDEAS

See Evanson, pp. 303–4, 306, 326–27; Chap. 1 above, the section under 'The European Reaction'.

J. Droz, *L'Allemagne et la Révolution française* (Paris, 1949), and *La pensée politique et morale des Cisrhénans* (Paris, 1940); R. Aris, *History of Political Thought in Germany from 1789 to 1815* (London, 1936); N. Hartmann, *Die Philosophie des deutschen Idealismus*, Vol. I (Berlin, 1923).

On counter-revolution, H. Moulinié, *Bonald* (Paris, 1915); P. Rohden, *Joseph de Maistre als politischer Theoretiker* (Munich, 1929); A. Omodeo, *Un reazionario: Il conte J. de Maistre* (Bari, 1939); O. Karmin, *Sir Francis d'Ivernois* (Geneva and Paris, 1920); F. Baldensperger, *Le mouvement des idées dans l'émigration française, 1789–1815*, 2 vols. (Paris, 1925).

On romanticism, see G. Lefebvre, *Napoléon* (Paris, 1935, 4th ed., 1953); H. Brunschwig, *La crise de l'État prussien à la fin du XVIIIe siècle et la genèse de la mentalité romantique* (Paris, 1947) and 'Jéna, la crise de l'état prussien et la genèse du romantisme', in *Annales: Économies—Sociétés—Civilisations*, I (1946), 306–13; H. Delacroix, 'Novalis et la formation de l'idéalisme magique', in *Revue de métaphysique et de morale*, XI (1903), 248–62.

For Italy, see preceding section under 'The European Reaction'.

Chapter 16. The Results of the War: International Politics

General works: Evanson, pp. 287–88, 313–14, and general works for Chap. 6 above.

THE ANGLO-FRENCH WAR

G. Lefebvre, *Napoléon* (Paris, 1935, 4th ed., 1953), Book I, Chap. 2, secs. 2, 4, 5.

THE WAR ON THE CONTINENT

See general works for Chap. 6 above.

Chapter 17. The Results of the War: The Rise of Capitalism in Great Britain; European Expansion in the World

General works: Evanson, pp. 287–96, for works on economic history and European expansion.

INTERNATIONAL TRADE

See preceding note; Dorothy B. Gobbell, 'British Trade and the Spanish Colonies, 1796–1823', in the *American Historical Review*, XLIII (1938), 288–320.

PRODUCTION

See Evanson, pp. 291–93, especially the works on price trends. See also the following portions of G. Lefebvre, *Études sur la Révolution française* (Paris, 1954): 'Le mouvement des prix et les origines de la Révolution française'; 'Les recherches relatives à la répartition de la propriété et de l'exploitation foncières à la fin de l'Ancien Régime'; 'Les études relatives à la vente des biens nationaux'; 'La Révolution française et les paysans'; 'Le meurtre du comte de Dampierre'; 'Sur Danton'; 'Le commerce extérieur en l'an II'; 'Sur la loi de prairial'; 'Les origines du communisme de Babeuf'; 'La place de la Révolution dans l'histoire du monde'.

EUROPEAN EXPANSION

See Evanson, pp. 289–90.

On the English in India, L. C. Bowring, *Haider Ali and Tipu Sultan* (Oxford, 1893); G. Saint-Yves, 'La chute de Tipou', in *Revue des questions historiques*, LXXXVIII (1910), 75–106; *Zemindary Settlement of Bengal*, 2 vols. (Calcutta, 1879); B. H. Baden Powell, *Land Systems of British India*, 3 vols. (Oxford, 1892).

On missions, see Evanson, pp. 290–91.

THE SHOCK TO COLONIAL EMPIRES

For colonies, Evanson, p. 324.

For Latin America, Evanson, pp. 289–90, 326–27; and for Miranda, Evanson, pp. 336–37.

Gen. Nemours, *Histoire militaire de la guerre de l'indépendance de Saint-Domingue*, 2 vols. (Paris, 1925–28); *Histoire des relations internationales de Toussaint Louverture* (Port-au-Prince, 1945).

Index

INDEX

Mauritius (Île de France), 215, 355, 357